Trigonometry

Algebra and Trigonometry
in four programmed volumes

I REAL NUMBERS AND ELEMENTARY ALGEBRA

II SETS AND FUNCTIONS

III TRIGONOMETRY

IV ALGEBRA: FUNCTIONS AND THEORY OF EQUATIONS

Algebra and Trigonometry
is also available as a regular one-volume textbook

Trigonometry

**ALGEBRA AND TRIGONOMETRY
IN FOUR PROGRAMMED VOLUMES**

THOMAS A. DAVIS
De Pauw University

HARCOURT BRACE JOVANOVICH, INC.
New York Chicago San Francisco Atlanta

ISBN: 0-15-502153-2

Library of Congress Catalog Card Number: 73-184416

Printed in the United States of America

Preface

Trigonometry considers, in programmed form, trigonometry as a study of six functions whose domains and ranges are sets of real numbers. It is a conceptual approach to what was once considered by many students a manipulative subject. The manipulation and graphing are there, too, but with meaning. This book and its three companion programmed volumes are designed for use in a variety of ways. Together, the four books constitute a basic college textbook in algebra and trigonometry. Individually, they may be used to cover a portion of the course; to supplement and reinforce another basic textbook; or to enable students, on their own, to acquire the necessary background for more advanced courses, such as calculus.

The virtues of programmed material are well known. A programmed text allows the student to proceed at his own rate, with the assurance that he has understood what he has learned. As, in part, a "self-teaching" and "self-testing" device, programming can free the instructor to use valuable class time for more advanced topics and for fuller explanation of particularly difficult concepts. Programming can also help compensate for the varying academic backgrounds students bring to their courses; each student can independently learn or review the concepts he needs to achieve the necessary level of preparation. Furthermore, I have found in my many classes at DePauw University that students enjoy working with programmed materials and profit from their use.

For instructors who like the content of the four programmed volumes but prefer a non-programmed approach, the identical material is also available as a single volume, non-programmed text, *Algebra and Trigonometry*. Some instructors will want to assign both versions, with the programmed volumes reinforcing what the student has learned from the non-programmed text. To make this dual use most effective, I have coordinated the two versions precisely: every exercise and every example in the two versions are numbered or lettered identically. But this coordination is merely a convenience and does not, of course, affect the use of the programmed volumes with any other textbook.

This book would not have been possible without the help of my wife Pat who read the material at each stage of its development. Her suggestions led to many improvements.

I also thank Dr. Michael Eraut, University of Sussex, who suggested many programming improvements, and Mrs. Patricia Gammon, who typed the many versions of the book as it evolved through testing and rewriting.

THOMAS A. DAVIS

To the Student

Programmed material such as this has the following characteristics:

(a) The subject matter is presented in carefully sequenced steps called frames.

(b) A written response is required at frequent intervals.

(c) Feedback about the correctness of the response is immediate.

To use the program effectively follow these instructions:

1. Cover the page with a piece of paper so that the frame you are working on is visible, but not its answer.

2. Read the frame carefully. Do not write your response until you have read the entire frame.

3. Make your response in the appropriate space(s) or on the appropriate diagram. If you have to solve a problem, derive a formula, or prove a theorem, put your work on a separate sheet of paper.

4. Now slide the covering paper down until the answer is visible.

5. Check your answer.

   If your answer is correct, go on to the next frame and repeat steps 2 to 5. Your answer need not be exactly the same as the one provided. Use your judgment about whether your answer is close enough to the one provided. If your answer is incorrect, try to discover why, and then go on to the next frame.

The frames in each part are numbered consecutively.

Since this is not a test, it is permissible to review previous steps if necessary.

Throughout the program are so-called express frames, terminal frames, and summary pages. If you answer the question in an express frame correctly, you are told in the answer to skip the next few frames. If you do not answer correctly, you are directed to the next frame, where you will begin a sequence that will teach you the correct response. An example of an express frame is frame 25 on page 10.

Terminal frames are usually labeled "exercise" and often occur at the end of a chapter. They are used to test your knowledge of a unit of material. If you answer the terminal frame correctly, you are directed to the next frame. If you do not answer it correctly, you are told which frames to review to enable you to do so. An example of a terminal frame is frame 148 on page 47.

Summary pages occur immediately after a sequence of frames in which a formula has been derived or a theorem has been proved. The summary pages pull together the complete proof or derivation as it should appear if you were asked to prove the theorem or derive the formula. The terminal frames and summary pages should prove especially useful in reviewing the material.

Finally, a quiz containing representative questions and problems is at the end of each chapter to help you in assessing how well you have learned the material in the chapter. To use the quiz for this purpose, write out the answers and solutions in detail and check them carefully against the answers in the back of the book. Otherwise, in glancing through the quiz, you may get the impression that you understand the material in the chapter when, in fact, you do not.

Contents

Trigonometry

PART 1

The word "trigonometry" is derived from two Greek words, *trigonon* and *metron*, and means "triangle measurement." Traditionally, trigonometry has been the study of triangles and their use in measuring distances, areas, and directions.

More recently, the emphasis has shifted to the study of periodic phenomena such as the phases of the moon, the swinging of a pendulum, alternating electric current, sound waves, and business cycles.

This unit is designed not as a complete course in trigonometry but as a prerequisite for a modern course in calculus. Because of this, we will emphasize the functional aspects of trigonometry rather than the study of triangles.

It is assumed that many of our readers already have had some traditional trigonometry. We shall begin with the study of angles but will soon advance to analytic trigonometry where we shall study trigonometry as circular functions whose domains and ranges are subsets of the real numbers.

1 Angles and Their Measure

Upon completing this chapter, you should be able to

I. Name the parts of an angle.

II. Given an angle,

(A) say whether it is positive, negative, or zero;
(B) say in which quadrant it lies;
(C) draw it in standard position.

III. Measure angles in radians and degrees. Change from one unit of measurement to another.

IV. (A) Define coterminal angles.
(B) Given an angle, name at least four angles that are coterminal with it.
(C) Given a number of angles, indicate which are coterminal.

V. Given an angle θ, give the arc length intercepted by that angle.

1. An **angle** is formed by two half-lines (or rays) that intersect at a point, as shown below. The point of intersection is called the **vertex**.

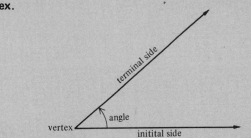

One side of the angle is called the **initial side**, the other the **terminal side**. And the angle is the amount of rotation about the vertex 0 that is required to make the initial side coincide with the terminal side.

In each figure below, label the inital side, terminal side, and vertex *I, T,* and 0, respectively.

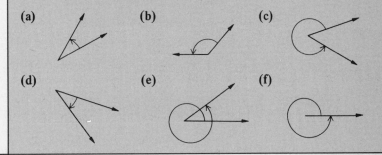

(a)   (b)   (c)

(d)   (e)   (f)

1.
(a)   (b)

(c)   (d)

(e)   (f)

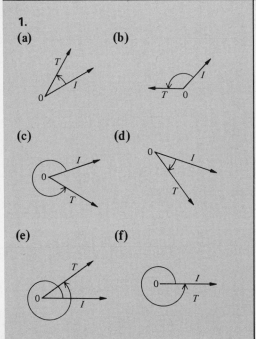

3

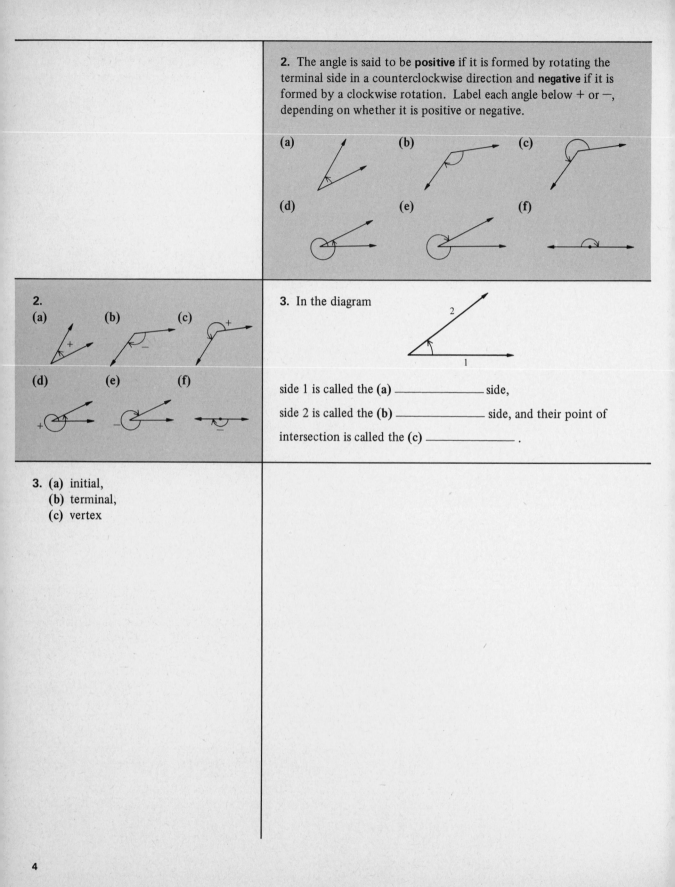

2. The angle is said to be **positive** if it is formed by rotating the terminal side in a counterclockwise direction and **negative** if it is formed by a clockwise rotation. Label each angle below + or −, depending on whether it is positive or negative.

(a)　　　　　(b)　　　　　(c)

(d)　　　　　(e)　　　　　(f)

2.
(a)　　(b)　　(c)

(d)　　(e)　　(f)

3. In the diagram

side 1 is called the **(a)** ——————— side,

side 2 is called the **(b)** ——————— side, and their point of

intersection is called the **(c)** ——————— .

3. (a) initial,
　(b) terminal,
　(c) vertex

4

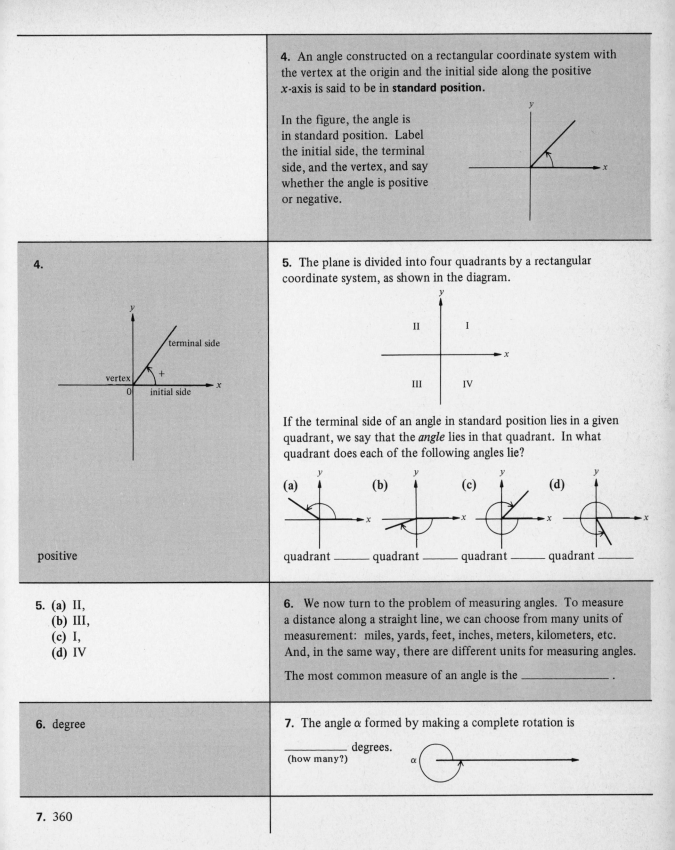

4. An angle constructed on a rectangular coordinate system with the vertex at the origin and the initial side along the positive x-axis is said to be in **standard position.**

In the figure, the angle is in standard position. Label the initial side, the terminal side, and the vertex, and say whether the angle is positive or negative.

4.

positive

5. The plane is divided into four quadrants by a rectangular coordinate system, as shown in the diagram.

If the terminal side of an angle in standard position lies in a given quadrant, we say that the *angle* lies in that quadrant. In what quadrant does each of the following angles lie?

(a) quadrant _____ (b) quadrant _____ (c) quadrant _____ (d) quadrant _____

5. (a) II,
(b) III,
(c) I,
(d) IV

6. We now turn to the problem of measuring angles. To measure a distance along a straight line, we can choose from many units of measurement: miles, yards, feet, inches, meters, kilometers, etc. And, in the same way, there are different units for measuring angles.

The most common measure of an angle is the _____.

6. degree

7. The angle α formed by making a complete rotation is

_____ degrees.
(how many?)

7. 360

8. A degree, denoted by °, is defined as $\frac{1}{360}$ of a complete rotation. Give the degree measures of the following angles.

(a)   (b)   (c)

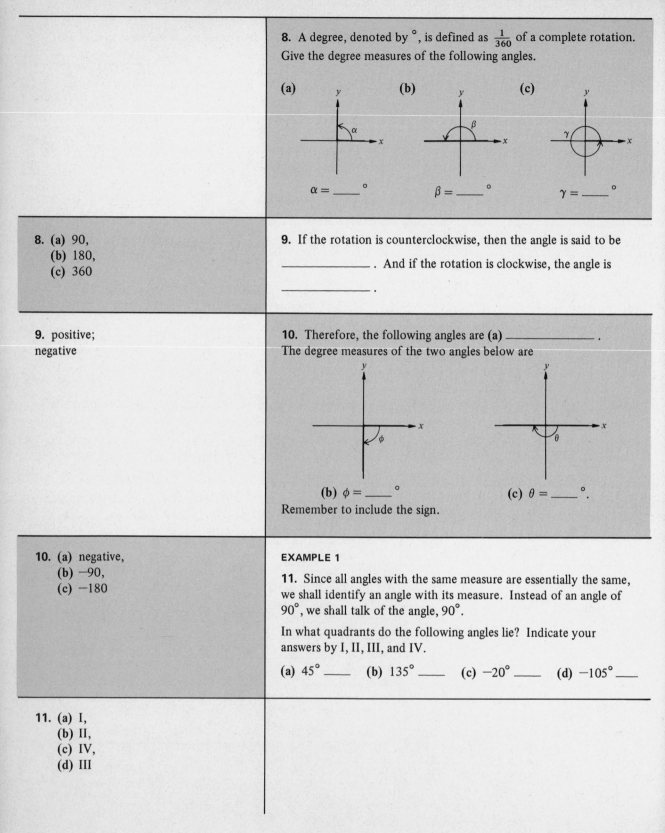

$\alpha = \underline{\quad}°$ $\beta = \underline{\quad}°$ $\gamma = \underline{\quad}°$

---

8. (a) 90,
   (b) 180,
   (c) 360

9. If the rotation is counterclockwise, then the angle is said to be

_____ . And if the rotation is clockwise, the angle is

_____ .

---

9. positive;
negative

10. Therefore, the following angles are **(a)** _____ .
The degree measures of the two angles below are

(b) $\phi = \underline{\quad}°$ **(c)** $\theta = \underline{\quad}°$.
Remember to include the sign.

---

10. (a) negative,
   (b) −90,
   (c) −180

EXAMPLE 1

11. Since all angles with the same measure are essentially the same, we shall identify an angle with its measure. Instead of an angle of 90°, we shall talk of the angle, 90°.

In what quadrants do the following angles lie? Indicate your answers by I, II, III, and IV.

(a) 45° ____   **(b)** 135° ____   **(c)** −20° ____   **(d)** −105° ____

---

11. (a) I,
   (b) II,
   (c) IV,
   (d) III

12. We can form angles that require more than one complete rotation.

Give the degree measures of the following angles.

(a)   (b)   (c)   (d)

$\alpha = $ _____ $^\circ$ $\beta = $ _____ $^\circ$ $\phi = $ _____ $^\circ$ $\theta = $ _____ $^\circ$

---

12. (a) 450,
   (b) 720,
   (c) −360,
   (d) −540

13. From the preceding examples, we see that it is impossible to determine the measure of an angle in standard position or even to tell if it is positive or negative from the position of its terminal side alone.

The angle $\alpha = 450^\circ$ (shown in frame 12) has the same terminal side as an angle of **(a)** _____ $^\circ$. And the angles β and ϕ in frame 12 have the same terminal side even though β is **(b)** _____ and
(positive, negative)

ϕ is **(c)** _____ .

---

13. (a) 90,
   (b) positive,
   (c) negative

14. DEFINITION: Angles that have the same terminal side (when placed in standard position) are called **coterminal**.

Thus the angles 45°, 405°, and -315° are coterminal. And the angles -540°, -180°, and 540° are all coterminal with the angle

_____ $^\circ$, which is between 0° and 360°.

---

14. 180

15. The angles ..., -720°, -360°, 0°, 360°, 720°, ... are all

_____ .

---

15. coterminal

16. In fact, if two angles are coterminal they differ by _____ $^\circ$ or

a multiple of _____ $^\circ$.

---

16. 360; 360

EXAMPLE 2

17. List five angles that are coterminal with the angle 60°.
Make three of them negative and two positive.

_____° _____° _____° _____° _____°

17. −300; −660; −1020; 420; 780

18. The only other measure of angles we will consider is **radian** measure. Consider the circle of radius r whose center is at the origin of a rectangular coordinate system.

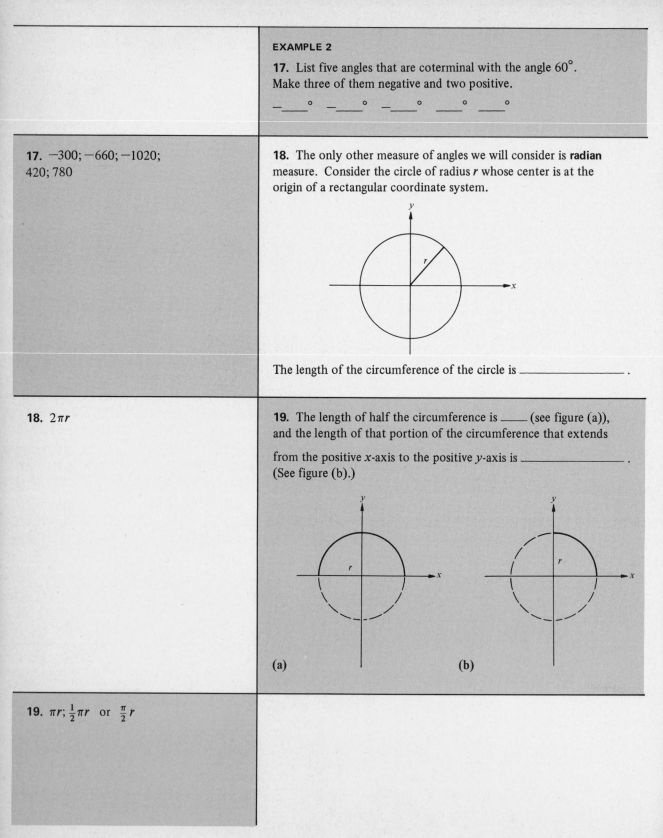

The length of the circumference of the circle is _____ .

18. $2\pi r$

19. The length of half the circumference is _____ (see figure (a)), and the length of that portion of the circumference that extends from the positive x-axis to the positive y-axis is _____ . (See figure (b).)

(a)   (b)

19. πr; $\frac{1}{2}\pi r$ or $\frac{\pi}{2} r$

8

20. That is, given a circle with radius r, the length of the arc intercepted by a $90°$ angle is _____ .

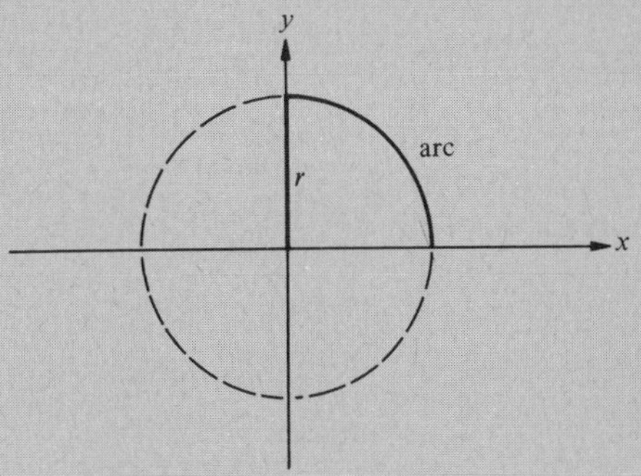

---

20. $\frac{\pi}{2} r$

21. The length of the arc intercepted by a $180°$ angle is _____ , and the length of the arc intercepted by a $45°$ angle is _____ .

---

21. πr; $\frac{\pi}{4} r$

22. Conversely, if the length of the arc intercepted by an angle $\alpha°$ is $\frac{\pi}{2} r$, then the angle $\alpha =$ _____ .

---

22. $90°$

EXAMPLE 3

23. Give the angles that intercept the following arcs.

angle in degrees	intercepts an arc of length
(a) _____	πr
(b) _____	$\frac{\pi}{4} r$
(c) _____	$\frac{2\pi}{3} r$
(d) _____	$\frac{\pi}{3} r \left(= \frac{2\pi}{6} r \right)$

---

23. (a) $180°$,
   (b) $45°$,
   (c) $120°$,
   (d) $60°$

24. Now we mark off an arc whose length is equal to *r* on our circle. What is the size of the angle θ that intercepts the arc with length *r*? _____

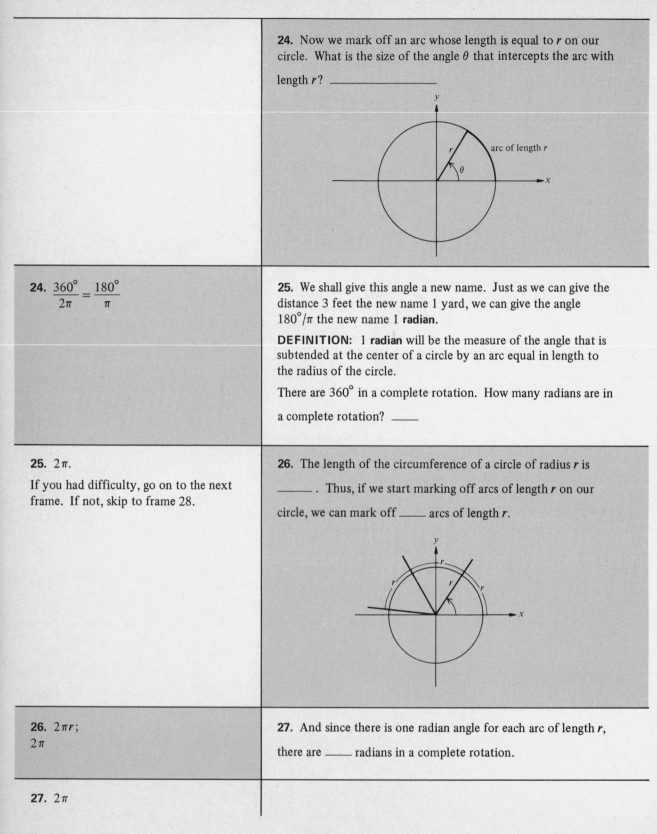

24. $\dfrac{360^\circ}{2\pi} = \dfrac{180^\circ}{\pi}$

25. We shall give this angle a new name. Just as we can give the distance 3 feet the new name 1 yard, we can give the angle $180^\circ/\pi$ the new name 1 **radian**.

DEFINITION: 1 **radian** will be the measure of the angle that is subtended at the center of a circle by an arc equal in length to the radius of the circle.

There are 360° in a complete rotation. How many radians are in a complete rotation? ____

25. 2π.

If you had difficulty, go on to the next frame. If not, skip to frame 28.

26. The length of the circumference of a circle of radius *r* is _____ . Thus, if we start marking off arcs of length *r* on our circle, we can mark off ____ arcs of length *r*.

26. $2\pi r$;
2π

27. And since there is one radian angle for each arc of length *r*, there are ____ radians in a complete rotation.

27. 2π

28. There are ____ radians in $\frac{1}{2}$ a rotation and ____ radians in $\frac{1}{4}$ of a rotation.

28. $\pi; \frac{\pi}{2}$

29. As we noted earlier, the length of the circumference of a circle of radius r is $2\pi r$, the length of half the circumference is

____ $\cdot r$, and the length of the arc intercepted by the

sides of the angle formed by $\frac{1}{4}$ of a rotation is ____ .

29. π since $(\frac{2\pi}{2} \cdot r = \pi \cdot r)$;

$\frac{\pi}{2}r \; (= \frac{2\pi}{4}r)$

30. Thus, we see that there are π radians in $\frac{1}{2}$ a rotation and the

length of $\frac{1}{2}$ the circumference is ____ $\cdot r$.

30. π

31. There are ____ radians in $\frac{1}{4}$ of a rotation, and the length of the arc intercepted by the sides of the angle formed by $\frac{1}{4}$ of a rotation

is ____ $\cdot r$.

31. $\frac{\pi}{2}; \frac{\pi}{2}$

32. And, in general, the length of the arc intercepted by an angle

of θ radians is ____ .

32. $\theta \cdot r$

33. That is, if we have a circle of radius r, and s is the length of the

arc intercepted by the angle of θ radians, then $s =$ ____ .

33. $\theta \cdot r$

34. If the radius of a circle is 2, then the length s of the arc intercepted by the angle $\frac{\pi}{8}$ radian is _____ .

---

34. $\dfrac{\pi}{4} = r \cdot \theta$

EXAMPLE 4

35. There are a number of advantages to using radian measure rather than degrees. This simple relationship between the radian measure of an angle and the length of the intercepted arc is only one of them. Radian measure is used almost exclusively in analytic trigonometry and calculus. However, we are used to thinking of angles in terms of degrees. One rotation is 2π radians, or $360°$. Thus,

(a) $360° = $ _____ radians,

(b) $180° = $ _____ radians,

(c) $\;\;90° = $ _____ radians,

(d) $\;\;45° = $ _____ radian,

(e) $-90° = $ _____ radians,

(f) $\;\;\;1° = $ _____ radian.

---

35. (a) 2π,

   (b) π,

   (c) $\frac{\pi}{2}$,

   (d) $\frac{\pi}{4}$,

   (e) $-\frac{\pi}{2}$,

   (f) $\dfrac{2\pi}{360} = \dfrac{\pi}{180}$

EXAMPLE 5

36. We can also see from the equation $360° = 2\pi$ radians that

(a) $\dfrac{2\pi}{3}$ radians $ = $ ____$°$,

(b) $\dfrac{\pi}{3}$ radians $ = $ ____$°$,

(c) $\dfrac{\pi}{6}$ radian $ = $ ____$°$,

(d) $-\dfrac{4\pi}{3}$ radians $ = $ ____$°$,

(e) $\dfrac{5\pi}{3}$ radians $ = $ ____$°$,

(f) $\;\;1$ radian $ = $ ____$°$,

---

36. (a) 120,

   (b) 60,

   (c) 30,

   (d) -240,

   (e) 300,

   (f) $\dfrac{180}{\pi}$

EXAMPLE 6

37. Express the following angles in degrees.

(a) $\dfrac{\pi}{4}$ radian $= $ ____

(b) $\dfrac{3\pi}{4}$ radians $= $ ____

(c) $\dfrac{5\pi}{4}$ radians $= $ ____

(d) $\dfrac{3\pi}{2}$ radians $= $ ____

---

37. (a) $45°$,
(b) $135°$,
(c) $225°$,
(d) $270°$

EXAMPLE 7

38. Express the following angles in radians.

(a) $720° = $ _____ radians

(b) $450° = $ _____ radians

(c) $-420° = $ _____ radians

(d) $-405° = $ _____ radians

---

38. (a) 4π,
(b) $\dfrac{5\pi}{2}$,
(c) $\dfrac{-7\pi}{3}$,
(d) $\dfrac{-9\pi}{4}$

39. In fact, since we know that **(a)** 1 radian $= $ ____ degrees and

(b) 1 degree $= $ _____ radian, we can convert the measure of any angle from degrees to radians or from radians to degrees.

(c) $15° = $ ____ radian

(d) _____ $= \dfrac{5\pi}{18}$ radian

(e) $-$_____ $= \dfrac{-4\pi}{9}$ radians

(f) $123° = $ ____ radians

---

39. (a) $\dfrac{180}{\pi}$, (b) $\dfrac{\pi}{180}$,

(c) $\dfrac{\pi}{12}$, (d) $50°$, (e) $80°$,

(f) $\dfrac{123\pi}{180}$.

If you had difficulty, go on to the next frame. If not, skip to frame 45.

40. Since

$1° = \dfrac{\pi}{180}$ radian, $\theta° = \left(\theta° \times \dfrac{\pi}{180}\right)$ radians.

So, to convert the measure of an angle from degrees to radians,

we multiply the number of degrees by _____ .

---

40. $\dfrac{\pi}{180}$

EXAMPLE 8

41. Express the following angles in radians.

(a) $25° =$ _____ radian

(b) $85° =$ _____ radians

(c) $-63° =$ _____ radians

(d) $227° =$ _____ radians

---

41. (a) $\dfrac{5\pi}{36}$,

(b) $\dfrac{17\pi}{36}$,

(c) $\dfrac{-7\pi}{20}$,

(d) $\dfrac{277\pi}{180}$

42. To convert the measure of angles from radians to degrees, we multiply the number of radians by _____ , since

θ radians $= (\phi \times$ _____ $)$ degrees.

---

42. $\dfrac{180}{\pi}$; $\dfrac{180}{\pi}$

43. 1 radian is _____ than 1 degree. Thus an angle θ
(larger, smaller)

will have _____ radians than degrees.
(fewer, more)

---

43. larger;
fewer

44. Therefore, to convert from degrees to radians, we multiply

by _____ , and to convert from radians to degrees we multiply

by _____ .

---

44. $\dfrac{\pi}{180}$; $\dfrac{180}{\pi}$

EXAMPLE 9

45. Express the following angles in degrees or radians as required.

(a) _____ radian = 20°

(b) $\frac{\pi}{17}$ radian = _____°

(c) $\frac{-\pi}{15}$ radian = _____°

(d) _____ radians = 390°

(e) 5 radians = _____°

---

45. (a) $\frac{\pi}{9}$

(b) $\frac{180}{17}$,

(c) -36,

(d) $\frac{13\pi}{6}$,

(e) $\frac{900}{\pi}$.

If you had difficulty, see frames 40 to 44.

46. We saw in frame 16 that two angles are coterminal if they differ by a complete rotation or any number of complete rotations. Thus, in terms of radians, two angles θ and ϕ are coterminal if

θ radians = $\phi \pm ($____$)n$, where n is any integer.

---

46. 2π

47. Thus, the angles $\frac{-7\pi}{2}$, $\frac{-3\pi}{2}$, $\frac{\pi}{2}$, $\frac{5\pi}{2}$, and $\frac{9\pi}{2}$ are all

_____ .

---

47. coterminal

EXAMPLE 10

48. List five angles (three negative and two positive) that are coterminal with $\frac{\pi}{3}$.

$-$____ $-$____ $-$____

$-$____ $-$____

---

48. $-\frac{17\pi}{3}$, $-\frac{11\pi}{3}$,

$-\frac{5\pi}{3}$, $\frac{7\pi}{3}$, $\frac{13\pi}{3}$

(since $\frac{\pi}{3} - 2\pi = -\frac{5\pi}{3}$,

$\frac{\pi}{3} - 2(2\pi) = -\frac{11\pi}{3}$, etc.)

QUIZ

If you cannot answer the following questions correctly, review the appropriate frames.

1. Label the parts of the angle in the diagram.

    (a) is _____ .

    (b) is _____ .

    (c) is _____ .

    (d) Draw the angle in standard position
         on the axes shown.

    (e) The angle is
         (1) positive,
         (2) negative,
         (3) zero.

    (f) The angle lies in quadrant
         (1) I, (2) II, (3) III, (4) IV.

2. Change the following from degrees to radians or from radians to degrees as needed.

degrees		radians	degrees		radians
60°	=	_____	_____	=	$\dfrac{3\pi}{4}$
270°	=	_____			
43°	=	_____	_____	=	$\dfrac{11\pi}{6}$
			_____	=	3

3. Two angles α and θ are coterminal if and only if _____ .

    Name three angles, two positive and one negative, that are coterminal with $\frac{\pi}{6}$.

4. For a circle of radius r, the arc length s intercepted by an angle θ, as shown in the

    diagram, is given by $s =$ _____ .

Answers are at end of book.

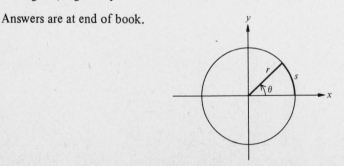

2 Definitions of Trigonometric Functions

Upon completing this chapter, you should be able to

I. Define the six trigonometric functions of angles and use their names and abbreviations correctly.

II. Write the five relationships among the trigonometric functions that are immediate consequences of the definitions.

III. State whether each trigonometric function is positive or negative in each of the four quadrants.

IV. Draw the appropriate triangles and give the six trigonometric values for 30°, 45°, and 60°.

V. Given the value of one of the trigonometric functions of an angle, calculate the five other trigonometric functions.

49. Consider the circle below, with radius r, whose center is at the origin. Let θ be an angle in standard position, and $P(x, y)$ be the point where the terminal side of the angle intersects the circle.

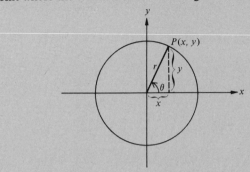

As you can see, there are three numbers associated with the angle θ: x, y, and r. From these three numbers we can form six trigonometric functions.

DEFINITION:

1. sine $\theta = \dfrac{y}{r} = \dfrac{\text{ordinate}}{\text{radius}}$

2. cosine $\theta = \dfrac{x}{r} = \dfrac{\text{abscissa}}{\text{radius}}$

3. tangent $\theta = \dfrac{y}{x} = \dfrac{\text{ordinate}}{\text{abscissa}}$

4. cotangent $\theta = \dfrac{x}{y} = \dfrac{\text{abscissa}}{\text{ordinate}}$

5. secant $\theta = \dfrac{r}{x} = \dfrac{\text{radius}}{\text{abscissa}}$

6. cosecant $\theta = \dfrac{r}{y} = \dfrac{\text{radius}}{\text{ordinate}}$

Thus, we see from the diagram that

(a) sine $\dfrac{\pi}{6} = $ _____ $= $ ____ ,

(b) cosine $\dfrac{\pi}{6} = $ _____ ,

(c) tangent $\dfrac{\pi}{6} = $ _____ ,

(d) cotangent $\dfrac{\pi}{6} = $ _____ ,

(e) secant $\dfrac{\pi}{6} = $ _____ ,

(f) cosecant $\dfrac{\pi}{6} = $ _____ .

49.
(a) $\dfrac{\text{ordinate}}{\text{radius}}$ $\dfrac{1}{2}$ (b) $\dfrac{\text{abscissa}}{\text{radius}} = \dfrac{\sqrt{3}}{2}$, (c) $\dfrac{\text{ordinate}}{\text{abscissa}} = \dfrac{1}{\sqrt{3}}$,

(d) $\dfrac{\text{abscissa}}{\text{ordinate}} = \sqrt{3}$, (e) $\dfrac{\text{radius}}{\text{abscissa}} = \dfrac{2}{\sqrt{3}}$, (f) $\dfrac{\text{radius}}{\text{ordinate}} = 2$

50. Sine θ is read "sine of θ," or "sine θ," and is abbreviated *sin θ*. Sin θ is defined by

$$\sin \theta = \underline{\hspace{5cm}} .$$

NOTE: You may already have learned the trigonometric functions in terms of the adjacent side, opposite side, and hypotenuse of a triangle. Look at the triangle in the figure and verify that our definitions agree with the ones you already know.

50. $\dfrac{\text{ordinate}}{\text{radius}} = \dfrac{y}{r}$

51. Cosine θ is read "cosine of θ" and is abbreviated *cos θ*. Cos θ is defined by

$$\cos \theta = \underline{\hspace{4cm}} .$$

51. $\dfrac{\text{abscissa}}{\text{radius}} = \dfrac{x}{r}$

52. Tangent θ is abbreviated *tan θ* and is defined by

$$\tan \theta = \underline{\hspace{4cm}} .$$

52. $\dfrac{\text{ordinate}}{\text{abscissa}} = \dfrac{y}{x}$

53. Cotangent θ is abbreviated *cot θ* and is defined by

$$\cot \theta = \underline{\hspace{4cm}} .$$

53. $\dfrac{\text{abscissa}}{\text{ordinate}} = \dfrac{x}{y}$

54. We write secant θ as *sec θ*. It is defined by

$$\sec \theta = \underline{\hspace{4cm}} .$$

54. $\dfrac{\text{radius}}{\text{abscissa}} = \dfrac{r}{x}$

55. And, finally, we write cosecant θ as *csc θ*. It is defined by

$$\csc \theta = \underline{\hspace{4cm}} .$$

55. $\dfrac{\text{radius}}{\text{ordinate}} = \dfrac{r}{y}$

56. It is clear from the definitions of the trigonometric functions that each function is the reciprocal of one of the others. That is,

(a) $\csc \theta = \dfrac{1}{\rule{3cm}{0.4pt}}$,

(b) $\sec \theta = \dfrac{}{\rule{3cm}{0.4pt}}$,

(c) $\cot \theta = \dfrac{}{\rule{3cm}{0.4pt}}$.

56.

(a) $\dfrac{1}{\sin \theta}\left(\csc \theta = \dfrac{r}{y} = \dfrac{1}{\dfrac{y}{r}} = \dfrac{1}{\sin \theta}\right)$,

(b) $\dfrac{1}{\cos \theta}\left(\sec \theta = \dfrac{r}{x} = \dfrac{1}{\dfrac{x}{r}} = \dfrac{1}{\cos \theta}\right)$,

(c) $\dfrac{1}{\tan \theta}\left(\cot \theta = \dfrac{x}{y} = \dfrac{1}{\dfrac{y}{x}} = \dfrac{1}{\tan \theta}\right)$.

57. Furthermore,

$\dfrac{\sin \theta}{\cos \theta} = \rule{3cm}{0.4pt}$ and

$\dfrac{\cos \theta}{\sin \theta} = \rule{3cm}{0.4pt}$.

57. $\tan \theta$;
$\cot \theta$

58. We now show that the trigonometric functions depend only on the size of the angle and *not* on the size of the circle.

Consider the concentric circles in the diagram where the terminal side of the angle θ cuts the circles at $P(x, y)$ and $P'(x', y')$.

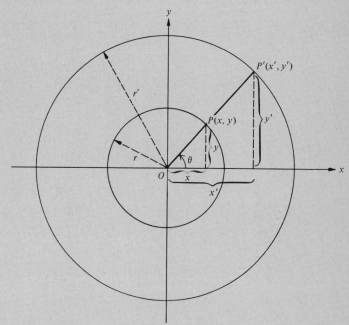

From plane geometry we know that the two triangles are similar and hence the ratios of the lengths of their corresponding sides are equal. That is, in terms of x', y', and r',

(a) $\dfrac{y}{r} =$ _____ , (b) $\dfrac{x}{r} =$ _____ , (c) $\dfrac{x}{y} =$ _____ ,

(d) $\dfrac{y}{x} =$ _____ , (e) $\dfrac{r}{x} =$ _____ , (f) $\dfrac{r}{y} =$ _____ .

Thus $\sin \theta$, $\cos \theta$, $\tan \theta$, $\cot \theta$, $\sec \theta$, and $\csc \theta$ depend only on θ and not on r.

58. (a) $\dfrac{y'}{r'}$ (b) $\dfrac{x'}{r'}$ (c) $\dfrac{x'}{y'}$

   (d) $\dfrac{y'}{x'}$ (e) $\dfrac{r'}{x'}$ (f) $\dfrac{r'}{y'}$

59. Using the appropriate abbreviations, name and define the six trigonometric functions in terms of x, y, and r.

(a) _____ = _____

(b) _____ = _____

(c) _____ = _____

(d) _____ = _____

(e) _____ = _____

(f) _____ = _____

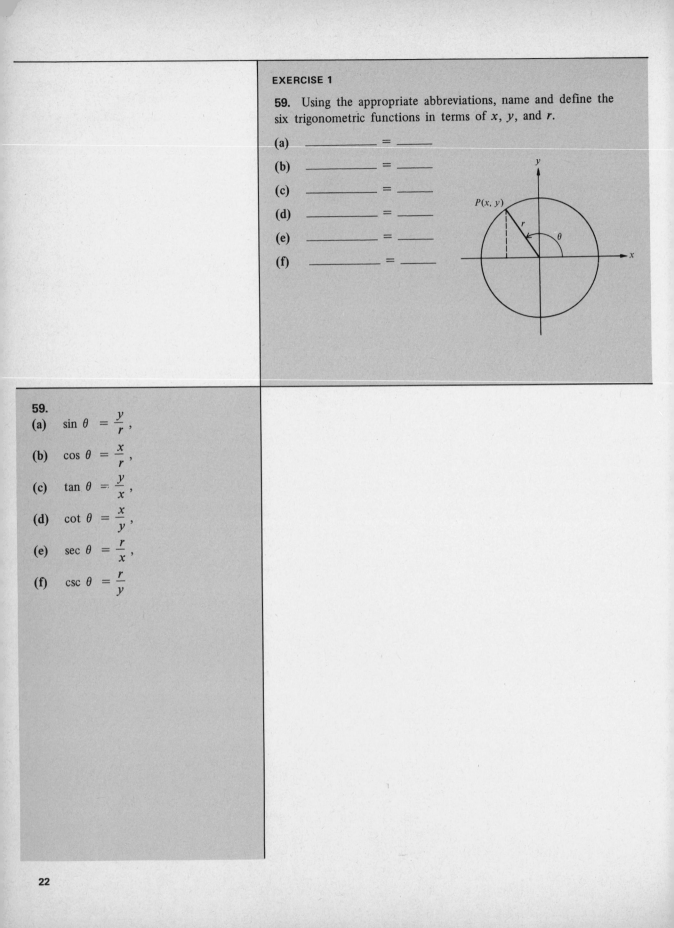

59.

(a) $\sin \theta = \dfrac{y}{r}$,

(b) $\cos \theta = \dfrac{x}{r}$,

(c) $\tan \theta = \dfrac{y}{x}$,

(d) $\cot \theta = \dfrac{x}{y}$,

(e) $\sec \theta = \dfrac{r}{x}$,

(f) $\csc \theta = \dfrac{r}{y}$

60. Now let us consider some specific angles. We may calculate the values of the trigonometric functions at three angles $30°(\pi/6)$, $45°(\pi/4)$, and $60°(\pi/3)$ without difficulty.

We shall look first at the angle $60°(\pi/3)$. In the figure, we have a right triangle with angles of $30°$ and $60°$.

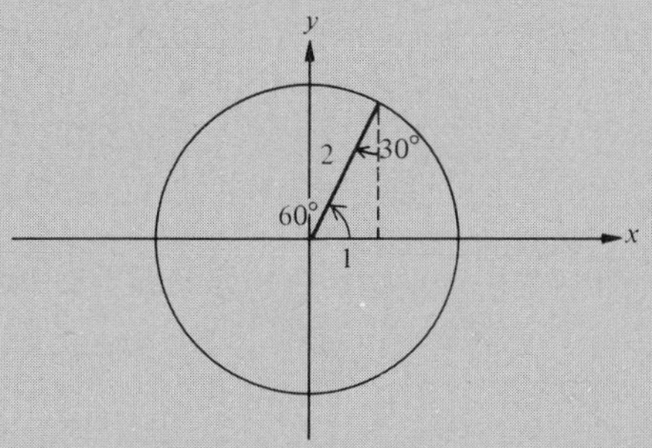

It is well known from geometry that if we choose the shortest side as one unit in length, the hypotenuse must be 2 units in length.

And by the Pythagorean theorem, the third side must be _____ units in length.

60. $\sqrt{3}$

61. Now that we know that **(a)** $x =$ ___ , **(b)** $y =$ ___ , and **(c)** $r =$ ___ , we can calculate the values of the six trigonometric functions at $60° = \pi/3$ radians.

(d) $\sin \frac{\pi}{3} =$ _____   **(e)** $\cos \frac{\pi}{3} =$ _____   **(f)** $\tan \frac{\pi}{3} =$ _____

(g) $\csc \frac{\pi}{3} =$ _____   **(h)** $\sec \frac{\pi}{3} =$ _____   **(i)** $\cot \frac{\pi}{3} =$ _____

61. (a) 1, **(b)** $\sqrt{3}$, **(c)** 2,

(d) $\frac{\sqrt{3}}{2}$,   **(e)** $\frac{1}{2}$,   **(f)** $\sqrt{3}$,

(g) $\frac{2}{\sqrt{3}}$ **(h)** 2,   **(i)** $\frac{1}{\sqrt{3}}$

62. If we draw a $30°\,(\pi/6)$ angle in standard position, then this time **(a)** $y = \underline{}$, $r = 2$, and **(b)** $x = \underline{}$. And the values of the six trigonometric functions at $30° = \frac{\pi}{6}$ radian are:

(c) $\sin \frac{\pi}{6} = \underline{}$,

(d) $\cos \frac{\pi}{6} = \underline{}$,

(e) $\tan \frac{\pi}{6} = \underline{}$,

(f) $\csc \frac{\pi}{6} = \underline{}$,

(g) $\sec \frac{\pi}{6} = \underline{}$,

(h) $\cot \frac{\pi}{6} = \underline{}$.

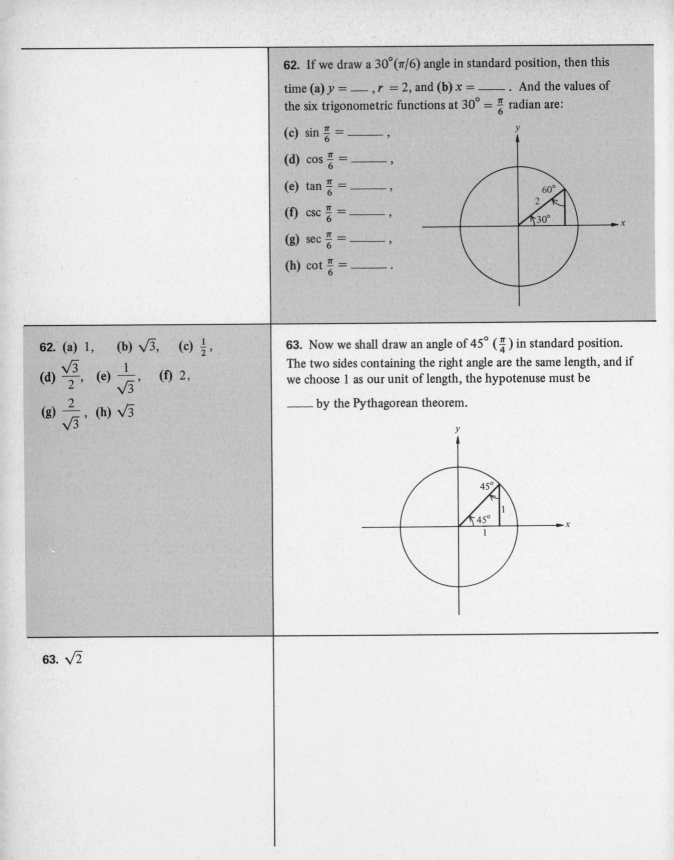

62. **(a)** 1, **(b)** $\sqrt{3}$, **(c)** $\frac{1}{2}$,

(d) $\frac{\sqrt{3}}{2}$, **(e)** $\frac{1}{\sqrt{3}}$, **(f)** 2,

(g) $\frac{2}{\sqrt{3}}$, **(h)** $\sqrt{3}$

63. Now we shall draw an angle of $45°\,\left(\frac{\pi}{4}\right)$ in standard position. The two sides containing the right angle are the same length, and if we choose 1 as our unit of length, the hypotenuse must be

$\underline{}$ by the Pythagorean theorem.

63. $\sqrt{2}$

64. Thus, since **(a)** $x = $ ____ , **(b)** $y = $ ____ , and **(c)** $r = $ ____ , we can calculate the values of the six trigonometric functions at $45° = \frac{\pi}{4}$ radian.

(d) $\sin \frac{\pi}{4} = $ ____   **(e)** $\cos \frac{\pi}{4} = $ ____   **(f)** $\tan \frac{\pi}{4} = $ ____

(g) $\csc \frac{\pi}{4} = $ ____   **(h)** $\sec \frac{\pi}{4} = $ ____   **(i)** $\cot \frac{\pi}{4} = $ ____

64. (a) 1,   **(b)** 1,   **(c)** $\sqrt{2}$,

(d) $\dfrac{1}{\sqrt{2}}$,   **(e)** $\dfrac{1}{\sqrt{2}}$,   **(f)** 1,

(g) $\sqrt{2}$,   **(h)** $\sqrt{2}$,   **(i)** 1

65. Insert the values of the six trigonometric functions for each angle listed.

θ	$\frac{\pi}{6}(30°)$	$\frac{\pi}{4}(45°)$	$\frac{\pi}{3}(60°)$
$\sin \theta$			
$\cos \theta$			
$\tan \theta$			
$\csc \theta$			
$\sec \theta$			
$\cot \theta$			

65.

θ	$\frac{\pi}{6}(30°)$	$\frac{\pi}{4}(45°)$	$\frac{\pi}{3}(60°)$
$\sin \theta$	$\dfrac{1}{2}$	$\dfrac{1}{\sqrt{2}}$	$\dfrac{\sqrt{3}}{2}$
$\cos \theta$	$\dfrac{\sqrt{3}}{2}$	$\dfrac{1}{\sqrt{2}}$	$\dfrac{1}{2}$
$\tan \theta$	$\dfrac{1}{\sqrt{3}}$	1	$\sqrt{3}$
$\csc \theta$	2	$\sqrt{2}$	$\dfrac{2}{\sqrt{3}}$
$\sec \theta$	$\dfrac{2}{\sqrt{3}}$	$\sqrt{2}$	2
$\cot \theta$	$\sqrt{3}$	1	$\dfrac{1}{\sqrt{3}}$

66. Most of our figures have shown θ in the first quadrant. However, the trigonometric functions are defined for all angles θ for which the denominator of the ratio does not equal zero. Thus, if θ is in the second quadrant, as shown below, then

x is **(a)** _____ , y is **(b)** _____ , and r is
(positive, negative)

always taken to be **(c)** _____ .

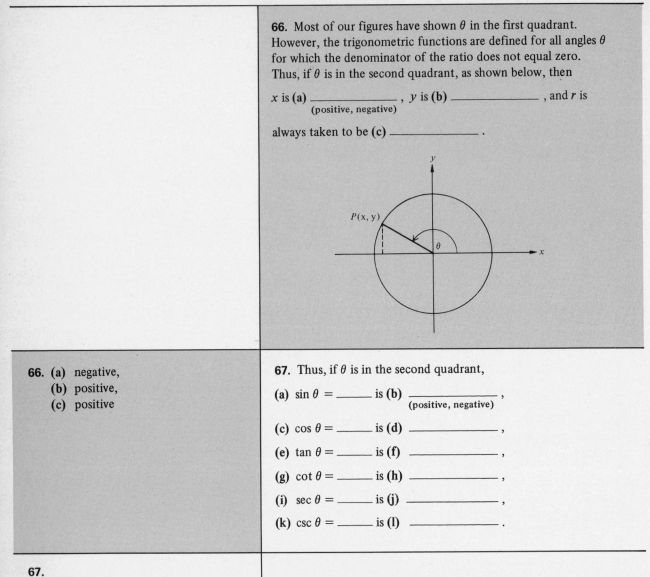

---

66. (a) negative,
   (b) positive,
   (c) positive

67. Thus, if θ is in the second quadrant,

(a) $\sin \theta =$ _____ is **(b)** _____ ,
(positive, negative)

(c) $\cos \theta =$ _____ is **(d)** _____ ,

(e) $\tan \theta =$ _____ is **(f)** _____ ,

(g) $\cot \theta =$ _____ is **(h)** _____ ,

(i) $\sec \theta =$ _____ is **(j)** _____ ,

(k) $\csc \theta =$ _____ is **(l)** _____ .

67.

(a) $\dfrac{y}{r}$,   **(b)** positive,

(c) $\dfrac{x}{r}$,   **(d)** negative,

(e) $\dfrac{y}{x}$,   **(f)** negative,

(g) $\dfrac{x}{y}$,   **(h)** negative,

(i) $\dfrac{r}{x}$,   **(j)** negative,

(k) $\dfrac{r}{y}$,   **(l)** positive

68. If θ is in the third quadrant, then x is _____ , and y is _____ .

---

68. negative; negative

69. Hence,

sin θ is **(a)** _____ ,

cos θ is **(b)** _____ ,

tan θ is **(c)** _____ ,

cot θ is **(d)** _____ ,

sec θ is **(e)** _____ ,

csc θ is **(f)** _____ .

---

69. (a) negative,
  (b) negative,
  (c) positive,
  (d) positive,
  (e) negative,
  (f) negative

70. If θ is in the fourth quadrant, then x is _____ and y is _____ .

---

70. positive; negative

71. Hence,

sin θ is **(a)** _____ ,

cos θ is **(b)** _____ ,

tan θ is **(c)** _____ ,

cot θ is **(d)** _____ ,

sec θ is **(e)** _____ ,

csc θ is **(f)** _____ .

---

71. (a) negative,
  (b) positive,
  (c) negative,
  (d) negative,
  (e) positive,
  (f) negative

72. Finally, if θ is in the first quadrant, all the trigonometric functions are _____ .

---

72. positive

73. Below is a coordinate system for each of the six trigonometric functions. Indicate in each quadrant, by using a + or −, whether the given function is positive or negative.

(a) sin θ

(b) cos θ

(c) tan θ

(d) csc θ

(e) sec θ

(f) cot θ

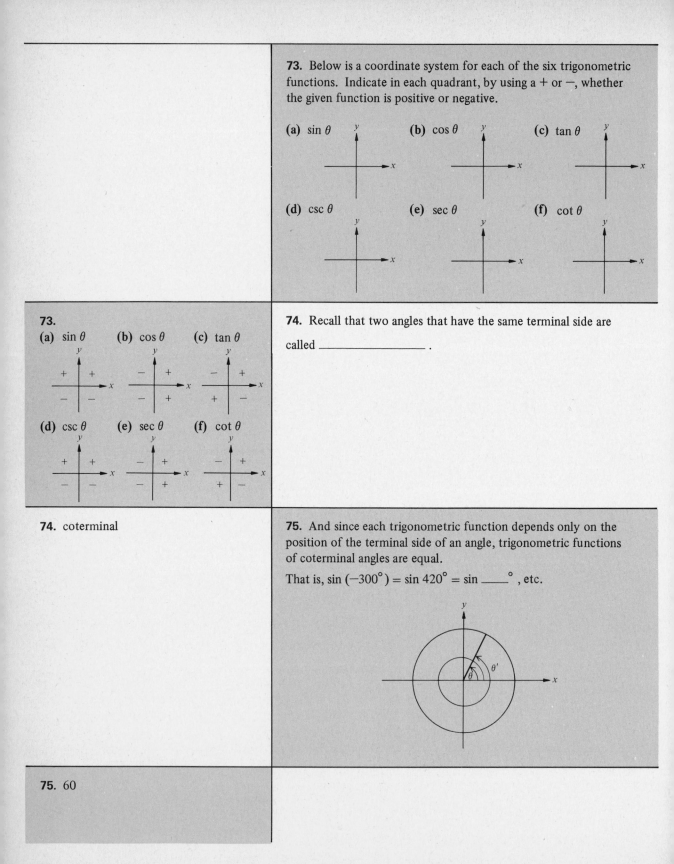

73.

(a) sin θ

−	+
+	+
−	−

(b) cos θ

−	+
−	+

(c) tan θ

−	+
+	−

(d) csc θ

+	+
−	−

(e) sec θ

−	+
−	+

(f) cot θ

−	+
+	−

74. Recall that two angles that have the same terminal side are called _____ .

74. coterminal

75. And since each trigonometric function depends only on the position of the terminal side of an angle, trigonometric functions of coterminal angles are equal.

That is, sin (−300°) = sin 420° = sin ____° , etc.

75. 60

76. Similarly $\tan\left(-\dfrac{5\pi}{3}\right) = \tan\dfrac{7\pi}{3} = \tan$ _____ , etc.

We could do the same for the four other trigonometric functions.

---

76. $\dfrac{\pi}{3}$

77. As we have noted, the trigonometric function of an angle θ is completely determined by the position of the terminal side of θ. Thus trigonometric functions have the same values at all angles

that are **(a)** _____ .

Give the following values.

(b) $\sin(-4\pi) =$ _____   **(c)** $\cos 7\pi$ = _____

(d) $\sin\dfrac{13\pi}{6}$ = _____   **(e)** $\tan\dfrac{9\pi}{4}$ = _____

(f) $\sin\dfrac{7\pi}{2}$ = _____   **(g)** $\tan\left(-\dfrac{3\pi}{2}\right) =$ _____

(h) $\cos\dfrac{13\pi}{3}$ = _____   **(i)** $\tan\dfrac{17\pi}{3}$ = _____

(j) $\cos\left(-\dfrac{11\pi}{6}\right) =$ _____

---

77. (a) coterminal,

(b) 0,   **(c)** -1,

(d) $\dfrac{1}{2}$,   **(e)** 1,

(f) -1,   **(g)** undefined,

(h) $-\dfrac{1}{2}$,   **(i)** $\sqrt{3}$

(j) $\dfrac{+\sqrt{3}}{2}$,

78. If we know the value of one of the trigonometric functions of an angle θ, and if we know what quadrant θ lies in, we can calculate the values of the other five trigonometric functions.

For example, let θ be in the first quadrant and let $\tan\theta = \dfrac{4}{3}$.

Since $\tan\theta$ is independent of the size of the circle, we can choose a circle of convenient size.

In this case, since

(a) $\dfrac{y}{x} = \tan\theta =$ _____ ,

it is clearly convenient to

choose the case where **(b)** $y =$ ___ and **(c)** $x =$ ___ .

---

78. (a) $\dfrac{4}{3}$,

(b) 4,

(c) 3

79. And by the Pythagorean theorem $r^2 = x^2 + y^2$. Hence, if in the preceding example, $x = 3$ and $y = 4$,

$r =$ _____ .

---

79. $\sqrt{(3)^2 + (4)^2} = \sqrt{25} = 5$

80. Thus, if θ is in the first quadrant and $\tan \theta = \frac{4}{3}$, then $x = 3, y = 4, r = 5$, and

(a) $\sin \theta =$ _____ , (b) $\cos \theta =$ _____ , $\tan \theta = \frac{4}{3}$,

(c) $\csc \theta =$ _____ , (d) $\sec \theta =$ _____ , (e) $\cot \theta =$ _____ .

---

80. (a) $\frac{4}{5}$, (b) $\frac{3}{5}$,

(c) $\frac{5}{4}$, (d) $\frac{5}{3}$, (e) $\frac{3}{4}$

EXAMPLE 1

81. Let θ be in the third quadrant and let $\sin \theta = -\dfrac{\sqrt{3}}{2}$.
Calculate the following:

(a) $\cos \theta =$ _____ , (b) $\tan \theta =$ _____ , (c) $\csc \theta =$ _____ ,

(d) $\sec \theta =$ _____ , (e) $\cot \theta =$ _____ .

---

81. (a) $-\frac{1}{2}$, (b) $\sqrt{3}$,

(c) $-\dfrac{2}{\sqrt{3}}$, (d) -2, (e) $\dfrac{1}{\sqrt{3}}$.

If you had difficulty, go on to the next frame. If not, skip to frame 85.

82. Since (a) $\dfrac{y}{r} = \sin \theta =$ _____ , we can take

(b) $y =$ _____ and (c) $r =$ _____ in our diagram.

---

82. (a) $-\dfrac{\sqrt{3}}{2}$, (b) $-\sqrt{3}$, (c) 2

83. And again by the Pythagorean theorem $r^2 = x^2 + y^2$ or $x^2 = r^2 - y^2$.

Since θ is in quadrant III, x is _____ and
(positive, negative)

$x =$ _____ .

---

83. negative;

$-\sqrt{r^2 - y^2} = -\sqrt{4 - 3} = -\sqrt{1} = -1$

84. Thus, if θ is in the third quadrant and
$\sin \theta = -\dfrac{\sqrt{3}}{2}$, then

(a) $\cos \theta =$ _____ , (b) $\tan \theta =$ _____ , (c) $\csc \theta =$ _____ ,

(d) $\sec \theta =$ _____ , (e) $\cot \theta =$ _____ .

---

84. (a) $-\frac{1}{2}$, (b) $\sqrt{3}$, (c) $-\dfrac{2}{\sqrt{3}}$,

(d) -2, (e) $\dfrac{1}{\sqrt{3}}$

(since $x = -1, y = -\sqrt{3}$, and $r = 2$)

EXAMPLE 2

85. Let $\cot \theta = -\sqrt{3}$ and let $\sin \theta$ be positive. Calculate the following:

(a) $\sin \theta =$ _____ ,   **(b)** $\cos \theta =$ _____ ,   **(c)** $\tan \theta =$ _____ ,

(d) $\csc \theta =$ _____ ,   **(e)** $\sec \theta =$ _____ .

---

85. (a) $\frac{1}{2}$, **(b)** $-\dfrac{\sqrt{3}}{2}$, **(c)** $-\dfrac{1}{\sqrt{3}}$,

(d) 2, **(e)** $-\dfrac{2}{\sqrt{3}}$.

If you had difficulty, go on to the next frame. If not, skip to frame 90.

86. First, we must determine in which quadrant θ lies. Since $\cot \theta$ is negative, θ is in either quadrant _____ or quadrant _____ .

---

86. II; IV

87. And since $\sin \theta$ is positive, θ is in either quadrant _____ or quadrant _____ .

---

87. I; II

88. To satisfy both requirements, θ must be in quadrant _____ .

---

88. II

89. Therefore, we know that θ lies in quadrant II and $\cot \theta = -\sqrt{3}$. Now calculate

(a) $\sin \theta =$ _____ ,   **(b)** $\cos \theta =$ _____ ,   **(c)** $\tan \theta =$ _____ ,

(d) $\csc \theta =$ _____ ,   **(e)** $\sec \theta =$ _____ .

---

89. (a) $\frac{1}{2}$, **(b)** $-\dfrac{\sqrt{3}}{2}$, **(c)** $-\dfrac{1}{\sqrt{3}}$,

(d) 2, **(e)** $-\dfrac{2}{\sqrt{3}}$.

If you had difficulty, see frames 78 to 84.

EXAMPLE 3

90. Let $\cos \theta = \dfrac{1}{\sqrt{2}}$ and let $\csc \theta$ be negative. Calculate the following:

(a) $\sin \theta =$ _____ , $\cos \theta = \dfrac{1}{\sqrt{2}}$,   **(b)** $\tan \theta =$ _____ ,

(c) $\csc \theta =$ _____ ,   **(d)** $\sec \theta =$ _____ ,   **(e)** $\cot \theta =$ _____ .

---

90. (a) $-\dfrac{1}{\sqrt{2}}$, **(b)** -1,

(c) $-\sqrt{2}$, **(d)** $\sqrt{2}$, **(e)** -1.

If you had difficulty, see frames 85 to 89.

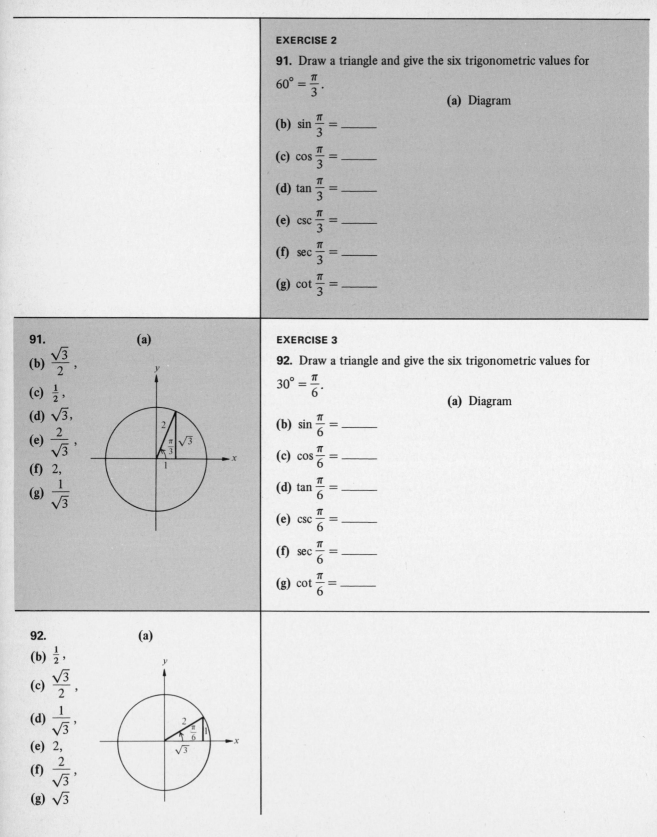

EXERCISE 2

91. Draw a triangle and give the six trigonometric values for $60° = \dfrac{\pi}{3}$.

(a) Diagram

(b) $\sin \dfrac{\pi}{3} =$ _____

(c) $\cos \dfrac{\pi}{3} =$ _____

(d) $\tan \dfrac{\pi}{3} =$ _____

(e) $\csc \dfrac{\pi}{3} =$ _____

(f) $\sec \dfrac{\pi}{3} =$ _____

(g) $\cot \dfrac{\pi}{3} =$ _____

91. **(a)**

(b) $\dfrac{\sqrt{3}}{2}$,

(c) $\dfrac{1}{2}$,

(d) $\sqrt{3}$,

(e) $\dfrac{2}{\sqrt{3}}$,

(f) 2,

(g) $\dfrac{1}{\sqrt{3}}$

EXERCISE 3

92. Draw a triangle and give the six trigonometric values for $30° = \dfrac{\pi}{6}$.

(a) Diagram

(b) $\sin \dfrac{\pi}{6} =$ _____

(c) $\cos \dfrac{\pi}{6} =$ _____

(d) $\tan \dfrac{\pi}{6} =$ _____

(e) $\csc \dfrac{\pi}{6} =$ _____

(f) $\sec \dfrac{\pi}{6} =$ _____

(g) $\cot \dfrac{\pi}{6} =$ _____

92. **(a)**

(b) $\dfrac{1}{2}$,

(c) $\dfrac{\sqrt{3}}{2}$,

(d) $\dfrac{1}{\sqrt{3}}$,

(e) 2,

(f) $\dfrac{2}{\sqrt{3}}$,

(g) $\sqrt{3}$

93. Draw a triangle and give the six trigonometric values for $45° = \dfrac{\pi}{4}$.

(a) Diagram

(b) $\sin \dfrac{\pi}{4} = $ _____

(c) $\cos \dfrac{\pi}{4} = $ _____

(d) $\tan \dfrac{\pi}{4} = $ _____

(e) $\csc \dfrac{\pi}{4} = $ _____

(f) $\sec \dfrac{\pi}{4} = $ _____

(g) $\cot \dfrac{\pi}{4} = $ _____

93.

(b) $\dfrac{1}{\sqrt{2}}$,

(c) $\dfrac{1}{\sqrt{2}}$,

(d) 1,

(e) $\sqrt{2}$,

(f) $\sqrt{2}$,

(g) 1

(a)

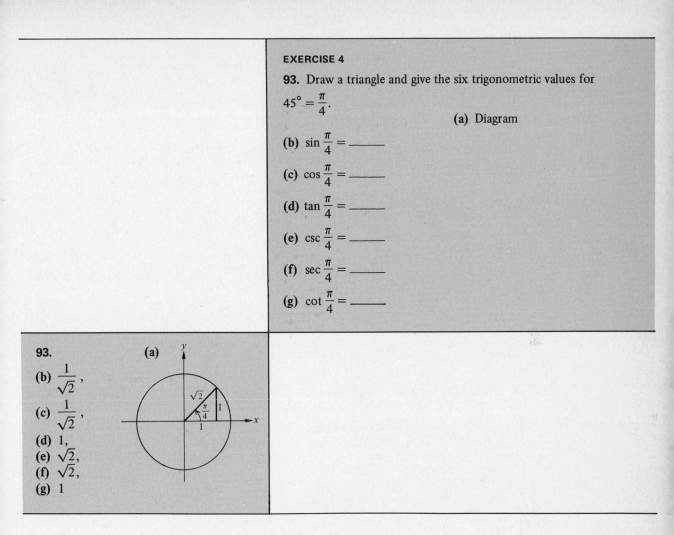

PROBLEMS

1. Let θ be in the second quadrant and let $\cos \theta = -\frac{1}{2}$. Calculate $\sin \theta$, $\tan \theta$, $\csc \theta$, $\sec \theta$, and $\cot \theta$.

2. Let θ be in quadrant III and let $\tan \theta = 4$. Calculate $\sin \theta$, $\cos \theta$, $\csc \theta$, $\sec \theta$, and $\cot \theta$.

3. Let $\sin \theta = -\frac{1}{2}$ and let $\cos \theta$ be positive. Calculate $\cos \theta$, $\tan \theta$, $\csc \theta$, $\sec \theta$, and $\cot \theta$.

4. Let $\cot \theta = \frac{3}{2}$ and let $\sec \theta$ be positive. Calculate $\sin \theta$, $\cos \theta$, $\tan \theta$, $\csc \theta$, and $\sec \theta$.

Answers are at end of book.

QUIZ

If you cannot answer the following questions correctly, review the appropriate frames.

1. Define each of the trigonometric functions in terms of x, y, and r.

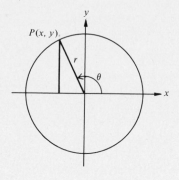

$\sin \theta = $ _____ $\cos \theta = $ _____ $\tan \theta = $ _____

$\csc \theta = $ _____ $\sec \theta = $ _____ $\cot \theta = $ _____

2. Fill in each blank below with the appropriate trigonometric function.

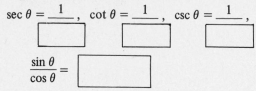

$\sec \theta = \dfrac{1}{\boxed{}}$, $\cot \theta = \dfrac{1}{\boxed{}}$, $\csc \theta = \dfrac{1}{\boxed{}}$,

$\dfrac{\sin \theta}{\cos \theta} = \boxed{}$

3. Below is a coordinate system for each of the six trigonometric functions. Indicate in each quadrant, by using a + or −, whether the given function is positive or negative.

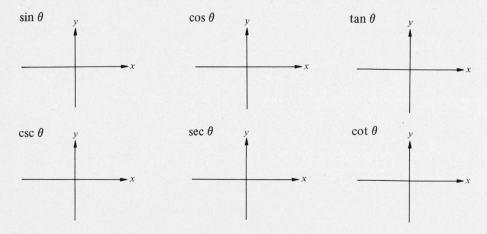

$\sin \theta$ $\cos \theta$ $\tan \theta$

$\csc \theta$ $\sec \theta$ $\cot \theta$

4. If $\cos \theta = -\frac{3}{5}$ and $\tan \theta$ is positive, then θ is in quadrant _____ and $\sin \theta = $ _____ .

5. Fill in the following table with the correct values.

θ	$30° = \dfrac{\pi}{6}$	$45° = \dfrac{\pi}{4}$	$60° = \dfrac{\pi}{3}$
$\sin \theta$			
$\cos \theta$			
$\tan \theta$			
$\csc \theta$			
$\sec \theta$			
$\cot \theta$			

Answers are at end of book.

3 Domain and Range of Trigonometric Functions

Upon completing this chapter, you should be able to

I. Define a quadrantal angle and give the values of the six trigonometric functions at each of the four basic quadrantal angles.

II. Specify the range of values for each of the six trigonometric functions in each of the four quadrants.

III. Give the domain and range of each of the six trigonometric functions.

---

94. We have called sine, cosine, etc. functions. In order to be functions, they must have

(a) a _____ , (b) a _____ ,

and (c) _____

_____

_____ .

---

94. (a) domain,
   (b) range (or second set),
   (c) a rule that assigns to each element in the domain one and only one element of the second set

95. The domain of each of the trigonometric functions is a set of

_____ . And the range is a set of _____
(angles, real numbers)

_____ .

---

95. angles;
real numbers

96. Given a circle with radius r, each angle θ has associated with it three numbers, x, y, and r. And the trigonometric functions are defined by the six ratios, $\dfrac{y}{r}, \dfrac{x}{r}, \dfrac{y}{x}, \dfrac{r}{y}, \dfrac{r}{x}$, and $\dfrac{x}{y}$.

Can the ratios be defined for *all* values of x, y, and r? _____

Why? _____

_____

96. No.
A ratio cannot be defined when its denominator is zero.

97. $x = 0$ if $\theta =$ _____ or _____ (choose values between 0 and 2π), and $y = 0$ if $\theta =$ _____ or _____ .

97. $\dfrac{\pi}{2}$; $\dfrac{3\pi}{2}$; 0; π

98. Thus, the trigonometric functions **(a)** _____ and

(b) _____ are undefined if $\theta = \dfrac{\pi}{2}$ or $\dfrac{3\pi}{2}$, and the

functions **(c)** _____ and **(d)** _____ are undefined if $\theta = 0$ or π.

98. **(a)** $\tan \theta = \dfrac{y}{x}$,

(b) $\sec \theta = \dfrac{r}{x}$,

(c) $\cot \theta = \dfrac{x}{y}$,

(d) $\csc \theta = \dfrac{r}{y}$

99. But we can always assume that $r > 0$ so the functions

_____ and _____ are always defined.

99. $\sin \theta = \dfrac{y}{r}$;

$\cos \theta = \dfrac{x}{r}$

100. Moreover, $x = 0$ for any angle θ that is coterminal with $\frac{\pi}{2}$ or $\frac{3\pi}{2}$. That is, $x = 0$ if and only if the terminal side of θ lies

_____ .

---

100. on the positive or negative y-axis

101. Thus, $x = 0$ if and only if θ equals one of the following

$..., -\frac{3\pi}{2}, -\frac{\pi}{2}, \frac{\pi}{2}, \frac{3\pi}{2}, \frac{5\pi}{2}, ...$

That is, $x = 0$ if and only if $\theta =$ _____ , $n = 0, 1, 2, ...$

---

101. $\frac{\pi}{2} \pm n\pi$

102. And the trigonometric functions **(a)** _____ $= \frac{y}{x}$ and

(b) _____ $= \frac{r}{x}$ are undefined if **(c)** $\theta =$ _____ .

---

102. **(a)** $\tan \theta$,
   (b) $\sec \theta$,
   (c) $\frac{\pi}{2} \pm n\pi$, $n = 0, 1, 2, ...$

103. Thus, the domain of $\tan \theta$ and $\sec \theta$ is the set of all angles

except $\theta =$ _____ .

---

103. $\frac{\pi}{2} \pm n\pi$, $n = 0, 1, 2, ...$

104. $y = 0$ for any angle θ that is coterminal with **(a)** ___ or

(b) ___ . That is, $y = 0$ if and only if the terminal side of θ lies

(c) _____ .

---

104. **(a)** 0, **(b)** π,
   (c) on the positive or negative x-axis

105. Thus $y = 0$ if and only if (iff) $\theta =$ _____ , $n = 0, 1, 2, ...$

---

105. $\pm n\pi$.
That is, $y = 0$ iff θ equals one of the following: $-3\pi, -2\pi, -\pi, 0, \pi, 2\pi, 3\pi, ...$

106. And the functions **(a)** _____ $= \frac{x}{y}$ and **(b)** _____ $= \frac{r}{y}$

are undefined if **(c)** $\theta =$ _____ . With these exceptions, all trigonometric functions are defined for all values of θ.

---

106. **(a)** $\cot \theta$, **(b)** $\csc \theta$,
   (c) $\pm n\pi, n = 0, 1, 2, ...$

107. Thus, the domain of $\cot \theta$ and $\csc \theta$ is the set of all angles

except $\theta =$ _____ .

---

107. $\pm n\pi$, $n = 0, 1, 2, ...$

108. The domain of $\sin \theta$ and $\cos \theta$ is _____

_____ .

---

108. the set of all angles

109. In general, then, we can say that all the trigonometric functions are defined for an angle θ unless the terminal side of θ lies _____ ,
in which case some of the trigonometric functions may not be defined.

---

109. on one of the coordinate axes

QUADRANTAL ANGLES

110. If the terminal side of an angle lies on one of the coordinate axes, we shall call it a **quadrantal angle**. A quadrantal angle is not considered to be in any quadrant.

List the first five non-negative quadrantal angles.

_____ _____ _____ _____ _____

---

110. $0; \dfrac{\pi}{2}; \pi; \dfrac{3\pi}{2}; 2\pi$

111. The first four negative quadrantal angles are

_____ _____ _____ _____ .

---

111. $-\dfrac{\pi}{2}; -\pi; -\dfrac{3\pi}{2}; -2\pi$

112. Moreover, any angle that is coterminal with 0, $\dfrac{\pi}{2}, \pi,$ or $\dfrac{3\pi}{2}$ is also a _____ since its

terminal side will also lie _____ .

---

112. quadrantal angle;
on a coordinate axis

113. Thus, the set of quadrantal angles is

$\{\theta \mid$ _____ $\}$.

---

113. $\theta = \pm n \dfrac{\pi}{2},\ n = 0, 1, 2, ...$

114. All six trigonometric functions are defined for all

_____ angles. But some trigonometric functions
(quadrantal, non-quadrantal)

are undefined for the _____ angles.

---

114. non-quadrantal;
quadrantal

115. $0, \dfrac{\pi}{2}, \pi$, and $\dfrac{3\pi}{2}$ are the four basic quadrantal angles. Every other quadrantal angle is _____ with one of these four.

115. coterminal

116. At each quadrantal angle, either x or y will equal zero while the other one will equal **(a)** $\pm$ ___ . Thus, the values of the trigonometric functions at the quadrantal angles will be **(b)** ___ , **(c)** $\pm$ ___ , or **(d)** _____ .

116. (a) r, **(b)** 0, **(c)** 1, **(d)** undefined

EXAMPLE 1

117. Fill in the table with $0, +1, -1$, or "undefined" as needed Draw the quadrantal angles if this will help.

θ	$0° = 0$ rad	$90° = \dfrac{\pi}{2}$ rad	$180° = \pi$ rad	$270° = \dfrac{3\pi}{2}$ rad
$\sin \theta$				
$\cos \theta$				
$\tan \theta$				
$\csc \theta$				
$\sec \theta$				
$\cot \theta$				

117.

$\sin \theta$	0	1	0	-1
$\cos \theta$	1	0	-1	0
$\tan \theta$	0	undef	0	undef
$\csc \theta$	undef	1	undef	-1
$\sec \theta$	1	undef	-1	undef
$\cot \theta$	undef	0	undef	0

118. Note that **(a)** $\csc \theta = 1/$ _____ , **(b)** $\sec \theta =$ _____ , and **(c)** $\cot \theta =$ _____ .
And whenever $\sin \theta$, $\cos \theta$, or $\tan \theta = 0$, then their reciprocal functions are **(d)** _____ .

118. (a) $\sin \theta$, **(b)** $\dfrac{1}{\cos \theta}$,

(c) $\dfrac{1}{\tan \theta}$,

(d) undefined

119. Look at the diagram. As θ increases from 0 to $\dfrac{\pi}{2}$ in quadrant I,

y **(a)** _____ from **(b)** ___ to **(c)** ___ .
(increases, decreases)

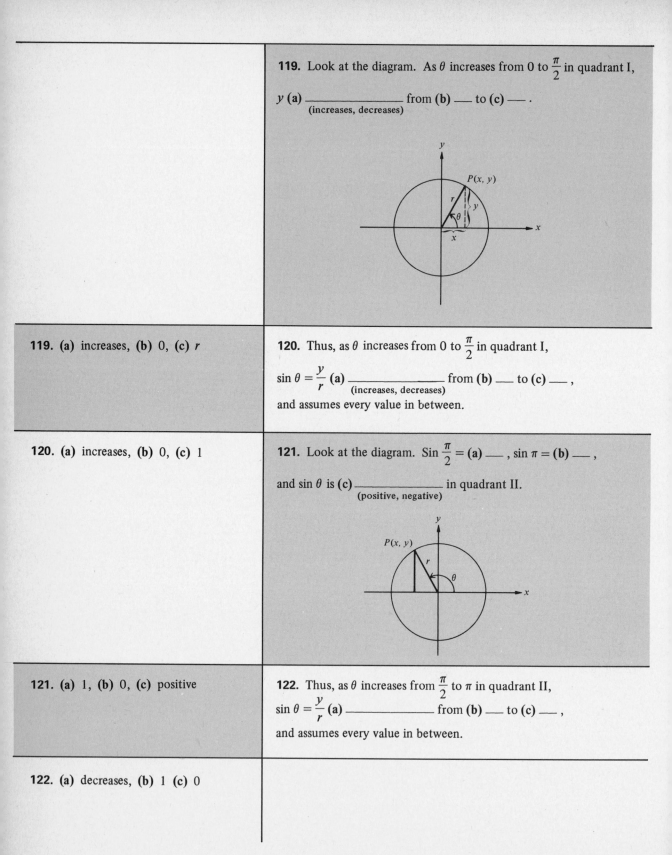

119. (a) increases, **(b)** 0, **(c)** r

120. Thus, as θ increases from 0 to $\dfrac{\pi}{2}$ in quadrant I,

$\sin \theta = \dfrac{y}{r}$ **(a)** _____ from **(b)** ___ to **(c)** ___ ,
(increases, decreases)
and assumes every value in between.

120. (a) increases, **(b)** 0, **(c)** 1

121. Look at the diagram. $\operatorname{Sin} \dfrac{\pi}{2} =$ **(a)** ___ , $\sin \pi =$ **(b)** ___ ,

and $\sin \theta$ is **(c)** _____ in quadrant II.
(positive, negative)

121. (a) 1, **(b)** 0, **(c)** positive

122. Thus, as θ increases from $\dfrac{\pi}{2}$ to π in quadrant II,
$\sin \theta = \dfrac{y}{r}$ **(a)** _____ from **(b)** ___ to **(c)** ___ ,
and assumes every value in between.

122. (a) decreases, **(b)** 1 **(c)** 0

123. As θ increases from π to $\dfrac{3\pi}{2}$ in quadrant III,

$\sin\theta$ **(a)** _____ from **(b)** ___ to **(c)** ___ , and assumes every value in between. (Draw a diagram if it will help.)

---

123. (a) decreases, **(b)** 0, **(c)** −1.

Recall from frames 68 and 69 that $\sin\theta$ is negative throughout quadrant III.

124. Finally, as θ increases from $\dfrac{3\pi}{2}$ to $2\pi = 0$ in quadrant IV,

$\sin\theta$ _____ .
(Again, draw a diagram if it will help.)

---

124. increases from −1 to 0

125. Thus, we see that in quadrants I and II, $\sin\theta = \dfrac{y}{r}$ assumes

all values **(a)** ___ $\leqslant z \leqslant$ ___ , and in quadrants III and IV, $\sin\theta$

assumes all values **(b)** ___ $\leqslant z \leqslant$ ___ .

Thus, $\sin\theta$ assumes all values **(c)** ___ $\leqslant z \leqslant$ ___ , but never

values outside **(d)** _____ .

---

125. (a) 0; 1,
    (b) −1; 0,
    (c) −1; 1,
    (d) $-1 \leqslant z \leqslant 1$

126. Thus, the range of $\sin\theta = \{z \in R \mid$ _____ $\}$.

---

126. $-1 \leqslant z \leqslant 1$

127. Now we want to determine the range of $\cos\theta$.

Look at the diagram.
In quadrants I and IV,
$\cos\theta = \dfrac{x}{r}$ assumes all values

(a) ___ $\leqslant z \leqslant$ ___ , and in
quadrants II and III, $\cos\theta$
assumes all values

(b) ___ $\leqslant z \leqslant$ ___ .

Thus, the range of **(c)** $\cos\theta = \{z \in R \mid$ _____ $\}$.

---

127. (a) 0; 1, **(b)** −1; 0,
    (c) $-1 \leqslant z \leqslant 1$.

Recall from frames 66 to 72 that $\cos\theta$ is positive in quadrants I and IV and negative in quadrants II and III.

If you had difficulty, go on to the next frame. If not, skip to frame 135.

128. Look at the diagram again. As θ increases from 0 to $\frac{\pi}{2}$ in quadrant I, **(a)** x _____ from **(b)** ___ to **(c)** ___ .
(increases, decreases)

---

128. (a) decreases, **(b)** r, **(c)** 0

129. Thus, as θ increases from 0 to $\frac{\pi}{2}$ in quadrant I,

$\cos \theta = \frac{x}{r}$ **(a)** _____ from **(b)** ___ to **(c)** ___ , and assumes every value in between.

---

129. (a) decreases, **(b)** 1, **(c)** 0

130. Look at the diagram. $\cos \frac{\pi}{2} =$ **(a)** ___ , $\cos \pi =$ **(b)** ___ ,

and $\cos \theta$ is **(c)** _____ in quadrant II.
(positive, negative)

---

130. (a) 0, **(b)** -1, **(c)** negative

131. Thus, as θ increases from $\frac{\pi}{2}$ to π in quadrant II,

$\cos \theta = \frac{x}{r}$ **(a)** _____ from **(b)** ___ to **(c)** ___ , and assumes every value in between.

---

131. (a) decreases, **(b)** 0, **(c)** -1

132. Draw a diagram if it will help you answer the following: As θ increases from π to $\frac{3\pi}{2}$ in quadrant III,

$\cos \theta$ **(a)** _____ from **(b)** ___ to **(c)** ___ , and assumes every value in between.

---

132. (a) increases, **(b)** -1, **(c)** 0

133. Finally, as θ increases from $\dfrac{3\pi}{2}$ to $2\pi = 0$ in quadrant IV, $\cos\theta$ **(a)** _____ from **(b)** ___ to **(c)** ___ , and assumes every value in between.

---

133. (a) increases, **(b)** 0, **(c)** 1

134. Thus, in quadrants I and IV, $\cos\theta = \dfrac{x}{r}$ assumes all values

(a) ___ $\leqslant z \leqslant$ ___ , and in quadrants II and III, $\cos\theta$ assumes all values **(b)** ___ $\leqslant z \leqslant$ ___ . Combining the two, we see that the range of $\cos\theta$ is **(c)** $\{z \in R \mid$ _____ $\}$.

---

134. (a) 0; 1,
  (b) $-1; 0$
  (c) $-1 \leqslant z \leqslant 1$

EXAMPLE 2

135. Draw a diagram and complete the following: In quadrant III, $\sin\theta$ assumes all values from ___ to ___ , and $\cos\theta$ assumes all values from ___ to ___ .

---

135. 0; -1; -1; 0
(since $\sin\pi = 0$, $\sin\dfrac{3\pi}{2} = -1$, and $\sin\theta$ is negative in quadrant III and $\cos\pi = -1$, $\cos\dfrac{3\pi}{2} = 0$, and $\cos\theta$ is negative in quadrant III).

136. We can repeat the preceding steps to determine the range of $\tan\theta$. Look at the diagram.

(a) Tan 0 = ___ , $\tan\theta = \dfrac{y}{x}$

is **(b)** _____
  (positive, negative)
throughout quadrant I, and as θ increases from 0 to $\dfrac{\pi}{2}$ in quadrant I,

$\tan\theta$ **(c)** _____ .
  (increases, decreases)

---

136. (a) 0,
  (b) positive,
  (c) increases

137. In fact, as θ increases from 0 to $\frac{\pi}{2}$, x becomes

(a) _____ and y increases from
(smaller and smaller, larger and larger)

(b) ___ to **(c)** ___ . Thus, $\tan \theta = \frac{y}{x}$ grows large without bound.

That is, $\tan \theta$ takes on all non-negative values $0 \leqslant z < \infty$.

---

137. (a) smaller and smaller
(b) 0, **(c)** r

---

138. Look at the diagram.

Tan θ is **(a)** _____ throughout quadrant II. Thus, for an
(positive, negative)

angle θ near $\frac{\pi}{2}$ in quadrant II, $\tan \theta = \frac{y}{x}$ is a very **(b)** _____
(small, large)

negative number, and **(c)** $\tan \pi =$ ___ .

---

138. (a) negative,
(b) large,
(c) 0

---

139. Thus, as θ increases from $\frac{\pi}{2}$ to π in quadrant II, $\tan \theta$ will be

(a) _____ and will **(b)** _____ from unbounded
(positive, negative)   (increase, decrease)

_____ numbers to **(d)** ___ .
(positive, negative)

---

139. (a) negative,
(b) increase,
(c) negative, **(d)** 0

---

140. That is, as θ increases from $\frac{\pi}{2}$ to π in quadrant II, $\tan \theta$

assumes all _____ values ___ $< z \leqslant$ ___ .
(non-positive, non-negative)

---

140. non-positive; $-\infty$; 0

141. Draw a diagram and answer the questions below. As θ increases from π to $\dfrac{3\pi}{2}$ in quadrant III, tan θ is (a) _____
(positive, negative)

and (b) _____ from (c) ___ to unbounded

(d) _____ values.
(positive, negative)

---

141. (a) positive,
(b) increases,
(c) 0, (d) positive

$P(x, y)$

If you had difficulty, go on to the next frame. If not, skip to frame 144.

142. Look at the diagram in frame 141.

Tan θ is (a) _____ in quadrant III. Thus, for an angle θ
(positive, negative)

near $\dfrac{3\pi}{2}$ in quadrant III, tan θ is a very large (b) _____
(positive, negative)

number and (c) tan $\pi =$ ___ .

---

142. (a) positive,
(b) positive,
(c) 0

143. Thus, as θ increases from π to $\dfrac{3\pi}{2}$ in quadrant III, tan θ

(a) _____ from (b) ___ to unbounded

(c) _____ values.
(positive, negative)

---

143. (a) increases,
(b) 0,
(c) positive

144. That is, as θ increases from π to $\dfrac{3\pi}{2}$ in quadrant III, tan θ

assumes all _____ values ___ $\leqslant z <$ ___.

---

144. non-negative; 0; ∞

145. Finally, draw a diagram to help you answer the question below.

As θ increases from $\frac{3\pi}{2}$ to 2π in quadrant IV,

tan θ is **(a)** _____ and **(b)** _____
(positive, negative)

from **(c)** _____

to **(d)** _____ .

---

145. (a) negative,
(b) increases,
(c) unbounded negative values,
(d) 0

If you had difficulty, use the following diagram and frames 141 to 144 for guidance.

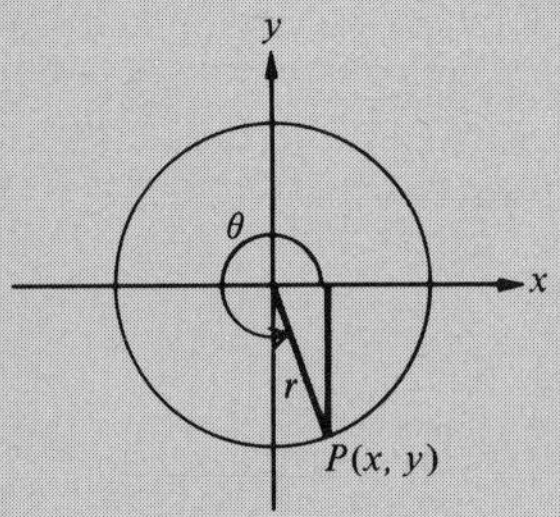

---

146. That is, as θ increases from $\frac{3\pi}{2}$ to 2π in quadrant IV, tan θ

assumes all _____ values ___ ___ z ___ ___ .

---

146. non-positive; $-\infty <$; $\leqslant 0$

---

147. In quadrants I and III, $\tan \theta = \frac{y}{x}$ assumes all values

(a) ___ ___ z ___ _____ , and in quadrants II and IV, tan θ assumes

all values **(b)** _____ . Thus, the range of tan θ is

(c) _____ .

---

147. (a) $0 \leqslant$; $< \infty$,
(b) $-\infty < z \leqslant 0$,
(c) R, the set of *all* real numbers

EXAMPLE 3

148. Draw a diagram and answer the following questions.

In quadrant II, sin θ is **(a)** _____ and
(positive, negative)

(b) _____ from **(c)** __ to **(d)** __ .
(increases, decreases)

Cos θ is **(e)** _____ and **(f)** _____

from **(g)** __ to **(h)** _____ , and tan θ is **(i)** _____

and **(j)** _____ from **(k)** _____

to **(l)** __ .

148.

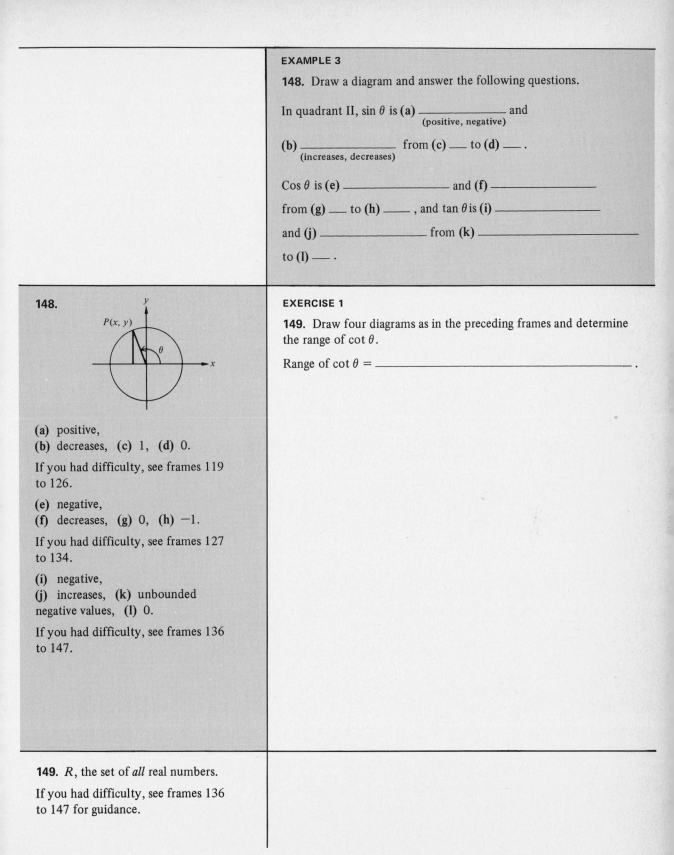

(a) positive,
(b) decreases, **(c)** 1, **(d)** 0.

If you had difficulty, see frames 119 to 126.

(e) negative,
(f) decreases, **(g)** 0, **(h)** −1.

If you had difficulty, see frames 127 to 134.

(i) negative,
(j) increases, **(k)** unbounded negative values, **(l)** 0.

If you had difficulty, see frames 136 to 147.

---

149. Draw four diagrams as in the preceding frames and determine the range of cot θ.

Range of cot θ = _____ .

---

149. R, the set of *all* real numbers.

If you had difficulty, see frames 136 to 147 for guidance.

150. Now let us consider the range of $\sec \theta = \dfrac{r}{x}$.

Draw a diagram and answer the questions below.

Sec θ is **(a)** _____ throughout quadrant I.
(positive, negative)

(b) Sec 0 = ____ , and for θ near $\dfrac{\pi}{2}$ in quadrant I,

sec θ is **(c)** _____ .

---

150. (a) positive, **(b)** 1,
(c) a large positive number

151. Thus, as θ increases from 0 to $\dfrac{\pi}{2}$ in quadrant I,

sec θ **(a)** _____ from **(b)** ___ to
(increases, decreases)

(c) _____ .

---

151. (a) increases,
(b) 1,
(c) unbounded positive values

152. Since sec 0 = **(a)** ___ and sec θ increases, sec $\theta \geqslant$ **(b)** ___ in quadrant I.

That is, as θ increases from 0 to $\dfrac{\pi}{2}$ in quadrant I, sec θ assumes

all values **(c)** ___ $\leqslant z <$ ___ .

---

152. (a) 1,
(b) 1,
(c) 1; ∞

153. Now let us look at sec θ in quadrant II.
Draw a diagram and answer the questions below.

Sec θ is **(a)** _____ throughout quadrant II,
(positive, negative)

for θ near $\dfrac{\pi}{2}$ in quadrant II, sec θ is

(b) _____ , and

(c) sec π = ____ .

---

153. (a) negative, **(b)** a large negative
number, **(c)** -1

154. Thus, as θ increases from $\frac{\pi}{2}$ to π in quadrant II,

$\sec \theta = \frac{r}{x}$ **(a)** _____ from **(b)** _____

_____ to **(c)** ____ .

---

154. (a) increases,
(b) unbounded negative values,
(c) -1

155. That is, as θ increases from $\frac{\pi}{2}$ to π in quadrant II, $\sec \theta$ takes

on all values ____ ____ z ____ ____ .

---

155. $-\infty < \, ; \, \leqslant -1$

EXAMPLE 4

156. Draw two more diagrams and finish determining the range of $\sec \theta$.

Range of $\sec \theta = \{ z \in R \mid$ _____ $\}$.

---

156. $z \leqslant -1 \ \text{or} \ z \leqslant 1$

If you had difficulty, go on to the next frame. If not, skip to frame 163.

157. Throughout quadrant III, sec θ is **(a)** _____ ,

(b) sec $\pi =$ _____ , and

(c) for θ near $\dfrac{3\pi}{2}$ in quadrant III, sec θ is

_____ .

---

157. (a) negative, **(b)** -1,
(c) a large negative number

158. Thus, as θ increases from π to $\dfrac{3\pi}{2}$ in quadrant III,

sec θ **(a)** _____ from **(b)** _____ to

(c) _____ .

---

158. (a) decreases,
   (b) -1,
   (c) unbounded negative values

159. That is, as θ increases from π to $\dfrac{3\pi}{2}$, sec θ assumes all

values _____ .

---

159. $-\infty < z \leqslant -1$

160. Finally, as θ increases from $\dfrac{3\pi}{2}$ to 2π in quadrant IV, sec θ

(a) _____ from **(b)** _____

to **(c)** _____ .

---

160. (a) decreases,
   (b) unbounded positive values,
   (c) 1

(since (1) sec θ is positive in quadrant IV,

(2) for θ near $\dfrac{3\pi}{2}$ in quadrant IV, sec θ is

a large positive number, and (3)
sec $2\pi = 1$)

161. That is, as θ increases from $\dfrac{3\pi}{2}$ to 2π in quadrant IV, sec θ assumes all values _____ .

---

161. $1 \leqslant z < \infty$

162. In quadrants I and IV, sec $\theta = \dfrac{r}{x}$ assumes all values _____ , and in quadrants II and III, sec θ assumes all values _____ .

---

162. $1 \leqslant z < \infty$;
$-\infty < z \leqslant -1$

163. Note that sec θ never assumes the values ___ $< z <$ ___ . Thus, the range of sec $\theta =$ $\{ z \in R \mid$ _____ $\}$.

---

163. $-1; 1;$
$z \leqslant -1$ or $z \geqslant 1$

EXAMPLE 5

164. Draw a diagram and answer the following questions.

In quadrant IV, tan θ **(a)** _____ from **(b)** _____
(increases, decreases)

_____ to **(c)** ___ , cot θ **(d)** _____

from **(e)** ___ to **(f)** _____ ,

sec θ **(g)** _____ from **(h)** _____

_____ to **(i)** ___ .

---

164. (a) increases, **(b)** unbounded negative values, **(c)** 0.
If you had difficulty, see frames 136 to 147.

(d) decreases, **(e)** 0, **(f)** unbounded negative values.
If you had difficulty, see frames 136 to 147.

(g) decreases, **(h)** unbounded positive values, **(i)** 1.
If you had difficulty, see frames 150 to 163.

165. Draw diagrams and determine the range of $\csc \theta = \dfrac{r}{y}$.

Range of $\csc \theta =$ _____ .

---

165. $\{z \in R \mid z \leqslant -1 \ \text{ or } \ z \geqslant 1\}$.

If you had difficulty, see frames 150 to 163 for guidance.

EXAMPLE 6

166. The values of a trigonometric function are either positive or negative throughout a given quadrant. Therefore, we can find the values of a trigonometric function by checking its value at the beginning of the quadrant and at the end of the quadrant and by knowing whether the function is positive or negative in that quadrant.

In quadrant I, $\csc \theta = \dfrac{r}{y}$ **(a)** _____
  (increases, decreases)

from **(b)** _____ to **(c)** ___ .

---

166. (a) decreases,
   (b) unbounded positive values,
   (c) 1.
(since (1) $\csc \theta$ is positive in quadrant I, (2) for θ near to 0 in quadrant I, $\csc \theta$ is a large positive number, and

(3) $\csc \dfrac{\pi}{2} = 1$).

EXAMPLE 7

167. In quadrant II,

csc θ **(a)** _____ from **(b)** __ to

(c) _____ ;

cot θ **(d)** _____ from **(e)** __ to

(f) _____ .

167. (a) increases, **(b)** 1,
(c) unbounded positive values,
(d) increases, **(e)** 0,
(f) unbounded positive values

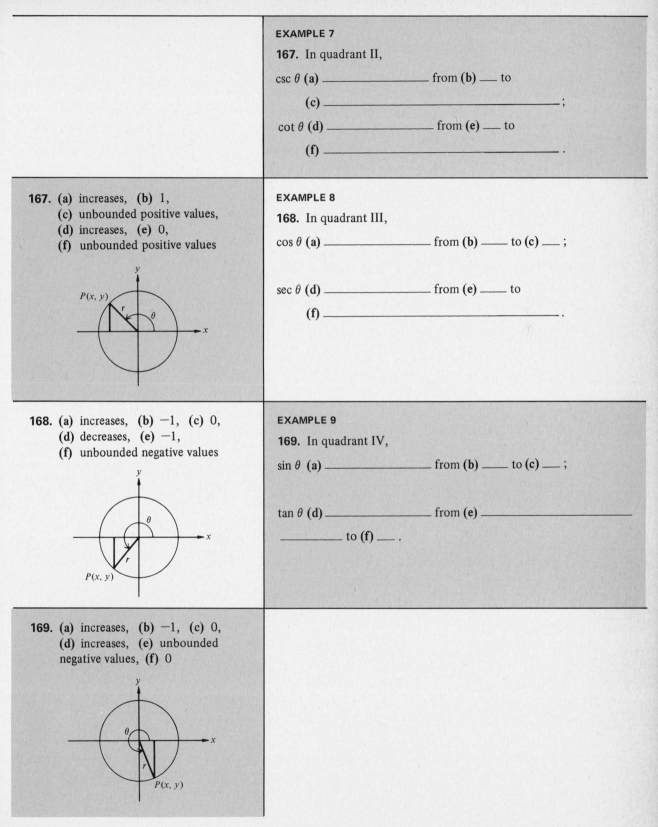

EXAMPLE 8

168. In quadrant III,

cos θ **(a)** _____ from **(b)** ____ to **(c)** __ ;

sec θ **(d)** _____ from **(e)** ____ to

(f) _____ .

168. (a) increases, **(b)** -1, **(c)** 0,
(d) decreases, **(e)** -1,
(f) unbounded negative values

EXAMPLE 9

169. In quadrant IV,

sin θ **(a)** _____ from **(b)** ____ to **(c)** __ ;

tan θ **(d)** _____ from **(e)** _____

_____ to **(f)** __ .

169. (a) increases, **(b)** -1, **(c)** 0,
(d) increases, **(e)** unbounded
negative values, **(f)** 0

170. The domain of each trigonometric function is a set of

_____ . And the range of each trigonometric function is

_____ .

170. angles;
a set of real numbers

EXERCISE 3

171. Give the domain and range of each of the six trigonometric functions.

Function	Domain	Range
$\sin \theta$		
$\cos \theta$		
$\tan \theta$		
$\csc \theta$		
$\sec \theta$		
$\cot \theta$		

171.

Function	Domain	Range
$\sin \theta$	set of all angles	$\{y \in R \mid -1 \leqslant y \leqslant 1\}$
$\cos \theta$	set of all angles	$\{y \in R \mid -1 \leqslant y \leqslant 1\}$
$\tan \theta$	set of all angles except $\{\frac{\pi}{2} \pm n\pi\}$	R
$\csc \theta$	set of all angles except $\{\pm n\pi\}$	$\{y \in R \mid y \leqslant -1$ or $y \geqslant 1\}$
$\sec \theta$	set of all angles except $\{\frac{\pi}{2} \pm n\pi\}$	$\{y \in R \mid y \leqslant -1$ or $y \geqslant 1\}$
$\cot \theta$	set of all angles except $\{\pm n\pi\}$	R

If you had difficulty, review frames 94 to 170.

PROBLEMS

1. In quadrant II,

$\cos \theta$ _____ from _____ to _____ ;
(increases, decreases)

$\sec \theta$ _____ from _____ to _____ .

2. In quadrant III,

$\sin \theta$ _____ from _____ to _____ ;

$\tan \theta$ _____ from _____ to _____ .

3. In quadrant IV,

$\csc \theta$ _____ from _____ to _____ ;

$\cot \theta$ _____ from _____ to _____ .

Answers are at end of book.

QUIZ

If you cannot answer the following questions correctly, review the appropriate frames.

1. The four basic quadrantal angles are **(a)** _____ , **(b)** _____ ,

(c) _____ , and **(d)** _____ .

2. Fill in the table with the correct value or the word "undefined" as needed.

θ	$0° = 0$ radian	$90° = \dfrac{\pi}{2}$ radians	$180° = \pi$ radians	$270° = \dfrac{3\pi}{2}$ radians
$\sin \theta$				
$\cos \theta$				
$\tan \theta$				
$\csc \theta$				
$\sec \theta$				
$\cot \theta$				

3. As θ increases from π to $\dfrac{3\pi}{2}$ in quadrant III,

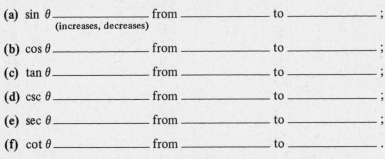

   (a) sin θ _____ from _____ to _____ ;
            _(increases, decreases)

   (b) cos θ _____ from _____ to _____ ;

   (c) tan θ _____ from _____ to _____ ;

   (d) csc θ _____ from _____ to _____ ;

   (e) sec θ _____ from _____ to _____ ;

   (f) cot θ _____ from _____ to _____ .

4. Give the domain and range of each of the six trigonometric functions.

	Domain	Range
sin θ		
cos θ		
tan θ		
csc θ		
sec θ		
cot θ		

Answers are at end of book.

4   Reduction Formulas

Upon completing this chapter, you should be able to

I. Draw the appropriate diagrams and relate the trigonometric values of the angles $\pi - \theta$, $\pi + \theta$, $-\theta$, $\frac{\pi}{2} - \theta$, and $\frac{\pi}{2} + \theta$ to the trigonometric values of θ.

II. Given any angle θ, use its reference angle and the reduction formulas to find the trigonometric values of θ to four decimal places.

Books of mathematical tables contain tables of trigonometric values for all angles between $0°$ (0 radians) and $90°$ ($\frac{\pi}{2}$ radians). It is possible to calculate the value of the trigonometric functions for any angle from these, as we shall see in this section.

172. Let θ be any angle. There are three other angles $\pi - \theta$, $\pi + \theta$, and $-\theta$ that are related to θ. Draw the angle $\pi - \theta$ on the diagram.

If the terminal side of the angle θ intersects the circle of radius r at the point $P(x, y)$, as shown, then the terminal side of the angle $\pi - \theta$ intersects the circle

at the point $Q(\underline{\quad}, \underline{\quad})$.

172.

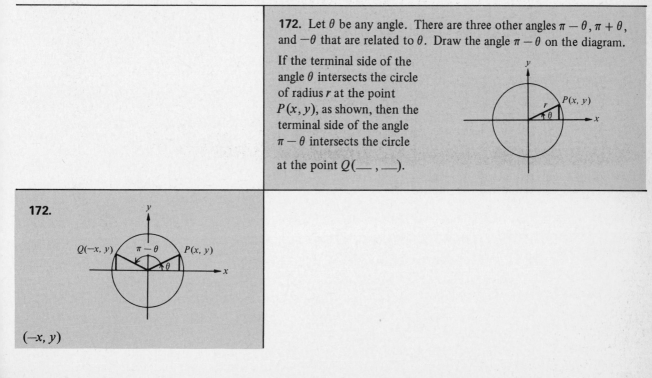

$(-x, y)$

173. Thus, **(a)** $\sin\,(\pi - \theta) =$ _____ $= \sin\theta$,

(b) $\cos\,(\pi - \theta) =$ _____ $=$ _____ ,

(c) $\tan\,(\pi - \theta) =$ _____ $=$ _____ ,

(d) $\csc\,(\pi - \theta) =$ _____ $=$ _____ ,

(e) $\sec\,(\pi - \theta) =$ _____ $=$ _____ ,

(f) $\cot\,(\pi - \theta) =$ _____ $=$ _____ .

173.

(a) $\dfrac{y}{r}$,

(b) $-\dfrac{x}{r}$; $-\cos\theta$,

(c) $\dfrac{y}{-x}$; $-\tan\theta$,

(d) $\dfrac{r}{y}$; $\csc\theta$,

(e) $\dfrac{r}{-x}$; $-\sec\theta$,

(f) $\dfrac{-x}{y}$; $-\cot\theta$

174. In frame 172 we drew θ in quadrant I. Here θ appears in the second quadrant. Draw in the angle $\pi - \theta$ and convince yourself that the preceding results do not depend on the quadrant in which θ lies. Again, the terminal side of $\pi - \theta$ intersects the circle at

(a) $Q($ _____ , _____ $)$ and we still have

(b) $\sin (\pi - \theta) =$ _____ $=$ _____ ,

(c) $\cos (\pi - \theta) =$ _____ $=$ _____ ,

(d) $\tan (\pi - \theta) =$ _____ $=$ _____ ,

(e) $\csc (\pi - \theta) =$ _____ $=$ _____ ,   **(h)**

(f) $\sec (\pi - \theta) =$ _____ $=$ _____ ,

(g) $\cot (\pi - \theta) =$ _____ $=$ _____ .

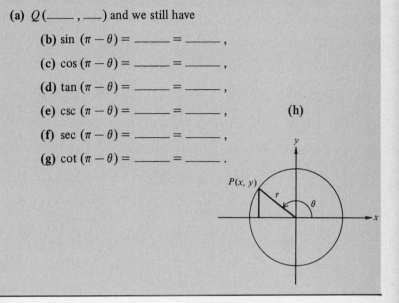

174. (a) $(-x, y)$,

(b) $\dfrac{y}{r}$; $\sin \theta$,

(c) $\dfrac{-x}{r}$; $-\cos \theta$,

(d) $\dfrac{y}{-x}$; $-\tan \theta$,

(e) $\dfrac{r}{y}$; $\csc \theta$,

(f) $\dfrac{r}{-x}$; $-\sec \theta$,

(g) $\dfrac{-x}{y}$; $-\cot \theta$,

(h)

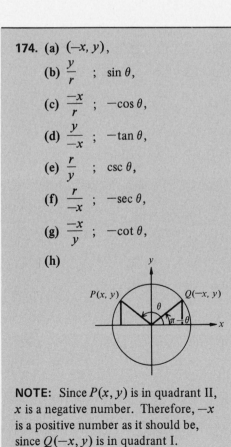

NOTE: Since $P(x, y)$ is in quadrant II, x is a negative number. Therefore, $-x$ is a positive number as it should be, since $Q(-x, y)$ is in quadrant I.

175. Here are two diagrams, one with θ in quadrant III and the other with θ in quadrant IV. In each diagram, draw the angle $\pi - \theta$, and label the coordinates of the point Q where the terminal side of $\pi - \theta$ intersects the circle.

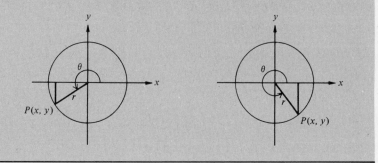

175.

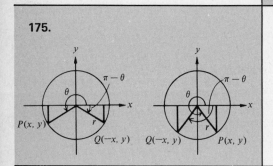

176. Again we get for θ in both quadrants III and IV, and hence for any angle θ,

(a) $\sin(\pi - \theta) = \underline{\hspace{1cm}}$, **(d)** $\csc(\pi - \theta) = \underline{\hspace{1cm}}$,

(b) $\cos(\pi - \theta) = \underline{\hspace{1cm}}$, **(e)** $\sec(\pi - \theta) = \underline{\hspace{1cm}}$,

(c) $\tan(\pi - \theta) = \underline{\hspace{1cm}}$, **(f)** $\cot(\pi - \theta) = \underline{\hspace{1cm}}$.

176.
(a) $\sin\theta$, **(d)** $\csc\theta$,
(b) $-\cos\theta$, **(e)** $-\sec\theta$,
(c) $-\tan\theta$ **(f)** $-\cot\theta$

177. We see that it is necessary only to draw a diagram with θ in quadrant I to recall the relationships between the values of the trigonometric functions at $\pi - \theta$ and θ.

   The same is true for $\pi + \theta$ and θ. **(a)** Draw $\pi + \theta$ in the diagram.

The terminal side of $\pi + \theta$ intersects the circle at the point

(b) $R\,(\underline{\hspace{1cm}}, \underline{\hspace{1cm}})$, and

(c) $\sin(\pi + \theta) = \underline{\hspace{1.5cm}}$,

(d) $\cos(\pi + \theta) = \underline{\hspace{1.5cm}}$,

(e) $\tan(\pi + \theta) = \underline{\hspace{1.5cm}}$,

(f) $\csc(\pi + \theta) = \underline{\hspace{1.5cm}}$,

(g) $\sec(\pi + \theta) = \underline{\hspace{1.5cm}}$,

(h) $\cot(\pi + \theta) = \underline{\hspace{1.5cm}}$.

(a)

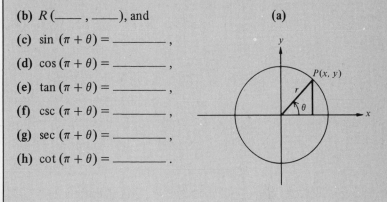

177. (a)

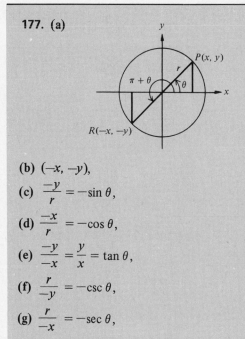

(b) $(-x, -y)$,

(c) $\dfrac{-y}{r} = -\sin\theta$,

(d) $\dfrac{-x}{r} = -\cos\theta$,

(e) $\dfrac{-y}{-x} = \dfrac{y}{x} = \tan\theta$,

(f) $\dfrac{r}{-y} = -\csc\theta$,

(g) $\dfrac{r}{-x} = -\sec\theta$,

(h) $\dfrac{-x}{-y} = \cot\theta$

178. Label the coordinates of the point R where the terminal side of the angle $\pi + \theta$ intersects the circle in each of the diagrams.

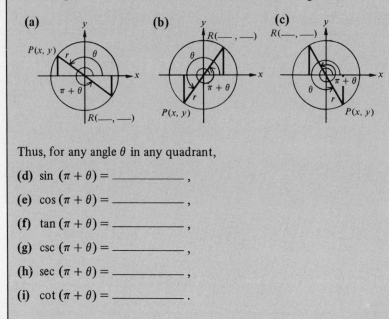

(a)

(b) $R(\text{---},\text{---})$

(c) $R(\text{---},\text{---})$

Thus, for any angle θ in any quadrant,

(d) $\sin(\pi + \theta) = $ _____ ,

(e) $\cos(\pi + \theta) = $ _____ ,

(f) $\tan(\pi + \theta) = $ _____ ,

(g) $\csc(\pi + \theta) = $ _____ ,

(h) $\sec(\pi + \theta) = $ _____ ,

(i) $\cot(\pi + \theta) = $ _____ .

178.

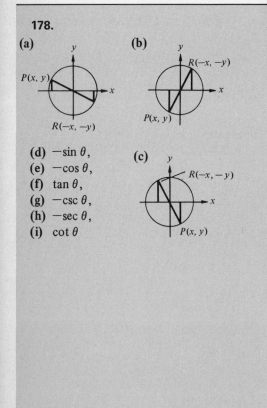

(a)

(b) $R(-x, -y)$

(c)

(d) $-\sin\theta$,
(e) $-\cos\theta$,
(f) $\tan\theta$,
(g) $-\csc\theta$,
(h) $-\sec\theta$,
(i) $\cot\theta$

179. Again we see that it is necessary only to draw a diagram with θ in quadrant I to recall the relationships between the values of the trigonometric functions at $\pi + \theta$ and θ.

The same is true for $-\theta$ and θ. Complete the following:

(a) $\sin(-\theta) = $ _____ $= $ _____ ,

(b) $\cos(-\theta) = $ _____ ,

(c) $\tan(-\theta) = $ _____ ,

(d) $\csc(-\theta) = $ _____ ,

(e) $\sec(-\theta) = $ _____ ,

(f) $\cot(-\theta) = $ _____ .

179.

(a) $\dfrac{-y}{r}$; $-\sin\theta$,

(b) $\dfrac{x}{r} = \cos\theta$,

(c) $\dfrac{-y}{x} = -\tan\theta$,

(d) $\dfrac{r}{-y} = -\csc\theta$,

(e) $\dfrac{r}{x} = \sec\theta$,

(f) $\dfrac{x}{-y} = -\cot\theta$

180. Label the coordinates of the point S where the terminal side of the angle $-\theta$ intersects the circle in each of the diagrams.

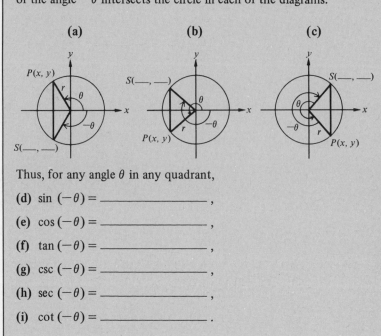

| (a) | (b) | (c) |

Thus, for any angle θ in any quadrant,

(d) $\sin(-\theta) =$ _____ ,

(e) $\cos(-\theta) =$ _____ ,

(f) $\tan(-\theta) =$ _____ ,

(g) $\csc(-\theta) =$ _____ ,

(h) $\sec(-\theta) =$ _____ ,

(i) $\cot(-\theta) =$ _____ .

180.

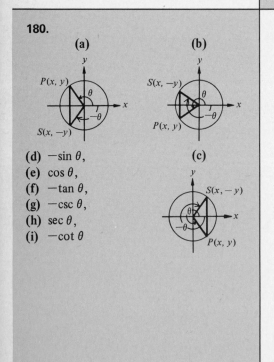

(a) (b) (c)

(d) $-\sin\theta$,
(e) $\cos\theta$,
(f) $-\tan\theta$,
(g) $-\csc\theta$,
(h) $\sec\theta$,
(i) $-\cot\theta$

EXAMPLE 1

181. Complete the diagrams and put a + or − in each of the following equations.

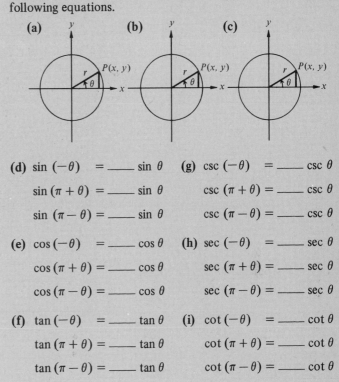

(a)   (b)   (c)

(d) $\sin(-\theta)$ = ____ $\sin\theta$ (g) $\csc(-\theta)$ = ____ $\csc\theta$

$\sin(\pi+\theta)$ = ____ $\sin\theta$ $\csc(\pi+\theta)$ = ____ $\csc\theta$

$\sin(\pi-\theta)$ = ____ $\sin\theta$ $\csc(\pi-\theta)$ = ____ $\csc\theta$

(e) $\cos(-\theta)$ = ____ $\cos\theta$ (h) $\sec(-\theta)$ = ____ $\sec\theta$

$\cos(\pi+\theta)$ = ____ $\cos\theta$ $\sec(\pi+\theta)$ = ____ $\sec\theta$

$\cos(\pi-\theta)$ = ____ $\cos\theta$ $\sec(\pi-\theta)$ = ____ $\sec\theta$

(f) $\tan(-\theta)$ = ____ $\tan\theta$ (i) $\cot(-\theta)$ = ____ $\cot\theta$

$\tan(\pi+\theta)$ = ____ $\tan\theta$ $\cot(\pi+\theta)$ = ____ $\cot\theta$

$\tan(\pi-\theta)$ = ____ $\tan\theta$ $\cot(\pi-\theta)$ = ____ $\cot\theta$

181.

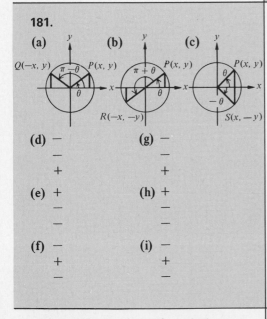

(a)   (b)   (c)

(d) −   (g) −
    −   −
    +   +

(e) +   (h) +
    −   −
    −   −

(f) −   (i) −
    +   +
    −   −

182. We already know the trigonometric values for the quadrantal angles. But draw a diagram and convince yourself that all the preceding results are still true if θ is a quadrantal angle.

182. NOTE: $0 = -0$. If you had difficulty, see frames 172 to 180 for guidance.

183. For each of the angles θ shown, either $\pi - \theta$, $\pi + \theta$, or $-\theta$ is in quadrant I. In each diagram draw the angle that is in quadrant I and label it correctly.

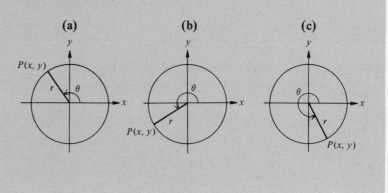

(a) (b) (c)

183.

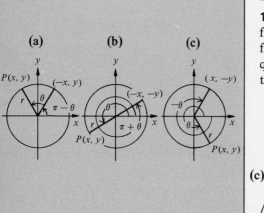

(a) (b) (c)

EXAMPLE 2

184. In each case one of the angles, $\pi - \theta$, $\pi + \theta$, or $-\theta$, lies in the first quadrant. For any angle θ we shall call the associated angle formed by the positive x-axis and the terminal line in the first quadrant, the **reference angle** of θ and label it θ'. Draw and label the *reference angle* for each angle shown.

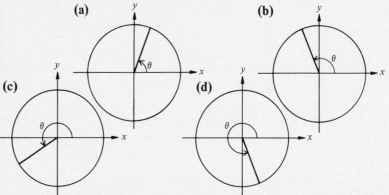

(a) (b) (c) (d)

184.

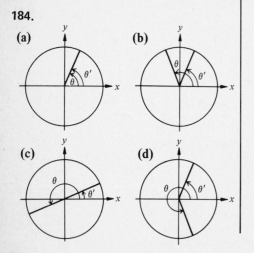

(a) (b) (c) (d)

185. The reference angle θ' for any angle θ is always between

_____° and _____°. That is, _____ radians $\leqslant \theta <$ _____ radians.

---

185. $0; 90;$

$0; \dfrac{\pi}{2}$

---

186. Let θ be an angle in the second quadrant. Its reference

angle will lie in quadrant ____ . Draw the reference angle in the diagram and label the coordinates of the point where the terminal line intersects the circle.

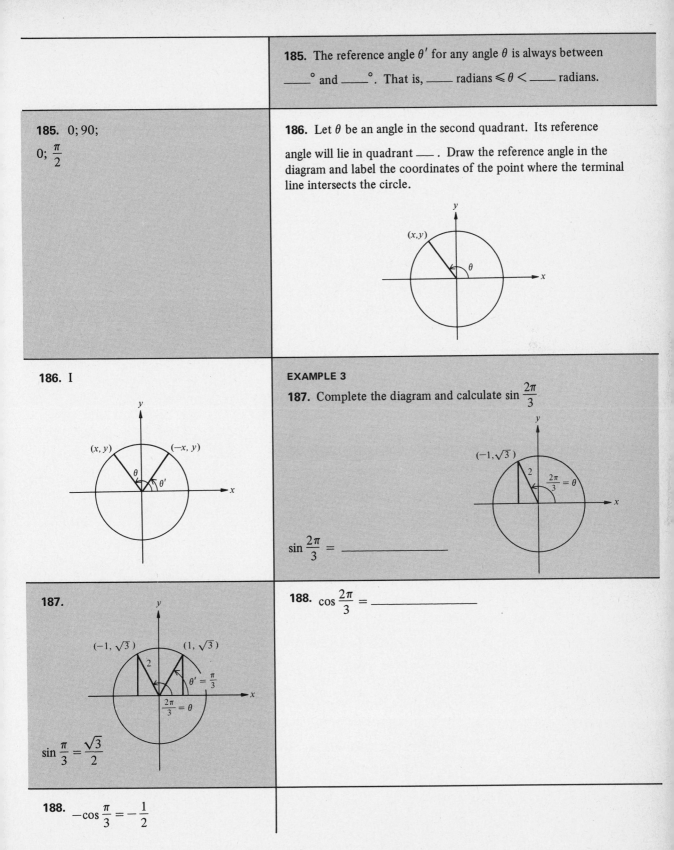

---

186. I

EXAMPLE 3

187. Complete the diagram and calculate $\sin \dfrac{2\pi}{3}$

$$\sin \dfrac{2\pi}{3} = \underline{\hspace{2cm}}$$

187.

$$\sin \dfrac{\pi}{3} = \dfrac{\sqrt{3}}{2}$$

188. $\cos \dfrac{2\pi}{3} = \underline{\hspace{2cm}}$

---

188. $-\cos \dfrac{\pi}{3} = -\dfrac{1}{2}$

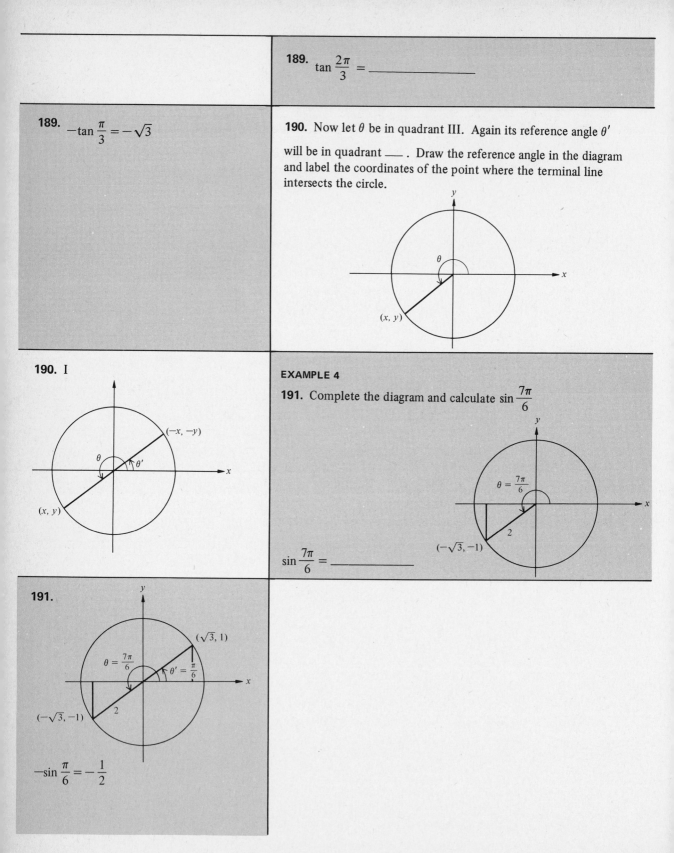

189.
$$\tan \frac{2\pi}{3} = \underline{\hspace{2cm}}$$

189.
$$-\tan \frac{\pi}{3} = -\sqrt{3}$$

190. Now let θ be in quadrant III. Again its reference angle θ' will be in quadrant ___ . Draw the reference angle in the diagram and label the coordinates of the point where the terminal line intersects the circle.

190. I

EXAMPLE 4

191. Complete the diagram and calculate $\sin \frac{7\pi}{6}$

$$\sin \frac{7\pi}{6} = \underline{\hspace{2cm}}$$

191.

$$-\sin \frac{\pi}{6} = -\frac{1}{2}$$

192.
$$\cos \frac{7\pi}{6} = \underline{\hspace{3cm}}$$

$$\tan \frac{7\pi}{6} = \underline{\hspace{3cm}}$$

192.
$$-\cos \frac{\pi}{6} = -\frac{\sqrt{3}}{2};$$

$$\tan \frac{\pi}{6} = \frac{1}{\sqrt{3}}$$

EXAMPLE 5

193. Finally, let θ lie in quadrant IV, and draw the reference angle θ' in the diagram.

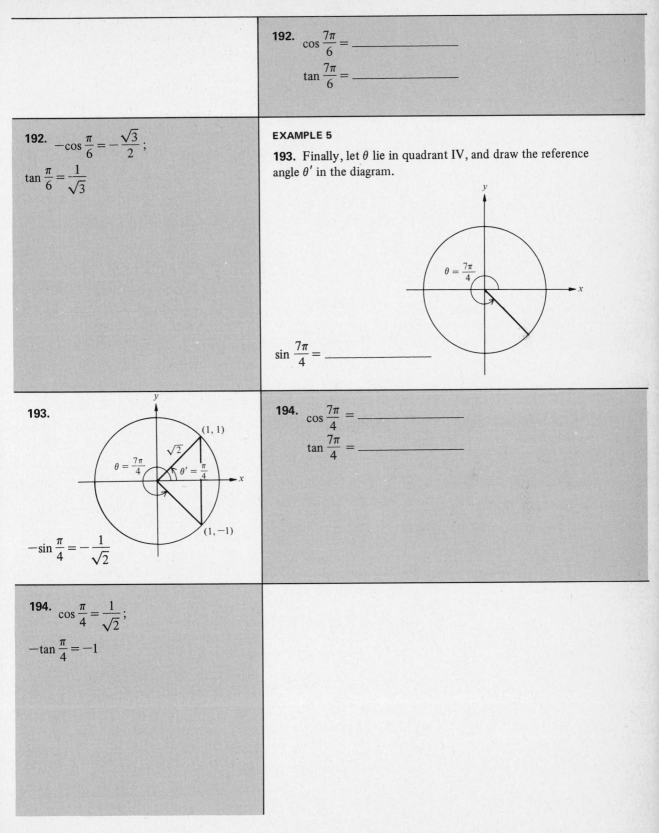

$$\sin \frac{7\pi}{4} = \underline{\hspace{3cm}}$$

193.

$$-\sin \frac{\pi}{4} = -\frac{1}{\sqrt{2}}$$

194.
$$\cos \frac{7\pi}{4} = \underline{\hspace{3cm}}$$

$$\tan \frac{7\pi}{4} = \underline{\hspace{3cm}}$$

194.
$$\cos \frac{\pi}{4} = \frac{1}{\sqrt{2}};$$

$$-\tan \frac{\pi}{4} = -1$$

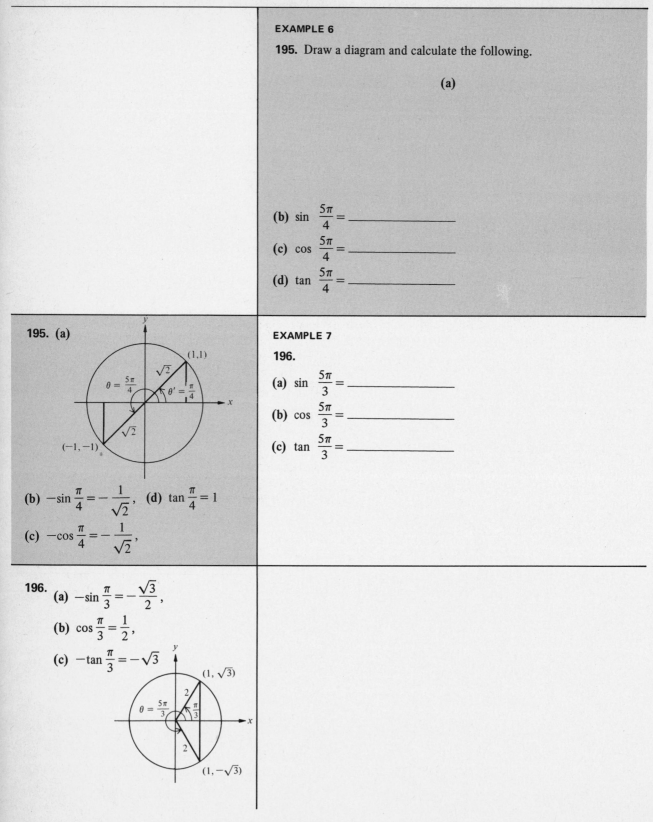

EXAMPLE 6

195. Draw a diagram and calculate the following.

(a)

(b) $\sin \dfrac{5\pi}{4} = $ _____

(c) $\cos \dfrac{5\pi}{4} = $ _____

(d) $\tan \dfrac{5\pi}{4} = $ _____

195. (a)

(b) $-\sin \dfrac{\pi}{4} = -\dfrac{1}{\sqrt{2}}$, (d) $\tan \dfrac{\pi}{4} = 1$

(c) $-\cos \dfrac{\pi}{4} = -\dfrac{1}{\sqrt{2}}$,

EXAMPLE 7

196.

(a) $\sin \dfrac{5\pi}{3} = $ _____

(b) $\cos \dfrac{5\pi}{3} = $ _____

(c) $\tan \dfrac{5\pi}{3} = $ _____

196.

(a) $-\sin \dfrac{\pi}{3} = -\dfrac{\sqrt{3}}{2}$,

(b) $\cos \dfrac{\pi}{3} = \dfrac{1}{2}$,

(c) $-\tan \dfrac{\pi}{3} = -\sqrt{3}$

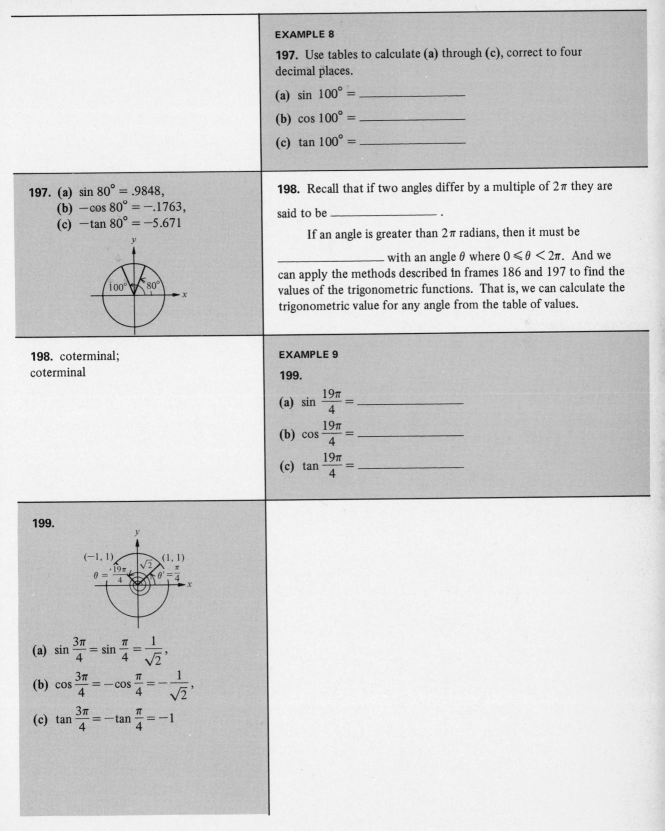

EXAMPLE 8

197. Use tables to calculate **(a)** through **(c)**, correct to four decimal places.

(a) sin $100°$ = _____

(b) cos $100°$ = _____

(c) tan $100°$ = _____

197. (a) sin $80°$ = .9848,
  (b) $-$cos $80°$ = $-$.1763,
  (c) $-$tan $80°$ = -5.671

198. Recall that if two angles differ by a multiple of 2π they are said to be _____ .

  If an angle is greater than 2π radians, then it must be _____ with an angle θ where $0 \leqslant \theta < 2\pi$. And we can apply the methods described in frames 186 and 197 to find the values of the trigonometric functions. That is, we can calculate the trigonometric value for any angle from the table of values.

198. coterminal; coterminal

EXAMPLE 9

199.

(a) sin $\dfrac{19\pi}{4}$ = _____

(b) cos $\dfrac{19\pi}{4}$ = _____

(c) tan $\dfrac{19\pi}{4}$ = _____

199.

(a) sin $\dfrac{3\pi}{4}$ = sin $\dfrac{\pi}{4}$ = $\dfrac{1}{\sqrt{2}}$,

(b) cos $\dfrac{3\pi}{4}$ = $-$cos $\dfrac{\pi}{4}$ = $-\dfrac{1}{\sqrt{2}}$,

(c) tan $\dfrac{3\pi}{4}$ = $-$tan $\dfrac{\pi}{4}$ = -1

200. We shall now investigate two other angles associated with an angle θ, $\frac{\pi}{2} - \theta$, and $\frac{\pi}{2} + \theta$. Draw the angle $\frac{\pi}{2} - \theta$ in the diagram and label the coordinates of the point (___ , ___) where the terminal side of the angle $\frac{\pi}{2} - \theta$ intersects the circle.

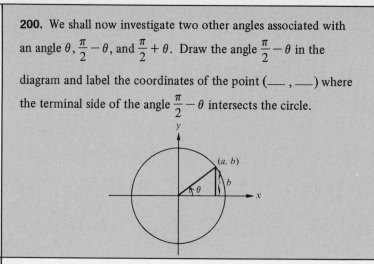

200. (b, a)

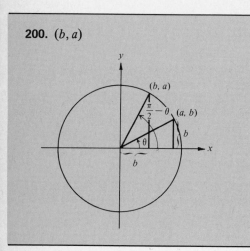

201. In the diagram we have drawn θ (in quadrant II) and the corresponding angle $\frac{\pi}{2} - \theta$. Label the coordinates where the terminal side of the angle $\frac{\pi}{2} - \theta$ intersects the circle.

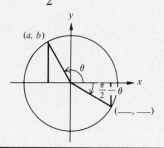

201. (b, a).

NOTE: For θ in quadrant II, the x-coordinate associated with θ is negative, and the y-coordinate is positive. The situation is reversed for $\frac{\pi}{2} - \theta$, since it is in quadrant IV.

202. Below are two diagrams, one with θ in quadrant III and the other with θ in quadrant IV. In each diagram, draw the angle $\frac{\pi}{2} - \theta$, and label the coordinates of the point where the terminal side of $\frac{\pi}{2} - \theta$ intersects the circle.

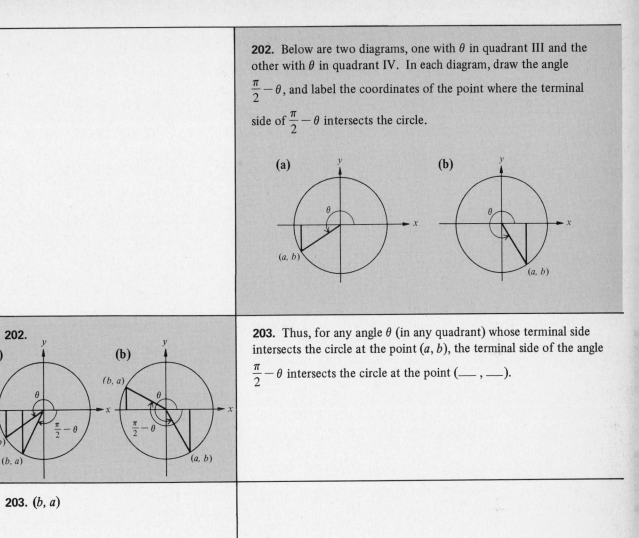

(a)

(b)

202.

(a)

(b)

203. (b, a)

203. Thus, for any angle θ (in any quadrant) whose terminal side intersects the circle at the point (a, b), the terminal side of the angle $\frac{\pi}{2} - \theta$ intersects the circle at the point (—— , ——).

204. It is necessary only to draw a diagram with θ in quadrant I to obtain the relationships between the trigonometric values of θ and $\frac{\pi}{2} - \theta$.

Draw the angle $\frac{\pi}{2} - \theta$ in the diagram and complete the following.

(a)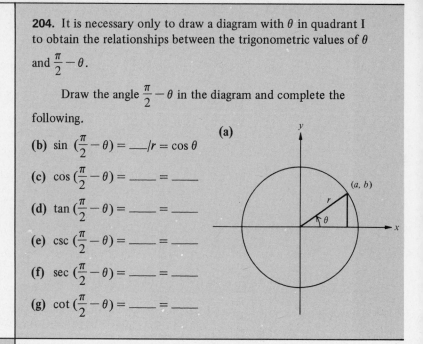

(b) $\sin\left(\frac{\pi}{2} - \theta\right) = $ ___$/r = \cos\theta$

(c) $\cos\left(\frac{\pi}{2} - \theta\right) = $ ___ $= $ ___

(d) $\tan\left(\frac{\pi}{2} - \theta\right) = $ ___ $= $ ___

(e) $\csc\left(\frac{\pi}{2} - \theta\right) = $ ___ $= $ ___

(f) $\sec\left(\frac{\pi}{2} - \theta\right) = $ ___ $= $ ___

(g) $\cot\left(\frac{\pi}{2} - \theta\right) = $ ___ $= $ ___

204. **(a)**

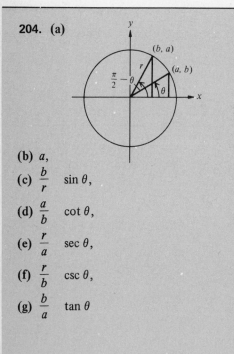

(b) a,

(c) $\dfrac{b}{r}$ $\sin\theta$,

(d) $\dfrac{a}{b}$ $\cot\theta$,

(e) $\dfrac{r}{a}$ $\sec\theta$,

(f) $\dfrac{r}{b}$ $\csc\theta$,

(g) $\dfrac{b}{a}$ $\tan\theta$

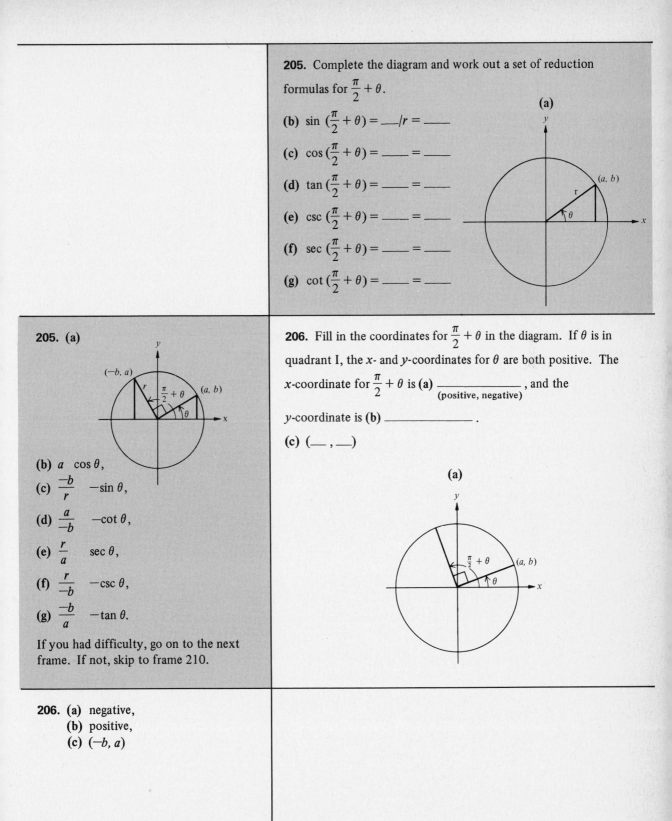

205. Complete the diagram and work out a set of reduction formulas for $\frac{\pi}{2} + \theta$.

(a)

(b) $\sin\left(\frac{\pi}{2} + \theta\right) = \underline{\quad}/r = \underline{\quad}$

(c) $\cos\left(\frac{\pi}{2} + \theta\right) = \underline{\quad} = \underline{\quad}$

(d) $\tan\left(\frac{\pi}{2} + \theta\right) = \underline{\quad} = \underline{\quad}$

(e) $\csc\left(\frac{\pi}{2} + \theta\right) = \underline{\quad} = \underline{\quad}$

(f) $\sec\left(\frac{\pi}{2} + \theta\right) = \underline{\quad} = \underline{\quad}$

(g) $\cot\left(\frac{\pi}{2} + \theta\right) = \underline{\quad} = \underline{\quad}$

205. (a)

(b) a $\cos\theta$,

(c) $\dfrac{-b}{r}$ $-\sin\theta$,

(d) $\dfrac{a}{-b}$ $-\cot\theta$,

(e) $\dfrac{r}{a}$ $\sec\theta$,

(f) $\dfrac{r}{-b}$ $-\csc\theta$,

(g) $\dfrac{-b}{a}$ $-\tan\theta$.

If you had difficulty, go on to the next frame. If not, skip to frame 210.

206. Fill in the coordinates for $\frac{\pi}{2} + \theta$ in the diagram. If θ is in quadrant I, the x- and y-coordinates for θ are both positive. The x-coordinate for $\frac{\pi}{2} + \theta$ is **(a)** $\underline{\hspace{3cm}}$, and the (positive, negative) y-coordinate is **(b)** $\underline{\hspace{3cm}}$.

(c) $(\underline{\quad}, \underline{\quad})$

(a)

206. (a) negative,
    (b) positive,
    (c) $(-b, a)$

207. In each diagram, label the coordinates of the point where the terminal side of the angle $\frac{\pi}{2} + \theta$ intersects the circle.

(a)

(b)

(c)

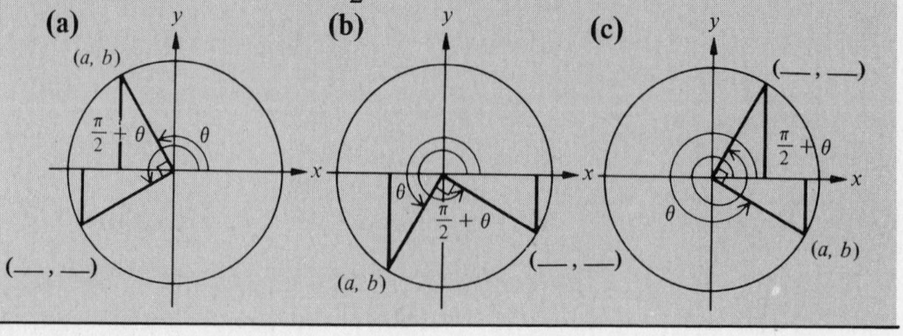

207. (a) $(-b, a)$
(b) $(-b, a)$
(c) $(-b, a)$

208. We see that for any angle θ (in any quadrant) whose terminal side intersects the circle at the point (a, b), the terminal side of the angle $\frac{\pi}{2} + \theta$ intersects the circle at the point (—, —);

208. $(-b, a)$

209. As with other reduction formulas, it is necessary only to draw a diagram with θ in quadrant I to obtain the relationships between the trigonometric values of θ and $\frac{\pi}{2} + \theta$. Draw the angle $\frac{\pi}{2} + \theta$ in the diagram and complete the following.

(a)

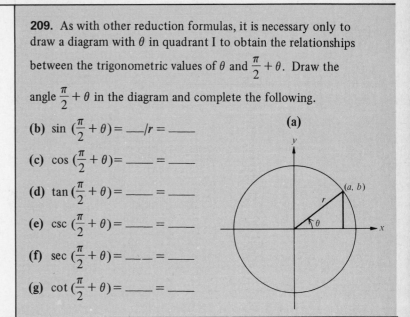

(b) $\sin\left(\frac{\pi}{2} + \theta\right) = \underline{\quad}/r = \underline{\quad}$

(c) $\cos\left(\frac{\pi}{2} + \theta\right) = \underline{\quad} = \underline{\quad}$

(d) $\tan\left(\frac{\pi}{2} + \theta\right) = \underline{\quad} = \underline{\quad}$

(e) $\csc\left(\frac{\pi}{2} + \theta\right) = \underline{\quad} = \underline{\quad}$

(f) $\sec\left(\frac{\pi}{2} + \theta\right) = \underline{\quad} = \underline{\quad}$

(g) $\cot\left(\frac{\pi}{2} + \theta\right) = \underline{\quad} = \underline{\quad}$

209. (a)

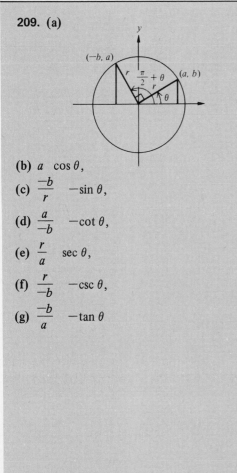

(b) $a \quad \cos\theta,$

(c) $\dfrac{-b}{r} \quad -\sin\theta,$

(d) $\dfrac{a}{-b} \quad -\cot\theta,$

(e) $\dfrac{r}{a} \quad \sec\theta,$

(f) $\dfrac{r}{-b} \quad -\csc\theta,$

(g) $\dfrac{-b}{a} \quad -\tan\theta$

210. Complete the diagrams and the following reduction formulas.

(a)

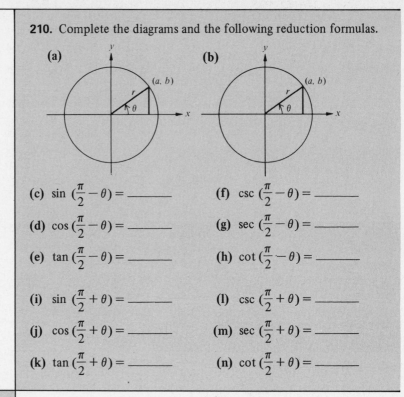

(b)

(c) $\sin\left(\dfrac{\pi}{2}-\theta\right) =$ _____

(f) $\csc\left(\dfrac{\pi}{2}-\theta\right) =$ _____

(d) $\cos\left(\dfrac{\pi}{2}-\theta\right) =$ _____

(g) $\sec\left(\dfrac{\pi}{2}-\theta\right) =$ _____

(e) $\tan\left(\dfrac{\pi}{2}-\theta\right) =$ _____

(h) $\cot\left(\dfrac{\pi}{2}-\theta\right) =$ _____

(i) $\sin\left(\dfrac{\pi}{2}+\theta\right) =$ _____

(l) $\csc\left(\dfrac{\pi}{2}+\theta\right) =$ _____

(j) $\cos\left(\dfrac{\pi}{2}+\theta\right) =$ _____

(m) $\sec\left(\dfrac{\pi}{2}+\theta\right) =$ _____

(k) $\tan\left(\dfrac{\pi}{2}+\theta\right) =$ _____

(n) $\cot\left(\dfrac{\pi}{2}+\theta\right) =$ _____

210.

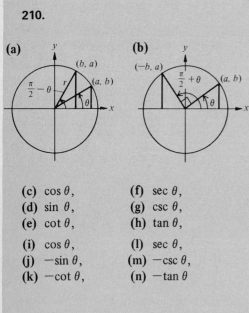

(a)

(b)

(c) $\cos\theta$,

(f) $\sec\theta$,

(d) $\sin\theta$,

(g) $\csc\theta$,

(e) $\cot\theta$,

(h) $\tan\theta$,

(i) $\cos\theta$,

(l) $\sec\theta$,

(j) $-\sin\theta$,

(m) $-\csc\theta$,

(k) $-\cot\theta$,

(n) $-\tan\theta$

EXAMPLE 10

211. Draw a diagram and calculate the following.

(a)

(b) $\sin \dfrac{3\pi}{4} = $ _____

(c) $\cos \dfrac{3\pi}{4} = $ _____

(d) $\tan \dfrac{3\pi}{4} = $ _____

(e) $\csc \dfrac{3\pi}{4} = $ _____

(f) $\sec \dfrac{3\pi}{4} = $ _____

(g) $\cot \dfrac{3\pi}{4} = $ _____

211. (a)

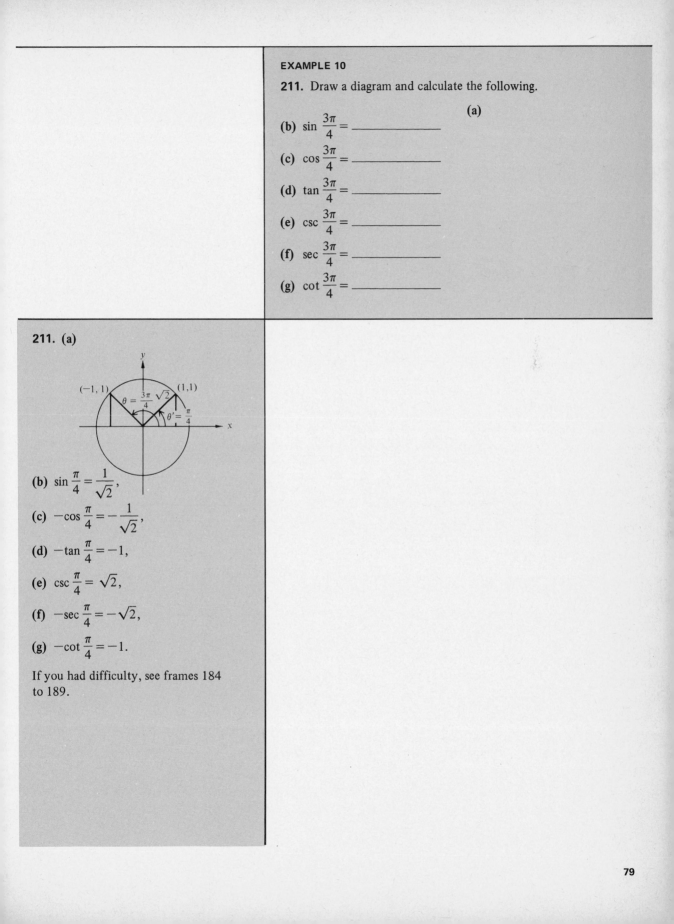

(b) $\sin \dfrac{\pi}{4} = \dfrac{1}{\sqrt{2}},$

(c) $-\cos \dfrac{\pi}{4} = -\dfrac{1}{\sqrt{2}},$

(d) $-\tan \dfrac{\pi}{4} = -1,$

(e) $\csc \dfrac{\pi}{4} = \sqrt{2},$

(f) $-\sec \dfrac{\pi}{4} = -\sqrt{2},$

(g) $-\cot \dfrac{\pi}{4} = -1.$

If you had difficulty, see frames 184 to 189.

EXAMPLE 11

212.

(a) $\sin \dfrac{4\pi}{3} =$ _____

(b) $\cos \dfrac{4\pi}{3} =$ _____

(c) $\tan \dfrac{4\pi}{3} =$ _____

212.

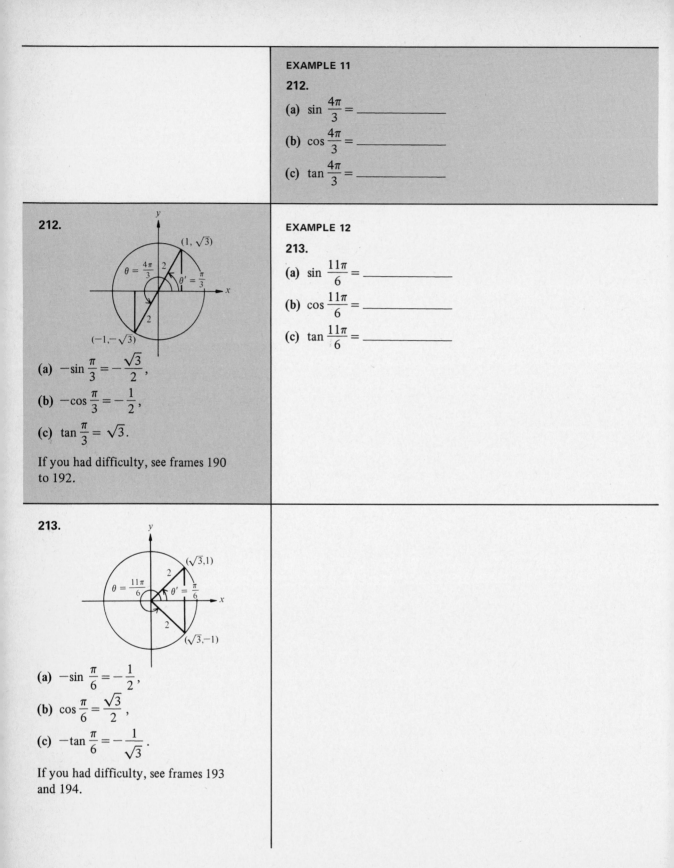

(a) $-\sin \dfrac{\pi}{3} = -\dfrac{\sqrt{3}}{2}$,

(b) $-\cos \dfrac{\pi}{3} = -\dfrac{1}{2}$,

(c) $\tan \dfrac{\pi}{3} = \sqrt{3}$.

If you had difficulty, see frames 190 to 192.

EXAMPLE 12

213.

(a) $\sin \dfrac{11\pi}{6} =$ _____

(b) $\cos \dfrac{11\pi}{6} =$ _____

(c) $\tan \dfrac{11\pi}{6} =$ _____

213.

(a) $-\sin \dfrac{\pi}{6} = -\dfrac{1}{2}$,

(b) $\cos \dfrac{\pi}{6} = \dfrac{\sqrt{3}}{2}$,

(c) $-\tan \dfrac{\pi}{6} = -\dfrac{1}{\sqrt{3}}$.

If you had difficulty, see frames 193 and 194.

EXAMPLE 13

214. Use the table to calculate **(a)** through **(c)**, correct to four decimal places.

(a) $\sin 200° =$ _____

(b) $\cos 200° =$ _____

(c) $\tan 200° =$ _____

214.

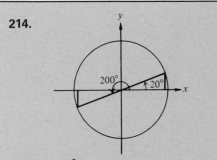

(a) $-\sin 20° = -.3420,$
(b) $-\cos 20° = -.9397$
(c) $\tan 20° = .3640.$

If you had difficulty, see frames 190 to 192 and 197.

EXERCISE 2

215. Complete the following reduction formulas.

(a) $\sin (\pi - \theta) =$ _____

(b) $\cos (\pi - \theta) =$ _____

(c) $\tan (\pi - \theta) =$ _____

(d) $\csc (\pi - \theta) =$ _____

(e) $\sec (\pi - \theta) =$ _____

(f) $\cot (\pi - \theta) =$ _____

215.

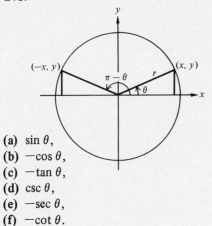

(a) $\sin \theta,$
(b) $-\cos \theta,$
(c) $-\tan \theta,$
(d) $\csc \theta,$
(e) $-\sec \theta,$
(f) $-\cot \theta.$

If you had difficulty, see frames 172 to 176.

EXERCISE 3

216.

(a) sin $(\pi + \theta) =$ _____

(b) cos $(\pi + \theta) =$ _____

(c) tan $(\pi + \theta) =$ _____

(d) csc $(\pi + \theta) =$ _____

(e) sec $(\pi + \theta) =$ _____

(f) cot $(\pi + \theta) =$ _____

216.

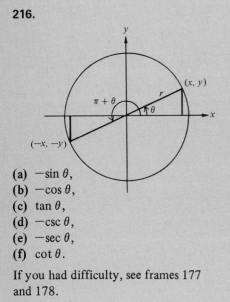

(a) $-\sin \theta,$
(b) $-\cos \theta,$
(c) $\tan \theta,$
(d) $-\csc \theta,$
(e) $-\sec \theta,$
(f) $\cot \theta.$

If you had difficulty, see frames 177 and 178.

EXERCISE 4

217.

(a) sin $(-\theta) =$ _____

(b) cos $(-\theta) =$ _____

(c) tan $(-\theta) =$ _____

(d) csc $(-\theta) =$ _____

(e) sec $(-\theta) =$ _____

(f) cot $(-\theta) =$ _____

217.

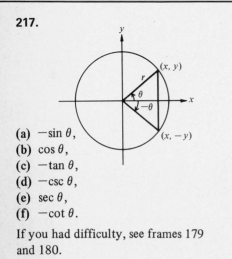

(a) $-\sin \theta,$
(b) $\cos \theta,$
(c) $-\tan \theta,$
(d) $-\csc \theta,$
(e) $\sec \theta,$
(f) $-\cot \theta.$

If you had difficulty, see frames 179 and 180.

218. Complete the following reduction formulas involving $\frac{\pi}{2}$.

(a) $\sin\left(\frac{\pi}{2}-\theta\right) =$ _____

(b) $\cos\left(\frac{\pi}{2}-\theta\right) =$ _____

(c) $\tan\left(\frac{\pi}{2}-\theta\right) =$ _____

(d) $\csc\left(\frac{\pi}{2}-\theta\right) =$ _____

(e) $\sec\left(\frac{\pi}{2}-\theta\right) =$ _____

(f) $\cot\left(\frac{\pi}{2}-\theta\right) =$ _____

218.

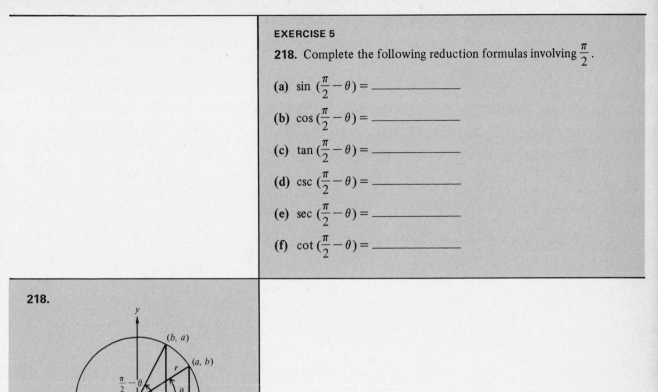

(a) $\cos\theta$,
(b) $\sin\theta$,
(c) $\cot\theta$,
(d) $\sec\theta$,
(e) $\csc\theta$,
(f) $\tan\theta$.

If you had difficulty, see frames 200 to 204.

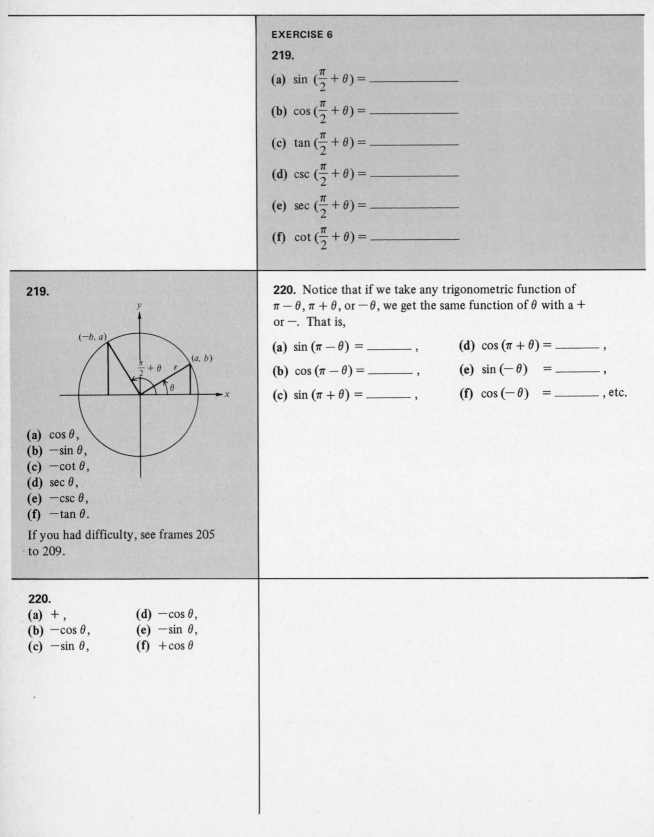

219.

(a) $\sin\left(\frac{\pi}{2} + \theta\right) =$ _____

(b) $\cos\left(\frac{\pi}{2} + \theta\right) =$ _____

(c) $\tan\left(\frac{\pi}{2} + \theta\right) =$ _____

(d) $\csc\left(\frac{\pi}{2} + \theta\right) =$ _____

(e) $\sec\left(\frac{\pi}{2} + \theta\right) =$ _____

(f) $\cot\left(\frac{\pi}{2} + \theta\right) =$ _____

219.

(a) $\cos\theta$,
(b) $-\sin\theta$,
(c) $-\cot\theta$,
(d) $\sec\theta$,
(e) $-\csc\theta$,
(f) $-\tan\theta$.

If you had difficulty, see frames 205 to 209.

220. Notice that if we take any trigonometric function of $\pi - \theta$, $\pi + \theta$, or $-\theta$, we get the same function of θ with a $+$ or $-$. That is,

(a) $\sin(\pi - \theta) =$ _____ ,   **(d)** $\cos(\pi + \theta) =$ _____ ,

(b) $\cos(\pi - \theta) =$ _____ ,   **(e)** $\sin(-\theta) =$ _____ ,

(c) $\sin(\pi + \theta) =$ _____ ,   **(f)** $\cos(-\theta) =$ _____ , etc.

220.

(a) $+$,   **(d)** $-\cos\theta$,
(b) $-\cos\theta$,   **(e)** $-\sin\theta$,
(c) $-\sin\theta$,   **(f)** $+\cos\theta$

221. On the other hand, if we take any trigonometric function of $\frac{\pi}{2} - \theta$ or $\frac{\pi}{2} + \theta$, we get the *co*-function of θ with a + or −. That is,

$$\text{sine } (\frac{\pi}{2} - \theta) = \text{cosine } \theta$$

$$\text{cosine } (\frac{\pi}{2} - \theta) = \text{sine } \theta$$

(a) tangent $(\frac{\pi}{2} - \theta) =$ _____   **(f)** $\cos (\frac{\pi}{2} + \theta) =$ _____

(b) _____ $(\frac{\pi}{2} - \theta) = \text{secant } \theta$ **(g)** $\tan (\frac{\pi}{2} + \theta) =$ _____

(c) secant $(\frac{\pi}{2} - \theta) =$ _____   **(h)** $\csc (\frac{\pi}{2} + \theta) =$ _____

(d) _____ $(\frac{\pi}{2} - \theta) = \text{tangent } \theta$ **(i)** $\sec (\frac{\pi}{2} + \theta) =$ _____

(e) $\sin (\frac{\pi}{2} + \theta) =$ _____   **(j)** $\cot (\frac{\pi}{2} + \theta) =$ _____

221.
(a) cotangent θ,   **(f)** $-\sin \theta$,

(b) cosecant,   **(g)** $-\cot \theta$,

(c) cosecant θ,   **(h)** $\sec \theta$,

(d) cotangent,   **(i)** $-\csc \theta$,

(e) $\cos \theta$,   **(j)** $-\tan \theta$

PROBLEMS

1. Calculate $\sin \frac{5\pi}{6}$, $\cos \frac{5\pi}{6}$, $\tan \frac{5\pi}{6}$.   **3.** Calculate $\sin \frac{13\pi}{4}$, $\cos \frac{13\pi}{4}$, $\tan \frac{13\pi}{4}$.

2. Calculate $\sin \frac{5\pi}{4}$, $\cos \frac{5\pi}{4}$, $\tan \frac{5\pi}{4}$.   **4.** Calculate $\sin \frac{11\pi}{3}$, $\cos \frac{11\pi}{3}$, $\tan \frac{11\pi}{3}$.

Answers are at end of book.

QUIZ

If you cannot answer the following questions correctly, review the appropriate frames.

1. Complete the following:

$\sin{(\pi + \theta)} = $ _____ $\sin{(\pi - \theta)} = $ _____ $\sin{(-\theta)} = $ _____

$\cos{(\pi + \theta)} = $ _____ $\cos{(\pi - \theta)} = $ _____ $\cos{(-\theta)} = $ _____

$\tan{(\pi + \theta)} = $ _____ $\tan{(\pi - \theta)} = $ _____ $\tan{(-\theta)} = $ _____

2. Complete the following:

$\sin{(\dfrac{\pi}{2} - \theta)} = $ _____ $\sin{(\dfrac{\pi}{2} + \theta)} = $ _____

$\cos{(\dfrac{\pi}{2} - \theta)} = $ _____ $\cos{(\dfrac{\pi}{2} + \theta)} = $ _____

$\tan{(\dfrac{\pi}{2} - \theta)} = $ _____ $\tan{(\dfrac{\pi}{2} + \theta)} = $ _____

3. Calculate the following:

$\sin{\dfrac{5\pi}{6}}$ $\cos{\dfrac{5\pi}{6}}$ $\tan{\dfrac{5\pi}{6}}$

Answers are at end of book.

Analytic Trigonometry

PART II

Up to now we have defined the trigonometric functions as functions from a set of angles to the set of real numbers. We have calculated their values at several special angles and found a number of relationships such as $\sin(\pi + \theta) = -\sin\theta$.

Now we want to give a more useful definition of trigonometric functions where the domain of the functions is also a subset of the set of real numbers. This will allow us to use the same methods in studying trigonometric functions that are used in studying other mathematical functions. Among other things we shall be able to graph the trigonometric functions and to study periodic phenomena.

We shall call the new functions, whose domains are subsets of real numbers, **circular** functions to distinguish them from the trigonometric functions, whose domains are sets of angles.

5 Circular Functions

Upon completing this chapter, you should be able to

I. Give the values of the six circular functions for any real numbers such as $0, \frac{\pi}{6}, \frac{\pi}{4}, \frac{\pi}{3}, \frac{\pi}{2}, \pi, 2\pi, \frac{15\pi}{2}$, etc.

II. Give the domain and range of each of the six circular functions.

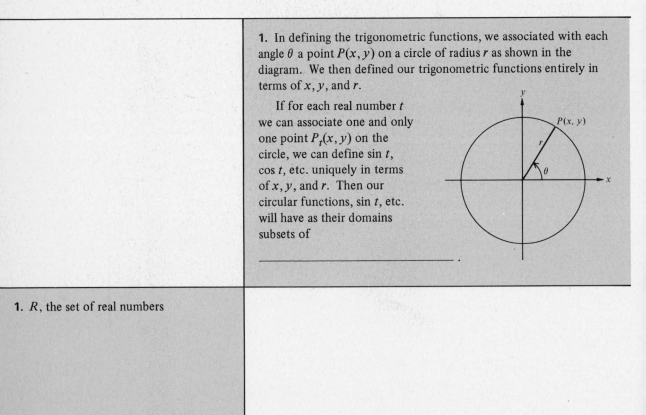

1. In defining the trigonometric functions, we associated with each angle θ a point $P(x, y)$ on a circle of radius r as shown in the diagram. We then defined our trigonometric functions entirely in terms of $x, y,$ and r.

If for each real number t we can associate one and only one point $P_t(x, y)$ on the circle, we can define $\sin t$, $\cos t$, etc. uniquely in terms of $x, y,$ and r. Then our circular functions, $\sin t$, etc. will have as their domains subsets of

_____ .

1. R, the set of real numbers

2. We now wish to assign to each real number t a unique point on a circle of radius r. See the diagram.

The center of the circle of radius r is placed at the origin of a rectangular coordinate system. And a vertical real number line is placed with its origin at the point $(r, 0)$. We choose *up* as the positive direction and r as the unit length. If we begin to wrap the positive half of the real number line counterclockwise around the circle, each point on the line will match a unique point on the circle.

What is the first real number that matches the point $(0, r)$ on the circle _____ ?

And the real number ____ will match the point $(-r, 0)$.

---

2. $\dfrac{\pi}{2}$;

π

3. If we continue to wind the positive half of the real number line around the circle, the real number _____ will be matched with the point $(0, -r)$.

And after one complete rotation, the real number _____ will also be associated with the point $(r, 0)$.

NOTE: 0 was already matched with point $(r, 0)$.

---

3. 3π;

2π

4. A second counterclockwise rotation by the positive half of the real number line will match the points $(0, r)$, $(-r, 0)$, $(0, -r)$, and $(r, 0)$ to the real numbers **(a)** _____ ,

(b) _____ , **(c)** _____ , and

(d) _____ , respectively.

4.
  (a) $\dfrac{\pi}{2} + 2\pi = \dfrac{5\pi}{2}$,
  (b) $\pi + 2\pi = 3\pi$,
  (c) $\dfrac{3\pi}{2} + 2\pi = \dfrac{7\pi}{2}$,
  (d) $2\pi + 2\pi = 4\pi$

5. As we continue to wind the positive half of the real number line around the circle, each non-negative real number is matched (or associated) with one and only one point on the circle. But it is clear that each point on the circle is matched to _____

_____ .

We have the following diagram.

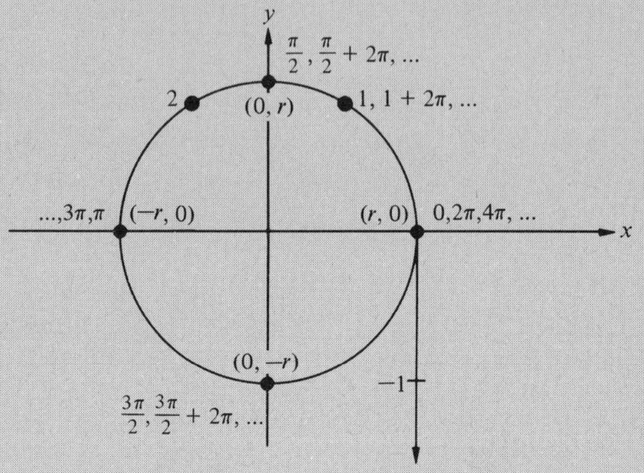

---

5. more than one real number

6. In the same way, we can wind the negative half of the real number line clockwise around the circle. And each negative real number will match a unique point on the circle. The negative

numbers **(a)** _____ , **(b)** _____ , **(c)** _____ , and **(d)** _____ will be matched with the points $(0, -r), (-r, 0), (0, r)$, and $(r, 0)$, respectively.

---

6. **(a)** $-\dfrac{\pi}{2}$, **(c)** $-\dfrac{3\pi}{2}$,

(b) $-\pi$, **(d)** -2π

7. Thus, to every real number t there is associated one and only one point $P_t(x, y)$ on the circle of radius r. And we can define our circular functions as

(a) $\sin t =$ _____ ,   **(d)** $\csc t =$ _____ ,

(b) $\cos t =$ _____ ,   **(e)** $\sec t =$ _____ ,

(c) $\tan t =$ _____ ,   **(f)** $\cot t =$ _____ .

---

7. **(a)** $\dfrac{y}{r}$,   **(d)** $\dfrac{r}{y}$,

(b) $\dfrac{x}{r}$,   **(e)** $\dfrac{r}{x}$,

(c) $\dfrac{y}{x}$,   **(f)** $\dfrac{x}{y}$

8. Let P_1 be the point on the circle associated with the real number 1.

Since we took the unit length from 0 to 1 along our real number line to be **(a)** ____ , the length of the arc from $(r, 0)$ to P_1 is **(b)** ____ , and the angle θ subtended by that arc will be **(c)** ____ radian(s).

8. (a) r,
   (b) r,
   (c) 1

9. Let t be any real number. Then the length of the arc from $(r, 0)$ to P_t will be _____ , and the angle subtended by that arc will be ____ radians.

9. $r \cdot t; t$

10. The sine of this angle, written sin (t radians), is equal to

(a) _____ (in terms of x, y, and r). But in frame 7 we also defined

(b) $\sin t =$ _____ for any real number t. So we can now define $\sin t$ for any real number t by the equation

(c) $\sin t = \sin ($_____$)$.

10.
   (a) $\dfrac{y}{r}$,

   (b) $\dfrac{y}{r}$,

   (c) t radians

11. Thus, if $0, \frac{\pi}{6}, \frac{\pi}{4}, \frac{\pi}{2},$ and π are real numbers,

(a) $\sin 0 =$ _____ ,   (f) $\cos 0 =$ _____ ,   (k) $\tan 0 =$ _____ ,

(b) $\sin \frac{\pi}{6} =$ _____ ,   (g) $\cos \frac{\pi}{6} =$ _____ ,   (l) $\tan \frac{\pi}{6} =$ _____ ,

(c) $\sin \frac{\pi}{4} =$ _____ ,   (h) $\cos \frac{\pi}{4} =$ _____ , (m) $\tan \frac{\pi}{4} =$ _____ ,

(d) $\sin \frac{\pi}{2} =$ _____ ,   (i) $\cos \frac{\pi}{2} =$ _____ ,   (n) $\tan \frac{\pi}{2} =$ _____ ,

(e) $\sin \pi =$ _____ ,   (j) $\cos \pi =$ _____ ,   (o) $\tan \pi =$ _____ .

11.
(a) 0,   (f) 1,   (k) 0,

(b) $\frac{1}{2}$,   (g) $\frac{\sqrt{3}}{2}$,   (l) $\frac{1}{\sqrt{3}}$,

(c) $\frac{1}{\sqrt{2}}$,   (h) $\frac{1}{\sqrt{2}}$,   (m) 1,

(d) 1,   (i) 0,   (n) undefined,
(e) 0,   (j) -1,   (o) 0

---

12. The domain of each of the circular functions may now be considered a subset of _____ .

---

12. R, the set of real numbers

---

13. But some trigonometric functions were not defined for all angles. Hence our new circular functions will not be defined for all real numbers since

$$\sin t = \sin (t \text{ radians}), \text{ etc.}$$

The domain of the circular function $\sin t$ is

_____ .

---

13. R, the set of all real numbers (since $\sin t = y/r$ and r is a positive constant and hence never equal to 0).

If you had difficulty, see frames 94 to 109 in Chapter 3.

---

14. Since the circular functions are also defined as ratios of x, y, and r, they will be undefined for those real numbers for which the denominator of the ratio is zero. As before, $x = 0$, for the

real numbers $t =$ _____ $\pm 2n\pi$ and $=$ _____ $\pm 2n\pi$,
$n = 0, 1, 2, \dots$.

---

14. $\frac{\pi}{2}; \frac{3\pi}{2}$

---

15. And $y = 0$ for the real numbers $t =$ _____ .

---

15. $\pm n\pi,\ n = 0, 1, 2, \dots$

16. Give the domains of the circular functions.

	Function	Domain
(a)	sin t	
(b)	cos t	
(c)	tan t	
(d)	csc t	
(e)	sec t	
(f)	cot t	

16.
(a) R, set of all real numbers,
(b) R, set of all real numbers,
(c) $\{t \in R \mid t \neq \frac{\pi}{2} \pm n\pi, n = 0, 1, 2, ...\}$,
(d) $\{t \in R \mid t \neq \pm n\pi, n = 0, 1, 2, ...\}$,
(e) $\{t \in R \mid t \neq \frac{\pi}{2} \pm n\pi, n = 0, 1, 2, ...\}$,
(f) $\{t \in R \mid t \neq \pm n\pi, n = 0, 1, 2, ...\}$.

If you had difficulty, see frames 94 to 109 in the chapter, "Domain and Range."

17. Since the circular functions assume the same set of values as the trigonometric functions, they have the same ranges. Give the ranges of the circular functions.

	Function	Range
(a)	sin t	
(b)	cos t	
(c)	tan t	
(d)	csc t	
(e)	sec t	
(f)	cot t	

17.
(a) $\{z \in R \mid -1 \leqslant z \leqslant 1\}$,
(b) $\{z \in R \mid -1 \leqslant z \leqslant 1\}$,
(c) R, the set of all real numbers,
(d) $\{z \in R \mid z \leqslant -1$ or $z \geqslant 1\}$,
(e) $\{z \in R \mid z \leqslant -1$ or $z \geqslant 1\}$,
(f) R, the set of all real numbers.

If you had difficulty, see frames 119 to 171 in the chapter, "Domain and Range."

18. The domains of the trigonometric functions are sets of

_____ , but the circular functions have sets of

_____ for their domains.

---

18. angles;
real numbers

19. But both the trigonometric functions and the circular functions have sets of _____ for their ranges.

---

19. real numbers

	20. A trigonometric function has the same value for all coterminal angles. That is, a trigonometric function has the same value for θ and $\theta \pm$ _____ .
20. $2n\pi$, $n = 1, 2, 3, \ldots$	**21.** Similarly, a circular function has the same value for all real numbers that differ by _____ . That is, a circular function has the same value for t and _____ . Thus, we have a regular repetition of values as the real number t changes by 2π.
21. $\pm 2n\pi$, $n = 1, 2, 3, \ldots$; $t \pm 2n\pi$, $n = 1, 2, 3, \ldots$	

QUIZ

If you cannot answer the following questions correctly, review the appropriate frames.

1. Consider the circle centered at the origin, with radius r, as shown in the diagram. Each real number can be associated with a point on the circumference of the circle.

Indicate the points on the circle that correspond to the real numbers.

(a) $\dfrac{\pi}{4}$ (b) π (c) $\dfrac{7\pi}{2}$

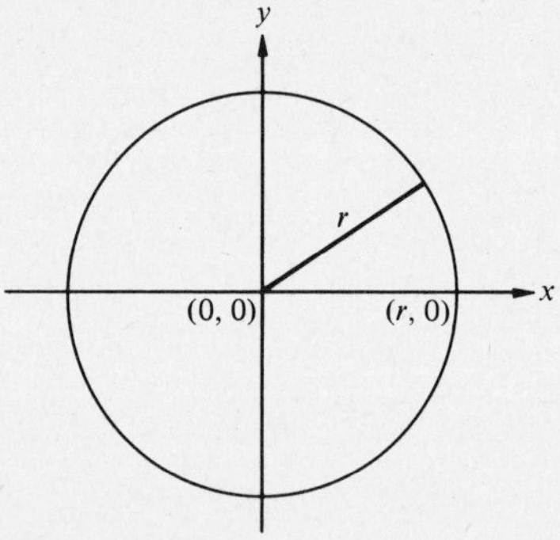

2. Give the domain and range of the following circular functions.

sin t

tan t

sec t

Answers are at end of book.

6 Periodic Functions

Upon completing this chapter, you should be able to

I. Define a periodic function.

II. Give the period of each of the six trigonometric functions.

III. Determine the period of a function from its graph.

IV. Use the following five theorems to determine the period of functions such as $y = a \sin x$, $y = \cos bx$, or $y = \tan (x + c)$:

Theorem 1. If $f(x)$ is a periodic function with period p, then for any number $a \neq 0$, the function $f(ax)$ is periodic with period $\dfrac{p}{a}$.

Theorem 2. If $f(x)$ is a periodic function with period p, then for any number a, the function $f(x + a)$ is periodic with period p.

Theorem 3. If $f(x)$ is a periodic function with period p, then for any number $K \neq 0$, the function $Kf(x)$ is periodic with period p.

Theorem 4. If f and g are periodic functions, both with period p, then (1) $f + g$, (2) $f - g$, (3) $f \cdot g$, and (4) $\dfrac{f}{g}$, $g \neq 0$ are periodic with period $\leqslant p$.

Theorem 5. Let g be a non-constant function and f be a periodic function with period p, then $g \circ f$ is periodic with period $\leqslant p$.

22. In the previous section we noted that the circular functions have a regular repetition of values. For example,

$$\sin t = \sin (t + 2\pi) \quad \text{for all } t \in R.$$

We shall call such a function **periodic** and make the following definition.

DEFINITION: A function f is **periodic** if there exists a real number $p > 0$ such that

$$f(x + p) = f(x)$$

for every x in the domain of f. If f is periodic and there is a smallest such number p, then this smallest p is called the primitive period or the **period** of f.

The period of $\sin t$ is **(a)** _____ since $\sin t$ clearly repeats every **(b)** _____ units. And **(c)** _____ is the smallest number for which $\sin t$ repeats, since $\sin \frac{\pi}{2} = 1$ and $\sin t$ does not equal 1 again until **(d)** $t =$ _____ .

---

22. (a) 2π,
　　(b) 2π,
　　(c) 2π,
　　(d) $\dfrac{5\pi}{2}$

23. Thus, we see that $\sin t$ is a _____ function with _____ 2π.

---

23. periodic; period

24. The graph of a periodic function has a repeating pattern. If p is the period of a periodic function, the graph will repeat every _____ units.

---

24. p

25. Look at the graph of a function f. Is the function periodic? _____

---

25. yes

26. What is the period of f as graphed in frame 25? _____

Why? _____

_____

---

26. 4.

The values repeat every four units, e.g., $f(-4) = f(0)$, $f(-2) = f(2)$, etc., and $p = 4$ is the smallest number for which $f(x + p) = f(x)$.

27. A function f is said to be periodic if there exists a $p > 0$ such that _____ for every x in the domain of f.

---

27. $f(x + p) = f(x)$

28. Cos t is also periodic, with period _____ since cos $0 = 1$ and cos t does not equal 1 again until $t =$ _____ .

---

28. 2π; 2π

29. Since all the circular functions repeat their values every 2π units, we know that

$$\tan(t + 2\pi) = \tan t \qquad \cot(t + 2\pi) = \cot t$$
$$\csc(t + 2\pi) = \csc t \qquad \sec(t + 2\pi) = \sec t.$$

Is 2π the smallest number for which each of these functions repeats? Answer and decide **(a)** through **(d)**.

(a) period of tan = _____

(b) period of cot = _____

(c) period of csc = _____

(d) period of sec = _____

---

29. (a) π,
 (b) π,
 (c) 2π,
 (d) 2π.

If you had difficulty, go on to the next frame. If not, skip to frame 34.

30. Let us look first at csc t. Csc t is the reciprocal of **(a)** _____ .

Therefore, $\csc \dfrac{\pi}{2} = 1$ and csc t does not equal 1 again until

(b) $t =$ _____ ; otherwise sin t would also equal 1 for that value of t. Therefore, the period of csc t is **(c)** _____ .

---

30. (a) sin t,
 (b) $\dfrac{5\pi}{2}$,
 (c) 2π

31. Similarly, sec t is the reciprocal of **(a)** _____ . Therefore,

(b) sec ___ $= 1$ and sec t does not equal 1 again until **(c)** $t =$ ___ .

Therefore, the period of sec t is **(d)** ___ .

---

31. (a) $\cos t$,
    (b) 0,
    (c) 2π,
    (d) 2π

32. Now let us look at tan t and cot t. Both are defined in terms of x and y. Look at the circle in this frame. If t is associated with the point $P_t(x, y)$, then _____ is associated with the point $(-x, -y)$. Draw in the point $(-x, -y)$.

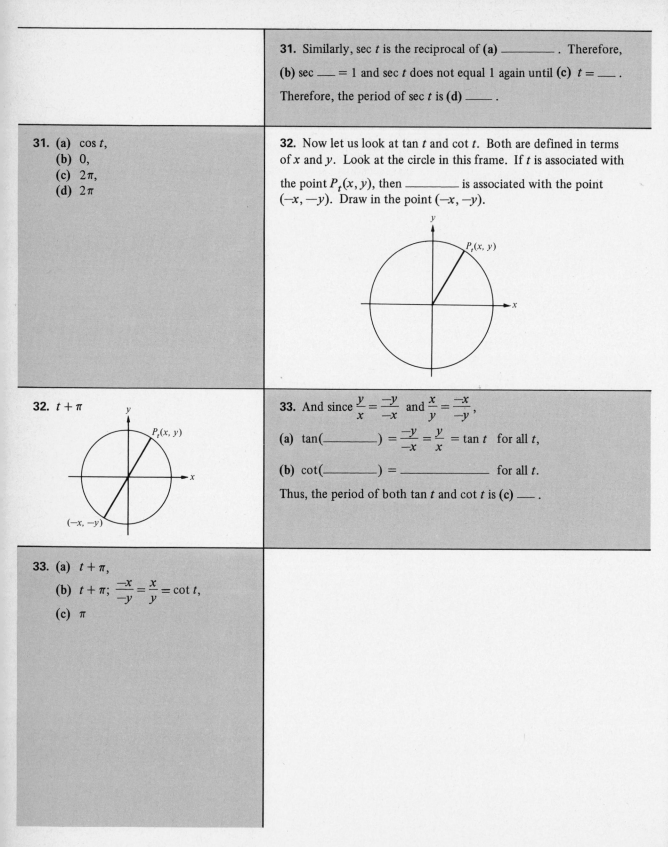

---

32. $t + \pi$

33. And since $\dfrac{y}{x} = \dfrac{-y}{-x}$ and $\dfrac{x}{y} = \dfrac{-x}{-y}$,

(a) $\tan(\underline{\hspace{1.5cm}}) = \dfrac{-y}{-x} = \dfrac{y}{x} = \tan t$ for all t,

(b) $\cot(\underline{\hspace{1.5cm}}) = \underline{\hspace{2.5cm}}$ for all t.

Thus, the period of both tan t and cot t is **(c)** ___ .

---

33. (a) $t + \pi$,
    (b) $t + \pi$; $\dfrac{-x}{-y} = \dfrac{x}{y} = \cot t$,
    (c) π

34. In summary then, the period of each of the circular functions is as follows.

Function	Period
(a) sin t	
(b) cos t	
(c) tan t	
(d) csc t	
(e) sec t	
(f) cot t	

34. **(a)** 2π,
(b) 2π,
(c) π,
(d) 2π,
(e) 2π,
(f) π

35. Note that since sine is the reciprocal of cosecant $\left(\text{i.e., } \csc t = \dfrac{1}{\sin t}\right)$, they have the same period, **(a)** ——— .

Similarly, cosine and **(b)** ———————— both have period **(c)** ——— .

And tangent and its reciprocal **(d)** ———————— both have period **(e)** ——— .

35. **(a)** 2π,
(b) secant,
(c) 2π,
(d) cotangent,
(e) π

36. We shall now prove five theorems about periodic functions that will be useful later. A function f is periodic if

_____

_____

_____ .

36. there exists a number $p > 0$ such that $f(x + p) = f(x)$ for all x in the domain of f

37. We shall use the periodic circular functions as examples to motivate the general theorems. From now on we shall let x represent a real number in the domain of the circular functions and write $\sin x$, $\cos x$, $\tan x$, etc.

Consider the new function $\sin 2x$. Compute the following values for $\sin 2x$:

x	0	$\dfrac{\pi}{4}$	$\dfrac{\pi}{2}$	$\dfrac{3\pi}{4}$	π	$\dfrac{5\pi}{4}$	$\dfrac{3\pi}{2}$	$\dfrac{7\pi}{4}$	2π
$2x$	0	$\dfrac{\pi}{2}$	π	$\dfrac{3\pi}{2}$	2π	$\dfrac{5\pi}{2}$	3π	$\dfrac{7\pi}{2}$	4π
$\sin 2x$									

37.
0   1   0   −1   0   1   0   −1   0

38. Thus the values of $\sin 2x$ repeat every time x increases by ____ units. That is, the period of $\sin 2x$ is ____ .

38. π;
π

39. We can *prove* that π is the period of $\sin 2x$ if we can replace x by $x + \pi$ in $\sin 2x$ and show that what we get is equal to $\sin 2x$. That is,

$$\sin 2x = \sin(2x + 2\pi) \quad \text{(since } \sin t = \sin(t + 2\pi) \text{ for all } t\text{).}$$

Therefore **(a)** $\sin 2x = \sin 2\,(\underline{\hspace{2cm}})$.

Since 2π is the smallest value of p for which

$\sin(x + p) = \sin x$, **(b)** ____ is the smallest value of K such that $\sin 2(x + K) = \sin 2x$ for all x.

Thus the period of $\sin 2x$ is **(c)** ____ .

39. (a) $x + \pi$,
(b) π,
(c) π

40. Now look at $\cos 3x$ and compute the following values for $\cos 3x$.

x	0	$\frac{\pi}{6}$	$\frac{\pi}{3}$	$\frac{\pi}{2}$	$\frac{2\pi}{3}$	$\frac{5\pi}{6}$	π	$\frac{7\pi}{6}$	$\frac{4\pi}{3}$	$\frac{3\pi}{2}$	$\frac{5\pi}{3}$	$\frac{11\pi}{6}$	2π
$3x$													
$\cos 3x$													

40.

$3x$	0	$\frac{\pi}{2}$	π	$\frac{3\pi}{2}$	2π	$\frac{5\pi}{2}$	3π	$\frac{7\pi}{2}$	4π	$\frac{9\pi}{2}$	5π	$\frac{11\pi}{2}$	6π
$\cos 3x$	1	0	-1	0	1	0	-1	0	1	0	-1	0	1

41. Thus the period of $\cos 3x$ is _____ , since the values of $\cos 3x$ repeat each time x increases by _____ units.

41. $\frac{2\pi}{3}$; $\frac{2\pi}{3}$

42. Again we can use the definition of a periodic function to *prove* that $\frac{2\pi}{3}$ is the period of $\cos 3x$ by showing that

$$\cos 3(x + \frac{2\pi}{3}) = \text{_____} .$$

42. $\cos 3x$

43. But
$$\cos 3(x + \frac{2\pi}{3}) = \text{_____} = \text{_____} \text{ since}$$
$\cos(t + 2\pi) = \cos t$ for all $t \in R$, and in particular for $t = 3x$.
Thus we have proved that the period of $\cos 3x$ is $\frac{2\pi}{3}$, since $\frac{2\pi}{3}$ is the smallest value of K for which $\cos 3(x + K) = \cos 3x$.

43. $\cos(3x + 2\pi)$; $\cos 3x$

EXAMPLE 1

44. The period of $\tan 2x$ is _____ .

44. $\frac{\pi}{2}$.

If you had difficulty, go on to the next frame. If not, skip to frame 47.

45. Calculate the values for tan $2x$.

x	0	$\dfrac{\pi}{8}$	$\dfrac{\pi}{4}$	$\dfrac{3\pi}{8}$	$\dfrac{\pi}{2}$	$\dfrac{5\pi}{8}$	$\dfrac{3\pi}{4}$	$\dfrac{7\pi}{8}$	π
$2x$									
tan $2x$									

45.

$2x$	0	$\dfrac{\pi}{4}$	$\dfrac{\pi}{2}$	$\dfrac{3\pi}{4}$	π	$\dfrac{5\pi}{4}$	$\dfrac{3\pi}{2}$	$\dfrac{7\pi}{4}$	2π
tan $2x$	0	1	∞	-1	0	1	∞	-1	0

46. Thus the period of tan $2x$ is _____ , since the values of tan $2x$ repeat each time x increases by _____ units.

46. $\dfrac{\pi}{2}$; $\dfrac{\pi}{2}$

47. We can prove that $\dfrac{\pi}{2}$ is the period of tan $2x$ by showing that

_____ .

47. $\tan 2(x + \dfrac{\pi}{2}) = \tan 2x$

48. But

$\tan 2(x + \dfrac{\pi}{2}) = $ _____ $=$ _____

since the period of tan x is π. That is, since $\tan(t + \pi) = \tan t$ for all t and in particular for $t = 2x$. Thus we have proved that the period of tan $2x$ is $\dfrac{\pi}{2}$, since $\dfrac{\pi}{2}$ is the smallest value of K for which $\tan 2(x + K) = \tan 2x$.

48. tan $(2x + \pi)$; tan $2x$

49. Sin x has period **(a)** _____ , and we have proved that sin $2x$ has period **(b)** _____ .

   Cos x has period **(c)** _____ , and we have proved that cos $3x$ has period **(d)** _____ .

   And tan x has period **(e)** _____ , and we have proved that tan $2x$ has period **(f)** _____ .

49.
(a) 2π,   (d) $\dfrac{2\pi}{3}$,

(b) π,   (e) π,

(c) 2π,   (f) $\dfrac{\pi}{2}$

50. Can you recognize a pattern? If $f(x)$ is a periodic function with period p, then

   $f(2x)$ has period **(a)** _____ ,

   $f(3x)$ has period **(b)** _____ ,

and, in general,

   $f(ax)$ has period **(c)** _____ .

---

50. (a) $\dfrac{p}{2}$, (b) $\dfrac{p}{3}$, (c) $\dfrac{p}{a}$.

If you had difficulty, go on to the next frame. If not, skip to frame 52.

51. Sin x has period 2π and sin $2x$ has period $\dfrac{2\pi}{2}$. Cos x has period 2π and cos $3x$ has period $\dfrac{2\pi}{3}$, and tan x has period π, and tan $2x$ has period $\dfrac{\pi}{2}$. The pattern seems to be, then, if $f(x)$ has period p, then we can find the period of $f(ax)$ by _____ .

---

51. dividing p by a

52. We have the following theorem:

THEOREM 1. If $f(x)$ is a periodic function with period p, then for any number $a > 0$, the function $f(ax)$ is periodic with period p/a.

NOTE: x represents elements in the domain in each case.

Proof: We can prove that $f(ax)$ has period $\dfrac{p}{a}$ by showing that

_____ .

52.
$$f\!\left(a\!\left(x + \frac{p}{a}\right)\right) = f(ax)\quad\text{for all }x$$

53. We are given that $f(x)$ has period p. That is, we know that

$f(x + p) =$ _____ .

---

53. $f(x)$ for all x

54. Now returning to $f\left(a\left(x + \dfrac{p}{a}\right)\right)$, we see that

$$f\left(a\left(x + \dfrac{p}{a}\right)\right) = f(ax + p) = \text{(a)} \underline{\hspace{2cm}}, \text{ since}$$

$f(x + p) = \text{(b)} \underline{\hspace{2cm}}$ for all real numbers and in particular for ax.

Thus we have proved that $f(ax)$ is (c) $\underline{\hspace{3cm}}$.

---

54. (a) $f(ax)$, **(b)** $f(x)$,
(c) periodic

55. We now show that $\dfrac{p}{a}$ is the smallest value K such that

$\quad f(a(x + K)) = f(ax)$ for all x.
$\quad$ If $f(a(x + K)) = f(ax + aK) = f(ax)$ for all x
it implies that $f(z + aK) = f(z)$ for all z.

But since p is *the* period of $f(x)$, $aK \geqslant \underline{\hspace{1cm}}$.

That is, $K \geqslant \underline{\hspace{1cm}}$.

---

55. p;
$\dfrac{p}{a}$

56. Thus $\dfrac{p}{a}$ is the smallest value K such that $f(a(x + K)) = f(ax)$

for all x. And we have proved that $f(ax)$ is periodic with

$\underline{\hspace{4cm}}$.

---

56. period $\dfrac{p}{a}$

SUMMARY

Theorem 1

If $f(x)$ is a periodic function with period p, then for any real number $a > 0$, the function
$f(ax)$ is periodic with period $\dfrac{p}{a}$.

Proof: We are given that $f(x)$ has period p. That is,

(1) $f(x + p) = f(x)$ for all x.

We must show that $f(ax)$ has period $\dfrac{p}{a}$. That is, we must show that

$$f\left(a\left(x + \dfrac{p}{a}\right)\right) = f(ax) \quad \text{for all } x.$$

But

$$f\left(a\left(x + \dfrac{p}{a}\right)\right) = f(ax + p) = f(ax)$$

by (1) above, since $f(x + p) = f(x)$ for all reals; it is in particular true for ax.

Furthermore $\dfrac{p}{a}$ is the smallest value of K for which $f(a(x + K)) = f(ax)$. For if $f(a(x + K)) = f(ax)$ for $K < \dfrac{p}{a}$, then $f(x + aK) = f(x)$ for all x, contradicting the fact that p is the smallest such value.

Thus we have proved that $f(ax)$ is periodic with period $\dfrac{p}{a}$.

	EXAMPLE 2 **57.** Use theorem 1 to find the period of the function $\cot 4x$. Period is ____ .
57. $\dfrac{\pi}{4}$. If you had difficulty, go on to the next frame. If not, skip to frame 59.	**58.** Cot x has period **(a)** ___ . Therefore to find the period of $\cot 4x$, the theorem tells us to divide **(b)** ___ by 4 to obtain **(c)** ___ .
58. (a) π, (b) π, (c) $\dfrac{\pi}{4}$	**EXAMPLE 3** **59.** The period of $\sec 8x$ is ____ .
59. $\dfrac{\pi}{4}$. If you had difficulty, see frames 37 to 58.	**EXAMPLE 4** **60.** The period of the function $\sin \frac{1}{2} x$ is ____ .
60. 4π. **NOTE:** The period of $\sin x$ is 2π and $2\pi / \frac{1}{2}$ is 4π.	**61.** If $f(x)$ is any periodic function with period p, the function $f(ax)$ is periodic with _____ .
61. period $\dfrac{p}{a}$	**62.** We shall label the following result a theorem, even though its proof is trivial, so that we may identify it for later use. **THEOREM 2.** If $f(x)$ is a periodic function with period p, then for any number a, the function $f(x + a)$ is periodic with period p. *Proof:* To prove that $f(x + a)$ has period p, we must show that _____ $= f(x + a)$ for all x.
62. $f((x + a) + p)$	

63. This is immediately true, since f has period p

$$f(t \text{\underline{\hspace{1cm}}}) = \text{\underline{\hspace{1cm}}} \quad \text{for all } t \in R,$$

and in particular it is true for $t = x + a$.

Thus $f(x + a)$ also has period $\text{\underline{\hspace{0.5cm}}}$ since p is the smallest value of K for which $f(x + a) + K) = f(x + a)$.
And our theorem is proved.

---

63. $+p; f(t);$
$\quad p$

64. Thus $\sin(x + \pi)$ has period $\text{\underline{\hspace{1cm}}}$.

---

64. 2π, since $\sin x$ has period 2π

65. $\text{Tan}(x + 17)$ has period $\text{\underline{\hspace{1cm}}}$.

---

65. π, since $\tan x$ has period π

EXAMPLE 5

66. What is the period of $\sin(2x + 8)$? $\text{\underline{\hspace{1cm}}}$

---

66. π.

If you had difficulty, go on to the next frame. If not, skip to frame 68.

67. $\text{Sin } 2x$ has period $\text{\underline{\hspace{0.5cm}}}$. And if we let $f(x) = \sin 2x$,

$f(x + 4) = \sin(2x + 8)$ has period $\text{\underline{\hspace{0.5cm}}}$ by theorem 2.

---

67. π;
$\quad \pi$

EXAMPLE 6

68. $\text{Cos}(3x + \pi)$ has period $\text{\underline{\hspace{1cm}}}$.

---

68. $\dfrac{2\pi}{3}$, since $\cos 3x$ has period $\dfrac{2\pi}{2}$

69. If $f(x)$ is any periodic function with period p,

$$f(ax) \text{ has period (a) } \text{\underline{\hspace{1cm}}} ,$$
and

$$f(ax + c) \text{ has period (b) } \text{\underline{\hspace{1cm}}} ,$$
while

$$f(x + c) \text{ has period (c) } \text{\underline{\hspace{1cm}}} .$$

---

69. (a) $\dfrac{p}{a}$, (b) $\dfrac{p}{a}$, (c) p,

since replacing x by $x + c$ or ax by $ax + c$ does not affect the period of $f(x)$ or $f(ax)$.

70. Finally, consider the function $4 \sin x$.

$4 \sin z$ has period _____ .

---

70. 2π, since the 4 affects not the period but only the magnitude of the values.

71. Again we state an immediate result as a theorem for future reference.

THEOREM 3. If $f(x)$ is a periodic function with period p, then for any number $K \neq 0$, the function $Kf(x)$ is periodic with period p.

Proof: It is immediate that $Kf(x)$ has period p since

_____ for all x.

---

71. $Kf(x + p) = Kf(x)$
$((Kf)(x + p) = K \cdot f(x + p)$
$= K \cdot f(x) = (Kf)(x)$
since $f(x + p) = f(x)$ for all x)

72. Thus the period of $7 \cos x$ is _____ .

---

72. 2π, since $\cos x$ has period 2π.

73. The period of $7 \cos 3x$ is _____ .

---

73. $\dfrac{2\pi}{3}$, since $\cos 3x$ has period $\dfrac{2\pi}{3}$.

74. And the period of $7 \cos(3x + 5)$ is _____ .

---

74. $\dfrac{2\pi}{3}$

75. If $f(x)$ is any periodic function with period p, then

$Kf(x)$ has period **(a)** _____ ,

$f(x + a)$ has period **(b)** _____ ,

but

$f(ax)$ has period **(c)** _____ ,

and

$Kf(ax + c)$ has period **(d)** _____ .

---

75. **(a)** p, **(b)** p, **(c)** $\dfrac{p}{a}$, **(d)** $\dfrac{p}{a}$,

since K and c do not affect the period.

76. In the volume on functions, we formed the new functions $f+g, f-g, f \cdot g, \dfrac{f}{g}, g \circ f$, and $f \circ g$ from two given functions. We now give two theorems that indicate whether the new functions are periodic if f and g are.

Let $f(x) = \sin x$ and $g(x) = \cos x$, then

$(f+g)(x) = $ _____ .

---

76. $\sin x + \cos x$

EXAMPLE 7

77. Is $\sin x + \cos x$ periodic? _____ If so, what is the period? _____

---

77. yes;
   2π.

If you had difficulty, go on to the next frame. If not skip to frame 80.

---

78. Compute the following values for $\sin x + \cos x$.

x	0	$\dfrac{\pi}{2}$	π	$\dfrac{3\pi}{2}$	2π	$\dfrac{5\pi}{2}$	3π	$\dfrac{7\pi}{2}$	4π
$\sin x + \cos x$									

78.

x	0	$\dfrac{\pi}{2}$	π	$\dfrac{3\pi}{2}$	2π	$\dfrac{5\pi}{2}$	3π	$\dfrac{7\pi}{2}$	4π
$\sin x$	0	1	0	-1	0	1	0	-1	0
$\cos x$	1	0	-1	0	1	0	-1	0	1
$\sin x + \cos x$	1	1	-1	-1	1	1	-1	-1	1

---

79. Thus the period of $\sin x + \cos x$ is _____ .

---

79. 2π

---

80. In this example, at least, $f(x)$ and $g(x)$ have period p, and $f + g$ has period _____ .

---

80. p

EXAMPLE 8

81. Let $f(x) = \cos 2x$ and $g(x) = \tan x$.

Then $(f \cdot g)(x) = $ _____ .

81. $\cos 2x \cdot \tan x$

82. Compute the following values of $\cos 2x \tan x$.

x	0	$\frac{\pi}{6}$	$\frac{\pi}{4}$	$\frac{\pi}{3}$	$\frac{\pi}{2}$	$\frac{2\pi}{3}$	$\frac{3\pi}{4}$	$\frac{5\pi}{6}$	π	$\frac{7\pi}{6}$	$\frac{5\pi}{4}$	$\frac{4\pi}{3}$	$\frac{3\pi}{2}$	$\frac{5\pi}{3}$	$\frac{7\pi}{4}$	$\frac{11\pi}{6}$	2π
$\cos 2x \cdot \tan x$																	

82.

x	0	$\frac{\pi}{6}$	$\frac{\pi}{4}$	$\frac{\pi}{3}$	$\frac{\pi}{2}$	$\frac{2\pi}{3}$	$\frac{3\pi}{4}$	$\frac{5\pi}{6}$	π	$\frac{7\pi}{6}$	$\frac{5\pi}{4}$	$\frac{4\pi}{3}$	$\frac{3\pi}{2}$	$\frac{5\pi}{3}$	$\frac{7\pi}{4}$	$\frac{11\pi}{6}$	2π
$\cos 2x$	1	$\frac{1}{2}$	0	$-\frac{1}{2}$	-1	$-\frac{1}{2}$	0	$\frac{1}{2}$	1	$\frac{1}{2}$	0	$-\frac{1}{2}$	-1	$-\frac{1}{2}$	0	$\frac{1}{2}$	1
$\tan x$	0	$\frac{1}{\sqrt{3}}$	1	$\sqrt{3}$	∞	$-\sqrt{3}$	-1	$-\frac{1}{\sqrt{3}}$	0	$\frac{1}{\sqrt{3}}$	1	$\sqrt{3}$	∞	$-\sqrt{3}$	-1	$\frac{1}{\sqrt{3}}$	0
$\cos 2x \cdot \tan x$	0	$-\frac{1}{2\sqrt{3}}$	0	$-\frac{\sqrt{3}}{2}$	∞	$\frac{\sqrt{3}}{2}$	0	$-\frac{1}{2\sqrt{3}}$	0	$\frac{1}{2\sqrt{3}}$	0	$\frac{\sqrt{3}}{2}$	∞	$\frac{\sqrt{3}}{2}$	0	$-\frac{1}{2\sqrt{3}}$	0

83. Thus the period of $\cos 2x \cdot \tan x$ is ___ .

83. π

84. Again, both $f(x)$ and $g(x)$ have period p and $f \cdot g$ has period ___ .

84. p

85. In general we can prove the following theorem.

THEOREM 4. If f and g are periodic functions, both with period p, then (1) $f + g$, (2) $f - g$, (3) $f \cdot g$, and (4) $\dfrac{f}{g}$, $g \neq 0$, are periodic with period $\leqslant p$.

Proof: (1) To prove that $f + g$ has period $\leqslant p$, we must show that $f + g$ repeats its values every p units. That is, we must show that

$$(f + g)(\underline{\hspace{1cm}}) = \underline{\hspace{2cm}} \text{ for all } x.$$

---

85. $x + p$; $(f + g)(x)$

86. But by definition of $f + g$,

$$(f + g)(x + p) = \underline{\hspace{3cm}} .$$

---

86. $f(x + p) + g(x + p)$

87. And since f and g both have period p,

$$f(x + p) = \underline{\hspace{1cm}} \text{ and } \underline{\hspace{1.5cm}} = \underline{\hspace{2cm}} \text{ for all } x.$$

---

87. $f(x)$; $g(x + p)$; $g(x)$

88. Thus by combining frames 86 and 87 we get

$$(f + g)(x + p) = \underline{\hspace{2cm}} = \underline{\hspace{2cm}} = \underline{\hspace{2cm}} .$$

Thus we have shown that $f + g$ repeats its values every p units. Hence p is periodic. But p may *not* be the smallest value of K for which $f + g$ repeats. Therefore all we can say is that the period of $f + g$ is $\leqslant p$.

---

88. $f(x + p) + g(x + p)$; $f(x) + g(x)$; $(f + g)(x)$

SUMMARY

Theorem 4

If f and g are periodic functions, both with period p, then (1) $f + g$, (2) $f - g$, (3) $f \cdot g$, and (4) $\dfrac{f}{g}$, $g \neq 0$, are periodic with period $\leqslant p$.

Proof: (1) To prove that $f + g$ has period $K \leqslant p$, we can show that $f + g$ repeats its values every p units. That is, we can show that

$$(f + g)(x + p) = (f + g)(x) \quad \text{for all } x.$$

By definition of $f + g$,

(a) $(f + g)(x + p) = f(x + p) + g(x + p)$

and since both f and g have period p,

(b) $f(x + p) = f(x)$ and $g(x + p) = g(x)$.

Thus combining (a) and (b) we get

$(f + g)(x + p) = f(x + p) + g(x + p) = f(x) + g(x) = (f + g)(x).$

Thus we have shown that $f + g$ repeats its values every p units. Hence $f + g$ is periodic. But p may *not* be the smallest value of K for which $f + g$ repeats. Hence the period of $f + g$ is $\leqslant p$.

The proofs for $f - g$, $f \cdot g$, and $\dfrac{f}{g}$ are similar.

---

89. Prove part (3) of theorem 4. That is, prove that if f and g have period p, then $f \cdot g$ has period $\leqslant p$.

---

89. To check your proof, see the summary preceding this frame.

90. To prove that $f \cdot g$ has period $\leqslant p$ you had to show that $f \cdot g$ repeats its values every p units. That is,

_____ .

---

90. $(f \cdot g)(x + p) = (f \cdot g)(x)$ for all x.

If you had difficulty, go on to the next frame. If not, skip to frame 92.

91. But by definition of $f \cdot g$,

   (a) _____

and, since f and g have period p.

   (b) _____.

Therefore by combining (a) and (b) we get

   (c) _____ for all x,

which shows that $f \cdot g$ repeats its values every p units. Hence $f \cdot g$ is periodic. But p may not be the smallest value of K for which $f \cdot g$ repeats. Hence the period of $f \cdot g$ is $\leqslant p$.

91.

(a) $(f \cdot g)(x + p) = f(x + p) \cdot g(x + p)$,

(b) $f(x + p) = f(x)$ and
    $g(x + p) = g(x)$ for all x,

(c) $(f \cdot g)(x + p) = f(x + p) \cdot g(x + p)$
    $= f(x) \cdot g(x) = (f \cdot g)(x)$

EXERCISE 1

92. Prove part (2) of theorem 4 above. That is, prove that if f and g have period p, then $f - g$ has period $\leqslant p$.

---

92. If you had difficulty, see frames 85 to 88 and the summary for guidance.

93. Use theorem 4 to answer the next three frames.

The period of $\sin x \cdot \cos x$ is $\leqslant$ _____ .

---

93. 2π,
since both $\sin x$ and $\cos x$ have period 2π, the result follows from theorem 4, part (3).

94. The period of $\dfrac{\sin 4x}{\tan 2x}$ is _____ .

---

94. $\leqslant \dfrac{\pi}{2}$.

NOTE: Don't forget the $\leqslant$.

95. The period of $\csc 3x - \sec 3x$ is _____ .

---

95. $\leqslant \dfrac{2\pi}{3}$.

NOTE: The period of both $\csc 3x$ and $\sec 3x$ is $\dfrac{2\pi}{3}$.

96. If $f(x)$ and $g(x)$ are both periodic with period p, then

$f(ax)$ has period **(a)** _____ ,

$f(x + c)$ has period **(b)** _____ ,

$Kf(x)$ has period **(c)** _____ ,

and $(f + g)(x), (f - g)(x), (f \cdot g)(x)$; and $\dfrac{f}{g}(x), g \neq 0$,

all have period **(d)** _____ .

96.
(a) $\dfrac{p}{a}$,
(b) p,
(c) p,
(d) $\leqslant p$

97. Now we turn to our final theorem, which deals with composite functions.

Let $h(x) = (\sin x)^2 + 1$.

Find $f(x)$ and $g(x)$ such that

$(g \circ f)(x) = h(x) = (\sin x)^2 + 1$.

$f(x) =$ _____

$g(x) =$ _____

97. $\sin x$;
$x^2 + 1$,
since $(g \circ f)(x) = g(f(x))$
$= g(\sin x) = (\sin x)^2 + 1$.

98. NOTE: $(\sin x)^2$ is usually denoted by $\sin^2 x$. Compute the following values for $h(x) = \sin^2 x + 1$.

x	0	$\dfrac{\pi}{4}$	$\dfrac{\pi}{2}$	$\dfrac{3\pi}{4}$	π	$\dfrac{5\pi}{4}$	$\dfrac{3\pi}{2}$	$\dfrac{7\pi}{4}$	2π	$\dfrac{9\pi}{4}$	$\dfrac{5\pi}{2}$	$\dfrac{11\pi}{4}$	3π	$\dfrac{13\pi}{4}$	$\dfrac{7\pi}{2}$	$\dfrac{15\pi}{4}$	4π
$\sin x$																	
$\sin^2 x + 1$																	

98.

x	0	$\dfrac{\pi}{4}$	$\dfrac{\pi}{2}$	$\dfrac{3\pi}{4}$	π	$\dfrac{5\pi}{4}$	$\dfrac{3\pi}{2}$	$\dfrac{7\pi}{4}$	2π	$\dfrac{9\pi}{4}$	$\dfrac{5\pi}{2}$	$\dfrac{11\pi}{4}$	3π	$\dfrac{13\pi}{4}$	$\dfrac{7\pi}{2}$	$\dfrac{15\pi}{4}$	4π
$\sin x$	0	$\dfrac{1}{\sqrt{2}}$	1	$\dfrac{1}{\sqrt{2}}$	0	$-\dfrac{1}{\sqrt{2}}$	-1	$-\dfrac{1}{\sqrt{2}}$	0	$\dfrac{1}{\sqrt{2}}$	1	$\dfrac{1}{\sqrt{2}}$	0	$-\dfrac{1}{\sqrt{2}}$	-1	$-\dfrac{1}{\sqrt{2}}$	0
$\sin^2 x + 1$	1	$\dfrac{3}{2}$	2	$\dfrac{3}{2}$	1	$\dfrac{3}{2}$	2	$\dfrac{3}{2}$	1	$\dfrac{3}{2}$	2	$\dfrac{3}{2}$	1	$\dfrac{3}{2}$	2	$\dfrac{3}{2}$	1

99. Is $h(x) = \sin^2 x + 1$ periodic? _____

---

99. yes

100. What is the period? ___

---

100. π, since $\sin^2 x + 1$ repeats each time x increases by π units.

101. In this example, $g(x) = x^2 + 1$ is not periodic,

$f(x) = \sin x$ has period _____ , and

$(g \circ f)(x) = \sin^2 x + 1$ has period _____ .

---

101. 2π; π
π

EXAMPLE 9

102. Now consider the function $h(x) = \sin^3 x$.

Find two functions f and g such that

$$(g \circ f)(x) = h(x) = \sin^3 x.$$

$f(x) = $ _____

$g(x) = $ _____

---

102. $\sin x$;
x^3, since
$(g \circ f)(x) = g(f(x)) = g(\sin x) = \sin^3 x.$

103. $h(x) = \sin^3 x$ has the following values. What is its period? _____

x	0	$\frac{\pi}{4}$	$\frac{\pi}{2}$	$\frac{3\pi}{4}$	π	$\frac{5\pi}{4}$	$\frac{3\pi}{2}$	$\frac{7\pi}{4}$	2π	$\frac{9\pi}{4}$	$\frac{5\pi}{2}$	$\frac{11\pi}{4}$	3π	$\frac{13\pi}{4}$	$\frac{7\pi}{2}$	$\frac{15\pi}{4}$	4π
$\sin x$	0	$\frac{1}{\sqrt{2}}$	1	$\frac{1}{\sqrt{2}}$	0	$-\frac{1}{\sqrt{2}}$	-1	$-\frac{1}{\sqrt{2}}$	0	$\frac{1}{\sqrt{2}}$	1	$\frac{1}{\sqrt{2}}$	0	$-\frac{1}{\sqrt{2}}$	-1	$-\frac{1}{\sqrt{2}}$	0
$\sin^3 x$	0	$\frac{1}{2\sqrt{2}}$	1	$\frac{1}{2\sqrt{2}}$	0	$-\frac{1}{2\sqrt{2}}$	-1	$-\frac{1}{2\sqrt{2}}$	0	$\frac{1}{2\sqrt{2}}$	1	$\frac{1}{2\sqrt{2}}$	0	$-\frac{1}{2\sqrt{2}}$	-1	$-\frac{1}{2\sqrt{2}}$	0

---

103. 2π

104. In the second example,

$g(x) = x^3$ **(a)** _____ ,

$f(x) = \sin x$ **(b)** _____ , and

$(g \circ f)(x) = \sin^3 x$ **(c)** _____ .

---

104. **(a)** is not periodic,
(b) has period 2π,
(c) has period 2π

105. In each of the two examples above, f was periodic with period p, g was not periodic, and $g \circ f$ was periodic. How were the periods of $g \circ f$ and f related?

period $g \circ f$ _____ period of f

---

105. $\leqslant$

106. In general we can state the following theorem.

THEOREM 5. Let g be a non-constant function and f be a periodic function with period p; then $g \circ f$ is periodic with period $\leqslant p$.

Proof: To prove that $g \circ f$ has a period $\leqslant p$, we can show that $g \circ f$ repeats every p units.

That is, we can show that

$(g \circ f)($ _____ $) = $ _____ for all x.

---

106. $x + p$; $(g \circ f)(x)$

107. By definition of $g \circ f$,

(1) $(g \circ f)(x + p) = $ _____ .

---

107. $g(f(x + p))$

108. And since f has period p,

(2) _____ for all x.

---

108. $f(x + p) = f(x)$

109. Thus by combining (1) and (2), we get

$(g \circ f)(x + p) = \underline{\hspace{5cm}}$,

and we have shown that $g \circ f$ repeats its values every p units.

(**NOTE:** This may not be the smallest value of K for which $g \circ f$ repeats.) Hence, its period is $\leqslant p$.

---

109. $g(f(x + p)) = g(f(x)) = (g \circ f)(x)$

SUMMARY

Theorem 5

Let g be a non-constant function and f be a periodic function with period p; then the composite function $g \circ f$ is periodic with period $\leqslant p$.

Proof: To prove that $g \circ f$ has period $K \leqslant p$, we can show that $g \circ f$ repeats its values every p units. That is, we can show that

$$(g \circ f)(x + p) = (g \circ f)(x) \quad \text{for all } x.$$

By definition of $g \circ f$,

(1) $(g \circ f)(x + p) = g(f(x + p))$

and since f has period p,

(2) $f(x + p) = f(x) \quad \text{for all } x.$

Thus by combining (1) and (2), we get

$$(g \circ f)(x + p) = g(f(x + p)) = g(f(x)) = (g \circ f)(x),$$

and we have shown that $g \circ f$ repeats its values every p units. Hence $g \circ f$ is periodic. But p may *not* be the smallest value of K for which $g \circ f$ repeats. Hence all we can say is that the period of $g \circ f$ is $\leqslant p$.

---

110. Note that, in each example and in the statement of the theorem f is periodic and g is not. Which did we show was periodic,

$f \circ g$ or $g \circ f$? $\underline{\hspace{2cm}}$

---

110. $g \circ f$

111. And in general it is not true that $(f \circ g)(x) = f(g(x))$ is periodic if f is periodic but g is not.

For example, let $f(x) = \sin x$ and $g(x) = x^2$.

Then $(f\triangle$ Then $(f \circ g)(x) =$ _____ .

---

111. $\sin x^2$. This is not the same as $\sin^2 x$.

---

112. Below is the graph of $\sin x^2$.

$$\sin(x^2)$$

Is $\sin x^2$ periodic? _____

---

112. No. As x increases at a constant rate, x^2 increases faster and faster and $\sin x^2$ repeats its values faster and faster, and hence there is *no* value K for which
$$\sin(x + K)^2 = \sin x^2$$
for all x

---

113. Thus, in general, if f is periodic and g is not, then

_____ $\equiv$ _____ is periodic
$(f \circ g)(x)$ or $(g \circ f)(x))$

while

_____ $\equiv$ _____ is not periodic.

---

113. $(g \circ f)(x)$; $g(f(x))$;
$(f \circ g)(x)$; $f(g(x))$

EXAMPLE 10

114. $h(x) = 3 \tan x + 1$ is periodic with period _____ .

---

114. $\leqslant \pi$.

If you had difficulty, go on to the next frame. If not, skip to frame 118.

---

115. Find two functions f and g such that
$$(g \circ f)(x) = h(x) = 3 \tan x + 1.$$

$f =$ _____

$g =$ _____

---

115. $f = \tan x$;
$g = 3x + 1$, since $(g \circ f)(x)$
$= g(\tan x) = 3 \tan x + 1$.

116. Therefore $3 \tan x + 1$ is a composite function $g \circ f$, where g is non-constant and f has period ___ .

---

116. π

117. Therefore, by theorem 5, $h(x) = 3 \tan x + 1 = (g \circ f)(x)$ is periodic with period $\leqslant$ ___ .

---

117. π

EXAMPLE 11
118. $h(x) = 4 \sin^2 2x - 3$ is periodic with period $\leqslant$ ___ .

---

118. π.

If you had difficulty, go on to the next frame. If not, skip to frame 121.

119. Find two functions f and g such that
$$g \circ f = h(x) = 4 \sin^2 (2x) - 3.$$

$f =$ _____

$g =$ _____

---

119. $\sin 2x$;
$4x^2 - 3$,
since $(g \circ f)(x) = g(f(x))$
$= g(\sin 2x) = 4 \sin^2 2x - 3.$

120. Thus $4 \sin^2 2x - 3$ is a composite function $(g \circ f)(x)$, where g is non-constant and f has period ___ . Therefore, by theorem 5, $h(x) = 4 \sin^2 (2x) - 3 = (g \circ f)(x)$ is periodic with period $\leqslant$ ___ .

---

120. π;
π

121. $h(x) = \cos 4x + 2$ is periodic with period $\leqslant$ _____ .

---

121. $\dfrac{2\pi}{3}$.

If you had difficulty, see frames 118 to 120.

122. If $f(x)$ is periodic with period p, then

$f(ax)$ has period **(a)** _____ ,

$f(x + c)$ has period **(b)** _____ ,

and

$Kf(x)$ has period **(c)** _____ ,

$Kf(ax + c)$ has period **(d)** _____ .

---

122. **(a)** $\dfrac{p}{a}$,   **(c)** p,

     (b) p,   **(d)** $\dfrac{p}{a}$

---

	123. If $f(x)$ is periodic with period p, and $g(x)$ is a non-constant function, then $g \circ f$ has period _____ .
123. $\leqslant p$	**124.** Finally, if both $f(x)$ and $g(x)$ are periodic with period p, then $f + g$, $f - g$, $f \cdot g$, and $\dfrac{f}{g}$, $g \neq 0$, all have period _____ .
124. $\leqslant p$	

PROBLEMS

What can you say about the period of each of the following function?

1. $\sin 3x$

2. $\csc 4x$

3. $\cot 2x$

4. $\cos (x + 3\pi)$

5. $\sec (x + 9)$

6. $\tan (2x + \pi)$

7. $5 \sin 2x$

8. $7 \cot \left(2x + \dfrac{1}{2}\right)$

9. $\sin 4x + \cot 2x$

10. $\sin 4x \cdot \cot 2x$

11. $\sin^2 (3x) - 1$

12. $\sqrt{\cos x}$

Answers are at end of book.

QUIZ

If you cannot answer the following questions correctly, review the appropriate frames.

1. Complete the following definition.

   A function f is periodic if

2. What is the period of the function f whose graph is shown below?

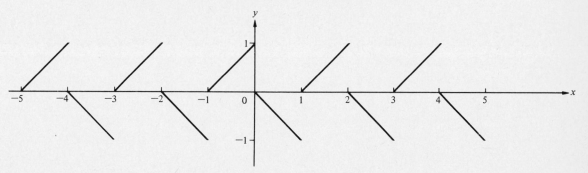

3. What is the period of the function $\sin 4x$?

4. What is the period of the function $\cos (x + \pi)$?

5. What is the period of the function $5 \sin x$?

6. If $f(x)$ and $g(x)$ are periodic both with period p, then for any number $a > 0$, give the period of each of the following:

(a) $f(ax)$

(b) $f(x + a)$

(c) $af(x)$

(d) $f + g$

(e) $f \cdot g$

(f) $\dfrac{f}{g}$, $g \neq 0$

Answers are at end of book.

7 Graphs of Trigonometric Functions

Upon completing this chapter, you should be able to

I. Graph the six trigonometric functions.

II. Identify each trigonometric function from its graph.

In this chapter we wish to graph the six trigonometric functions. If a function is defined by an equation such as $y = \sin x$, then, as we saw in the volume on functions, its graph consists of the set of all points (x, y) that satisfy the equation.

We know several things about the trigonometric functions that will help us greatly in graphing them. We know the domains and ranges, their values at several special and quadrantal angles, and the period of each.

We shall construct the graphs on rectangular coordinate axes with the same unit length on each axis. And, since we know the period of each function, it will be necessary only to plot points corresponding to the x-values in one period.

We shall begin with the graph of $\sin x$.

THE GRAPH OF SIN x

125. We shall graph $\sin x$ by plotting a number of points and connecting them by a smooth curve.

Since $\sin x$ has period _____ , we need only plot points for $x, 0 \leqslant x < $ _____ .

125. 2π;
2π

126. Fill in the following values for sin x.

x	0	$\frac{\pi}{6}$	$\frac{\pi}{4}$	$\frac{\pi}{3}$	$\frac{\pi}{2}$	$\frac{2\pi}{3}$	$\frac{3\pi}{4}$	$\frac{5\pi}{6}$	π	$\frac{7\pi}{6}$	$\frac{5\pi}{4}$	$\frac{4\pi}{3}$	$\frac{3\pi}{2}$	$\frac{5\pi}{3}$	$\frac{7\pi}{4}$	$\frac{11\pi}{6}$	2π
sin x																	

126.

x	0	$\frac{\pi}{6}$	$\frac{\pi}{4}$	$\frac{\pi}{3}$	$\frac{\pi}{2}$	$\frac{2\pi}{3}$	$\frac{3\pi}{4}$	$\frac{5\pi}{6}$	π	$\frac{7\pi}{6}$	$\frac{5\pi}{4}$	$\frac{4\pi}{3}$	$\frac{3\pi}{2}$	$\frac{5\pi}{3}$	$\frac{7\pi}{4}$	$\frac{11\pi}{6}$	2π
sin x	0	$\frac{1}{2}$	$\frac{1}{\sqrt{2}}$	$\frac{\sqrt{3}}{2}$	1	$\frac{\sqrt{3}}{2}$	$\frac{1}{\sqrt{2}}$	$\frac{1}{2}$	0	$-\frac{1}{2}$	$-\frac{1}{\sqrt{2}}$	$-\frac{\sqrt{3}}{2}$	-1	$-\frac{\sqrt{3}}{2}$	$-\frac{1}{\sqrt{2}}$	$-\frac{1}{2}$	0
decimal approx. for sin x	0	.5	.71	.87	1.0	.87	.71	.5	0	$-.5$	$-.71$	$-.87$	-1.0	-7.8	$-.71$	$-.5$	0

127. On the coordinate system, mark off some convenient numbers on the x-axis.

127.

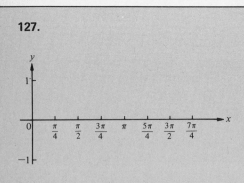

Since our values are given for $\frac{\pi}{6}, \frac{\pi}{4}, \frac{\pi}{3}$, etc. these are the numbers we need on our x-axis.

128. Plot several points on the coordinate system in frame 127 and connect them with a smooth line.

128.

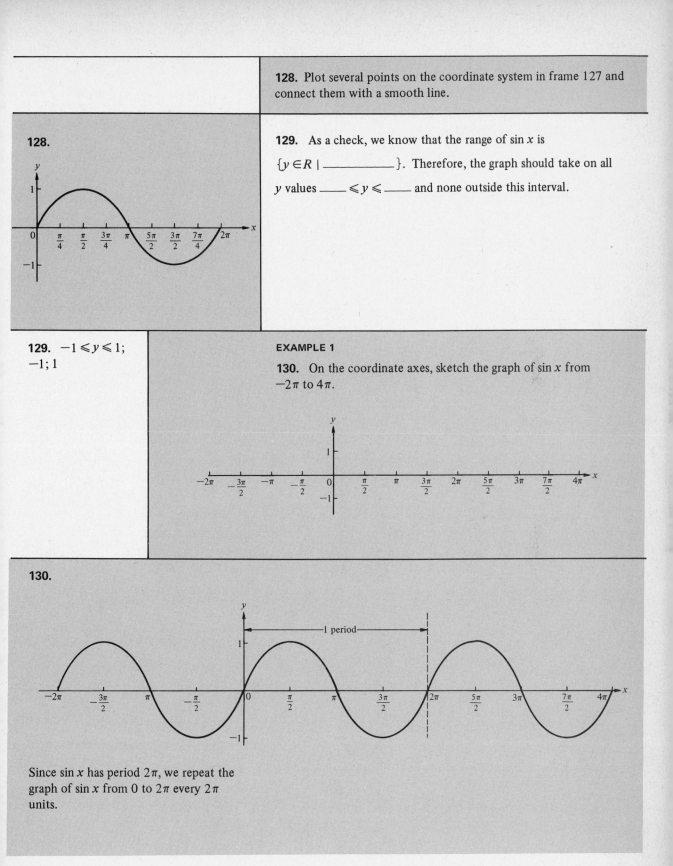

129. As a check, we know that the range of sin x is

$\{y \in R \mid$ _____ $\}$. Therefore, the graph should take on all

y values ___ $\leqslant y \leqslant$ ___ and none outside this interval.

129. $-1 \leqslant y \leqslant 1$;
$-1; 1$

EXAMPLE 1

130. On the coordinate axes, sketch the graph of sin x from -2π to 4π.

130.

Since sin x has period 2π, we repeat the graph of sin x from 0 to 2π every 2π units.

131. Now let us turn to the graph of cos *x*. Cos *x* also has period _____ . And we can graph cos *x*, as we did sin *x*, by plotting several points for *x* in _____ *x* _____ and connecting them with a smooth curve.

131. 2π;
$0 \leqslant \ \leqslant 2\pi$

132. Insert the appropriate values for cos *x*.

x	0	$\frac{\pi}{6}$	$\frac{\pi}{4}$	$\frac{\pi}{3}$	$\frac{\pi}{2}$	$\frac{3\pi}{4}$	π	$\frac{5\pi}{4}$	$\frac{3\pi}{2}$	$\frac{7\pi}{4}$	2π
cos *x*											

132.

x	0	$\frac{\pi}{6}$	$\frac{\pi}{4}$	$\frac{\pi}{3}$	$\frac{\pi}{2}$	$\frac{3\pi}{4}$	π	$\frac{5\pi}{4}$	$\frac{3\pi}{2}$	$\frac{7\pi}{4}$	2π
cos *x*	1	$\frac{\sqrt{3}}{2}$	$\frac{1}{\sqrt{2}}$	$\frac{1}{2}$	0	$-\frac{1}{\sqrt{2}}$	-1	$-\frac{1}{\sqrt{2}}$	0	$\frac{1}{\sqrt{2}}$	1
decimal approx. for cos *x*	1	.87	.71	.5	0	−.71	−1.0	−.71	0	.71	1

133. Graph cos *x* by plotting a few points and joining them with a smooth curve.

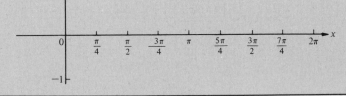

133.

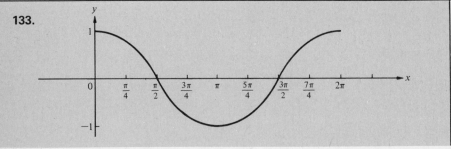

EXAMPLE 2

134. Graph $\cos x$ from -2π to 4π.

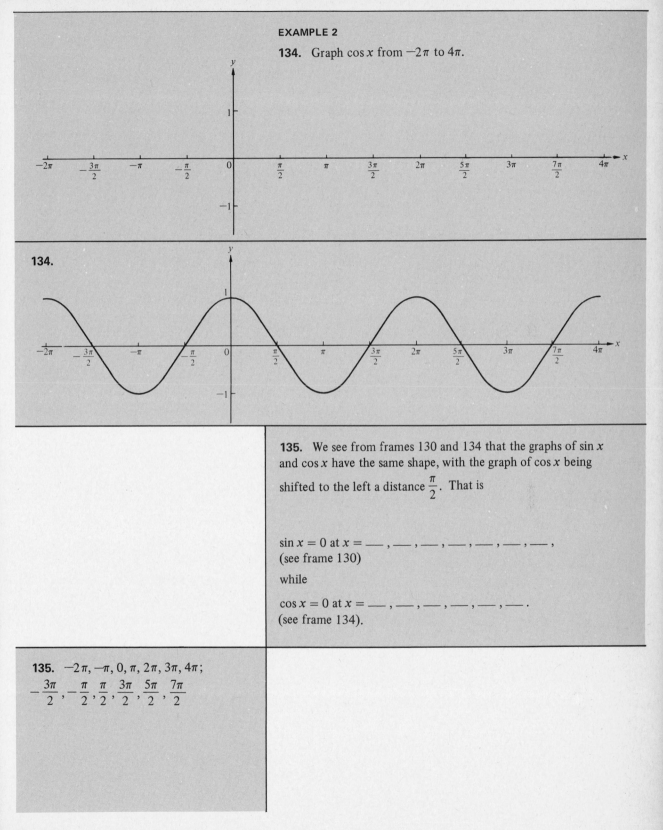

134.

135. We see from frames 130 and 134 that the graphs of $\sin x$ and $\cos x$ have the same shape, with the graph of $\cos x$ being shifted to the left a distance $\dfrac{\pi}{2}$. That is

$\sin x = 0$ at $x =$ ___ , ___ , ___ , ___ , ___ , ___ , ___ ,
(see frame 130)
while
$\cos x = 0$ at $x =$ ___ , ___ , ___ , ___ , ___ , ___ .
(see frame 134).

135. $-2\pi, -\pi, 0, \pi, 2\pi, 3\pi, 4\pi$;
$-\dfrac{3\pi}{2}, -\dfrac{\pi}{2}, \dfrac{\pi}{2}, \dfrac{3\pi}{2}, \dfrac{5\pi}{2}, \dfrac{7\pi}{2}$

136. Since we know the basic shape of the graphs of $\sin x$ and $\cos x$, we need check only a few points.

$\text{Sin } 0 = $ **(a)** ___ , $\sin \dfrac{\pi}{2} = $ **(b)** ___ , $\sin \pi = $ **(c)** ___ ,

$\sin \dfrac{3\pi}{2} = $ **(d)** ___ , and $\sin 2\pi = $ **(e)** ___ ,

while

$\cos 0 = $ **(f)** ___ , $\cos \dfrac{\pi}{2} = $ **(g)** ___ , $\cos \pi = $ **(h)** ___ ,

$\cos \dfrac{3\pi}{2} = $ **(i)** ___ , $\cos 2\pi = $ **(j)** ___ .

---

136. **(a)** 0, **(b)** 1, **(c)** 0, **(d)** −1, **(e)** 0, **(f)** 1, **(g)** 0, **(h)** −1, **(i)** 0, **(j)** 1

EXERCISE 1

137. Graph $\sin x$ and $\cos x$ on the axes shown.

137.

138. Now we turn to the graph of csc x. We could graph $f(x) = \csc x$ by plotting points from known values. However, we shall use the graph of sin x and the relationship

csc $x = 1/$_____ .

---

138. sin x

139. If sin $x = y$ at a point x, then at the same point x

csc $x =$ _____ .

Thus, since sin x is always in the interval $-1 \leqslant y \leqslant 1$, csc x is *never* in the interval _____ $< y <$ _____ .

---

139. $\dfrac{1}{y}$;

-1 ; 1

140. That is, the *range* of sin x is $\{y \in R \mid -1 \leqslant y \leqslant 1\}$ and the range of csc x is

$\{y \in R \mid$ _____ $\}$.

---

140. $y \leqslant -1$ or $y \geqslant 1$

141. If sin $x = 1$, then csc $x =$ _____ , and csc x is undefined whenever sin $x =$ _____ , but csc x is defined for all other values of x.

---

141. $1 ; 0$

142. Therefore, csc $x = 1$ when sin $x =$ **(a)** ___ , and we will have a vertical asymptote for csc x whenever sin $x = 0$. That is, the graph of csc x will grow large without bound in a positive or

negative direction whenever sin x approaches **(b)** ___ Graph csc x on the coordinate axes. We have sketched the graph of sin x as a guide.

(c)

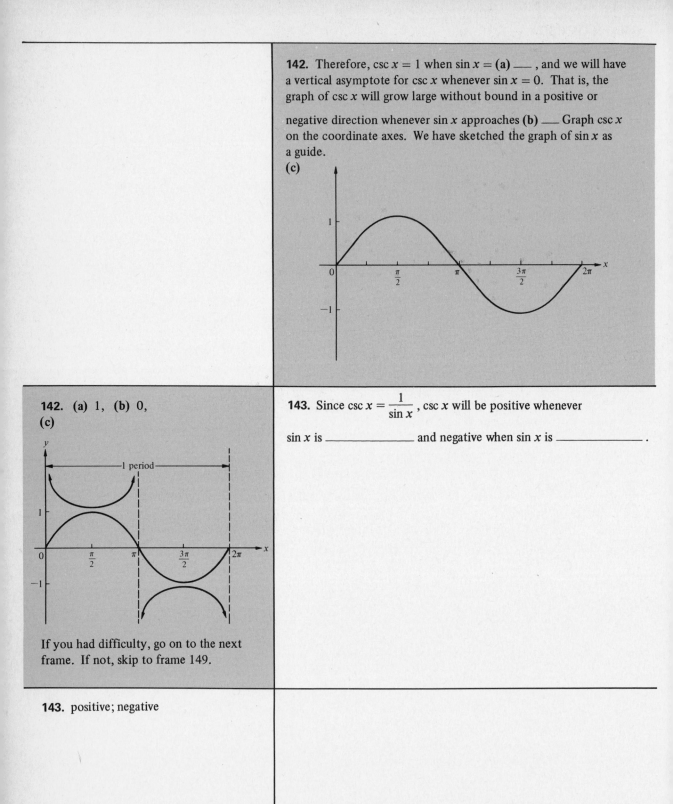

142. (a) 1, **(b)** 0,
(c)

If you had difficulty, go on to the next frame. If not, skip to frame 149.

143. Since csc $x = \dfrac{1}{\sin x}$, csc x will be positive whenever

sin x is _____ and negative when sin x is _____ .

143. positive; negative

144. Moreover at $\frac{\pi}{2}$, $\sin x = 1$; therefore, $\csc \frac{\pi}{2} = 1$. And as we take values of x closer and closer to π, $\sin x$ approaches _____ , and hence $\csc x$ grows large without bound in a _____ direction. That is, we have a vertical asymptote at $x = \pi$.

---

144. 0; positive

145. Similarly, as x moves from $\frac{\pi}{2}$ to 0, $\sin x$ approaches _____ , and again $\csc x$ _____ _____ and we have a vertical asymptote at $x = 0$.

---

145. 0; grows large without bound in a positive direction

146. At $\frac{3\pi}{2}$, $\sin x = $ _____ , and hence $\csc x = $ _____ at $\frac{3\pi}{2}$.

---

146. $-1; -1$

147. And as x moves toward either π or 2π from $\frac{3\pi}{2}$, $\sin x$ approaches _____ , and hence $\csc x$ _____ in a negative direction this time, since $\sin x$ and hence $\csc x$ are negative in the interval $\pi < x < 2\pi$.

---

147. 0; grows large without bound

148. Now use this information to sketch the graph of $\csc x$ on the coordinate axes. Again use the graph of $\sin x$ as a guide.

148.

149. In a similar way, we can use the fact that $\sec x = \dfrac{1}{\cos x}$ to graph $\sec x$.

Graph $\csc x$ on the coordinate axes. We have sketched the graph of $\cos x$ as a guide.

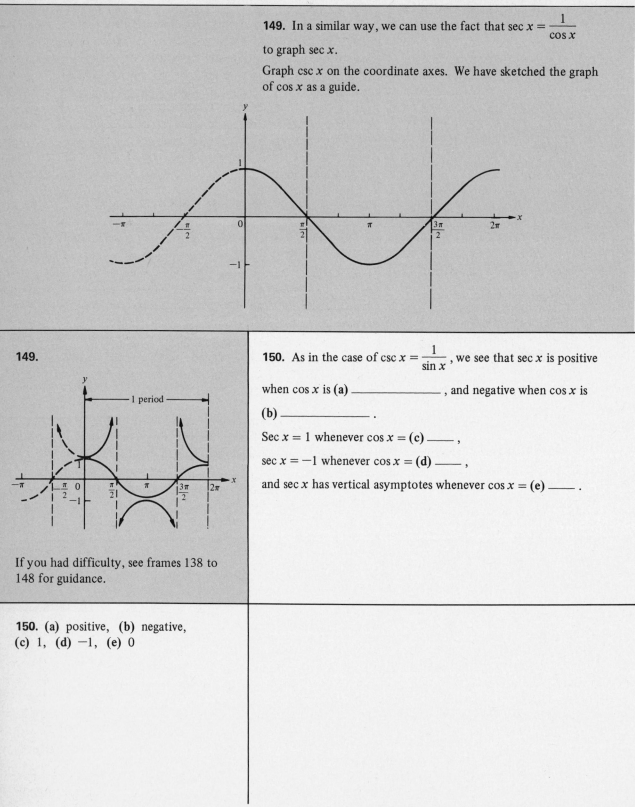

149.

If you had difficulty, see frames 138 to 148 for guidance.

150. As in the case of $\csc x = \dfrac{1}{\sin x}$, we see that $\sec x$ is positive when $\cos x$ is **(a)** _____ , and negative when $\cos x$ is **(b)** _____ .

Sec $x = 1$ whenever $\cos x =$ **(c)** _____ ,

sec $x = -1$ whenever $\cos x =$ **(d)** _____ ,

and $\sec x$ has vertical asymptotes whenever $\cos x =$ **(e)** _____ .

150. (a) positive, **(b)** negative, **(c)** 1, **(d)** −1, **(e)** 0

151. Next we turn to the graphs of first $\tan x$ and then $\cot x$. To graph $\tan x$ we must again plot several points and join them with a smooth curve.

Use the values in the table to graph $\tan x$. Since $\tan x$ has period ____ , we need plot only those points for which ____ $\leqslant x \leqslant$ ____ .

x	0	$\dfrac{\pi}{6}$	$\dfrac{\pi}{4}$	$\dfrac{\pi}{3}$	$\dfrac{\pi}{2}$	$\dfrac{2\pi}{3}$	$\dfrac{3\pi}{4}$	$\dfrac{5\pi}{6}$	π
$\tan x$	0	$\dfrac{1}{\sqrt{3}}$	1	$\sqrt{3}$	undefined	$-\sqrt{3}$	-1	$-\dfrac{1}{\sqrt{3}}$	0
decimal approx.	0	.58	1.0	1.73	undefined	-1.73	-1.0	$-.58$	0

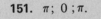

151. π; 0; π.

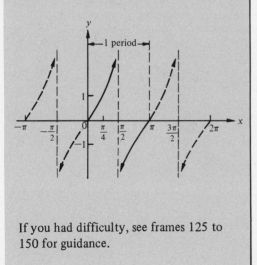

If you had difficulty, see frames 125 to 150 for guidance.

152. We see that $\tan x = 0$ (in the interval from 0 to 2π) at

$x =$ **(a)** _____ , _____ , _____ , and $\tan x$ has vertical asymptotes at

$x =$ **(b)** _____ , _____ , and $\tan x$ **(c)** _____ as x increases
(increases, decreases)

from left to right.

---

152. (a) $0, \pi, 2\pi,$

(b) $\dfrac{\pi}{2}, \dfrac{3\pi}{2},$

(c) increases

GRAPH OF COT x

153. Finally, we can use the fact that $\cot x = \dfrac{1}{\tan x}$ to graph $\cot x$.

Graph $\cot x$ on the coordinate axes. We have sketched the graph of $\tan x$ as a guide.

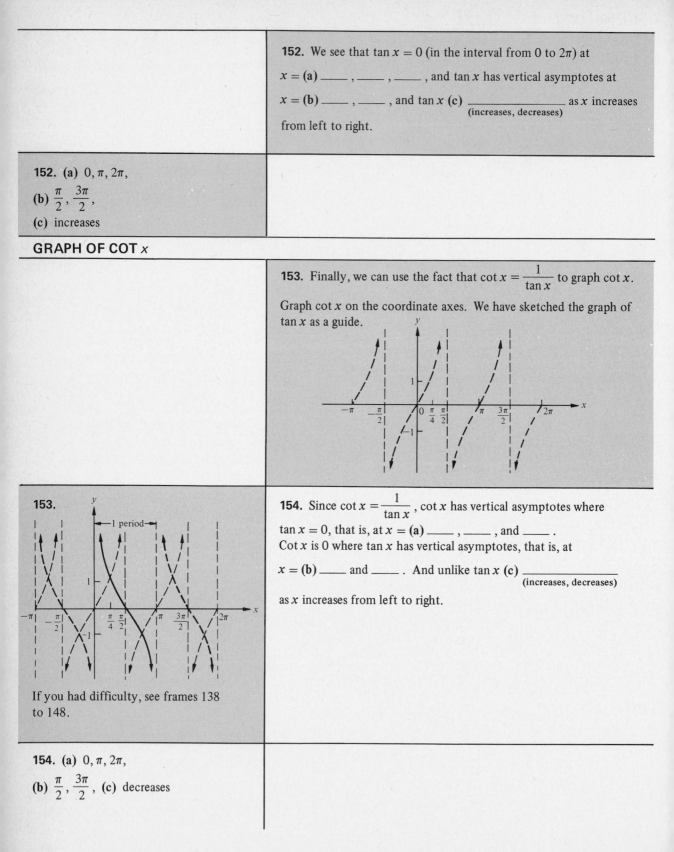

153.

If you had difficulty, see frames 138 to 148.

154. Since $\cot x = \dfrac{1}{\tan x}$, $\cot x$ has vertical asymptotes where

$\tan x = 0$, that is, at $x =$ **(a)** _____ , _____ , and _____ .
Cot x is 0 where $\tan x$ has vertical asymptotes, that is, at

$x =$ **(b)** _____ and _____ . And unlike $\tan x$ **(c)** _____
(increases, decreases)

as x increases from left to right.

---

154. (a) $0, \pi, 2\pi,$

(b) $\dfrac{\pi}{2}, \dfrac{3\pi}{2},$ **(c)** decreases

EXAMPLE 3

155. Here are sketches of the six trigonometric functions. Label each one correctly.

(a)

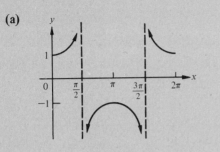

(d)

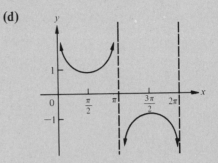

(b)

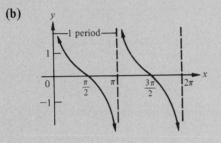

(e)

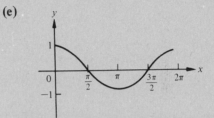

(c)

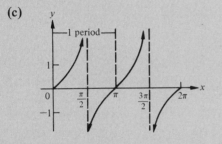

(f)

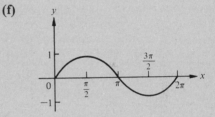

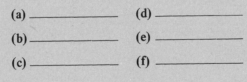

(a) _____ (d) _____

(b) _____ (e) _____

(c) _____ (f) _____

---

155. (a) $\sec x$, (d) $\cos x$,
(b) $\csc x$, (e) $\tan x$,
(c) $\cot x$, (f) $\sin x$

156. As a check, you could use the fact that both $\tan x$ and $\cot x$ have period _____ , while $\sin x$, $\cos x$, $\csc x$ and $\sec x$ all have period _____ .

156. π; 2π

157. You could also have checked that the graphs fell in the correct ranges. Give the ranges of the six circular functions.

Function	Range
$\sin x$	$\{y \in R \mid \qquad\qquad\qquad\qquad\qquad \}$
$\cos x$	
$\tan x$	
$\csc x$	
$\sec x$	
$\cot x$	

157.

Function	Range
$\sin x$	$\{y \in R \mid -1 \leqslant y \leqslant 1\}$
$\cos x$	$\{y \in R \mid -1 \leqslant y \leqslant 1\}$
$\tan x$	R, the set of all real numbers
$\csc x$	$\{y \in R \mid y \leqslant -1 \text{ or } y \geqslant 1\}$
$\sec x$	$\{y \in R \mid y \leqslant -1 \text{ or } y \geqslant 1\}$
$\cot x$	R, the set of all real numbers

158. You could distinguish between $\sec x$ and $\csc x$ by comparing them with $\cos x$ and $\sin x$.

Sec $x = 1$ where **(a)** _____ $= 1$, and has vertical asymptotes where **(b)** _____ $= 0$.

Csc $x = 1$ where **(c)** _____ and has vertical asymptotes where **(d)** _____ .

158. **(a)** $\cos x$, **(b)** $\cos x$, **(c)** $\sin x = 1$, **(d)** $\sin x = 0$

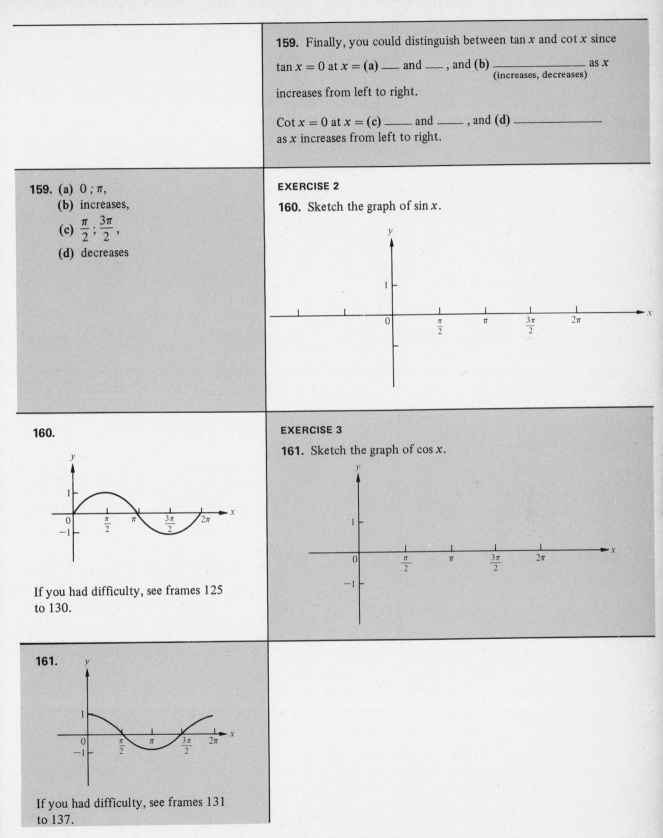

159. Finally, you could distinguish between $\tan x$ and $\cot x$ since

$\tan x = 0$ at $x =$ **(a)** ____ and ____, and **(b)** _____ as x increases from left to right. $\underset{\text{(increases, decreases)}}{}$

$\cot x = 0$ at $x =$ **(c)** ____ and ____, and **(d)** _____ as x increases from left to right.

---

159. (a) $0\,;\pi,$
    (b) increases,
    (c) $\dfrac{\pi}{2}\,;\dfrac{3\pi}{2},$
    (d) decreases

EXERCISE 2

160. Sketch the graph of $\sin x$.

160.

If you had difficulty, see frames 125 to 130.

EXERCISE 3

161. Sketch the graph of $\cos x$.

161.

If you had difficulty, see frames 131 to 137.

162. Sketch the graph of csc x.

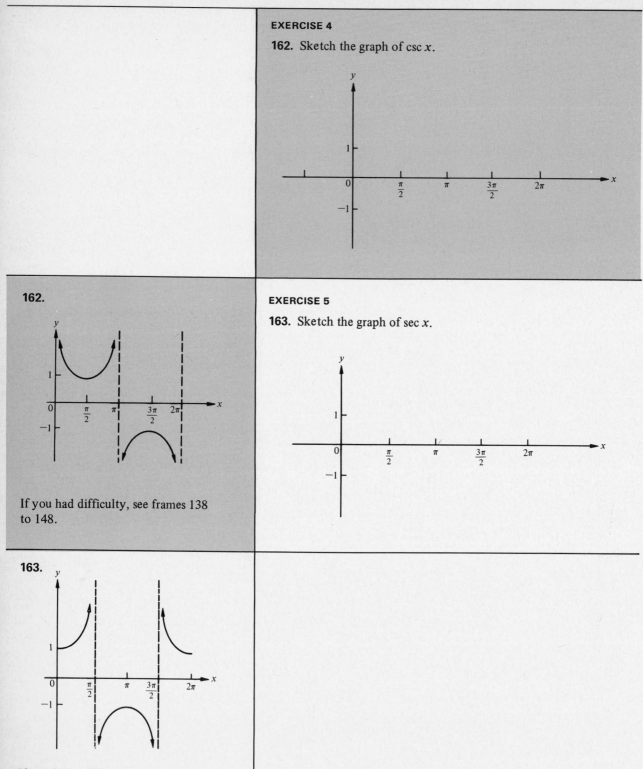

162.

If you had difficulty, see frames 138 to 148.

163. Sketch the graph of sec x.

163.

If you had difficulty, see frames 149 to 150.

164. Sketch the graph of tan x.

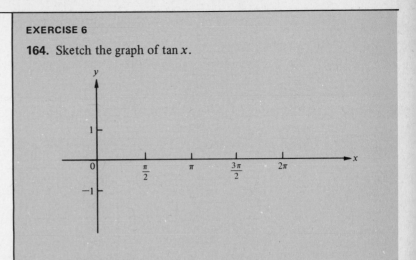

164.

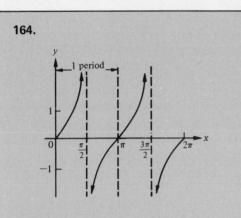

If you had difficulty, see frames 151 and 152.

165. Sketch the graph of cot x.

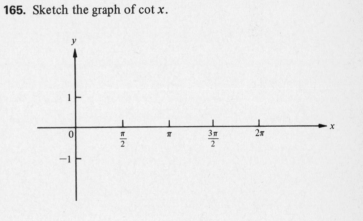

165.

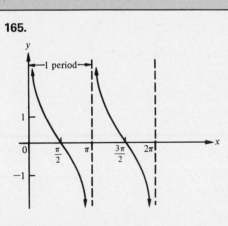

If you had difficulty, see frames 153 and 154.

QUIZ

If you cannot answer the following questions correctly, review the appropriate frames.

1. Complete the following table.

Function	Period
sin x	2π
cos x	
tan x	
cot x	
csc x	
sec x	

2. Sketch the graph of sin x. Indicate one period.

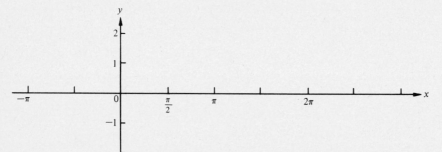

3. Sketch the graph of csc x on the axes in question 2. Indicate one period.

4. Sketch the graph of cos x on the coordinate axes below. Indicate one period.

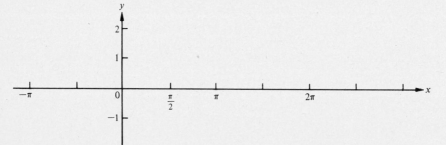

5. Sketch the graph of sec x on the axes in question 4. Indicate one period.

6. Sketch the graph of tan x on the axes below. Indicate one period.

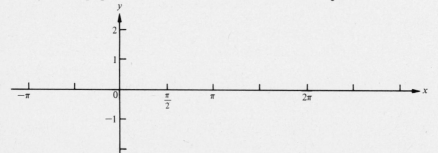

7. Sketch the graph of cot x on the axes below. Indicate one period.

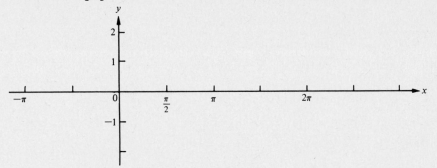

Answers are at end of book.

8 Generalized Circular Functions

We have already studied the period of a function. Now we wish to look at two more properties of circular functions, *amplitude* and *phase shift*, and their effects on the graphs of the circular functions.

Functions of the form $y = a \sin(bx + c)$ and $y = a \cos(bx + c)$ are related to the circular functions $y = \sin x$ and $y = \cos x$. We shall use this relationship and our knowledge of the graphs $y = \sin x$ and $y = \cos x$ to sketch the graphs of $y = a \sin(bx + c)$ and $y = a \cos(bx + c)$. We could make careful graphs by plotting special points, but the sketches will show us the essential features of the graphs.

The generalized sine function is defined by $y = a \sin(bx + c)$. We shall study the effect of each of the constants $a, b,$ and c on the graph.

Upon completing this chapter, you should be able to

I. Define phase shift and amplitude.

II. Given a function of the form

$y = a \sin(bx + c), y = a \cos(bx + c),$ or
$y = a \tan(bx + c), a \neq 0, b \neq 0$

(A) find the (1) amplitude,
             (2) period,
             (3) phase shift;

(B) sketch the graph of the function.

166. Sin x has period **(a)** _____ . And we proved in the section on the period of a function that if $f(x)$ has period p then $f(ax)$ has period **(b)** _____ . Thus sin $2x$ will have period **(c)** _____ .

---

166. (a) 2π,
(b) $\dfrac{p}{a}$
(c) $\dfrac{2\pi}{2} = \pi$.

If you had difficulty, see frames 22 to 52.

167. We want to see how the 2 affects the graph of $y = \sin x$. Since sin x has period 2π, one complete oscillation is _____ units long. Sin $x = 0$ at $x =$ _____ , _____ , and _____ . See the graph.

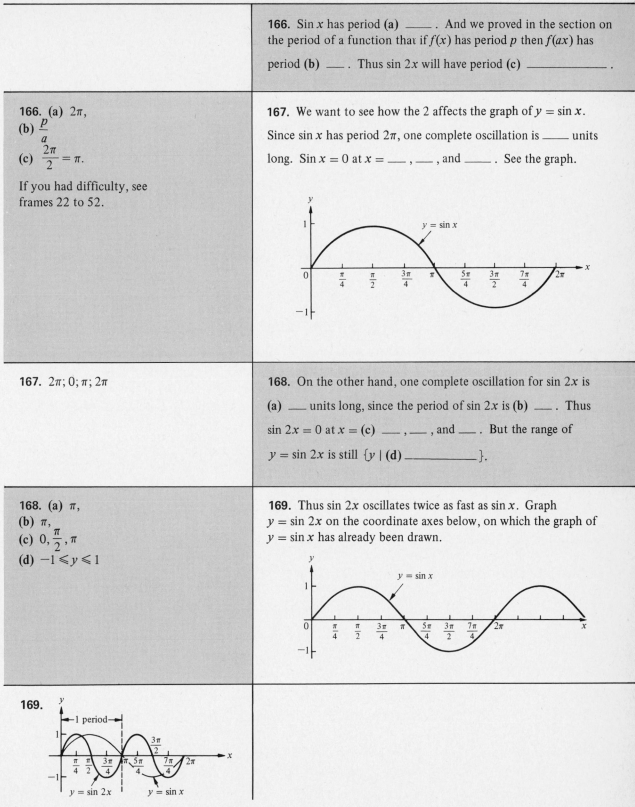

$y = \sin x$

---

167. $2\pi; 0; \pi; 2\pi$

168. On the other hand, one complete oscillation for sin $2x$ is **(a)** _____ units long, since the period of sin $2x$ is **(b)** _____ . Thus sin $2x = 0$ at $x =$ **(c)** _____ , _____ , and _____ . But the range of $y = \sin 2x$ is still $\{y \mid$ **(d)** _____ $\}$.

---

168. (a) π,
(b) π,
(c) $0, \dfrac{\pi}{2}, \pi$
(d) $-1 \leqslant y \leqslant 1$

169. Thus sin $2x$ oscillates twice as fast as sin x. Graph $y = \sin 2x$ on the coordinate axes below, on which the graph of $y = \sin x$ has already been drawn.

$y = \sin x$

169.

$y = \sin 2x$ $y = \sin x$

170. The three zero y-values that occur at the beginning, middle, and end of the period of the graph of $y = \sin x$ are $(0, 0)$, $(\pi, 0)$, and $(2\pi, 0)$. These three zero y-values for $y = \sin 2x$ occur at

(a) $(\underline{\quad}, 0), (\underline{\quad}, 0),$ and $(\underline{\quad}, 0)$.

The maximum y-value, 1, of the graph of $y = \sin x$ occurs at

(b) $\left(\dfrac{}{2}, 1\right)$ while the maximum y-value, 1, of the graph of

$y = \sin 2x$ occurs at **(c)** $(\underline{\quad}, 1)$.

The minimum y-value, -1, of the graph of $y = \sin x$ occurs at

$\left(\dfrac{3\pi}{2}, -1\right)$ while the minimum y-value, -1, of the graph of $y = \sin 2x$

occurs at **(d)** $(\underline{\quad}, -1)$.

And, in general, a y-value k that occurs at (x, k) on the graph of

$y = \sin x$ will occur on the graph of $y = \sin 2x$ at **(e)** $(\underline{\quad}, \underline{\quad})$.

---

170. (a) $0, \dfrac{\pi}{2}, \pi$, (b) π,

(c) $\dfrac{\pi}{4}$, (d) $\dfrac{3\pi}{4}$, (e) $(\dfrac{x}{2}, k)$

---

171. Now look at $\sin 4x$. The period of $\sin 4x$ is **(a)** $\underline{\quad}$, $\sin 4x = 0$ at

$x =$ **(b)** $\underline{\quad}, \underline{\quad}$, and $\underline{\quad}$, which are the beginning, middle, and end of the period.

---

171. (a) $\dfrac{\pi}{2}$, since $\sin x$

has period 2π,

(b) $0, \dfrac{\pi}{4}, \dfrac{\pi}{2}$

---

172. Sin $4x$ oscillates **(a)** $\underline{\quad\quad}$ times as fast as $\sin x$. The

maximum y-value, 1, of $\sin 4x$ occurs at **(b)** $(\underline{\quad}, 1)$; the minimum

y-value, -1, occurs at **(c)** $(\underline{\quad}, -1)$; and in general a y-value, k,

that occurs a (x, k) on the graph of $y = \sin x$ will occur on the graph

of $y = \sin 4x$ at **(d)** $(\underline{\quad}, \underline{\quad})$. That is, the graph is compressed

horizontally toward the y-axis by a factor of $\frac{1}{4}$.

---

172. (a) four, (b) $\dfrac{\pi}{8}$,

(c) $\dfrac{3\pi}{8}$, (d) $(\dfrac{x}{4}, k)$

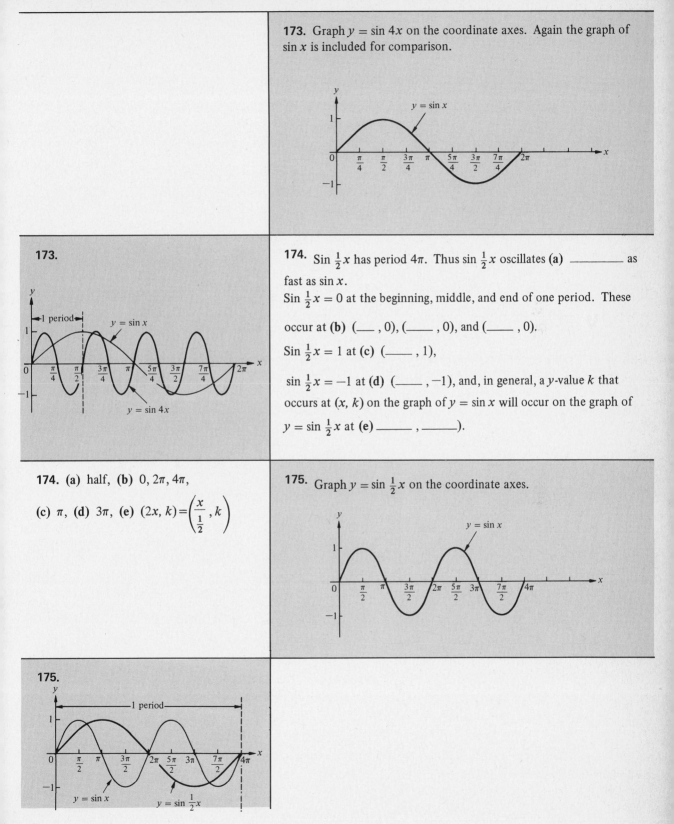

173. Graph $y = \sin 4x$ on the coordinate axes. Again the graph of $\sin x$ is included for comparison.

173.

174. Sin $\frac{1}{2}x$ has period 4π. Thus $\sin \frac{1}{2}x$ oscillates **(a)** _____ as fast as $\sin x$.

Sin $\frac{1}{2}x = 0$ at the beginning, middle, and end of one period. These occur at **(b)** (__ , 0), (___ , 0), and (___ , 0).

Sin $\frac{1}{2}x = 1$ at **(c)** (___ , 1),

$\sin \frac{1}{2}x = -1$ at **(d)** (___ , −1), and, in general, a y-value k that occurs at (x, k) on the graph of $y = \sin x$ will occur on the graph of $y = \sin \frac{1}{2}x$ at **(e)** _____ , _____).

174. **(a)** half, **(b)** $0, 2\pi, 4\pi$,

(c) π, **(d)** 3π, **(e)** $(2x, k) = \left(\dfrac{x}{\frac{1}{2}} , k \right)$

175. Graph $y = \sin \frac{1}{2}x$ on the coordinate axes.

175.

176. In general a function $y = \sin ax$ has period _____ , and $\sin ax$ oscillates _____ as fast as $\sin x$.

---

176. $\dfrac{2\pi}{a}$; a times

177. Sin $ax = 0$ at the beginning, middle, and end of one period. These occur at **(a)** (___ , 0), (___ , 0), and (_____ , 0).

Sin $ax = 1$ at **(b)** (_____ , 0),

$\sin ax = -1$ at **(c)** (_____ , −1), and, in general, a y-value k that occurs at (x, k) on the graph of $y = \sin x$ will occur on the graph of $y = \sin ax$ at **(d)** (___ , ___).

That is, the graph is compressed or expanded along the x-axis by a factor of **(e)** ___ .

177.
(a) $0, \dfrac{\pi}{a}, \dfrac{2\pi}{a},$

(b) $\dfrac{\pi}{2a}$, **(c)** $\dfrac{3\pi}{2a},$

(d) $\dfrac{x}{a}, k,$ **(e)** $\dfrac{1}{a}$

EXAMPLE 1

178. The same theory applies to any of the circular functions. We can sketch the graph of $\cos ax$, $y = \tan ax$, etc. from the graph of $y = \cos x, y = \tan x$, etc.

Graph $y = \cos 2x$ on the coordinate axes. The graph of $y = \cos x$ is included.

178.

If you had difficulty, go on to the next frame. If not, skip to frame 183.

179. π;
twice

180. Cos $2x =$ ____ at the beginning and end of one period. These occur at (____ , ____) and (____ , ____).

180. 1;
0, 1; π, 1

181. Cos $x = 0$ at $\dfrac{\pi}{2}$ and $\dfrac{3\pi}{2}$, while cos $2x = 0$ at **(a)** (____ , 0) and (____ , 0), cos $x = -1$ at π, while cos $2x = -1$ at (____ , -1); and, in general, a y-value k that occurs at (x, k) on the graph of $y = \cos x$ will occur on the graph of $y = \cos 2x$ at **(c)** (____ , ____).

181. **(a)** $\dfrac{\pi}{4}$, $\dfrac{3\pi}{4}$,

(b) $\dfrac{\pi}{2}$, **(c)** $\dfrac{x}{2}$, k

182. Now graph $y = \cos 2x$ on the coordinate axes.

182.

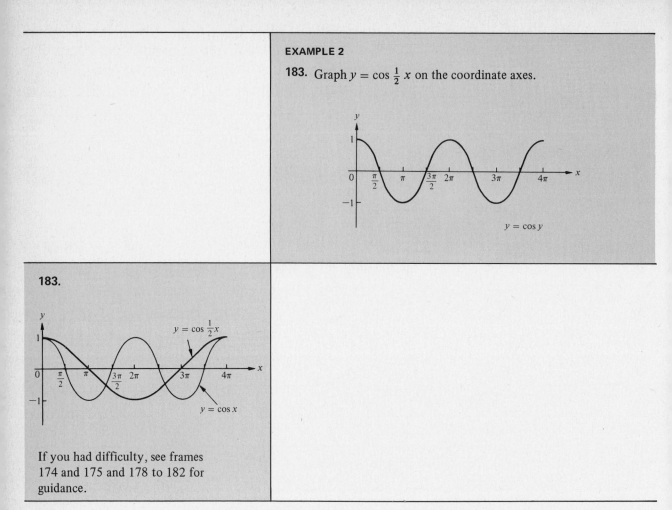

EXAMPLE 2

183. Graph $y = \cos \frac{1}{2} x$ on the coordinate axes.

$y = \cos y$

183.

If you had difficulty, see frames 174 and 175 and 178 to 182 for guidance.

PHASE SHIFT

184. In this section we want to look at the graphs of $y = \sin(x + c)$, $y = \cos(x - c)$, etc. We saw in the section on the period of a function that if $f(x)$ has period p, then $f(x + c)$ has period ____ .

Thus $\sin(x + c$, will have period ____ for any number c.

184. p;
2π.

If you had difficulty, see frames 62 to 65.

185. How then does replacing x by $x + c$ affect the graph of $y = \sin x$? Let us look at $\sin(x + \frac{\pi}{2})$. As we observed above,

its period is ____ , and
$$\sin x = 0 \text{ at } x = 0, \quad \pi, \text{ and } 2\pi$$
while
$$\sin\left(x + \frac{\pi}{2}\right) = 0 \text{ at } x = \text{\_\_\_} , \text{\_\_\_} , \text{ and \_\_\_} .$$

185. 2π;
$$-\frac{\pi}{2} ; \frac{\pi}{2} ; \frac{3\pi}{2}$$

186. The range of $y = \sin(x + \frac{\pi}{2})$ is still $\{y \in R \mid \textbf{(a)}\text{_____}\}$.
$$\text{Sin } x = 1 \text{ at } x = \frac{\pi}{2}$$
$$\text{and } \sin x = -1 \text{ at } x = \frac{3\pi}{2}$$
while
$$\sin\left(x + \frac{\pi}{2}\right) = 1 \text{ at } x = \textbf{(b)}\text{\_\_\_}$$
$$\text{and } \sin\left(x + \frac{\pi}{2}\right) = -1 \text{ at } x = \textbf{(c)}\text{\_\_\_} .$$

186. (a) $-1 \leqslant y \leqslant 1$,
(b) 0, **(c)** π

187. Thus the effect of replacing x by $x + \frac{\pi}{2}$ is to slide (translate) the graph ____ units to the ____.
(left, right)

187. $\frac{\pi}{2}$; left

188. Graph $y = \sin \left(x + \dfrac{\pi}{2}\right)$ on the coordinate axes. Once more, we have included the graph of $\sin x$ for comparison.

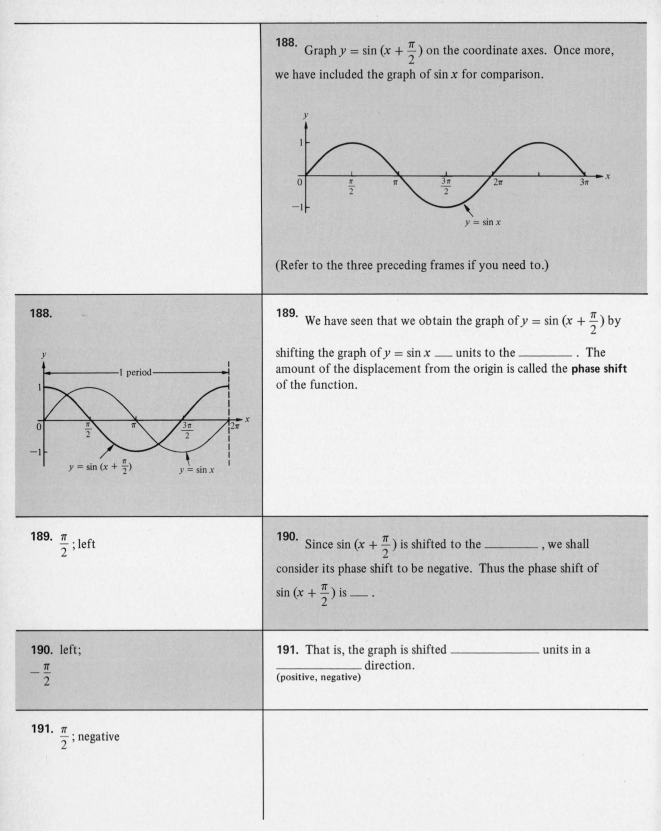

(Refer to the three preceding frames if you need to.)

188.

189. We have seen that we obtain the graph of $y = \sin \left(x + \dfrac{\pi}{2}\right)$ by shifting the graph of $y = \sin x$ ____ units to the _____ . The amount of the displacement from the origin is called the **phase shift** of the function.

---

189. $\dfrac{\pi}{2}$; left

190. Since $\sin \left(x + \dfrac{\pi}{2}\right)$ is shifted to the _____ , we shall consider its phase shift to be negative. Thus the phase shift of $\sin \left(x + \dfrac{\pi}{2}\right)$ is ___ .

---

190. left;

$-\dfrac{\pi}{2}$

191. That is, the graph is shifted _____ units in a _____ direction.
(positive, negative)

---

191. $\dfrac{\pi}{2}$; negative

192. Thus $-\dfrac{\pi}{2}$ is the _____ _____ of $\sin\left(x + \dfrac{\pi}{2}\right)$.

---

192. phase shift

193. Sin $(x - \pi)$ still has period 2π. But $\sin(x - \pi) = 0$ at the positive values $x =$ ___ , ___ , and ___ .

---

193. π; 2π; 3π

194. The range of $\sin(x - \pi)$ i still $\{y \in R \mid -1 \leqslant y \leqslant 1\}$ but $\sin(x - \pi) = 1$ at $x =$ ___ and $\sin(x - \pi) = -1$ at ___ .

---

194. $\dfrac{3\pi}{2}$; $\dfrac{5\pi}{2}$

195. Thus the effect of replacing x by $x - \pi$ is to shift the graph ___ units to the _____ .

---

195. π; right

196. Thus the phase shift of $\sin(x - \pi)$ is ___ .

---

196. $+\pi$

197. Graph $\sin(x - \pi)$ on the coordinate axes. (Refer to the four previous frames if you need to.)

197.

NOTE: Since $\sin(x - \pi) = \sin(x + \pi)$, a phase shift of π to the right produces the same graph as a phase shift of π to the left.

149

198. We obtain the graph of $y = \sin(x - \pi)$ by shifting the graph of $y = \sin x$ **(a)** ___ units to the **(b)** _____ . And we observed above that the phase shift of $\sin(x - \pi)$ is **(c)** ___ .

198. (a) π,
(b) right,
(c) $+\pi$

199. Thus if we replace x by x *plus* $\dfrac{\pi}{2}$, the shift is to the

_____ , and the phase shift is ___ ___ .
(left, right)   (+, −)

199. left; $-\dfrac{\pi}{2}$

200. And if we replace x by x *minus* $\dfrac{\pi}{2}$, the shift is to the

_____ , and the phase shift is ___ .

200. right; $+\dfrac{\pi}{2}$

EXAMPLE 3

201. Give the phase shift of $y = \sin\left(x - \dfrac{\pi}{4}\right)$ and graph the function on the coordinate axes.

Phase shift is ___ .

$y = \sin x$

201. $+\dfrac{\pi}{4}$

EXAMPLE 4

202. Phase shift is defined in the same way for all six circular functions, and the graphs of $y = \cos(x + c)$, $y = \tan(x + c)$, etc. are found by shifting the graphs of $y = \cos x$, $y = \tan x$, etc.

Graph $y = \tan(x + \frac{\pi}{2})$ on the coordinate axes. The graph of $y = \tan x$ is included. Recall that the period of $\tan x$ is ___.

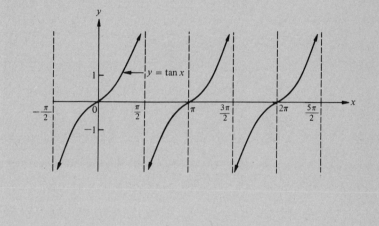

202. π

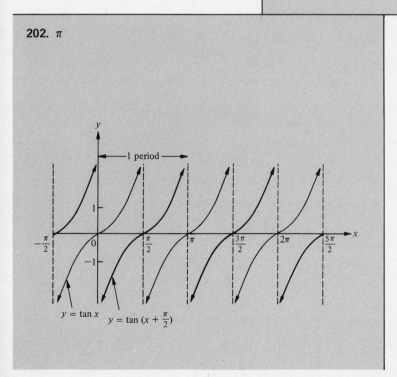

203. Now let us consider functions of the form $y = \sin(bx + c)$. That is, let us discover how multiplying by b and replacing x by $x + c$ affects the graph of $\sin x$.

First consider $\sin 2\left(x + \dfrac{\pi}{2}\right)$. We saw in frames 167 to 170 that $\sin 2x$ has period ___ and that the graph of $\sin 2x$ is compressed toward the y-axis by a factor of ___ .

---

203. $\pi; \dfrac{1}{2}$

204. Moreover replacing x by $x + \dfrac{\pi}{2}$ in any function $f(x)$ causes the graph of $f(x)$ to shift ___ units to the _____ .

---

204. $\dfrac{\pi}{2}$; left

205. In particular, replacing x by $x + \dfrac{\pi}{2}$ in $\sin 2x$ causes the graph of $\sin 2x$ to shift ___ units to the _____ .

---

205. $\dfrac{\pi}{2}$; left

206. Graph $y = \sin 2\left(x + \dfrac{\pi}{2}\right)$ on the coordinate axes. The graph of $y = \sin x$ is included.

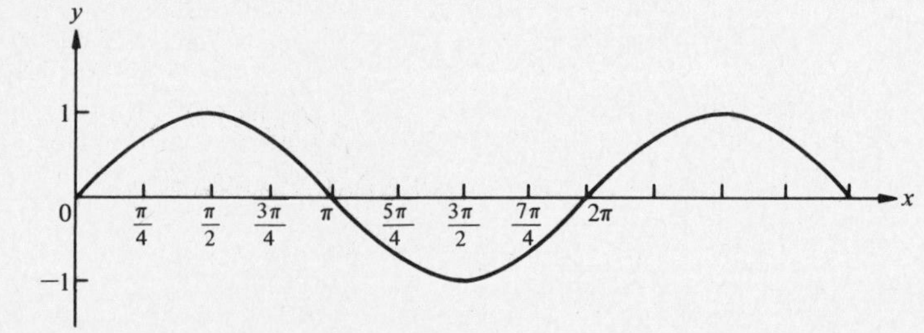

---

206. If you had difficulty, go on to the next frame. If not skip to frame 209.

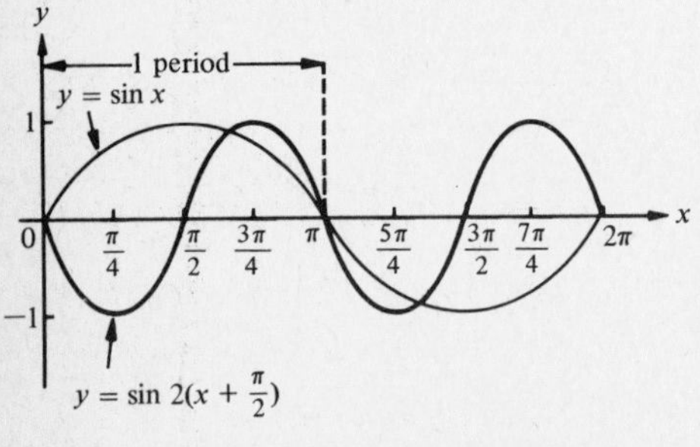

207. Probably the easiest way to graph $y = \sin 2(x + \frac{\pi}{2})$ is to first visualize (or actually sketch) the graph of $y = \sin 2x$ and then shift it $\frac{\pi}{2}$ units to the left. That is, treat the 2 and $\frac{\pi}{2}$ separately.

Graph $y = \sin 2x$ on the coordinate axes.

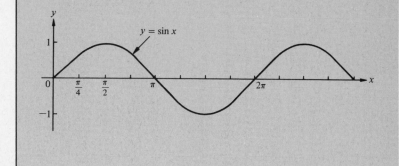

207.

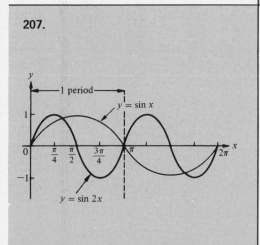

If you had difficulty, see frames 185 to 189.

208. Now graph $y = \sin 2(x + \frac{\pi}{2})$ on the coordinate axes by shifting the graph of **(a)** _____ **(b)** ___ units to the **(c)** _____ .

The graphs of $y = \sin x$ and $y = \sin 2x$ are included.

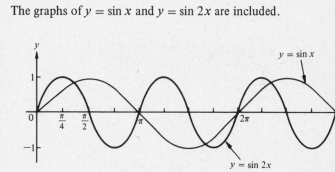

208. (a) $y = \sin 2x$,

(b) $\frac{\pi}{2}$,

(c) left.

If you had difficulty, see frames 185 to 189.

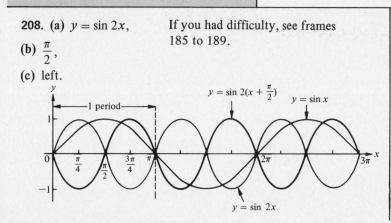

209. To convince yourself that the graph of $y = \sin 2\left(x + \frac{\pi}{2}\right)$, given in the answer to frame 208, is correct, calculate the values of $\sin 2\left(x + \frac{\pi}{2}\right)$ at $x = 0, \frac{\pi}{4}, \frac{\pi}{2}, \frac{3\pi}{4}$, and π and plot them on the coordinate axes there.

x	0	$\frac{\pi}{4}$	$\frac{\pi}{2}$	$\frac{3\pi}{4}$	π
$x + \frac{\pi}{2}$					
$2\left(x + \frac{\pi}{2}\right)$					
$\sin 2\left(x + \frac{\pi}{2}\right)$					

209.

x	0	$\frac{\pi}{4}$	$\frac{\pi}{2}$	$\frac{3\pi}{4}$	π
$x + \frac{\pi}{2}$	$\frac{\pi}{2}$	$\frac{3\pi}{4}$	π	$\frac{5\pi}{4}$	$\frac{3\pi}{2}$
$2\left(x + \frac{\pi}{2}\right)$	π	$\frac{3\pi}{2}$	2π	$\frac{5\pi}{2}$	3π
$\sin 2\left(x + \frac{\pi}{2}\right)$	0	-1	0	1	0

210. Multiply through by 2 and put $\sin 2\left(x + \frac{\pi}{2}\right)$ in the form $\sin(bx + c)$. We get _____ .

---

210. $\sin(2x + \pi)$

211. Since $y = \sin(2x + \pi)$ is of the form $y = \sin(bx + c)$ the constant c is ___ , but, as we have seen from the graph of $y = \sin 2\left(x + \frac{\pi}{2}\right) = \sin(2x + \pi)$, the phase shift is _____ .

---

211. $\pi; -\frac{\pi}{2}$

212. In the discussion of phase shift, we shifted the graphs by replacing ___ by $x + c$, not by replacing $2x$ by $2x + c$.

---

212. x

213. Thus to find the phase shift of $\sin(bx + c)$, we must put it in the form $\sin b\left(x + \frac{c}{b}\right)$ and the phase shift will be ___ .

---

213. $-\frac{c}{b}$

214. To find the phase shift of $\sin(3x + 6)$ we write $\sin(3x + 6)$ as $\sin 3(x + 2)$. Hence the phase shift is _____ .

214. -2

EXAMPLE 5

215. Find the phase shift of $y = \sin(2x + \frac{\pi}{2})$ and graph the function on the coordinate axes.

Phase shift is **(a)** _____ , and the period is **(b)** _____ .
(c)

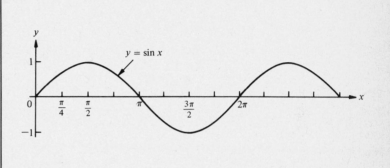

215. **(a)** $-\frac{\pi}{4}$, since

$$\sin(2x + \frac{\pi}{2}) = \sin 2(x + \frac{\pi}{4}),$$

(b) π, **(c)**

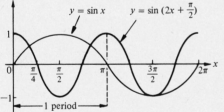

If you had difficulty, see frames 203 to 214.

EXAMPLE 6

216. Find the phase shift of $y = \sin(4x - \pi)$ and graph the function on the coordinate axes.

The phase shift is **(a)** _____ , and the period is **(b)** ___ .
(c)

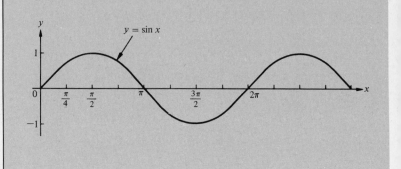

---

216. (a) $+\dfrac{\pi}{4}$, since

$$\sin(4x - \pi) = \sin 4\left(x - \frac{\pi}{4}\right),$$

(b) $\dfrac{\pi}{2}$,

(c)

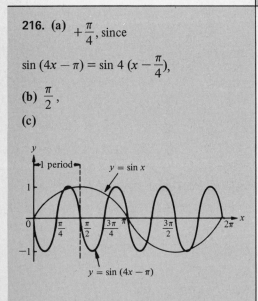

If you had difficulty, see frames 171 to 173 and 211 to 215.

EXAMPLE 7

217. Now find the phase shift of $y = \sin\left(\frac{1}{2}x - \frac{\pi}{8}\right)$ and graph the

function on the coordinate axes. The phase shift is **(a)** ___ , and

the period is **(b)** ___ .

(c)

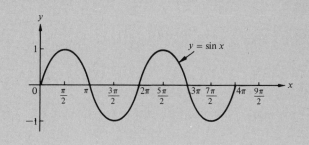

217.
(a) $+\frac{\pi}{4}$, since $\sin\left(\frac{1}{2}x - \frac{\pi}{8}\right) =$

$\sin\frac{1}{2}\left(x - \frac{\pi}{4}\right)$, **(b)** 4π,

(c)

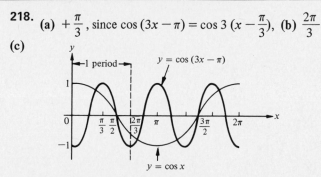

If you had difficulty, see frames 174, 175
and 211 to 215.

EXAMPLE 8

218. Once more the same procedure works for all six circular
functions. Find the phase shift of $y = \cos(3x - \pi)$ and graph the
function on the coordinate axes. The graph of $y = \cos x$ is
included. The phase shift is **(a)** ___ , and the period of

$y = \cos(3x - \pi)$ is **(b)** ___ .

(c)

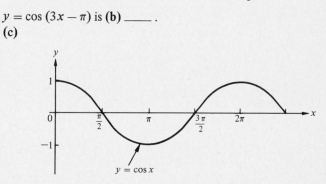

---

218. **(a)** $+\frac{\pi}{3}$, since $\cos(3x - \pi) = \cos 3\left(x - \frac{\pi}{3}\right)$, **(b)** $\frac{2\pi}{3}$

(c)

If you had difficulty, see frames 219 to
221. If not skip to frame 222.

157

Cos $3x$ also has period $\frac{2\pi}{3}$; hence $\cos 3x = 1$ at $(0, 1)$ and

(a) (_____ , 1), and $\cos 3x = -1$ at **(b)** (___ , -1), and $\cos 3x = 0$ at **(c)** (_____ , 0) and (_____ , 0).

---

219. **(a)** $\frac{2\pi}{3}$,

(b) $\frac{\pi}{3}$, **(c)** $\frac{\pi}{6}$, $\frac{3\pi}{6}$

---

220. We obtain the graph of $y = \cos(3x - \pi)$ by shifting the graph of $y = \cos 3x$ **(a)** ___ units to the **(b)** _____.
(left, right)

Thus $\cos(3x - \pi) = 1$ at **(c)** (_____ , 1) and (_____ , 1),

$\cos(3x - \pi) = -1$ at **(d)** (_____ , -1),

$\cos(3x - \pi) = 0$ at **(e)** (___ , 0), (_____ , 0), and (_____ , 0),

and $\cos(3x - \pi) =$ **(f)** _____ at $x = 0$.

---

220. **(a)** $\frac{\pi}{3}$, **(b)** right,

(c) $\frac{\pi}{3}$, π, **(d)** $\frac{2\pi}{3}$,

(e) $\frac{\pi}{6}$, $\frac{3\pi}{6}$, $\frac{5\pi}{6}$, **(f)** -1

---

221. Now graph $y = \cos(3x - \pi)$.

$y = \cos x$

221.

$y = \cos(3x - \pi)$

$y = \cos x$

222. In this section we want to connect the graphs of $y = a \sin x$, $y = a \cos x$, etc. We saw in the chapter on the period of a function that if $f(x)$ has period p, then $af(x)$ has period ____ . Thus $y = a \sin x$ will have period ____ for any number $a > 0$.

---

222. p;

2π

223. What then is the effect of multiplying $\sin x$ by a, $a > 0$?

Sin $x = 0$ at $x = 0, \pi$, and 2π, and $a \sin x = 0$ at $x =$ ____ , ____ ,

and ____ .

---

223. 0, π, 2π

224. Thus multiplying $\sin x$ by a does not compress the graph in the x-direction nor shift it along the x-axis. However,

$\sin \dfrac{\pi}{2} = 1$ and $\sin \dfrac{3\pi}{2} = 1$ while

$a \sin \dfrac{\pi}{2} =$ ___ and $a \sin \dfrac{3\pi}{2} =$ _____ .

---

224. $a; a \cdot -1 = -a$

225. The effect of multiplying $\sin x$ by a is to multiply each

y-value by ___ .

---

225. a

226. Thus multiplying by a causes the graph of $y = \sin x$ to expand

or contract in the _____ direction by a factor of ___ .
 (x-, y-)

---

226. y-; a

EXAMPLE 9

227. Graph $y = 2 \sin x$ on the coordinate axes. The graph of $y = \sin x$ is included.

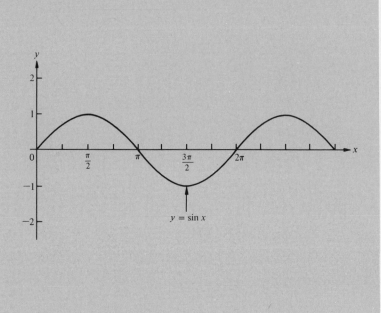

227.

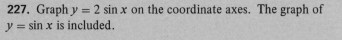

If you had difficulty, see frames 222 to 226.

228. Thus we see that the only change in the graph of $y = \sin x$ is that the y-value at each point x is _____ . And the range of $y = 2 \sin x$ is $\{ y \in R \mid$ _____ $\}$.

228. doubled;
$-2 \leqslant y \leqslant 2$

229. We have the following definition:

DEFINITION: The **amplitude** of a periodic function is one-half of the maximum value minus the minimum value of the function. That is, amplitude = $\frac{1}{2}$ (max − min).

Thus the amplitude of $\sin x$ is **(a)** ___ , since the maximum value sine assumes is **(b)** ___ , and the minimum is **(c)** ___ .

---

229. (a) 1, since amp = $\frac{1}{2}$ (max − min),
(b) 1, **(c)** −1

230. The amplitude of $y = 2 \sin x$ is ___ .

---

230. 2, since the maximum value is 2 and the minimum value is −2.

231. And, in general, the amplitude of $y = a \sin x$ is ___ .

---

231. a

EXAMPLE 10

232. Graph $y = \frac{1}{2} \sin x$ on the coordinate axes. The amplitude of $y = \frac{1}{2} \sin x$ is ___ .

---

232. $\frac{1}{2}$

EXAMPLE 11

233. Graph $y = 3 \cos x$ on the coordinate axes. The amplitude is **(a)** _____ , and the period is **(b)** _____ . The graph of $y = \cos x$ is included.
(c)

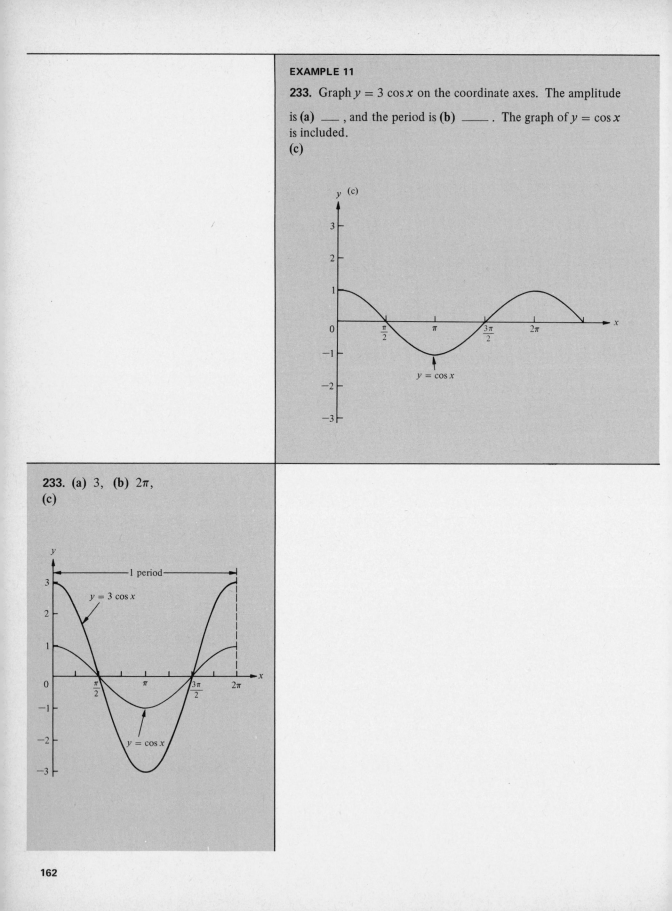

233. (a) 3, **(b)** 2π,
(c)

234. If we wish to graph functions such as $y = 3 \sin 2x$ or $y = 2 \sin (x + \frac{\pi}{2})$, we can calculate the effects of the change in amplitude a, the multiple b, or the phase shift c separately.

If we consider $y = 3 \sin 2x$, the 3 affects the ＿＿＿＿＿＿＿, and the 2 affects the ＿＿＿＿＿ .

234. amplitude; period

EXAMPLE 12

235. Graph $y = 3 \sin 2x$ on the coordinate axes. The amplitude is **(a)** ＿ , and the period is **(b)** ＿ . The graph of $y = \sin x$ is included.

(c)

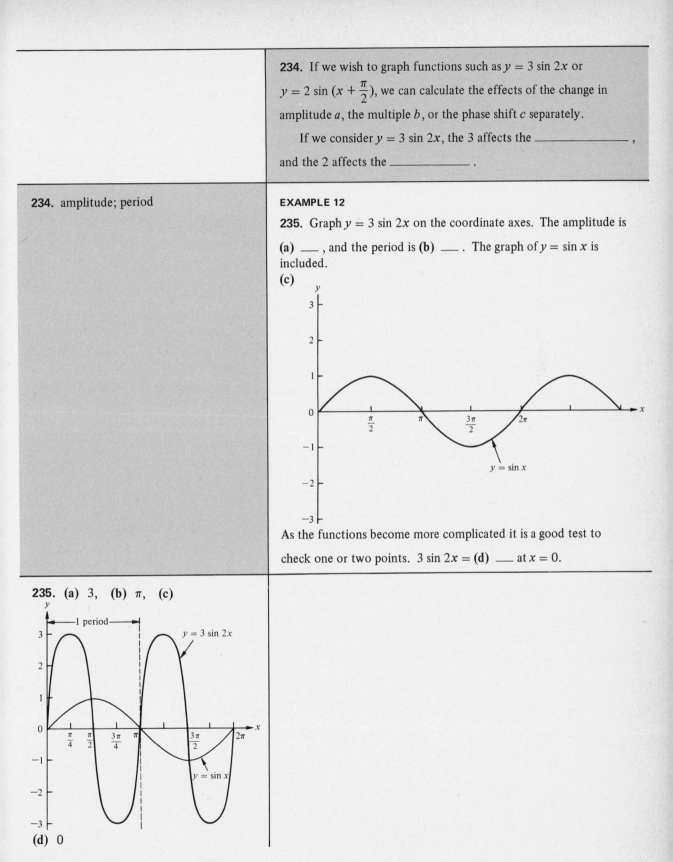

As the functions become more complicated it is a good test to check one or two points. $3 \sin 2x =$ **(d)** ＿ at $x = 0$.

235. (a) 3, **(b)** π, **(c)**

(d) 0

236.
Consider $y = 2 \sin (x + \frac{\pi}{2})$. The 2 affects the _____ ,
and the $\frac{\pi}{2}$ indicates the _____ .

236. amplitude;
phase shift

EXAMPLE 13

237.
Graph $y = 2 \sin (x + \frac{\pi}{2})$ on the coordinate axes. The
amplitude is **(a)** ____ , the phase shift is **(b)** ____ , and the period
is **(c)** ____ .
(d)

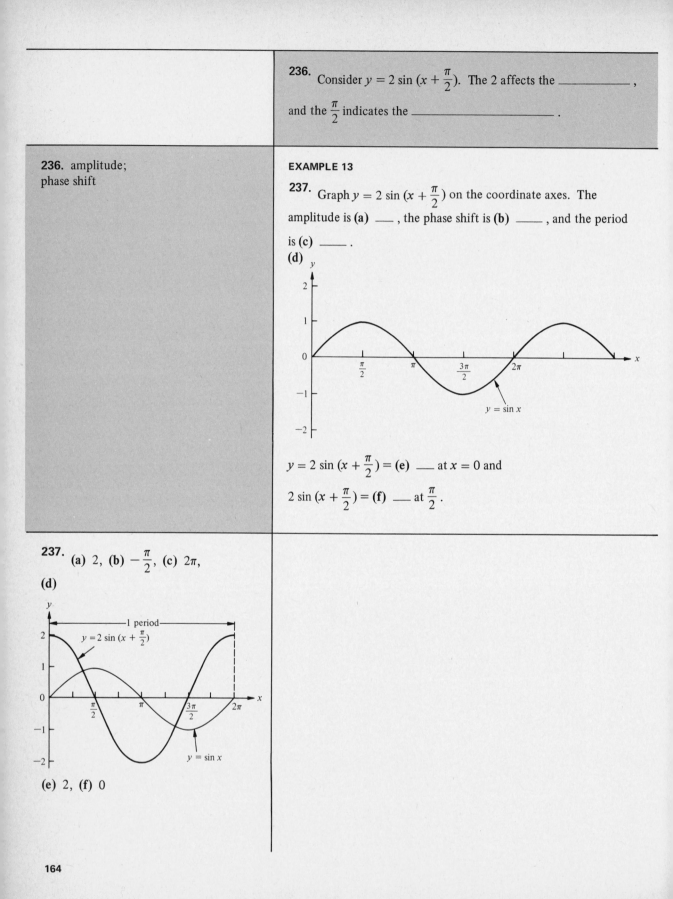

$y = 2 \sin (x + \frac{\pi}{2}) = $ **(e)** ____ at $x = 0$ and

$2 \sin (x + \frac{\pi}{2}) = $ **(f)** ____ at $\frac{\pi}{2}$.

237. **(a)** 2, **(b)** $-\frac{\pi}{2}$, **(c)** 2π,

(d)

(e) 2, **(f)** 0

EXAMPLE 14

238. Graph $y = \frac{3}{2} \cos(x - \pi)$ on the coordinate axes. The amplitude is **(a)** _____ , the phase shift is **(b)** _____ , and the period is **(c)** _____ .

(d)

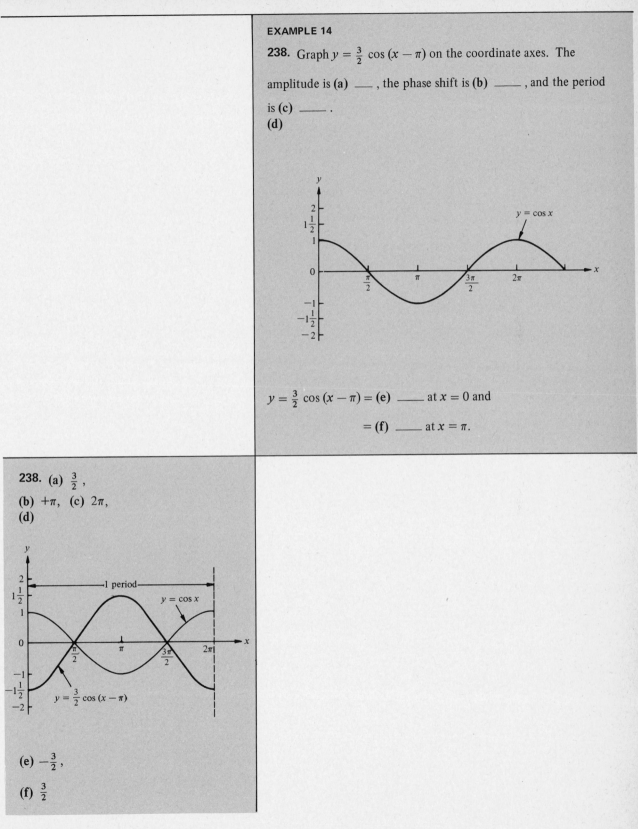

$y = \frac{3}{2} \cos(x - \pi) = $ **(e)** _____ at $x = 0$ and

$$= \textbf{(f)} \text{\_\_\_\_\_ at } x = \pi.$$

238. **(a)** $\frac{3}{2}$,

(b) $+\pi$, **(c)** 2π,

(d)

(e) $-\frac{3}{2}$,

(f) $\frac{3}{2}$

239. In general if $a > 0, b > 0$, and $y = a \sin bx$, then the amplitude is ____ , the period is ____ , and the phase shift is 0.

239. $a; \dfrac{2\pi}{b}$

240. If $a > 0$ and $y = a \sin (x + c)$, then the amplitude is **(a)** ____ , the phase shift is **(b)** ____ , and the period is **(c)** ____ .

240. (a) a, **(b)** $-c$, **(c)** 2π

241. Finally, if $a > 0, b > 0$, and $y = a \sin (bx + c)$, the amplitude is **(a)** ____ , the period is **(b)** ____ , and the phase shift is **(c)** ____ .

241. **(a)** a, **(b)** $\dfrac{2\pi}{b}$,

(c) $-\dfrac{c}{b}$, since $a \sin (bx + c) =$

$a \sin b \left(x + \dfrac{c}{b}\right)$.

EXAMPLE 15

242. Graph the function $y = 3 \sin(2x - \pi)$ on the coordinate axes.

The amplitude is **(a)** ____ , the period is **(b)** ____ , and the phase shift

is **(c)** _____ .

(d)

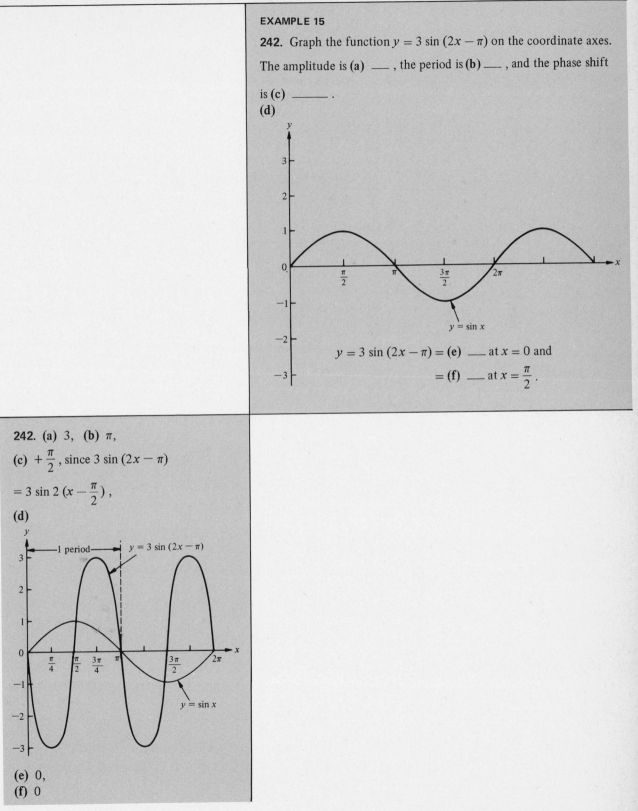

$y = 3 \sin(2x - \pi) =$ **(e)** ____ at $x = 0$ and

$\qquad\qquad\qquad = $ **(f)** ____ at $x = \dfrac{\pi}{2}$.

242. (a) 3, **(b)** π,

(c) $+\dfrac{\pi}{2}$, since $3 \sin(2x - \pi)$

$= 3 \sin 2\left(x - \dfrac{\pi}{2}\right)$,

(d)

(e) 0,
(f) 0

167

EXAMPLE 16

243. Graph the function $y = 2 \cos (\frac{1}{2}x + \frac{\pi}{4})$ on the coordinate axes. The amplitude is **(a)** ___ , the period is **(b)** ___ , and the phase shift is **(c)** ___ .

(d)

$y = 2 \cos (\frac{1}{2}x + \frac{\pi}{4}) =$ **(e)** ___ at $x = 0$, and

$= $ **(f)** ___ at $x = \frac{\pi}{2}$.

243. (a) 2, **(b)** 4π,

(c) $-\frac{\pi}{2}$,

(d)

(e) $\dfrac{2}{\sqrt{2}} = \sqrt{2}$,

(f) 0

244. Up to now we have considered the graphy of $y = a \sin(bx + c)$ where $a > 0$, $b > 0$, and c is any real number.

a gives the **(a)** _____ , 2π is the **(b)** _____ ,

and $-\dfrac{c}{b}$ is the **(c)** _____ .

244. (a) amplitude,
  (b) period,
  (c) phase shift

245. Now let us see what happens to ghe graphs of
$y = a \sin(bx + c)$ and $y = a \cos(bx + c)$ if we let $a < 0$.

Recall that the graph of the general sine function $y = a \sin bx$ passes through the origin for any real numbers a and b. If we introduce c, the graph of $y = a \sin(bx + c)$ is translated to the right or left. The phase shift measures the distance of this shift from the origin. That is, the phase shift measures the directed distance to which the graph of $y = a \sin(bx + c)$ is translated from the graph of $y = a \sin bx$.

Now, we shall investigate $a < 0$. For example, compute a few values for $y = -\sin x$ and sketch the graph on the coordinate axes below.

x					
$-\sin x$					

245.

x	0	$\dfrac{\pi}{2}$	π	$\dfrac{3\pi}{2}$	2
$-\sin x$	0	-1	0	1	0

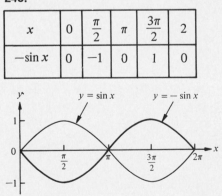

246. Thus we see that $y = -\sin x$ is a reflection of $y = \sin x$ in the _____. That is, the graphs of $y = \sin x$ and $y = -\sin x$ (or $-y = \sin x$) are symmetric with respect to the _____.

246. x-axis; x-axis

247. This should come as no surprise since the test for symmetry with respect to the x-axis is as follows. A curve is symmetric with respect to the x-axis if its equation is unchanged when y is replaced by $-y$.

Thus two graphs are symmetric with respect to the x-axis if we can obtain the equation of one of the graphs by replacing ___ by _____ in the other equation.

247. y; $-y$

248. If we have a function $y = f(x)$ and its graph, then the graph of $y = -f(x)$ is the reflection of the graph of $f(x)$ in the _____.

248. x-axis

EXAMPLE 17

249. Graph $y = -\cos x$ on the coordinate axes.

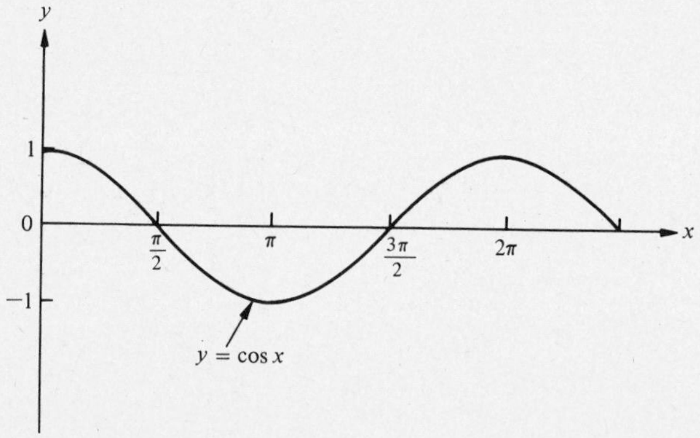

$y = \cos x$

249.

$y = -\cos x$

$y = \cos x$

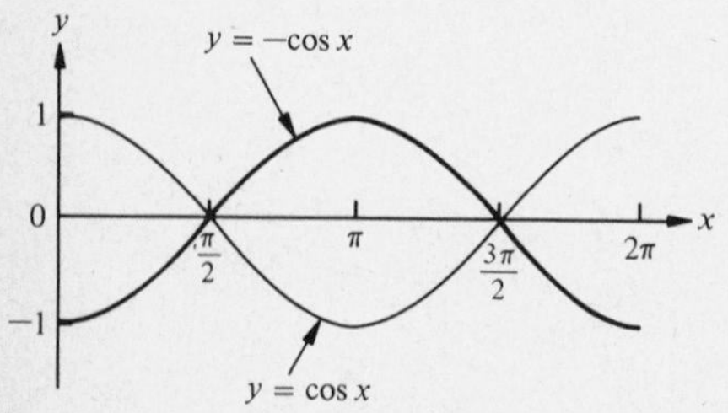

EXAMPLE 18

250. Graph $y = -2 \sin x$ on the coordinate axes. The graph will
be the reflection of the graph of **(a)** _____ in the
x-axis. Hence the amplitude will be **(b)** ___ , the period **(c)** ___ ,
and the phase shift **(d)** ___ .
(e)

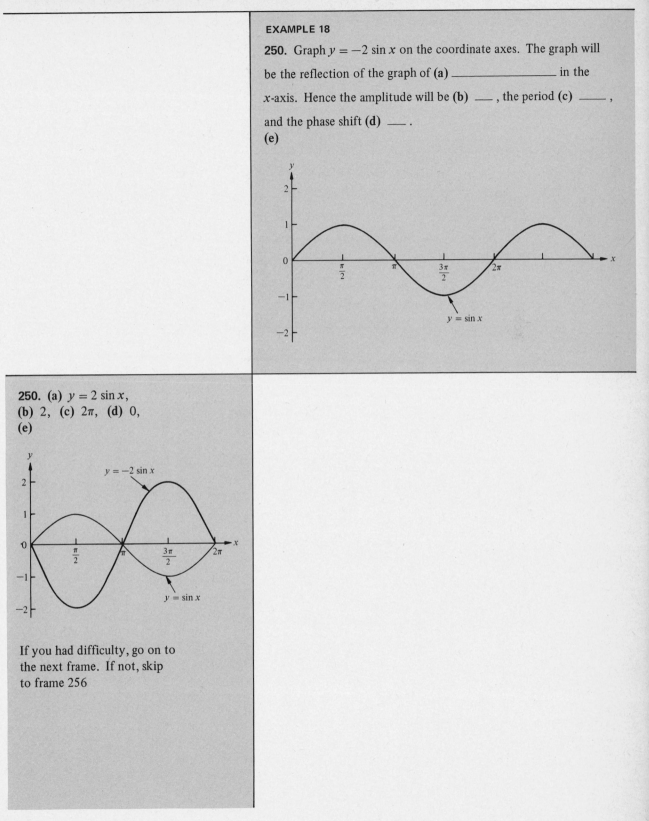

250. (a) $y = 2 \sin x$,
(b) 2, **(c)** 2π, **(d)** 0,
(e)

If you had difficulty, go on to
the next frame. If not, skip
to frame 256

251. Since we can get $y = -2 \sin x$ by replacing y by $-y$ in $y = 2 \sin x$, $y = -2 \sin x$ and $y = 2 \sin x$ are symmetric with respect to the **(a)** _____ . That is, the graph of $y = -2 \sin x$ will be the reflection of the graph of **(b)** _____ in the **(c)** _____ .

---

251. **(a)** x-axis,
  (b) $y = 2 \sin x$,
  (c) x-axis

252. Therefore $y = -2 \sin x$ has the same amplitude, period, and phase shift as $y = 2 \sin x$. Thus $y = -2 \sin x$ has amplitude **(a)** ___ , period **(b)** _____ , and phase shift **(c)** ___ .

---

252. **(a)** 2, **(b)** 2π,
(c) 0

253. Since the phase shift is 0, the graph of $y = -2 \sin x$ will pass through the origin, and since the period is 2π, $y = -2 \sin x$ will also be 0 at (___ , 0) and (___, 0).

---

253. π; 2π

254. Now we need only decide if the graph ascends or descends from the origin. But at $x = \dfrac{\pi}{2}$, $y = -2 \sin x = ($_____ , $\dfrac{\pi}{2})$. Thus the graph _____ from the origin.
  (ascends, descends)

---

254. -2;
descends

255. Now graph $y = -2 \sin x$ on the coordinate axes.

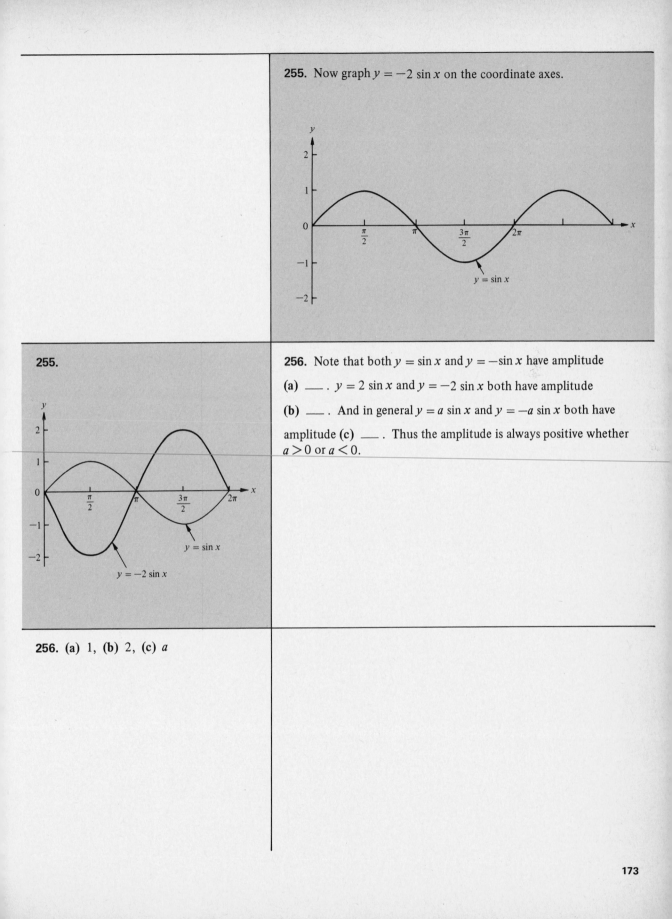

255.

256. Note that both $y = \sin x$ and $y = -\sin x$ have amplitude

(a) ___ . $y = 2 \sin x$ and $y = -2 \sin x$ both have amplitude

(b) ___ . And in general $y = a \sin x$ and $y = -a \sin x$ both have

amplitude **(c)** ___ . Thus the amplitude is always positive whether $a > 0$ or $a < 0$.

256. (a) 1, **(b)** 2, **(c)** a

EXAMPLE 19

257. Graph $y = -\sin 2x$ on the coordinate axes. The graph will be the reflection of the graph of **(a)** _____ in the x-axis. Hence the amplitude will be **(b)** ___ , the period **(c)** ___ , and the phase shift **(d)** ___ .

Check a point to show that the graph **(e)** _____ to the

$$\text{(ascends, descends)}$$

right of the origin.

(f)

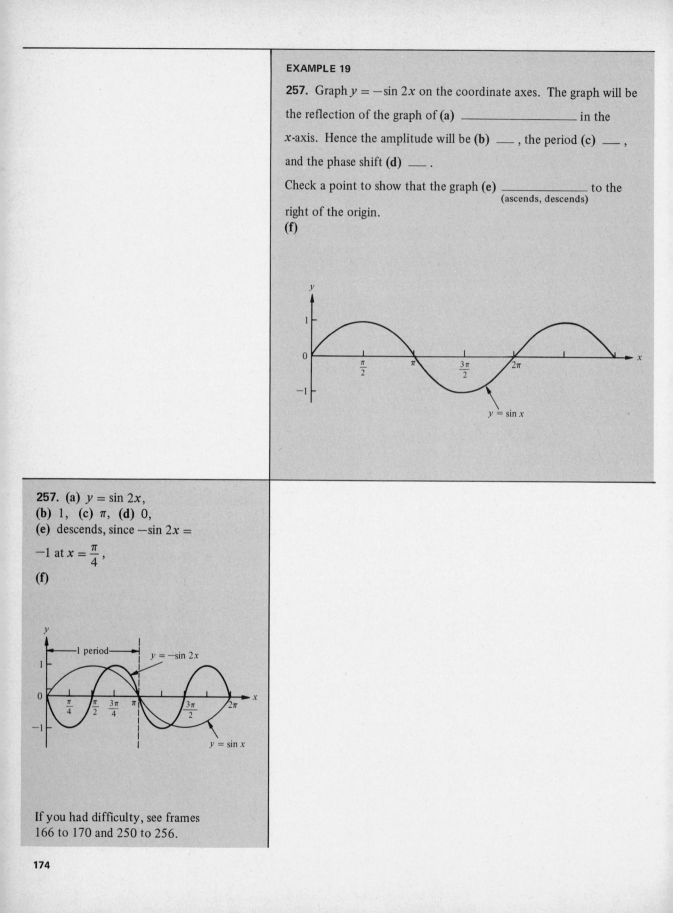

257. **(a)** $y = \sin 2x$,
(b) 1, **(c)** π, **(d)** 0,
(e) descends, since $-\sin 2x =$
-1 at $x = \dfrac{\pi}{4}$,

(f)

If you had difficulty, see frames
166 to 170 and 250 to 256.

EXAMPLE 20

258. Graph $y = -2 \cos (x + \frac{\pi}{2})$ on the coordinate axes. The amplitude is **(a)** ____ , the period is **(b)** ____ , and the phase shift is **(c)** ____ . At $x = 0$, $y = -2 \cos (x + \frac{\pi}{2}) = $ **(d)** ____ .

Check a point to show that the graph **(e)** _____ to (ascends, descends) the right of the origin.

(f)

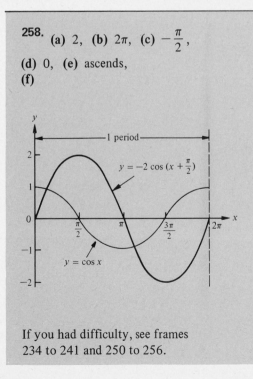

258. **(a)** 2, **(b)** 2π, **(c)** $-\frac{\pi}{2}$,

(d) 0, **(e)** ascends,

(f)

If you had difficulty, see frames 234 to 241 and 250 to 256.

259. If we have $y = a \sin (bx + c)$ or $y = a \cos (bx + c)$ with $a > 0$ and $b > 0$, then the amplitude is **(a)** ___ , the period is **(b)** ___ , and the phase shift is **(c)** ___ .

We get the graph of $y = a \sin (bx + c)$ by compressing or expanding the graph of $y = \sin x$ in both the x- and y-directions and then shifting it along the x-axes **(d)** ___ units.

259. **(a)** a, **(b)** $\dfrac{2\pi}{b}$,

(c) $-\dfrac{c}{b}$, **(d)** $\dfrac{c}{b}$

260. If we have $y = -a \sin (bx + c)$ where $a > 0$ ($-a < 0$) and $b > 0$, then the amplitude is **(a)** ___ , the period **(b)** ___ , and the phase shift **(c)** ___ .

The graph of $y = -a \sin (bx + c)$ is the reflection of the graph of **(d)** ___ in the x-axis.

260. **(a)** a, **(b)** $\dfrac{2\pi}{b}$,

(c) $-\dfrac{c}{b}$,

(d) $y = a \sin (bx + c)$

PROBLEMS

Find the amplitude, period, phase shift, and graph of each of the following.

1. $y = \sin 3x$

2. $y = \cos 4x$

3. $y = \sin (x + \dfrac{\pi}{2})$

4. $y = 2 \cos x$

5. $y = 3 \sin (x - \dfrac{\pi}{2})$

6. $y = \sin (\dfrac{1}{2}x + \dfrac{\pi}{2})$

7. $y = 3 \cos (2x + \pi)$

8. $y = \tan (\dfrac{1}{4}x - \dfrac{\pi}{8})$

9. $y = 2 \sin (3x + \pi)$

10. $y = -3 \sin (x - \dfrac{\pi}{2})$

Answers are at end of book.

QUIZ

If you cannot answer the following questions correctly, review the appropriate frames.

1. Give the period and sketch the graph of $y = \sin 3x$ on the coordinate axes.

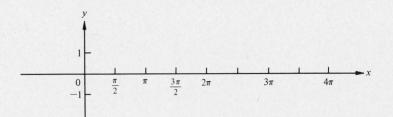

2. Give the phase shift of $y = \sin \left(x + \dfrac{\pi}{4}\right)$ and sketch its graph on the coordinate axes.

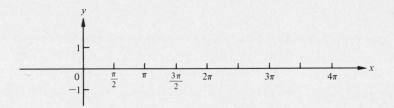

3. Give the phase shift and period of $y = \sin (4x - \pi)$ and sketch the graph on the coordinate axes.

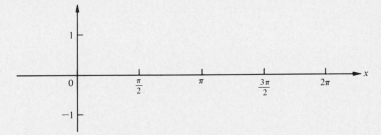

4. Give the amplitude of $y = 3 \sin x$ and sketch the graph on the coordinate axes.

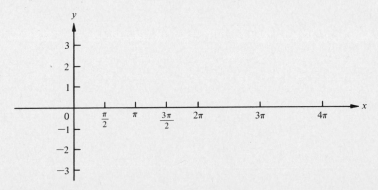

5. Give the amplitude, period, and phase shift of $y = 3 \sin (4x - \pi)$ and sketch the graph on the coordinate axes.

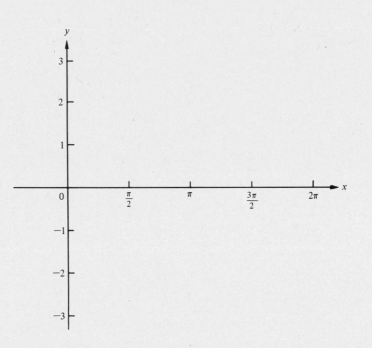

6. Graph $y = -\sin x$ on the coordinate axes.

Answers are at end of book.

9 Trigonometric Identities

In trigonometric equations one or more of the expressions contain a trigonometric function. In this chapter we shall consider trigonometric identities in which every expression is made up of trigonometric functions or constants.

We shall prove a number of basic identities and then use them to prove other identities.

Upon completing this chapter, you should be able to

I. Determine, from a trigonometric equation in x, those values of x for which the equation is
   (A) undefined,
   (B) defined but not true,
   (C) true,
   and classify the equation as (1) an identity or (2) a conditional equation.

II. Derive and write
   (A) The three reciprocal identities

   $$(1)\quad \csc x = \frac{1}{\sin x}$$

   $$(2)\quad \sec x = \frac{1}{\cos x}$$

   $$(3)\quad \cot x = \frac{1}{\tan x}$$

   (B) The two ratio or quotient identities

   $$(4)\quad \tan x = \frac{\sin x}{\cos x}$$

   $$(5)\quad \cot x = \frac{\cos x}{\sin x}$$

   (C) The three Pythagorean or square identities
   $$(6)\quad \sin^2 x + \cos^2 x = 1$$
   $$(7)\quad 1 + \tan^2 x = \sec^2 x$$
   $$(8)\quad \cot^2 x + 1 = \csc^2 x$$

III. Prove identities using the eight basic identities.

261. Three categories of real numbers are determined by the equation csc $x = 1$.

(1) Csc $x = 1$ is undefined for some values of x (that is, one side of the quation—or maybe both—is undefined.

(2) Csc $x = 1$ is a true statement for some values of x.

(3) Csc $x = 1$ is defined but not true for some values of x.

Csc x is undefined for $x =$ _____.

---

261. $\pm n\pi, n = 0, 1, 2, \ldots$.

If you had difficulty, see frames 107 to 171 in chapter 3 on the domain of csc x.

262. Csc $x = 1$ is true for $x =$ _____.
And csc $x = 1$ is not true for all other values of x.

---

262. $\dfrac{\pi}{2} \pm 2n\pi, n = 0, 1, 2, \ldots ,$

since csc $x = \dfrac{1}{\sin x} = 1$ if and

263. DEFINITION: An equation that is true for all values for which both sides are defined is said to be an **identical equation** or an **identity**.

Csc $x = 1$ _____ an identity.
$\quad\quad\quad\quad$ (is, is not)

Why? _____

_____

---

263. Is not.
It is not true for all values for which csc x is defined. For example,
csc $\dfrac{\pi}{4} \neq 1$.

264. DEFINITION: An equation that is not true for at least one value at which both sides of the equation are defined is called a **conditional equation** or **equation**.

Is sin $x =$ tan x an identity or a conditional equation?

_____

Why? _____

_____

_____

---

264. Conditional equation.
It is a conditional equation since sin $x =$ tan x is not true for all values of x for which both sin x and tan x are defined. For example,
$\dfrac{1}{\sqrt{2}} = \sin \dfrac{\pi}{4} \neq \tan \dfrac{\pi}{4} = 1.$

265. Sin $x = \tan x$ is undefined when $x = $ _____ .

---

265. $\dfrac{\pi}{2} \pm n\pi, n = 0, 1, 2, ...$

266. If an equation is true for all values for which both sides are defined, it is called a(n) _____ .

---

266. identity

267. If an equation is *not* true for all values at which both sides are defined, it is called a(n) _____ .

---

267. conditional equation or equation

268. For the most part, we shall drop the word "conditional" and speak about identities and equations.

There are eight identities that are immediate consequences of the definitions of our trigonometric functions. There are three **reciprocal identities:**

(1) $\csc x = \dfrac{1}{\sin x}$ (2) _____ and

(3) _____ .

268.
$$\sec x = \frac{1}{\cos x} \, ;$$
$$\cot x = \frac{1}{\tan x}$$

269. The identity (1) $\csc x = \dfrac{1}{\sin x}$ is not defined when

$x = $ _____ .

---

269. $\pm n\pi, n = 0, 1, 2, ...$

270. The identity (2) $\sec x = \dfrac{1}{\cos x}$ is not defined when

$x = $ _____ .

---

270. $\dfrac{\pi}{2} \pm n\pi, n = 0, 1, 2, ...$

271.

And the identity (3) $\cot x = \dfrac{1}{\tan x}$ is undefined if

$x =$ _____ .

---

271. $\dfrac{\pi}{2} \pm n\pi$ or $\pm n\pi, n = 0, 1, 2, \ldots$

Since $\tan x$ is undefined if

$x = \dfrac{\pi}{2} \pm n\pi, n = 0, 1, 2, \ldots$, and $\cot x$

is undefined if $x = \pm n\pi, n = 0, 1, 2, \ldots$,
we can combine these two and derive

that $\cot x = \dfrac{1}{\tan x}$ is undefined if

$x = \pm n\dfrac{\pi}{2}, n = 0, 1, 2, \ldots$.

272. The next two identities are the **quotient** or **ratio identities**.

(4) $\tan x = \dfrac{\sin x}{\cos x}$ (5) $\cot x =$ _____

---

272. $\dfrac{\cos x}{\sin x}$

273. The identity (4) $\tan x = \dfrac{\sin x}{\cos x}$ is undefined if

$x =$ _____ .

---

273. $\dfrac{\pi}{2} \pm n\pi, n = 0, 1, 2, \ldots$

274.

And the identity (5) $\cot x = \dfrac{\cos x}{\sin x}$ is undefined if

$x =$ _____ .

---

274. $\pm n\pi, n = 0, 1, 2, \ldots$

275. The remaining three fundamental identities are called the **Pythagorean identities** or **identities involving squares**. Consider the figure. By the Pythagorean theorem
(i) $x^2 + y^2 = r^2$ or,
on dividing both sides of
(i) by r^2, we get
(ii) $\left(\dfrac{x}{r}\right)^2 + \underline{\quad} = \underline{\quad}$.

---

275. $\left(\dfrac{y}{r}\right)^2 ; 1$

276. But sin t and cos t are defined by sin $t = $ ___ and

cos $t = $ ___ .

Thus, by substituting sin t and cos t into (ii) in frame 275 we get our sixth identity.

(6) _____

---

276. $\dfrac{y}{r}, \dfrac{x}{r}$;

$\sin^2 t + \cos^2 t = 1$

277. For $x \neq 0$, we divide (i) $x^2 + y^2 = r^2$ on both sides by x^2.

We get (iii) _____ , $x \neq 0$.

If we substitute in the appropriate trigonometric functions we get the seventh identity.

(7) _____

---

277. $1 + \left(\dfrac{y}{x}\right)^2 = \left(\dfrac{r}{x}\right)^2$;

$1 + \tan^2 t = \sec^2 t$

278. Finally, if $y \neq 0$, we divide (i) $x^2 + y^2 = r^2$ on both sides

by y^2 and get (iv) _____ , $y \neq 0$.

And if we substitute in the appropriate trigonometric functions, we get the eighth fundamental identity.

(8) _____

---

278. $\left(\dfrac{x}{y}\right)^2 + 1 = \left(\dfrac{r}{y}\right)^2$;

$\cot^2 t + 1 = \csc^2 t$

279. The identity (6) $\sin^2 t + \cos^2 t = 1$ is undefined if

$t = $ _____ .

---

279. No values. Sin t and cos t are both defined for all values.

280. The identity (7) $1 + \tan^2 t = \sec^2 t$ is undefined if

$t = $ _____ .

---

280. $\dfrac{\pi}{2} \pm n\pi, n = 0, 1, 2, ...$

281. And the identity (8) $\cot^2 t + 1 = \csc^2 t$ is undefined if

$t = $ _____ .

---

281. $\pm n\pi, n = 0, 1, 2, ...$

282. The three Pythagorean identities were all dervied from the Pythagorean theorem, which states that **(i)** $x^2 + y^2 = r^2$. The first identity was obtained by dividing both sides of **(i) (a)** by _____ , giving us **(ii) (b)** _____ .
And substituting in the appropriate trigonometric function gave us

(6) (c) _____ .

---

282. (a) r^2 ,

(b) $\left(\dfrac{x}{r}\right)^2 + \left(\dfrac{y}{r}\right)^2 = 1$,

(c) $\sin^2 t + \cos^2 t = 1$

---

283. We obtained the second identity by dividing both sides of **(i)** by **(a)** _____ , which gave us **(iii) (b)** _____

if **(c)** ___ $\neq 0$, which led to **(7) (d)** _____ .

---

283. (a) x^2 ,

(b) $1 + \left(\dfrac{y}{r}\right)^2 = \left(\dfrac{r}{x}\right)^2$ **(c)** x ,

(d) $1 + \tan^2 t = \sec^2 t$

---

284. And, finally, we obtained the third Pythagorean identity by dividing both sides of **(i)** by **(a)** _____ , which gave

(iv) (b) _____ if **(c)** ___ $\neq 0$,

and led to **(8) (d)** _____ .

---

284. (a) y^2 ,

(b) $\left(\dfrac{x}{y}\right)^2 + 1 = \left(\dfrac{r}{y}\right)^2$, **(c)** y ,

(d) $\cot^2 t + 1 = \csc^2 t$

285. In some of our identities, we used t to represent the elements of the domains to distinguish them from the x-values that appear in the definitions of the trigonometric functions. We shall return to using the letter x to represent elements of the domains. List the eight fundamental identities.

The reciprocal identities:

(1) _____

(2) _____

(3) _____

The ratio or quotient identities:

(4) _____

(5) _____

The Pythagorean identities:

(6) _____

(7) _____

(8) _____

These are all very important and should be memorized. Note that they are *not* defined for all values of x.

285.

(1) $\csc x = \dfrac{1}{\sin x}$,

(2) $\sec x = \dfrac{1}{\cos x}$,

(3) $\cot x = \dfrac{1}{\tan x}$,

(4) $\tan x = \dfrac{\sin x}{\cos x}$,

(5) $\cot x = \dfrac{\cos x}{\sin x}$,

(6) $\sin^2 x + \cos^2 x = 1$,

(7) $1 + \tan^2 x = \sec^2 x$

(8) $\cot^2 x + 1 = \csc^2 x$.

If you had difficulty, review the identities until you can write all eight down quickly.

286. There are many other trigonometric identities that are based on the eight fundamental ones listed above.

If we are given a trigonometric equation such as

(i) $\tan x \cdot \csc x = \sec x$

the first step is to note the values of x for which the equation is undefined.

$\operatorname{Tan} x \cdot \csc x = \sec x$ is undefined if $x =$ _____.

---

286. $\dfrac{\pi}{2} \pm n\pi$ or $\pm n\pi, n = 0, 1, 2, ...,$

since tan and sec are undefined for

$x = \dfrac{\pi}{2} \pm n\pi$ and csc is undefined for

$x = \pm n\pi, n = 0, 1, 2, ...$ That is,

$x = \pm n\dfrac{\pi}{2}, n = 0, 1, 2, ...$

---

287. Next we might substitute in a few values, and if there are no obvious values for which the equation is *not* valid, we can try to prove that it is an identity by using the eight fundamental identities.

Which three of the fundamental identities can we apply immediately to the equation

(i) $\tan x \cdot \csc x = \sec x$?

(a) _____

(b) _____

(c) _____

287.

(a) (1) $\csc x = \dfrac{1}{\sin x}$,

(b) (2) $\sec x = \dfrac{1}{\cos x}$,

(c) (4) $\tan x = \dfrac{\sin x}{\cos x}$,

since $\csc x$, $\sec x$, and $\tan x$ are the three terms appearing in the equation.

---

288. If we substitute these values in the left-hand side of

(i) $\tan x \cdot \csc x = \sec x$

we get

(ii) $\tan x \cdot \csc x =$ (iii) (a)_____.

For what values of x is the left-hand side of (ii) undefined?

$x =$ (b)_____.

In making substitutions, have we introduced any new values at

which the equation is undefined? (c) _____

288.

(a) $\dfrac{\sin x}{\cos x} \cdot \dfrac{1}{\sin x}$,

(b) $\dfrac{\pi}{2} \pm n\pi$ or $\pm n\pi, n = 0, 1, 2, ...$ That is

is, $x = \pm n\dfrac{\pi}{2}, n = 0, 1, 2, ...,$ (c) no

---

289. Finally, if we replace $\dfrac{\sin x}{\sin x}$ by 1 in the left-hand side of (ii),

we get

(ii) $\dfrac{\sin x}{\cos x} \cdot \dfrac{1}{\sin x} =$ _____.

But this equals the right-hand side, and our identity is proved.

---

289. $\dfrac{1}{\cos x}$

290. We have proved that the equation $\tan x \cdot \csc x = \sec x$

is an identity, since we have proved that it is _____

_____.

---

290. true for all values of x for which both sides are defined

291. In proving an identity, we may use any of the normal algebraic operations (if we are careful to avoid dividing by 0) or one of the eight fundamental identities. Using the identities we can make substitutions like:

Substitute (a) ____ for $\sin^2 x + \cos^2 x$,

substitute (b) _____ for $\cot x$, or

substitute (c) _____ for $\csc^2 x$.

---

291. (a) 1,

(b) $\dfrac{\cos x}{\sin x}$,

(c) $1 + \cot^2 x$

292. Given the equation
$$\csc^2 x + 2\cot x = (1 + \cot x)^2$$

we first _____

_____,

and then, if there are no obvious values of x for which the equation is *not* true, we can try to prove that it is an identity by using the

ordinary algebraic operations and the _____

_____ .

---

292. note the values of x for which the equation is undefined; eight fundamental identities

293. $\csc^2 x + 2\cot x = (1 + \cot x)^2$ is undefined for

$x =$ _____ .

---

293. $\pm n\pi, n = 0, 1, 2, \dots$, since $\csc x$ and $\cot x$ are undefined if $x = \pm n\pi, n = 0, 1, 2, \dots$.

294. There is no set procedure for proving an identity. However, there are two basic approaches:

(1) We can transform one side of the equation (usually the more complicated one) by using algebraic operations and the fundamental identities until it is the same as the other side.

(2) We can transform each side separately until they are both equal to some third expression.

List substitutions that we might make in

$$\csc^2 x + 2 \cot x = (1 + \cot x)^2$$

using the eight fundamental identities.

(a) _____

(b) _____

(c) _____

(d) _____

294.

(a) (1) $\csc^2 x = \dfrac{1}{\sin^2 x}$,

(b) (3) $\cot x = \dfrac{\cos x}{\sin x}$,

(c) (5) $\cot x = \dfrac{1}{\tan x}$,

(d) (8) $\csc^2 x = \cot^2 x + 1$

---

295. Let us choose $\csc^2 x + 2 \cot x$ as the more complicated side. Which of the four identities listed in the previous answer should we use?_____

---

295. (8) $\csc^2 x = \cot^2 x + 1$, since replacing $\csc^2 x$ by $\dfrac{1}{\sin^2 x}$ and $\cot x$ by either $\dfrac{\cos x}{\sin x}$ or $\dfrac{1}{\tan x}$ would make the expression more complicated.

---

296. Therefore, if we replace $\csc^2 x$ by $\cot^2 x + 1$ in the left-hand side of the equation, we get

$$\csc^2 x + 2 \cot x = \underline{\hspace{4cm}}.$$

---

296. $(\cot^2 x + 1) + 2 \cot x$

---

297. But $(\cot^2 x + 1) + 2 \cot x = \cot^2 x + 2 \cot x + 1 =$

$$\underline{\hspace{4cm}}.$$

---

297. $(1 + \cot x)^2$

298. Thus, the two sides of the equation are the same. And we have proved that the equation

$$\csc^2 x + 2\cot x = (1 + \cot x)^2$$

is an identity by proving that it is _____

_____ .

---

298. true for all values of x for which both sides are defined

299. Given a trigonometric equation, we

_____

_____ ,

and if there are no obvious values for which the equation is *not* true, we

_____

_____

_____

The only way to become proficient at proving identities is to know the eight fundamental identities well and to practice. However, some suggestions that might be useful in proving identities are listed in the following summary.

---

299. note the values of x for which the equation is undefined,
try to prove it is an identity using the ordinary algebraic equations and the eight fundamental identities

SUMMARY

Proving Identities

Given a trigonometric equation,

 (I) note all the values of x for which the equation is undefined, and

 (II) try to prove that the equation is an identity by using ordinary algebra and the eight fundamental identities.

The following list may be useful in proving identities:

 (A) Transform one side (usually the more complicated side) until it is the same as the second side.

 (B) Or transform each side separately until they are both equal to some third expression.

In transforming a side,

   (1) factoring an expression, or the numerator or denominator of an expression, may suggest a solution.

   (2) If the side contains a sum of fractions, it may be helpful to combine them into a single fraction.

   (3) Or, if the numerator of a fraction has more than one term, it may be helpful to split the fraction into a sum of fractions.

   (4) If nothing else is obvious, write all the expressions in terms of sines and cosines.

   (5) If you are simplifying one side, always keep in mind the other side for comparison and guidance.

   (6) Check to see that each operation you perform is valid for all defined values.

EXAMPLE 1

300. There are many ways to prove the same identity. In the following frames, your approach may not agree with the answer given, but it may still be correct.

In the following cases, prove the identity. Check the answer only *after* you have completed your proof or *after* you have tried and failed.

Prove the identity

$$\cos x = \frac{1}{\cos x} - \frac{\sin^2 x}{\cos x}.$$

300. $\dfrac{1}{\cos x} - \dfrac{\sin^2 x}{\cos x}$

$= \dfrac{1 - \sin^2 x}{\cos x}$

$= \dfrac{\cos^2 x}{\cos x}$ by (6)

$= \cos x$

EXAMPLE 2

301. Prove the identity

$$\tan x \sin x + \cos x = \sec x.$$

301. $\tan x \sin x + \cos x$

$= \dfrac{\sin x}{\cos x} \cdot \sin x + \cos x$ by (4)

$= \dfrac{\sin^2 x + \cos^2 x}{\cos x}$ by (6)

$= \dfrac{1}{\cos x}$

$= \sec x$ by (2)

EXAMPLE 3

302. Prove the identity

$$\csc x \sec x = \tan x + \cot x.$$

302. $\tan x + \cot x$

$= \dfrac{\sin x}{\cos x} + \dfrac{\cos x}{\sin x}$ by (4) and (5)

$= \dfrac{\sin^2 x + \cos^2 x}{\cos x \sin x}$

$= \dfrac{1}{\cos x \sin x}$ by (6)

$= \dfrac{1}{\cos x} \cdot \dfrac{1}{\sin x}$ by (1) and (2)

$= \sec x \cdot \csc x$

EXAMPLE 4

303. Prove the identity

$$\csc^2 x \tan^2 x = 1 + \tan^2 x.$$

303. $\csc^2 x \tan^2 x$

$$= \frac{1}{\sin^2 x} \cdot \frac{\sin^2 x}{\cos^2 x} \quad \text{by (1) and (4)}$$

$$= \frac{1}{\cos^2 x}$$

$$= \sec^2 x \qquad \text{by (2)}$$

$$= 1 + \tan^2 x \qquad \text{by (7)}$$

EXAMPLE 5

304. Prove the identity

$$\sec^2 x \cdot \csc^2 x = \sec^2 x + \csc^2 x.$$

304. $\sec^2 x + \csc^2 x$

$$= \frac{1}{\cos^2 x} + \frac{1}{\sin^2 x} \qquad \text{by (1) and (2)}$$

$$= \frac{\sin^2 x + \cos^2 x}{\cos^2 x \sin^2 x}$$

$$= \frac{1}{\cos^2 x \cdot \sin^2 x} \qquad \text{by (6)}$$

$$= \frac{1}{\cos^2 x} \cdot \frac{1}{\sin^2 x}$$

$$= \sec^2 x \cdot \csc^2 x \qquad \text{by (1) and (2)}$$

EXAMPLE 6

305. Prove the identity

$$\cot^2 x \cdot \cos^2 x = \cot^2 x - \cos^2 x.$$

305. $\cot^2 x - \cos^2 x$

$$= \frac{\cos^2 x}{\sin^2 x} - \cos^2 x \qquad \text{by (5)}$$

$$= \cos^2 x \left(\frac{1}{\sin^2 x} - 1 \right)$$

$$= \cos^2 x \, (\csc^2 x - 1) \quad \text{by (1)}$$

$$= \cos^2 x \cdot \cot^2 x \qquad \text{by (8)}$$

EXAMPLE 7

306. Prove the identity

$$\cos^2 x = (1 - \sin x)(1 + \sin x).$$

306. $\cos^2 x = 1 - \sin^2 x$

$$= (1 - \sin x)(1 + \sin x) \quad \text{by (6)}$$

EXAMPLE 8

307. Prove the identity

$$\frac{\sin x}{1 + \cos x} = \frac{1 - \cos x}{\sin x}.$$

307. It is often helpful to start with a known identity. We shall use (6)

$$\sin^2 x + \cos^2 x = 1.$$

Therefore

$$\sin^2 x \sin^2 x = 1 - \cos^2 x.$$

Therefore

$$\sin^2 x = (1 - \cos x)(1 + \cos x)$$

and

$$\frac{\sin^2 x}{\sin x (1 + \cos x)} = \frac{(1 - \cos x)(1 + \cos x)}{\sin x (1 + \cos x)}$$

if $\sin x \neq 0$ and $1 + \cos x \neq 0$. Thus

$$\frac{\sin x}{1 + \cos x} = \frac{1 - \cos x}{\sin x}.$$

EXAMPLE 9

308. Prove the identity

$$1 - 2 \sin^2 x = \frac{\cot x - \tan x}{\cot x + \tan x}.$$

308. $\dfrac{\cot x - \tan x}{\cot x + \tan x}$

$$= \frac{\dfrac{\cos x}{\sin x} - \dfrac{\sin x}{\cos x}}{\dfrac{\cos x}{\sin x} + \dfrac{\sin x}{\cos x}}$$

by (4) and (5)
($\sin x \neq 0$,
$\cos x \neq 0$)

$$= \frac{\dfrac{\cos^2 x - \sin^2 x}{\sin x \cos x}}{\dfrac{\cos^2 x + \sin^2 x}{\sin x \cos x}}$$

$$= \cos^2 x - \sin^2 x \qquad \text{by (6)}$$
$$= 1 - \sin^2 x - \sin^2 x \quad \text{by (6)}$$
$$= 1 - 2 \sin^2 x$$

EXAMPLE 10

309. Prove the identity

$$(\csc x - \cot x)^2 = \frac{1 - \cos x}{1 + \cos x}.$$

309. $(\csc x - \cot x)^2 =$

$$\left(\frac{1}{\sin x} - \frac{\cos x}{\sin x} \right)^2 \quad (\sin x \neq 0)$$

$$= \frac{(1 - \cos x)^2}{\sin^2 x} \qquad \text{by (1) and (5)}$$

$$= \frac{(1 - \cos x)^2}{1 - \cos^2 x} \qquad \text{by (6)}$$

$$= \frac{(1 - \cos x)^2}{(1 - \cos x)(1 + \cos x)}$$

$$= \frac{1 - \cos x}{1 + \cos x}$$

If you cannot answer the following questions correctly, review the appropriate frames.

1. Draw a diagram and derive the three Pythagorean (or square) identities.

2. List the eight basic trigonometric identities.

3. Prove the identity $1 + \cos x = \dfrac{\sin^2 x}{1 - \cos x}$.

Answers are at end of book.

10 Addition Formulas

Previously we worked only with identities containing a single variable x. In this chapter we shall establish some fundamental identities that involve two or more real numbers or multiples of real numbers.

We shall let $\alpha, \beta, \ldots, \theta$, etc. represent real numbers. Our first six identities involve expressions for $\sin(\alpha + \beta)$, $\cos(\alpha + \beta)$, $\tan(\alpha + \beta)$, $\sin(\alpha - \beta)$, $\cos(\alpha - \beta)$, and $\tan(\alpha - \beta)$. These are the so-called **addition formulas.**

Upon completing this chapter, you should be able to

I. Derive and write the addition identities:

(1) $\cos(\alpha - \beta) = \cos\alpha \cos\beta + \sin\alpha \sin\beta$

(2) $\cos(\alpha + \beta) = \cos\alpha \cos\beta - \sin\alpha \sin\beta$

(3) $\sin(\alpha + \beta) = \sin\alpha \cos\beta + \cos\alpha \sin\beta$

(4) $\sin(\alpha - \beta) = \sin\alpha \cos\beta - \cos\alpha \sin\beta$

(5) $\tan(\alpha + \beta) = \dfrac{\tan\alpha + \tan\beta}{1 - \tan\alpha \tan\beta}$

(6) $\tan(\alpha - \beta) = \dfrac{\tan\alpha - \tan\beta}{1 + \tan\alpha \tan\beta}$

II. Prove other identities using these six addition identities.

III. Use the addition identities to calculate the values of $\sin\dfrac{\pi}{12}$, $\cos\dfrac{7\pi}{8}$, etc.

310. We first establish the identity for $\cos(\alpha - \beta)$.

Look at the diagram and label the coordinates of the points P and Q in terms of $\cos\alpha$, $\sin\alpha$, $\cos\beta$, and $\sin\beta$. The circle with radius r is centered at the origin of a rectangular coordinate system.

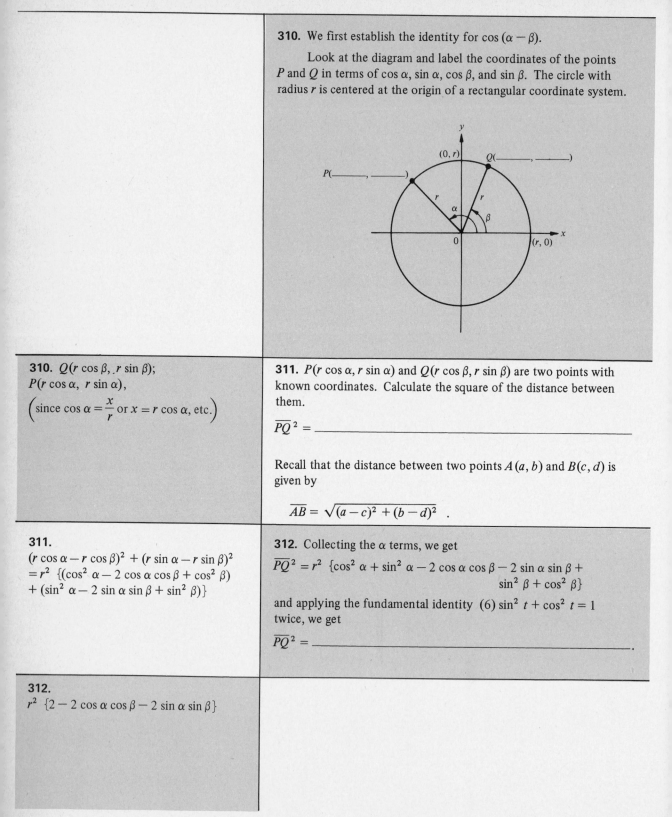

310. $Q(r\cos\beta,\, r\sin\beta)$;
$P(r\cos\alpha,\, r\sin\alpha)$,

$\left(\text{since } \cos\alpha = \dfrac{x}{r} \text{ or } x = r\cos\alpha, \text{ etc.}\right)$

311. $P(r\cos\alpha, r\sin\alpha)$ and $Q(r\cos\beta, r\sin\beta)$ are two points with known coordinates. Calculate the square of the distance between them.

$\overline{PQ}^2 = $ _____

Recall that the distance between two points $A(a, b)$ and $B(c, d)$ is given by

$$\overline{AB} = \sqrt{(a - c)^2 + (b - d)^2}\ .$$

311.
$(r\cos\alpha - r\cos\beta)^2 + (r\sin\alpha - r\sin\beta)^2$
$= r^2\ \{(\cos^2\alpha - 2\cos\alpha\cos\beta + \cos^2\beta)$
$+ (\sin^2\alpha - 2\sin\alpha\sin\beta + \sin^2\beta)\}$

312. Collecting the α terms, we get
$$\overline{PQ}^2 = r^2\ \{\cos^2\alpha + \sin^2\alpha - 2\cos\alpha\cos\beta - 2\sin\alpha\sin\beta + \sin^2\beta + \cos^2\beta\}$$
and applying the fundamental identity (6) $\sin^2 t + \cos^2 t = 1$ twice, we get

$\overline{PQ}^2 = $ _____.

312.
$r^2\ \{2 - 2\cos\alpha\cos\beta - 2\sin\alpha\sin\beta\}$

313. In the diagram, label the angle $\alpha - \beta$.

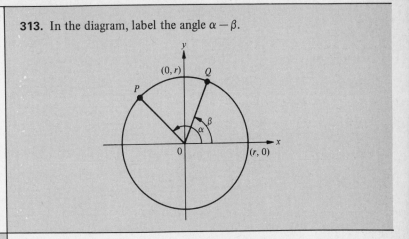

313.

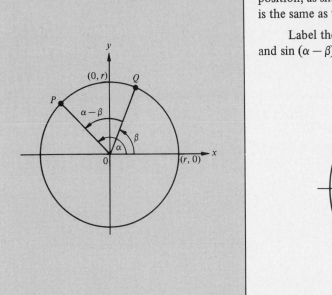

314. If we rotate the angle $\alpha - \beta$ clockwise until it is in standard position, as shown on the diagram, the distance between P' and Q' is the same as the distance $\overline{PQ}$, as shown in frame 313.

Label the coordinates of P' and Q' in terms of r, $\cos(\alpha - \beta)$, and $\sin(\alpha - \beta)$.

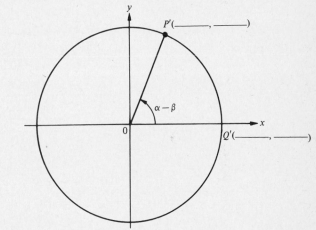

314.

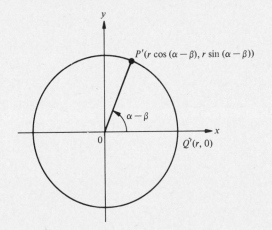

315. Calculate the square of the distance between P' and Q' in terms of the coordinates of P' and Q'.

$$\overline{P'Q'}\,^2 = \underline{\hspace{8cm}}$$

$$\underline{\hspace{10cm}}$$

315.
$(r - r \cos (\alpha - \beta))^2 + (r \sin (\alpha - \beta))^2 =$
$r^2 - 2r^2 \cos (\alpha - \beta) + r^2 \cos^2 (\alpha - \beta) +$
$r^2 \sin^2 (\alpha - \beta) = r^2 \{1 - 2 \cos (\alpha - \beta) +$
$\cos^2 (\alpha - \beta) + \sin^2 (\alpha - \beta)\}$

316. Again by using the fundamental identity (6) $\sin^2 t + \cos^2 t = 1$, we get

$$\overline{P'Q'}\,^2 = \underline{\hspace{7cm}} .$$

---

316. $r^2 \{2 - 2 \cos (\alpha - \beta)\}$

317. Since $\overline{PQ} = \overline{P'Q'}$, we get our desired identity by setting $\overline{PQ}\,^2 = \overline{P'Q'}\,^2$, and solving for $\cos (\alpha - \beta)$.

$$\overline{PQ}\,^2 = \text{(a)} \underline{\hspace{3cm}} = \text{(b)} \underline{\hspace{3cm}} = \overline{P'Q'}\,^2;$$

hence

$$(9)\ \cos (\alpha - \beta) = \text{(c)} \underline{\hspace{6cm}} .$$

317.
(a) $r^2 \{2 - 2 \cos \alpha \cos \beta - 2 \sin \alpha \sin \beta\}$,
(b) $r^2 \{2 - 2 \cos (\alpha - \beta)\}$,
(c) $\cos \alpha \cos \beta + \sin \alpha \sin \beta$

318. In establishing the formula, we pictured the angles in the first and second quadrants. There was nothing special about these, and we could have chosen α and β in any quadrants. Therefore, for any real numbers α and β,

$$(9)\ \cos (\alpha - \beta) = \underline{\hspace{6cm}} .$$

---

318. $\cos \alpha \cos \beta + \sin \alpha \sin \beta$

Proof of the identity

(9) $\cos(\alpha - \beta) = \cos\alpha\cos\beta + \sin\alpha\sin\beta$

The points where the terminal sides of the angles α and β intersect the circumference of the circle of radius r are labeled P and Q, respectively. If the center of the circle is at the origin, the coordinates of P and Q are $P(r\cos\alpha, r\sin\alpha)$ and $Q(r\cos\beta, r\sin\beta)$.

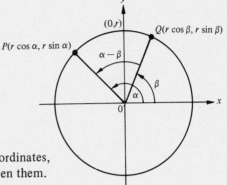

The points P and Q have known coordinates, so we may calculate the distance between them.

$$\overline{PQ}^2 = (r\cos\alpha - r\cos\beta)^2 + (r\sin\alpha - r\sin\beta)^2$$
$$= r^2(\cos^2\alpha - 2\cos\alpha\cos\beta + \cos^2\beta) + r^2(\sin^2\alpha - 2\sin\alpha\sin\beta + \sin^2\beta)$$
$$= r^2\{\cos^2\alpha + \sin^2\alpha - 2\cos\alpha\cos\beta - 2\sin\alpha\sin\beta + \cos^2\beta + \sin^2\beta\}.$$

And replacing $\cos^2\alpha + \sin^2\alpha$ and $\cos^2\beta + \sin^2\beta$ by 1, we get

$$\overline{PQ}^2 = r^2\{2 - 2\cos\alpha\cos\beta - 2\sin\alpha\sin\beta\}.$$

On the other hand, if we rotate the angle $\alpha - \beta$ until it is in standard position, as shown in the diagram, the distance between P' and Q' is the same as the distance $\overline{PQ}$. The coordinates of P' and Q' are $P'(r\cos(\alpha-\beta), r\sin(\alpha-\beta))$ and $Q'(r, 0)$, respectively. And in terms of the coordinates of P' and Q',

$$\overline{P'Q'}^2 = (r - r\cos(\alpha-\beta))^2 + (r\sin(\alpha-\beta))^2$$
$$= r^2 - 2r^2\cos(\alpha-\beta) + r^2\cos^2(\alpha-\beta) + r^2\sin^2(a-\beta)$$
$$= r^2\{1 - 2\cos(\alpha-\beta) + \cos^2(\alpha-\beta) + \sin^2(\alpha-\beta)\}.$$

And if we replace $\cos^2(\alpha-\beta) + \sin^2(\alpha-\beta)$ by 1, we get

$$\overline{P'Q'}^2 = r^2\{2 - 2\cos(\alpha-\beta)\}.$$

Since $\overline{PQ} = \overline{P'Q'}$, we get our desired identity by setting $\overline{PQ}^2 = \overline{P'Q'}^2$, and solving for $\cos(\alpha-\beta)$, we get

$$\overline{PQ}^2 = r^2\{2 - 2\cos\alpha\cos\beta - 2\sin\alpha\sin\beta\} = r^2\{2 - 2\cos(\alpha-\beta)\} = \overline{P'Q'}^2$$

or $2 - 2\cos\alpha\cos\beta - 2\sin\alpha\sin\beta = 2 - 2\cos(\alpha-\beta)$ and (9) $\cos(\alpha - \sigma)$
$= \cos\alpha\cos\beta + \sin a\sin\beta$.

199

EXAMPLE 1

319. We established earlier a formula for $\cos(\pi - \theta)$ by direct methods. Let $\alpha = \pi$ and $\beta = \theta$ and show that the result is the same.

$\cos(\pi - \theta) = $ _____ _____ + _____ _____ = _____

319.

$\cos \pi \cos \theta + \sin \pi \sin \theta =$
$(-1) \cos \theta + 0 \cdot \sin \theta = -\cos \theta$

EXAMPLE 2

320. We also established a formula for $\cos(\frac{\pi}{2} - \theta)$. Use identity (9) to show that it gives the same result.

$\cos(\frac{\pi}{2} - \theta) = $ _____

320.

$\cos \frac{\pi}{2} \cos \theta + \sin \frac{\pi}{2} \sin \theta$
$= 0 \cdot \cos \theta + 1 \cdot \sin \theta = \sin \theta.$

For a comparison, see frame 204 in chapter 4.

EXAMPLE 3

321. Finally, we established a formula for $\cos(-\theta)$. Let $\alpha = 0$, and use identity (9) to show the result is the same.

$\cos(-\theta) = $ _____

321.

$\cos(0 - \theta) = \cos 0 \cos \theta + \sin 0 \sin \theta$
$= 1 \cdot \cos \theta + 0 \cdot \sin \theta$
$= \cos \theta.$

See frame 179 of chapter 4 for comparison.

EXERCISE 1

322. The six addition formulas, like the first eight fundamental identities, are important and should be memorized. Complete the addition formula.

(9) $\cos(\alpha - \beta) = $ _____

---

322. $\cos \alpha \cos \beta + \sin \alpha \sin \beta.$

NOTE: As a memory device, $\cos(\alpha \ minus \ \beta) = \cos \alpha \cos \beta \ plus$ $\sin \alpha \sin \beta.$

323. We can use the reduction formulas we proved earlier to establish the five remaining addition formulas from the one we have just derived.

Since $\cos(-\theta) = $ _____ and $\sin(-\theta) = $ _____ for all θ, we can establish the identity for $\cos(\alpha + \beta)$ by replacing β by $-\beta$ in identity (9).

---

323. $\cos \theta; -\sin \theta$

324. Therefore, from (9),

(10) $\cos (\alpha + \beta) =$ _____ .

---

324. $\cos (\alpha - (-\beta)) =$
$\cos \alpha \cos (-\beta) + \sin \alpha \sin (-\beta)$
$= \cos \alpha \cos \beta + \sin \alpha (-\sin \beta)$
$= \cos \alpha \cos \beta - \sin \alpha \sin \beta$

325. Note this time that

(10) $\cos (\alpha \text{ } plus \text{ } \beta) = \cos \alpha \cos \beta$ _____ $\sin \alpha \sin \beta$.

   Use identity (10) to show that

$\cos (\pi + \theta) =$ _____ .

NOTE: The result is the same as we obtained earlier.

---

325. minus;
$\cos \pi \cos \theta - \sin \pi \sin \theta$
$= (-1) \cos \theta - 0 \cdot \sin \theta$
$= -\cos \theta$.

See frame 177 of chapter 4 for comparison.

326. Use identity (10) to show that

$\cos (\dfrac{\pi}{2} + \theta) =$ _____

for all θ as before.

326.
$\cos (\dfrac{\pi}{2}) \cos \theta - \sin (\dfrac{\pi}{2}) \sin \theta$
$= 0 \cdot \cos \theta - 1 \cdot \sin \theta$
$= -\sin \theta$.

See frame 205 of chapter 4 for comparison.

327. If you remember that

(9) $\cos (\alpha - \beta) = \cos \alpha \cos \beta + \sin \alpha \sin \beta$

you can always get the formula

(10) $\cos (\alpha + \beta) = $ **(a)** _____

by replacing **(b)** ___ by **(c)** ___ in (9).

327.
(a) $\cos \alpha \cos \beta - \sin \alpha \sin \beta$,
(b) β,   **(c)** $-\beta$

EXERCISE 2

328. $\cos (\alpha - \beta) =$ _____

   $\cos (\alpha + \beta) =$ _____

---

328. $\cos \alpha \cos \beta + \sin \alpha \sin \beta$;
$\cos \alpha \cos \beta - \sin \alpha \sin \beta$

329. Now we shall establish the formulas for $\sin(\alpha + \beta)$ and $\sin(\alpha - \beta)$.

To establish the formula for $\sin(\alpha + \beta)$ we shall use (9) and the fact derived in the section on reduction formulas that

$$\cos\left(\frac{\pi}{2} - \theta\right) = \underline{\hspace{3cm}}, \text{ and}$$

$$\sin\left(\frac{\pi}{2} - \theta\right) = \underline{\hspace{3cm}} \text{ for all } \theta.$$

---

329. $\sin\theta$; $\cos\theta$.

If you had difficulty, see frames 200 to 204 of chapter 4.

---

330. From the second equation in frame 329, we have

$$\sin(\alpha + \beta) = \cos\left(\frac{\pi}{2} - (\alpha + \beta)\right)$$

$$= \cos\left(\left(\frac{\pi}{2} - \alpha\right) - \beta\right)$$

and by (9)

$$(11)\ \sin(\alpha + \beta) = \cos\left(\left(\frac{\pi}{2} - \alpha\right) - \beta\right)$$

$$= \underline{\hspace{6cm}}.$$

330.

$$\cos\left(\frac{\pi}{2} - \alpha\right)\cos\beta + \sin\left(\frac{\pi}{2} - \alpha\right)\sin\beta$$

$$= \sin\alpha\cos\beta + \cos\alpha\sin\beta$$

since $\cos\left(\frac{\pi}{2} - \alpha\right) = \sin\alpha$ and

$$\sin\left(\frac{\pi}{2} - \alpha\right) = \cos\alpha\ .$$

SUMMARY

Proof of the identity

$(11)\ \sin(\alpha + \beta) = \sin\alpha\cos\beta + \cos\alpha\sin\beta$.

Since $\cos\left(\frac{\pi}{2} - \theta\right) = \sin\theta$ for all θ, we can write

$$\sin(\alpha + \beta) = \cos\left(\frac{\pi}{2} - (\alpha + \beta)\right)$$

$$= \cos\left(\left(\frac{\pi}{2} - \alpha\right) - \beta\right).$$

Now we can apply

(9) $\cos(\alpha - \beta) = \cos\alpha\cos\beta + \sin\alpha\sin\beta$ for all α and β.

We get

$$\sin(\alpha + \beta) = \cos\left(\left(\frac{\pi}{2} - \alpha\right) - \beta\right) = \cos\left(\frac{\pi}{2} - \alpha\right)\cos\beta + \sin\left(\frac{\pi}{2} - \alpha\right)\sin\beta.$$

And, finally, we get

(11) $\sin(\alpha + \beta) = \sin\alpha\cos\beta + \cos\alpha\sin\beta$

since $\cos\left(\frac{\pi}{2} - \alpha\right) = \sin\alpha$ and $\sin\left(\frac{\pi}{2} - \alpha\right) = \cos\alpha$.

---

	331. Use identity (11) to show that $\sin(\pi + \theta) = $ _____ for all θ as before.
331. $\sin\pi\cos\theta + \cos\pi\sin\theta$ $= 0 \cdot \cos\theta + (-1)\sin\theta$ $= -\sin\theta$. See frame 177 of chapter 4 for a comparison.	**332.** Use identity (11) to show that $\sin\left(\frac{\pi}{2} + \theta\right) = $ _____ for all θ as before.
332. $\sin\dfrac{\pi}{2}\cos\theta + \cos\dfrac{\pi}{2}\sin\theta$ $= 1 \cdot \cos\theta + 0 \cdot \sin\theta$ $= \cos\theta$. See frame 205 of chapter 4 for comparison.	**333.** Again, if you remember that (9) $\cos(\alpha - \beta) = \cos\alpha\cos\beta + \sin\alpha\sin\beta$ and that $\sin\theta = \cos\left(\frac{\pi}{2} - \theta\right)$ and $\sin\left(\frac{\pi}{2} - \theta\right) = \cos\theta$ you can establish the identity (11) $\sin(\alpha + \beta) = $ _____.
333. $\sin\alpha\cos\beta + \cos\alpha\sin\beta$, since $\sin(\alpha + \beta) = \cos\left(\dfrac{\pi}{2} - (\alpha + \beta)\right)$ $\qquad = \cos\left(\left(\dfrac{\pi}{2} - \alpha\right) - \beta\right)$ We apply (9) with $\dfrac{\pi}{2} - \alpha$ replacing α.	

334. Now we can establish $\sin(\alpha - \beta)$ by replacing

(a) _____ by (b) _____ in

(c) _____ .

---

334. (a) β, (b) $-\beta$,
(c) (11) $\sin(\alpha + \beta) =$
$\sin \alpha \cos \beta + \cos \alpha \sin \beta$

335. If we replace β by $-\beta$ in (11) we get

(12) $\sin(\alpha - \beta) = \sin(\alpha + (-\beta))$

$= $ _____ .

---

335. $\sin \alpha \cos(-\beta) + \cos \alpha \sin(-\beta)$
$= \sin \alpha \cos \beta + \cos \alpha (-\sin \beta)$
$= \sin \alpha \cos \beta - \cos \alpha \sin \beta$

336. Note that in the formulas for $\sin(\alpha + \beta)$ and $\sin(\alpha - \beta)$, unlike $\cos(\alpha - \beta)$ and $\cos(\alpha + \beta)$,

(11) $\sin(\alpha \text{ plus } \beta) = \sin \alpha \cos \beta \underset{\text{(plus, minus)}}{\underline{\hspace{2cm}}} \cos \alpha \sin \beta$, and ,

(12) $\sin(\alpha \text{ minus } \beta) = \sin \alpha \cos \beta \underline{\hspace{2cm}} \cos \alpha \sin \beta$.

---

336. plus;
minus

337. Use identity (12) to show that

$\sin(\pi - \theta) = $ _____
for all θ as before.

---

337. $\sin \pi \cos \theta - \cos \pi \sin \theta$
$= 0 \cdot \cos \theta - (-1) \sin \theta$
$= \sin \theta$.

See frame 173 of chapter 4 for comparison.

338. Use identity (12) to show that

$\sin(\frac{\pi}{2} - \theta) = $ _____
for all θ as before.

---

338. $\sin \frac{\pi}{2} \cos \theta - \cos \frac{\pi}{2} \sin \theta$

$= 1 \cdot \cos \theta - 0 \cdot \sin \theta = \cos \theta$.

See frame 204 of chapter 4 for comparison.

339. Finally, use identity (12) to show that

$\sin(-\theta) = $ _____
for all θ as before.

339.
$\sin(0 - \theta) = \sin 0 \cos \theta - \cos 0 \sin \theta$
$\qquad = 0 \cdot \cos \theta - 1 \cdot \sin \theta$
$\qquad = -\sin \theta$.

See frame 180 of chapter 4 for comparison.

340. $\sin (\alpha + \beta) =$ _____

$\sin (\alpha - \beta) =$ _____

---

340. $\sin \alpha \cos \beta + \cos \alpha \sin \beta$;
$\sin \alpha \cos \beta - \cos \alpha \sin \beta$

EXERCISE 3

341.

(9) $\cos (\alpha - \beta) =$ _____

(10) $\cos (\alpha + \beta) =$ _____

(11) $\sin (\alpha + \beta) =$ _____

(12) $\sin (\alpha - \beta) =$ _____

---

341. (9) $\cos \alpha \cos \beta + \sin \alpha \sin \beta$;
(10) $\cos \alpha \cos \beta - \sin \alpha \sin \beta$;
(11) $\sin \alpha \cos \beta + \cos \alpha \sin \beta$;
(12) $\sin \alpha \cos \beta - \cos \alpha \sin \beta$.

If you had difficulty, review frames 310 to 340 until you can write these formulas quickly.

342. In frames 60 to 65 of chapter 2, Definitions of Trigonometric Functions, we drew the diagram shown and found that

$\sin \dfrac{\pi}{3} =$ **(a)** _____,

$\cos \dfrac{\pi}{3} =$ **(b)** _____,

$\tan \dfrac{\pi}{3} =$ **(c)** _____.

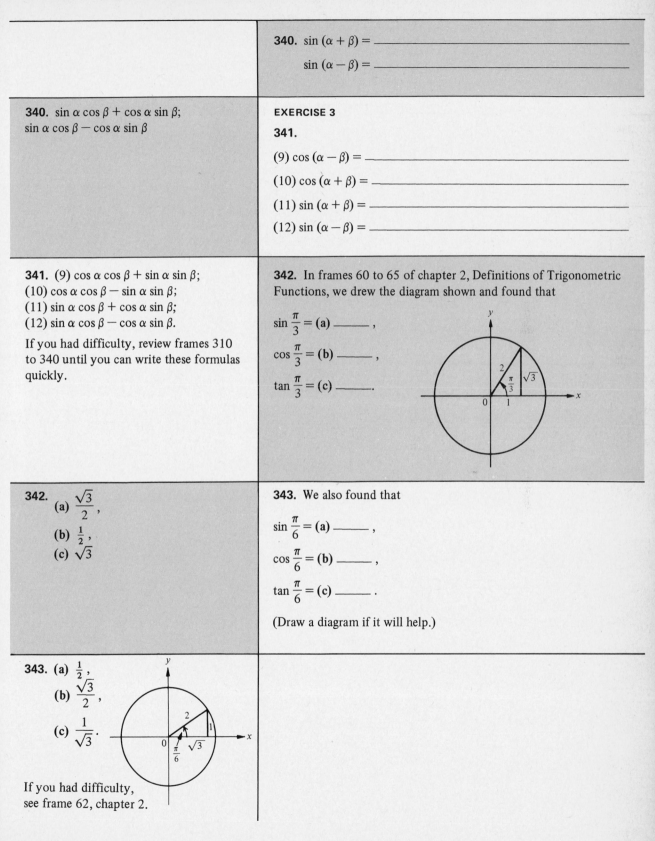

342.
(a) $\dfrac{\sqrt{3}}{2}$,

(b) $\dfrac{1}{2}$,

(c) $\sqrt{3}$

343. We also found that

$\sin \dfrac{\pi}{6} =$ **(a)** _____,

$\cos \dfrac{\pi}{6} =$ **(b)** _____,

$\tan \dfrac{\pi}{6} =$ **(c)** _____.

(Draw a diagram if it will help.)

---

343. (a) $\dfrac{1}{2}$,

(b) $\dfrac{\sqrt{3}}{2}$,

(c) $\dfrac{1}{\sqrt{3}}$.

If you had difficulty,
see frame 62, chapter 2.

344. Finally,

$$\sin \frac{\pi}{4} = \text{(a)} \underline{\quad\quad},$$

$$\cos \frac{\pi}{4} = \text{(b)} \underline{\quad\quad},$$

$$\tan \frac{\pi}{4} = \text{(c)} \underline{\quad\quad}.$$

---

344. (a) $\dfrac{1}{\sqrt{2}}$,

(b) $\dfrac{1}{\sqrt{2}}$,

(c) 1.

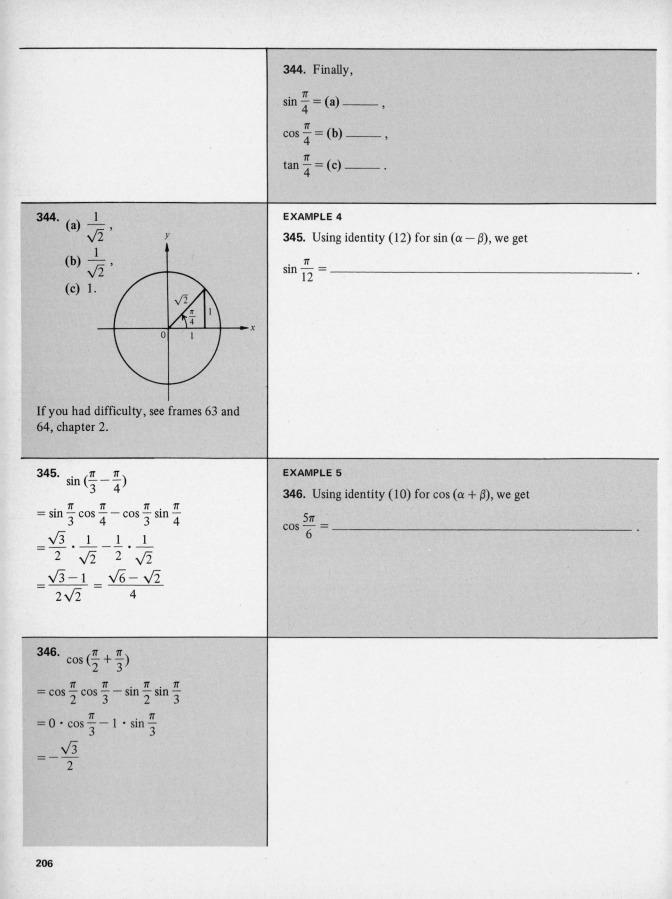

If you had difficulty, see frames 63 and 64, chapter 2.

EXAMPLE 4

345. Using identity (12) for $\sin(\alpha - \beta)$, we get

$$\sin \frac{\pi}{12} = \underline{\hspace{8cm}}.$$

345.
$$\sin\left(\frac{\pi}{3} - \frac{\pi}{4}\right)$$

$$= \sin \frac{\pi}{3} \cos \frac{\pi}{4} - \cos \frac{\pi}{3} \sin \frac{\pi}{4}$$

$$= \frac{\sqrt{3}}{2} \cdot \frac{1}{\sqrt{2}} - \frac{1}{2} \cdot \frac{1}{\sqrt{2}}$$

$$= \frac{\sqrt{3} - 1}{2\sqrt{2}} = \frac{\sqrt{6} - \sqrt{2}}{4}$$

EXAMPLE 5

346. Using identity (10) for $\cos(\alpha + \beta)$, we get

$$\cos \frac{5\pi}{6} = \underline{\hspace{8cm}}.$$

346.
$$\cos\left(\frac{\pi}{2} + \frac{\pi}{3}\right)$$

$$= \cos \frac{\pi}{2} \cos \frac{\pi}{3} - \sin \frac{\pi}{2} \sin \frac{\pi}{3}$$

$$= 0 \cdot \cos \frac{\pi}{3} - 1 \cdot \sin \frac{\pi}{3}$$

$$= -\frac{\sqrt{3}}{2}$$

TAN $(\alpha + \beta)$ AND TAN $(\alpha - \beta)$

347. Finally, we can establish the formulas for $\tan(\alpha + \beta)$ and $\tan(\alpha - \beta)$ from the four addition formulas already established and the quotient identity

(4) $\tan \theta = $ _____ .

---

347. $\dfrac{\sin \theta}{\cos \theta}$

348. When is the identity

(4) $\tan \theta = \dfrac{\sin \theta}{\cos \theta}$ undefined? **(a)** _____

That is, the identity $\tan \theta = \dfrac{\sin \theta}{\cos \theta}$ is undefined

if $\theta = $ **(b)** _____ . And if we use this identity to prove our addition formula, then the addition formula

will also be undefined at **(c)** _____ ,

that is, at $\theta = $ **(d)** _____ .

---

348. (a) $\cos \theta = 0$,

(b) $\theta = \dfrac{\pi}{2} \pm n\pi$, $n = 0, 1, 2, ...,$,

(c) $\cos \theta = 0$,

(d) $\dfrac{\pi}{2} \pm n\pi$, $n = 0, 1, 2, ...$

349. If $\cos(\alpha + \beta) \neq 0$,

$\tan(\alpha + \beta) = $ _____ by identity (4)

$= $ _____ by identities (10) and (11).

---

349. $\dfrac{\sin(\alpha + \beta)}{\cos(\alpha + \beta)}$,

$\dfrac{\sin \alpha \cos \beta + \cos \alpha \sin \beta}{\cos \alpha \cos \beta - \sin \alpha \sin \beta}$

350. When $\cos \alpha \cos \beta \neq 0$, we can divide each term of the numerator and denominator in

(13) $\tan (\alpha + \beta) = \dfrac{\sin \alpha \cos \beta + \cos \alpha \sin \beta}{\cos \alpha \cos \beta - \sin \alpha \sin \beta}$

by $\cos \alpha \cos \beta$, and get $\tan (\alpha + \beta)$

$=$ _____

_____

by the identities $\tan \alpha = \dfrac{\sin \alpha}{\cos \alpha}$ and $\tan \beta = \dfrac{\sin \beta}{\cos \beta}$.

---

350. $\dfrac{\dfrac{\sin \alpha \cos \beta}{\cos \alpha \cos \beta} + \dfrac{\cos \alpha \sin \beta}{\cos \alpha \cos \beta}}{\dfrac{\cos \alpha \cos \beta}{\cos \alpha \cos \beta} - \dfrac{\sin \alpha \sin \beta}{\cos \alpha \cos \beta}}$;

$\dfrac{\tan \alpha \cdot 1 + 1 \cdot \tan \beta}{1 - \tan \alpha \tan \beta}$

---

351. We put two restrictions on our identity. We assumed that

$\cos (\alpha + \beta) \neq 0$ and that _____ .

---

351. $\cos \alpha \cos \beta \neq 0$

---

352. Thus, the identity

(13) $\tan (\alpha + \beta) = \dfrac{\tan \alpha + \tan \beta}{1 - \tan \alpha \tan \beta}$

is undefined for all values of α and β for which

_____ , _____ , or _____ .

---

352. $\cos (\alpha + \beta) = 0$; $\cos \alpha = 0$
$\cos \beta = 0$

Proof of the identity

(13) $\tan(\alpha + \beta) = \dfrac{\tan \alpha + \tan \beta}{1 - \tan \alpha \tan \beta}$

If $\cos(\alpha + \beta) \neq 0$, we can write

$\tan(\alpha + \beta) = \dfrac{\sin(\alpha + \beta)}{\cos(\alpha + \beta)}$ \qquad by (4)

$= \dfrac{\sin \alpha \cos \beta + \cos \alpha \sin \beta}{\cos \alpha \cos \beta - \sin \alpha \sin \beta}$ \quad by (10 and (11).

And for all values of α and β for which $\cos \alpha \cos \beta \neq 0$, we can divide each term of the numerator and denominator above by $\cos \alpha \cos \beta$, and get

(13) $\tan(\alpha + \beta) = \dfrac{\dfrac{\sin \alpha \cos \beta}{\cos \alpha \cos \beta} + \dfrac{\cos \alpha \sin \beta}{\cos \alpha \cos \beta}}{\dfrac{\cos \alpha \cos \beta}{\cos \alpha \cos \beta} - \dfrac{\sin \alpha \sin \beta}{\cos \alpha \cos \beta}}$

$= \dfrac{\tan \alpha \cdot 1 + 1 \cdot \tan \beta}{1 - \tan \alpha \tan \beta}$ \quad by identities $\tan \alpha = \dfrac{\sin \alpha}{\cos \alpha}$ and $\tan \beta = \dfrac{\sin \beta}{\cos \beta}$.

$= \dfrac{\tan \alpha + \tan \beta}{1 - \tan \alpha \tan \beta}$,

for all values of α and β for which $\cos(\alpha + \beta) \neq 0$, $\cos \alpha \neq 0$, and $\cos \beta \neq 0$, that is, for all values of α and β except α, β, or $\alpha + \beta = \dfrac{\pi}{2} \pm n\pi$, $n = 0, 1, 2, ...$).

---

353. Use identity (13) to show that

$\tan(\pi + \theta) = $ _____ for all θ,

$\theta \neq \dfrac{\pi}{2} \pm n\pi$, $n = 0, 1, 2, ...$, as before.

---

353. $\dfrac{\tan \pi + \tan \theta}{1 - \tan \pi \tan \theta}$

$= \dfrac{0 + \tan \theta}{1 - 0 \cdot \tan \theta}$

$= \tan \theta$.

See frame 177 of chapter 4 for comparison.

354. Now use identity (13) to show that

$\tan{(\frac{\pi}{2} + \theta)} = $ _____ for all θ as before.

---

354. It cannot be done.

The identity is *not* valid here, since $\tan{\frac{\pi}{2}}$ is undefined. And the identity is valid only if $\tan{(\frac{\pi}{2} + \theta)}$, $\tan{\frac{\pi}{2}}$, and $\tan{\theta}$ are all defined.

355. Similarly, we can establish the formula for $\tan{(\alpha - \beta)}$ from

identities (4) $\tan{\alpha} = $ **(a)** _____ ,

(9) $\cos{(\alpha - \beta)} = $ **(b)** _____ ,

(12) $\sin{(\alpha - \beta)} = $ **(c)** _____ .

---

355. **(a)** $\dfrac{\sin{\alpha}}{\cos{\alpha}}$,

(b) $\cos{\alpha}\cos{\beta} + \sin{\alpha}\sin{\beta}$

(c) $\sin{\alpha}\cos{\beta} - \cos{\alpha}\sin{\beta}$

EXERCISE 4

356. Use identities (4), (9), and (12) to establish the formula for

$\tan{(\alpha - \beta)}$. _____

356.

(14) $\tan{(\alpha - \beta)} = \dfrac{\tan{\alpha} - \tan{\beta}}{1 + \tan{\alpha}\tan{\beta}}$

for all values of α and β for which $\cos{(\alpha - \beta)} \neq 0$, $\cos{\alpha} \neq 0$, and $\cos{\beta} \neq 0$.

If you had difficulty, see frames 347 to 352 and the summary on page 209 for guidance.

357. However, a simpler way to establish the formula for

$\tan{(\alpha - \beta)}$ is to replace **(a)** ____ by **(b)** ____ in the identity.

(13) $\tan{(\alpha + \beta)} = $ **(c)** _____ .

---

357. **(a)** β, **(b)** $-\beta$,

(c) $\dfrac{\tan{\alpha} + \tan{\beta}}{1 - \tan{\alpha}\tan{\beta}}$

358. Use identity (13) to establish the formula

(14) $\tan{(\alpha - \beta)} = $ _____ .

358.

$\tan{(\alpha + (-\beta))} = \dfrac{\tan{\alpha} + \tan{(-\beta)}}{1 - \tan{\alpha}\tan{(-\beta)}}$

$= \dfrac{\tan{\alpha} - \tan{\beta}}{1 + \tan{\alpha}\tan{\beta}}$,

since $\tan{(-\theta)} = -\tan{\theta}$ for all θ

359. Use identity (14) to show that

$\tan(\pi - \theta) = $ _____ for all θ,

$\theta \neq \dfrac{\pi}{2} \pm n\pi, n = 0, 1, 2, \dots$, as before.

---

359. $\dfrac{\tan \pi - \tan \theta}{1 + \tan \pi \cdot \tan \theta}$

$= \dfrac{0 - \tan \theta}{1 + 0 \cdot \tan \theta}$

$= -\tan \theta.$

See frame 173 of chapter 4 for comparison.

360. Use identity (14) to show that

$\tan(-\theta) = $ _____ for all θ,

$\theta \neq \dfrac{\pi}{2} \pm n\pi, n = 0, 1, 2, \dots$, as before.

360.
$\tan(0 - \theta) = \dfrac{\tan 0 - \tan \theta}{1 + \tan 0 \cdot \tan \theta}$

$\qquad\qquad = \dfrac{0 - \tan \theta}{1 + 0 \cdot \tan \theta}$

$\qquad\qquad = -\tan \theta$

See frame 179 of chapter 4 for comparison.

361. Can we use identity (14) to show that $\tan\left(\dfrac{\pi}{2} - \theta\right) = \cot \theta$?

_____

Why? _____

_____

---

361. No.

Tan $\dfrac{\pi}{2}$ is not defined, and the identity

(14) is valid only if $\tan\left(\dfrac{\pi}{2} - \theta\right)$, $\tan \dfrac{\pi}{2}$,

and $\tan \theta$ are all defined.

362.
$\tan(\alpha + \beta) = $ _____

$\tan(\alpha - \beta) = $ _____

---

362. $\dfrac{\tan \alpha + \tan \beta}{1 - \tan \alpha \tan \beta}$;

$\dfrac{\tan \alpha - \tan \beta}{1 + \tan \alpha \tan \beta}$

363.

(9) $\cos(\alpha - \beta) = $ _____

(10) $\cos(\alpha + \beta) = $ _____

(11) $\sin(\alpha + \beta) = $ _____

(12) $\sin(\alpha - \beta) = $ _____

(13) $\tan(\alpha + \beta) = $ _____

(14) $\tan(\alpha - \beta) = $ _____

363. (9) $\cos\alpha\cos\beta + \sin\alpha\sin\beta$,

(10) $\cos\alpha\cos\beta - \sin\alpha\sin\beta$,

(11) $\sin\alpha\cos\beta + \cos\alpha\sin\beta$,

(12) $\sin\alpha\cos\beta - \cos\alpha\sin\beta$,

(13) $\dfrac{\tan\alpha + \tan\beta}{1 - \tan\alpha\tan\beta}$,

(14) $\dfrac{\tan\alpha - \tan\beta}{1 + \tan\alpha\tan\beta}$.

If you had difficulty, review frames 310 to 362.

SUMMARY

List of Addition Formulas

(9) $\cos(\alpha - \beta) = \cos\alpha\cos\beta + \sin\alpha\sin\beta$

(10) $\cos(\alpha + \beta) = \cos\alpha\cos\beta - \sin\alpha\sin\beta$

(11) $\sin(\alpha + \beta) = \sin\alpha\cos\beta + \cos\alpha\sin\beta$

(12) $\sin(\alpha - \beta) = \sin\alpha\cos\beta - \cos\alpha\sin\beta$

(13) $\tan(\alpha + \beta) = \dfrac{\tan\alpha + \tan\beta}{1 - \tan\alpha\tan\beta}$

(14) $\tan(\alpha - \beta) = \dfrac{\tan\alpha - \tan\beta}{1 + \tan\alpha\tan\beta}$

364. Draw any diagrams you need, and use the distance formula to establish the addition formula for $\cos(\alpha - \beta)$.

364. $\cos(\alpha - \beta) = \cos\alpha\cos\beta + \sin\alpha\sin\beta$

If you had difficulty, see frames 310 to 318 and the summary.

365. Use the identity

$(9) \cos(\alpha - \beta) = \cos\alpha \cos\beta + \sin\alpha \sin\beta$

to establish the addition formula (10) for $\cos(\alpha + \beta)$.

---

365. If you had difficulty, see frames 323 and 324.

EXERCISE 8

366. Use identity (9) to establish the addition formula (11) for $\sin(\alpha + \beta)$.

---

366. If you had difficulty, see frames 329 and 330 and the summary.

367. Use the identity

(11) $\sin (\alpha + \beta) = \sin \alpha \cos \beta + \cos \alpha \sin \beta$

to establish the addition formula (12) for $\sin (\alpha - \beta)$.

---

367. If you had difficulty, see frames 334 and 335.

368. Use identities (4), (10), and (11) to establish the addition formula (13) for $\tan (\alpha + \beta)$.

---

368. If you had difficulty, see frames 347 to 352 and the summary.

369. Use the identity

$$(13)\ \tan{(\alpha + \beta)} = \frac{\tan{\alpha} + \tan{\beta}}{1 - \tan{\alpha}\tan{\beta}}$$

to establish the addition formula (14) for $\tan{(\alpha - \beta)}$.

369. If you had difficulty, see frame 358.

EXAMPLE 6

370. As with the eight fundamental identities, we can use the six addition formulas to prove other identities. The approach is the same.

Prove (A) $\sin(\alpha + \beta) + \sin(\alpha - \beta) = 2 \sin \alpha \cos \beta$.

370. If you had difficulty, go on to the next frame. It not, skip to frame 373.

371. There are many ways to prove an identity, but the most obvious way of proving that

(A) $\sin(\alpha + \beta) + \sin(\alpha - \beta) = 2\sin\alpha\cos\beta$

is to use the addition formulas (11) and (12) and replace

$\sin(\alpha + \beta)$ by _____

and $\sin(\alpha - \beta)$ by _____
in the left-hand side.

---

371. $\sin\alpha\cos\beta + \cos\alpha\sin\beta$; $\sin\alpha\cos\beta - \cos\alpha\sin\beta$

372. We get

$\sin(\alpha + \beta) + \sin(\alpha - \beta)$
$= \sin\alpha\cos\beta + \cos\alpha\sin\beta + \sin\alpha\cos\beta - \cos\alpha\sin\beta$

and collecting terms gives _____
and our identity is proved.

---

372. $2\sin\alpha\cos\beta$

EXAMPLE 7
373. Prove the identity

(E) $\sin\alpha + \sin\beta = 2\sin\left(\dfrac{\alpha + \beta}{2}\right)\cos\left(\dfrac{\alpha - \beta}{2}\right)$.

---

373. If you had difficulty, go on to the next frame. If not, skip to frame 377.

374. We shall use the identity

(A) $\sin(\theta + \phi) + \sin(\theta - \phi) = 2\sin\theta\cos\phi$

we have just proved.   Let (i) $\alpha = \theta + \phi$ and

(ii) $\beta = $ _____ .

---

374. $\theta - \phi$

375. Then, in terms of α and β,

$\theta = $ (a) _____ ,

since, from (i), $\theta = $ (b) _____ and, from

(ii), $\theta = $ (c) _____ .

Hence $2\theta = $ (d) _____ .

375.
(a) $\dfrac{\alpha + \beta}{2}$,

(b) $\alpha - \phi$,
(c) $\beta + \phi$,
(d) $\alpha + \beta$

376. Similarly, $\phi = $ _____ in terms of α and β, and substituting α and β into identity (A) in frame 374, we get

_____

and our identity is proved.

---

376. $\dfrac{\alpha - \beta}{2}$;

$\sin \alpha + \sin \beta = $

$2 \sin\left(\dfrac{\alpha + \beta}{2}\right) \cos\left(\dfrac{\alpha - \beta}{2}\right)$

EXAMPLE 8

377. As mentioned before there are many ways to prove an identity. In the following frames, your approach may vary from the answer given, and still be correct. Check the answer only *after* you have completed the proof or after you have tried and failed.

Prove the identity

(B) $\cos(\alpha + \beta) + \cos(\alpha - \beta) = 2 \cos \alpha \cos \beta$.

---

377. Substituting identities

(9) $\cos(\alpha - \beta) = \cos \alpha \cos \beta + \sin \alpha \sin \beta$

and

(10) $\cos(\alpha + \beta) = \cos \alpha \cos \beta - \sin \alpha \sin \beta$.

Substituting these in the left-hand side of (B), we get

$\cos(\alpha + \beta) + \cos(\alpha - \beta) = \cos \alpha \cos \beta - \sin \alpha \sin \beta + \cos \alpha \cos \beta + \sin \alpha \sin \beta$

and collecting terms on the left gives us $2 \cos \alpha \cos \beta$, and the identity is proved.

EXAMPLE 9

378. Prove the identity

(C) $\cos(\alpha + \beta) - \cos(\alpha - \beta) = 2 \sin \alpha \sin \beta$.

---

378. If you had difficulty, see frame 377. The proof differs only by a minus sign.

EXAMPLE 10

379. Prove the identity

(D) $\sin (\alpha + \beta) - \sin (\alpha - \beta) = 2 \cos \alpha \sin \beta$.

---

379. If you had difficulty, see frames 370 to 372. The proof differs only by a minus sign.

EXAMPLE 11

380. Prove the identity

(F) $\cos \alpha \cos \beta = 2 \cos \left(\dfrac{\alpha + \beta}{2}\right) \cos \left(\dfrac{\alpha - \beta}{2}\right)$.

---

380. We shall use the identity

(B) $\cos (\theta + \phi) + \cos (\theta - \phi) = 2 \cos \theta \cos \phi$.

Let $\alpha = \theta + \phi$ and $\beta = \theta - \phi$.

Then $\theta = \left(\dfrac{\alpha + \beta}{2}\right)$ and $\theta = \left(\dfrac{\alpha - \beta}{2}\right)$.

And substituting α and β into (B), we get

$\cos \alpha \cos \beta = 2 \cos \left(\dfrac{\alpha + \beta}{2}\right) \cos \left(\dfrac{\alpha - \beta}{2}\right)$.

And the identity is proved.

If you still have difficulty, see frames 373 to 376. The proof is similar.

EXAMPLE 12

381. Prove the identity

$$(G) \cos \alpha - \cos \beta = -2 \sin\left(\frac{\alpha + \beta}{2}\right) \sin\left(\frac{\alpha - \beta}{2}\right).$$

381. If you had difficulty, see identity (C) in frames 378 and see frame 380 for guidance.

EXAMPLE 13

382. Prove the identity

$$(H) \sin \alpha - \sin \beta = 2 \cos\left(\frac{\alpha + \beta}{2}\right) \sin\left(\frac{\alpha - \beta}{2}\right).$$

382. If you had difficulty, see frames 373 to 376 for guidance.

SUMMARY

List of Proven Identities

(A) $\sin(\alpha + \beta) + \sin(\alpha - \beta) = 2\sin\alpha\cos\beta$

(B) $\cos(\alpha + \beta) + \cos(\alpha - \beta) = 2\cos\alpha\cos\beta$

(C) $\cos(\alpha + \beta) - \cos(\alpha - \beta) = -2\sin\alpha\sin\beta$

(D) $\sin(\alpha + \beta) - \sin(\alpha - \beta) = 2\cos\alpha\sin\beta$

(E) $\sin\alpha + \sin\beta = 2\sin\left(\dfrac{\alpha+\beta}{2}\right)\cos\left(\dfrac{\alpha-\beta}{2}\right)$

(F) $\cos\alpha + \cos\beta = 2\cos\left(\dfrac{\alpha+\beta}{2}\right)\cos\left(\dfrac{\alpha-\beta}{2}\right)$

(G) $\cos\alpha - \cos\beta = -2\sin\left(\dfrac{\alpha+\beta}{2}\right)\sin\left(\dfrac{\alpha-\beta}{2}\right)$

(H) $\sin\alpha - \sin\beta = 2\cos\left(\dfrac{\alpha+\beta}{2}\right)\sin\left(\dfrac{\alpha-\beta}{2}\right)$

QUIZ

If you cannot answer the following questions correctly, review the appropriate frames.

1. Draw any diagrams you need and establish the addition formula for $\cos(\alpha - \beta)$.

2. Complete the following identities.

(a) $\cos(\alpha + \beta) = $ _____

(b) $\cos(\alpha - \beta) = $ _____

(c) $\tan(\alpha - \beta) = $ _____

3. Use the identity (a) above for $\cos(\alpha + \beta)$ to establish the addition formula for $\sin(\alpha + \beta)$.

4. Prove that $\cos\alpha + \cos\beta = 2\cos\left(\dfrac{\alpha+\beta}{2}\right)\cos\left(\dfrac{\alpha-\beta}{2}\right)$.

5. $\sin\dfrac{\pi}{12} = $ _____ $\cos\dfrac{\pi}{12} = $ _____

Answers are at end of book.

11 Formulas for Multiples and Fractions of θ

Upon completing this chapter, you should be able to

I. Derive and write the identities

(1) $\sin 2\theta = 2 \sin\theta \cos\theta$

(2) $\cos 2\theta = \begin{cases} \cos^2\theta - \sin^2\theta \\ 1 - 2\sin^2\theta \\ 2\cos^2\theta - 1 \end{cases}$

(3) $\tan 2\theta = \dfrac{2\tan\theta}{1 - \tan^2\theta}$

(4) $\sin^2\dfrac{\theta}{2} = \dfrac{1 - \cos\theta}{2}$

(5) $\cos^2\dfrac{\theta}{2} = \dfrac{1 + \cos\theta}{2}$

(6) $\tan\dfrac{\theta}{2} = \dfrac{\sin\theta}{1 + \cos\theta} = \dfrac{1 - \cos\theta}{\sin\theta}$

II. Use these identities to calculate values of $\sin\dfrac{2\pi}{3}$, $\cos\dfrac{\pi}{8}$, etc.

III. Use these identities to prove other identities.

DOUBLE-ANGLE FORMULAS

383. We can establish the formulas for $\sin 2\theta$, $\cos 2\theta$, and $\tan 2\theta$, by replacing both α and β by θ in the addition formulas (10), (11), and (13), respectively.

Use identity (11) for $\sin(\alpha + \beta)$ to prove that

(15) $\sin 2\theta = $ _____ for all θ.

383. $2\sin\theta\cos\theta$.

If you had difficulty, go on to the next frame. If not, skip to frame 385.

384. If we substitute θ for both α and β in (11) $\sin(\alpha + \beta) = \sin \alpha \cos \beta$, we get

$\sin 2\theta =$ _____ .
and collecting terms we get

(15) $\sin 2\theta =$ _____

---

384. $\sin \theta \cos \theta + \cos \theta \sin \theta$; $2 \sin \theta \cos \theta$

EXAMPLE 1
385. Using identity (15) for $\sin 2\theta$, we get $\sin$

$\sin \dfrac{2\pi}{3} =$ _____ .

---

385. $\sin \left(2 \cdot \dfrac{\pi}{3}\right) = 2 \sin \dfrac{\pi}{3} \cos \dfrac{\pi}{3}$

$= 2 \cdot \dfrac{\sqrt{3}}{2} \cdot \dfrac{1}{2}$

$= \dfrac{\sqrt{3}}{2}$

386. Use identity (10) for $\cos(\alpha + \beta)$ to prove that

(16) $\cos 2\theta =$ _____ for all θ.

---

386. $\cos^2 \theta - \sin^2 \theta$.

If you had difficulty, go on to the next frame. If not, skip to frame 388.

387. If we substitute θ for both α and β in

(10) $\cos(\alpha + \beta) = \cos \alpha \cos \beta - \sin \alpha \sin \beta$, we get

$\cos 2\theta$ _____ .

That is, (16) $\cos 2\theta =$ _____ .

---

387. $\cos \theta \cos \theta - \sin \theta \sin \theta$; $\cos^2 \theta - \sin^2 \theta$

EXAMPLE 2
388. Using identity (16) for $\cos 2\theta$, we get

$\cos \dfrac{2\pi}{3} =$ _____ .

---

388. $\cos \left(2 \cdot \dfrac{\pi}{3}\right) = \cos^2 \left(\dfrac{\pi}{3}\right) - \sin^2 \left(\dfrac{\pi}{3}\right)$

$= \left(\dfrac{1}{2}\right)^2 - \left(\dfrac{\sqrt{3}}{2}\right)^2$

$= \dfrac{1}{4} - \dfrac{3}{4} = -\dfrac{1}{2}$

EXAMPLE 3
389. Using identity (15) for $\sin 2\theta$ and the results of frames 385 to 388, we get

$\sin \dfrac{4\pi}{3} =$ _____ .

---

389. $\sin \left(2 \cdot \dfrac{2\pi}{3}\right) = 2 \sin \dfrac{2\pi}{3} \cos \dfrac{2\pi}{3}$

$= 2 \cdot \dfrac{\sqrt{3}}{2} \cdot \left(-\dfrac{1}{2}\right)$

$= -\dfrac{\sqrt{3}}{2}$

390. Complete the following double-angle formulas.

(15) $\sin 2\theta = $ _____

(16) $\cos 2\theta = $ _____

---

390. $2\sin\theta\cos\theta$;
$\cos^2\theta - \sin^2\theta$

391. Use identity (13) for $\tan(\alpha + \beta)$ to prove that

(17) $\tan 2\theta = $ _____ .

---

391. $\dfrac{2\tan\theta}{1 - \tan^2\theta}$.

If you had difficulty, go on to the next frame. If not, skip to frame 393.

392. If we substitute θ for both α and β in

(13) $\tan(\alpha + \beta) = \dfrac{\tan\alpha + \tan\beta}{1 - \tan\alpha\tan\beta}$

we get $\tan 2\theta = $ _____ .

That is, (17) $\tan 2\theta = $ _____ .

---

392. $\dfrac{\tan\theta + \tan\theta}{1 - \tan\theta\tan\theta}$;

$\dfrac{2\cdot\tan\theta}{1 - \tan^2\theta}$

EXAMPLE 4

393. Using identity (17) for $\tan 2\theta$, we get

$\tan\dfrac{2\pi}{3} = $ _____ .

---

393. $\tan\left(2\cdot\dfrac{\pi}{3}\right) = \dfrac{2\tan(\pi/3)}{1 - \tan^2(\pi/3)}$

$= \dfrac{2\cdot\sqrt{3}}{1 - (\sqrt{3})^2}$

$= \dfrac{2\sqrt{3}}{1 - 3} = -\sqrt{3}$

EXERCISE 1

394.

(15) $\sin 2\theta = $ **(a)** _____

(16) $\cos 2\theta = $ **(b)** _____

(17) $\tan 2\theta = $ **(c)** _____

---

394. (a) $2\sin\theta\cos\theta$,

(b) $\cos^2\theta - \sin^2\theta$,

(c) $\dfrac{2\tan\theta}{1 - \tan^2\theta}$

395. Use identity (16) for $\cos 2\theta$ and identity
(6), $\sin^2\theta + \cos^2\theta = 1$, to get two more useful identities for $\cos 2\theta$.

(18) $\cos 2\theta = $ _____

(19) $\cos 2\theta = $ _____

---

395. $1 - 2\sin^2\theta$;
$2\cos^2\theta - 1$.

If you had difficulty, go on to the next frame. If not, skip to frame 398.

396. First let us use (6) $\sin^2 \theta + \cos^2 \theta = 1$ and replace

$\cos^2 \theta$ by **(a)** —————— in (16). We get

$\cos 2\theta = $ **(b)** ——————————— .

That is, (18) $\cos 2\theta = $ **(c)** —————— .

---

396. (a) $1 - \sin^2 \theta$,
   (b) $(1 - \sin^2 \theta) - \sin^2 \theta$,
   (c) $1 - 2\sin^2 \theta$

397. Next replace $\sin^2 \theta$ by **(a)** —————— in (16).

We get $\cos 2\theta = $ **(b)** ——————————— .

That is, (19) $\cos 2\theta = $ **(c)** —————— .

---

397. (a) $1 - \cos^2 \theta$,
   (b) $\cos^2 \theta - (1 - \cos^2 \theta)$,
   (c) $2\cos^2 \theta - 1$

EXERCISE 2

398. Complete the following double-angle formulas.

(16) $\cos 2\theta = $ **(a)** ———————————————

(18) $\cos 2\theta = $ **(b)** ———————————————

(19) $\cos 2\theta = $ **(c)** ———————————————

---

398. (a) $\cos^2 \theta - \sin^2 \theta$,
   (b) $1 - 2\sin^2 \theta$,
   (c) $2\cos^2 \theta - 1$

FORMULAS FOR HIGHER MULTIPLES OF θ

399. Now that we have identities for $\sin(\alpha + \beta)$, $\cos(\alpha + \beta)$, and $\tan(\alpha + \beta)$, and $\sin 2\theta$, $\cos 2\theta$, and $\tan 2\theta$, we can establish identities for $\sin n\theta$, $\cos n\theta$, and $\tan n\theta$, $n = 3, 4, 5, \ldots$. These identities may appear in many different forms depending on how they are established.

Use identity (15) for $\sin 2\theta$ to prove that in terms of 2θ

$\sin 4\theta = $ ——————————————————————— .

---

399. $\sin 2(2\theta) = 2\sin 2\theta \cos 2\theta$

400. Now use the identities for $\sin 2\theta$ and $\cos 2\theta$ to express $\sin 4\theta$ in terms of θ.

$\sin 4\theta =$ _____

_____

_____

400. $2 \sin 2\theta \cos 2\theta$
$= 2(2 \sin \theta \cos \theta)(\cos^2 \theta - \sin^2 \theta)$
$= 4 (\sin \theta \cos^3 \theta - \cos \theta \sin^3 \theta).$

NOTE: We could equally well have replaced $\cos 2\theta$ by $1 - 2 \sin^2 \theta$ or by $2 \cos^2 \theta - 1$ and thus have arrived at

$\sin 4\theta = 4 (\sin \theta \cos \theta - 2 \cos \theta \sin^3 \theta)$

or

$\sin 4\theta = 4 (\sin \theta \cos^3 \theta - \sin \theta \cos \theta)$

EXAMPLE 5

401. Prove the identity $\sin 3\theta = 3 \sin \theta - 4 \sin^3 \theta$.

(You may wish to use separate paper for this.)

401.
$\sin 3\theta = \sin (\theta + 2\theta)$
$\quad = \sin \theta \cos 2\theta + \cos \theta \sin 2\theta \quad \text{by (11)}$
$\quad = \sin \theta (1 - 2 \sin^2 \theta) + \cos \theta (2 \sin \theta \cos \theta) \quad \text{by (18) and (15)}$
$\quad = \sin \theta - 2 \sin^3 \theta + 2 \cos^2 \theta \sin \theta$
$\quad = \sin \theta - 2 \sin^3 \theta + 2 (1 - \sin^2 \theta) \sin \theta \quad \text{by (6)}$
$\quad = \sin \theta - 2 \sin^3 \theta + 2 \sin \theta - 2 \sin^3 \theta$
$\quad = 3 \sin \theta - 4 \sin^3 \theta$

EXAMPLE 6

402. Prove the identity

$$\cos 3\theta = 4 \cos^3 \theta - 3 \cos \theta.$$

402.

(1) $\cos 3\theta = \cos (\theta + 2\theta)$

(2) $\qquad = \cos \theta \cos 2\theta - \sin \theta \sin 2\theta$

(3) $\qquad = \cos \theta (2 \cos^2 \theta - 1) - \sin \theta (2 \sin \theta \cos \theta)$

(4) $\qquad = 2 \cos^3 \theta - \cos \theta - 2 \sin^2 \theta \cos \theta$

(5) $\qquad = 2 \cos^3 \theta - \cos \theta - 2 (1 - \cos^2 \theta) \cos \theta$ by (6)

(6) $\qquad = 2 \cos^3 \theta - \cos \theta - 2 \cos \theta + 2 \cos^3 \theta$

(7) $\qquad = 4 \cos^3 \theta - 3 \cos \theta$

NOTE: In step (3) we replaced $\cos 2\theta$ by $2 \cos^2 \theta - 1$. Had we replaced $\cos 2\theta$ by $\cos^2 \theta - \sin^2 \theta$, we would not have gotten the required identity.

403. Complete the following double-angle formulas.

(15) $\sin 2\theta =$ **(a)** _____

(16) $\cos 2\theta =$ **(b)** _____

(18) $\cos 2\theta =$ **(c)** _____

(19) $\cos 2\theta =$ **(d)** _____

(17) $\tan 2\theta =$ **(e)** _____

403. (a) $2 \sin \theta \cos \theta$,

$\quad$ **(b)** $\cos^2 \theta - \sin^2 \theta$,

$\quad$ **(c)** $1 - 2 \sin^2 \theta$,

$\quad$ **(d)** $2 \cos^2 \theta - 1$,

$\quad$ **(e)** $\dfrac{2 \tan \theta}{1 - \tan^2 \theta}$

404. We can now establish the formulas for $\sin \frac{\theta}{2}$, $\cos \frac{\theta}{2}$, and $\tan \frac{\theta}{2}$. We can establish $\sin \frac{\theta}{2}$ and $\cos \frac{\theta}{2}$ by replacing θ by $\frac{\theta}{2}$ in identities (18) and (19), respectively.

Use identity (18) $\cos 2\theta = 1 - 2 \sin^2 \theta$ to prove that

$(20')$ $\sin^2 \left(\frac{\theta}{2} \right) =$ _____ .

---

404. $\frac{1 - \cos \theta}{2}$.

If you had difficulty, go on to the next frame. If not, skip to frame 407.

405. If we substitute $\frac{\theta}{2}$ for θ in

(18) $\cos 2\theta = 1 - 2 \sin^2 \theta$, we get $\cos \theta = \cos (2 \cdot (\frac{\theta}{2}) =$

_____ .

---

405. $1 - 2 \sin^2 \left(\frac{\theta}{2} \right)$

406. And solving the preceding equation for $\sin^2 \left(\frac{\theta}{2} \right)$, we get

$(20')$ $\sin^2 \left(\frac{\theta}{2} \right) =$ _____ .

---

406. $\frac{1 - \cos \theta}{2}$

407. By taking the square root of both sides of $(20')$ we get

(20) $\sin \frac{\theta}{2} =$ _____ .

---

407. $\pm \sqrt{\dfrac{1 - \cos \theta}{2}}$

EXAMPLE 7

408. Using formula (20) for $\sin \frac{\theta}{2}$, we get $\sin \frac{\pi}{8} =$ _____

_____ .

408.

$$\sin \left(\frac{1}{2} \cdot \frac{\pi}{4} \right) = \pm \sqrt{\frac{1 - \cos (\pi/4)}{2}}$$

$$= \pm \sqrt{\frac{1 - (1/\sqrt{2})}{2}} = \pm \sqrt{\frac{\sqrt{2} - 1}{2\sqrt{2}}} .$$

Thus, $\sin \frac{\pi}{8} = + \sqrt{\dfrac{2 - \sqrt{2}}{4}} = + \frac{1}{2} \sqrt{2 - \sqrt{2}}$,

since $\frac{\pi}{8}$ is in the first quadrant.

409. Use identity (19) $\cos 2\theta = 2 \cos^2 \theta - 1$ to prove that

(21') $\cos^2 \left(\dfrac{\theta}{2} \right) = $ _____ .

---

409. $\dfrac{1 + \cos \theta}{2}$.

If you had difficulty, go on to the next frame. If not, skip to frame 412.

410. If we substitute $\dfrac{\theta}{2}$ for θ in (19) $\cos 2\theta = 2 \cos^2 \theta - 1$,

we get $\cos \theta = \cos \left(2 \cdot \dfrac{\theta}{2} \right) = $ _____ .

---

410. $2 \cos^2 \left(\dfrac{\theta}{2} \right) - 1$

411. And solving for $\cos^2 \dfrac{\theta}{2}$ gives

(21') $\cos^2 \left(\dfrac{\theta}{2} \right) = $ _____ .

---

411. $\dfrac{1 + \cos \theta}{2}$

412. Finally, by taking the square root of both sides of (21'), we get

(21) $\cos \dfrac{\theta}{2} = $ _____ .

---

412. $\pm \sqrt{\dfrac{1 + \cos \theta}{2}}$

EXAMPLE 8

413. Using formula (21) for $\cos \dfrac{\theta}{2}$, we get $\cos \dfrac{\pi}{8} = $ _____

_____ .

413.

$$\cos \left(\dfrac{1}{2} \cdot \dfrac{\pi}{4} \right) = \pm \sqrt{\dfrac{1 + \cos(\pi/4)}{2}}$$

$$= \pm \sqrt{\dfrac{1 + (1/\sqrt{2})}{2}} = \pm \sqrt{\dfrac{\sqrt{2} + 1}{2\sqrt{2}}} .$$

Thus, $\cos \dfrac{\pi}{8} = + \sqrt{\dfrac{2 + \sqrt{2}}{4}} = + \dfrac{1}{2} \sqrt{2 + \sqrt{2}}$,

since $\dfrac{\pi}{8}$ is in the first quadrant

414. Complete the following half-angle formulas:

$(20')\ \sin^2\left(\dfrac{\theta}{2}\right) =$ **(a)** _____

$(20)\ \sin\dfrac{\theta}{2} =$ **(b)** _____

$(21')\ \cos^2\left(\dfrac{\theta}{2}\right) =$ **(c)** _____

$(21)\ \cos\dfrac{\theta}{2} =$ **(d)** _____

414. **(a)** $\dfrac{1 - \cos\theta}{2}$,

(b) $\pm\sqrt{\dfrac{1 - \cos\theta}{2}}$

(c) $\dfrac{1 + \cos\theta}{2}$,

(d) $\pm\sqrt{\dfrac{1 + \cos\theta}{2}}$

415. **NOTE:** In the formula for $\sin^2\left(\dfrac{\theta}{2}\right)$ we have

$$\frac{1 \underline{} \cos\theta}{2}$$

while in the formula for $\cos^2\left(\dfrac{\theta}{2}\right)$, we have

$$\frac{1 \underline{} \cos\theta}{2}$$

415. $-$;
$+$

416. Finally, from identities (4), (20), and (21), we get

$(22)\ \tan\dfrac{\theta}{2} = \dfrac{\sin(\theta/2)}{\cos(\theta/2)} =$ _____ .

416.

$$\frac{\pm\sqrt{\dfrac{1 - \cos\theta}{2}}}{\pm\sqrt{\dfrac{1 + \cos\theta}{2}}} = \pm\sqrt{\dfrac{1 - \cos\theta}{1 + \cos\theta}}$$

EXAMPLE 9

417. Using formula (22), we get $\tan \dfrac{\pi}{8} =$ _____

_____ .

417.
$$\tan\left(\frac{1}{2} \cdot \frac{\pi}{4}\right) = \pm \sqrt{\frac{1 - \cos \theta}{1 + \cos \theta}}$$

$$= \pm \sqrt{\frac{1 - (1/\sqrt{2})}{1 + (1/\sqrt{2})}} = \pm \sqrt{\frac{\sqrt{2} - 1}{\sqrt{2} + 1}} .$$

Since $\dfrac{\pi}{8}$ is in the first quadrant,

$$\tan \frac{\pi}{8} = + \sqrt{\frac{\sqrt{2} - 1}{\sqrt{2} + 1}} .$$

418. We can obtain a formula for $\tan \dfrac{\theta}{2}$ that does not contain a square root as follows.

If we multiply the numerator and denominator in the right-hand side of

$$\tan \frac{\theta}{2} = \frac{\sin (\theta/2)}{\cos (\theta/2)}$$

by $2 \cos \dfrac{\theta}{2}$, we get $\tan \dfrac{\theta}{2} =$ _____ .

418.
$$\frac{2 \sin \dfrac{\theta}{2} \cos \dfrac{\theta}{2}}{2 \cos^2 \left(\dfrac{\theta}{2}\right)}$$

419. But by identity (15)

$2 \sin \dfrac{\theta}{2} \cos \dfrac{\theta}{2} =$ _____ , and by identity (19) $2 \cos^2 \left(\dfrac{\theta}{2}\right) =$ _____ .

419. $\sin \theta$;
$1 + \cos \theta,$

since $\cos \theta = \cos \left(2 \cdot \dfrac{\theta}{2}\right)$

$$= 2 \cos^2 \left(\frac{\theta}{2}\right) - 1.$$

420. Hence

(23) $\tan \dfrac{\theta}{2} =$ _____ .

420. $\dfrac{\sin \theta}{1 + \cos \theta}$

421. Or since

$$\frac{\sin \theta}{1 + \cos \theta} = \frac{1 - \cos \theta}{\sin \theta}$$

we may write (24) $\tan \dfrac{\theta}{2} =$ _____ .

421. $\dfrac{1 - \cos \theta}{\sin \theta}$

EXAMPLE 10

422. Using formula (23) for $\tan \dfrac{\theta}{2}$, we get $\tan \dfrac{\pi}{12} =$

_____

_____.

422. $\tan \left(\dfrac{1}{2} \cdot \dfrac{\pi}{6} \right) = \dfrac{\sin (\pi/6)}{1 + \cos (\pi/6)}$

$= \dfrac{\frac{1}{2}}{1 + \dfrac{\sqrt{3}}{2}} = \dfrac{1}{2 + \sqrt{3}}$

EXERCISE 3

423. Complete the following half-angle formulas.

(20′) $\sin^2 \left(\dfrac{\theta}{2} \right) =$ **(a)** _____

(20) $\sin \dfrac{\theta}{2} =$ **(b)** _____

(21′) $\cos^2 \left(\dfrac{\theta}{2} \right) =$ **(c)** _____

(21) $\cos \dfrac{\theta}{2} =$ **(d)** _____

(22) $\left\{ \rule{0pt}{8ex} \right.$ $\tan \dfrac{\theta}{2} =$ **(e)** _____

(23) $\tan \dfrac{\theta}{2} =$ **(f)** _____

(24) $\tan \dfrac{\theta}{2} =$ **(g)** _____

423. **(a)** $\dfrac{1 - \cos \theta}{2}$,

(b) $\pm \sqrt{\dfrac{1 - \cos \theta}{2}}$,

(c) $\dfrac{1 + \cos \theta}{2}$,

(d) $\pm \sqrt{\dfrac{1 + \cos \theta}{2}}$,

(e) $\pm \sqrt{\dfrac{1 - \cos \theta}{1 + \cos \theta}}$,

(f) $\dfrac{\sin \theta}{1 + \cos \theta}$,

(g) $\dfrac{1 - \cos \theta}{\sin \theta}$.

If you had difficulty, review frames 404 to 421.

424. Use the identity (11) $\sin(\alpha + \beta) = \sin\alpha\cos\beta + \cos\alpha\sin\beta$ to establish formula (15) for $\sin 2\theta$.

(15) _____

---

424. $\sin 2\theta = 2\sin\theta\cos\theta$.

If you had difficulty, see frames 383 and 384.

EXERCISE 5

425. Use the identity (10) $\cos(\alpha + \beta) = \cos\alpha\cos\beta - \sin\alpha\sin\beta$ to establish formula (16) for $\cos 2\theta$.

(16) _____

---

425. $\cos 2\theta = \cos^2\theta - \sin^2\theta$.

If you had difficulty, see frames 386 and 387.

426. Use identity (16) $\cos 2\theta = \cos^2 \theta - \sin^2 \theta$ to establish formulas (18) and (19) for $\cos 2\theta$.

(18) _____

(19) _____

---

426. $\cos 2\theta = 1 - 2 \sin^2 \theta$;
$\cos 2\theta = 2 \cos^2 \theta - 1$.

If you had difficulty, see frames 395 to 397.

427. Use the identity (13) $\tan(\alpha + \beta) = \dfrac{\tan \alpha + \tan \beta}{1 - \tan \alpha \tan \beta}$ to establish the formula (17) for $\tan 2\theta$.

(17) _____

---

427. $\tan 2\theta = \dfrac{2 \tan \theta}{1 - \tan^2 \theta}$.

If you had difficulty, see frames 391 and 392.

428. Use identity (18) $\cos 2\theta = 1 - 2 \sin^2 \theta$ to establish the formula (20') for $\sin^2 \left(\dfrac{\theta}{2}\right)$.

(20') _____

---

428. $\sin^2 \left(\dfrac{\theta}{2}\right) = \dfrac{1 - \cos \theta}{2}$.

If you had difficulty, see frames 404 to 406.

429. Use identity (19) $\cos 2\theta = 2 \cos^2 - 1$ to establish formula (21′) for $\cos^2 \left(\dfrac{\theta}{2} \right)$.

(21′) _____

429. $\cos^2 \left(\dfrac{\theta}{2} \right) = \dfrac{1 + \cos \theta}{2}$.

If you had difficulty, see frames 409 to 411.

EXERCISE 10

430. Use identities

(20) $\sin \dfrac{\theta}{2} = \pm \sqrt{\dfrac{1 - \cos \theta}{2}}$ and

(21) $\cos \dfrac{\theta}{2} = \pm \sqrt{\dfrac{1 + \cos \theta}{2}}$

to establish formula (22) for $\tan \dfrac{\theta}{2}$.

(22) _____

430. $\tan \dfrac{\theta}{2} = \pm \sqrt{\dfrac{1 - \cos \theta}{1 + \cos \theta}}$.

If you had difficulty, see frame 416.

SUMMARY

List of Multiple-Angle Formulas

(15) $\sin 2\theta = 2 \sin \theta \cos \theta$

(16) $\cos 2\theta = \cos^2 \theta - \sin^2 \theta$

(18) $\cos 2\theta = 1 - 2 \sin^2 \theta$

(19) $\cos 2\theta = 2 \cos^2 \theta - 1$

(17) $\tan 2\theta = \dfrac{2 \tan \theta}{1 - \tan^2 \theta}$

(20') $\sin^2 \dfrac{\theta}{2} = \dfrac{1 - \cos \theta}{2}$

(20) $\sin \dfrac{\theta}{2} = \pm \sqrt{\dfrac{1 - \cos \theta}{2}}$

(21') $\cos^2 \dfrac{\theta}{2} = \dfrac{1 + \cos \theta}{2}$

(21) $\cos \dfrac{\theta}{2} = \pm \sqrt{\dfrac{1 + \cos \theta}{2}}$

(22) $\tan \dfrac{\theta}{2} = \pm \sqrt{\dfrac{1 - \cos \theta}{1 + \cos \theta}}$

(23) $\tan \dfrac{\theta}{2} = \dfrac{\sin \theta}{1 + \cos \theta}$

(24) $\tan \dfrac{\theta}{2} = \dfrac{1 - \cos \theta}{\sin \theta}$

EXAMPLE 11

431. We can use the ten multiple-angle formulas to prove other identities as we have done in previous sections. The approach is the same. (See the summary following frame 299.)

Prove the identity

(A) $\cos^4 \theta - \sin^4 \theta = \cos 2\theta$.

---

431. If you had difficulty, go on to the next frame. If not, skip to frame 434.

	432. We can factor the left side (which is the more complicated) into $$\cos^4\theta - \sin^4\theta = (\cos^2\theta - \sin^2\theta)\,(\underline{\hspace{5cm}})\,.$$
432. $\cos^2\theta + \sin^2\theta$	**433.** But $\cos^2\theta + \sin^2\theta = \textbf{(a)}\ \underline{\hspace{1cm}}$; hence we have $$\cos^4\theta - \sin^4\theta = \textbf{(b)}\ \underline{\hspace{3cm}}$$ $$= \textbf{(c)}\ \underline{\hspace{3cm}}\ \text{(by identity (16))}.$$ Hence, identity (A) is proved.
433. (a) 1, **(b)** $\cos^2\theta - \sin^2\theta$, **(c)** $\cos 2\theta$	

List of Proved Identities

$$\sin 4\theta = 4\,(\sin\theta\cos^3\theta - \cos\theta\sin^3\theta)$$
$$\sin 4\theta = 4\,(\sin\theta\cos\theta - 2\cos\theta\sin^3\theta)$$
$$\sin 4\theta = 4\,(\sin\theta\cos^3\theta - \sin\theta\cos\theta)$$
$$\sin 3\theta = 3\sin\theta - 4\sin^3\theta$$
$$\cos 3\theta = 4\cos^3\theta - 3\cos\theta$$
$$\cos^4\theta - \sin^4\theta = \cos 2\theta$$

EXAMPLE 12

434. In the following frames, your approach may vary from the answer given and still be correct. Check the answer only after you have completed the proof of the identity or after you have tried and failed.

Prove the identity

$\cot \theta = \cot 2\theta + \csc 2\theta.$

(Hint: By identity (23)

$$\frac{\cos \alpha + 1}{\sin \alpha} = \frac{1}{\tan \alpha/2} \text{ for all } \alpha.)$$

434.

$$\cot 2\theta + \csc 2\theta = \frac{\cos 2\theta}{\sin 2\theta} + \frac{1}{\sin 2\theta}$$

$$= \frac{\cos 2\theta + 1}{\sin 2\theta}$$

$$= \frac{1}{\tan \theta} \quad \text{by (23)}$$

$$= \cot \theta \quad \text{by (3)}$$

EXAMPLE 13

435. Prove the identity

$$\sin \theta = 2 \sin 2\theta \cos \theta - \sin 3\theta.$$

435.

$2 \sin 2\theta \cos \theta - \sin 3\theta$

$= 2 \sin 2\theta \cos \theta - (\sin 2\theta \cos \theta + \cos 2\theta \sin \theta) \quad \text{by (11)}$

$= \sin 2\theta \cos \theta - \cos 2\theta \sin \theta$

$= \sin (2\theta - \theta) \quad \text{by (12)}$

$= \sin \theta$

EXAMPLE 14

436. Prove the identity

$$\frac{\sin 2\theta}{\sin \theta} - \frac{\cos 2\theta}{\cos \theta} = \sec \theta.$$

436. $\dfrac{\sin 2\theta}{\sin \theta} - \dfrac{\cos 2\theta}{\cos \theta}$

$= \dfrac{\sin 2\theta \cos \theta - \cos 2\theta \sin \theta}{\sin \theta \cos \theta}$

$= \dfrac{\sin (2\theta - \theta)}{\sin \theta \cos \theta}$ by (12)

$= \dfrac{1}{\cos \theta}$

$= \sec \theta$ by (2)

EXAMPLE 15

437. Prove the identity

$$\tan \theta = \frac{\sin 3\theta - \sin \theta}{\cos 3\theta + \cos \theta}.$$

437. $\dfrac{\sin 3\theta - \sin \theta}{\cos 3\theta + \cos \theta}$

$= \dfrac{2 \cos 2\theta \sin \theta}{2 \cos 2\theta \cos \theta}$ by (G) and (H)

$= \tan \theta.$

If you had difficulty, look up identities (G) and (H) in frames 381 to 382.

EXAMPLE 16

438. Prove the identity

$$\tan \theta = \frac{\sin 4\theta - \sin 2\theta}{\cos 4\theta + \cos 2\theta}.$$

438. $\dfrac{\sin 4\theta - \sin 2\theta}{\cos 4\theta + \cos 2\theta}$

$= \dfrac{2 \cos 3\theta \sin \theta}{2 \cos 3\theta \cos \theta}$ by (G) and (H)

$= \tan \theta$

EXAMPLE 17

439. Prove the identity

$$\sin 3\theta = 2 \sin 2\theta \cos \theta - \sin \theta.$$

439.

$\sin 3\theta + \sin \theta = 2 \sin 2\theta \cos \theta$ by (E).

If you had difficulty, see identity (E) in frame 373.

EXAMPLE 18

440. Prove the identity

$$\sin 3\theta = 4 \sin \theta \cos^2 \theta - \sin \theta.$$

440. $\sin 3\theta + \sin \theta$
$= 2 \sin 2\theta \cos \theta$ by (E)
$= 4 \sin \theta \cos \theta \cdot \cos \theta$ by (15)
$= 4 \sin \theta \cos^2 \theta$

EXAMPLE 19

441. Prove the identity

$$\cos 3\theta = \frac{\cos \theta}{\sec 4\theta} + \frac{\sec \theta}{\csc 4\theta}.$$

441. $\dfrac{\cos \theta}{\sec 4\theta} + \dfrac{\sec \theta}{\csc 4\theta}$

$= \cos \theta \cdot \cos 4\theta + \sin \theta \sin 4\theta$ by (2) and (1)

$= \cos 3\theta$ by (9)

EXAMPLE 20

442. Prove the identity

$$\cos 4\theta = 8 \cos^4 \theta - 8 \cos^2 \theta + 1.$$

442. $\cos 4\theta$
$= 2 \cos^2 (2\theta) - 1$ by (19)
$= 2 (2 \cos^2 \theta - 1)^2 - 1$ by (19)
$= 2 (4 \cos^4 \theta - 4 \cos^2 \theta + 1) - 1$
$= 8 \cos^4 \theta - 8 \cos^2 \theta + 1$

EXAMPLE 21

443. Prove the identity

$$\cos 4\theta = 8 \cos^4 \theta - 4 \cos 2\theta - 3.$$

443. $\cos 4\theta$
$= 2 \cos^2 (2\theta) - 1$ by (19)
$= 2 (2 \cos^2 \theta - 1)^2) - 1$ by (19)
$= 2 (4 \cos^4 \theta - 4 \cos^2 \theta + 1) - 1$
$= 8 \cos^4 \theta - 4(2 \cos^2 \theta - 1) - 3$
$= 8 \cos^4 \theta - 4 \cos 2\theta - 3$ by (19)

EXAMPLE 22

444. Prove the identity

$$\tan \frac{\theta}{2} = \frac{\sin \theta - \cos \theta + 1}{\sin \theta + \cos \theta + 1}.$$

444. $\dfrac{\sin \theta - \cos \theta + 1}{\sin \theta + \cos \theta + 1}$

$$= \frac{2 \sin \dfrac{\theta}{2} \cos \dfrac{\theta}{2} + 2 \sin^2 \dfrac{\theta}{2}}{2 \sin \dfrac{\theta}{2} \cos \dfrac{\theta}{2} + 2 \cos^2 \dfrac{\theta}{2}}$$

by (15), (18), (19)

$$= \frac{2 \sin \dfrac{\theta}{2} \left(\cos \dfrac{\theta}{2} + \sin \dfrac{\theta}{2}\right)}{2 \cos \dfrac{\theta}{2} \left(\sin \dfrac{\theta}{2} + \cos \dfrac{\theta}{2}\right)}$$

$$= \tan \frac{\theta}{2} \quad \text{by (4)}$$

EXAMPLE 23

445. Prove the identity

$$\cos (\alpha + \beta) \cdot \cos (\alpha - \beta) = \cos^2 \alpha - \sin^2 \beta.$$

445. $\cos (\alpha + \beta) \cdot \cos (\alpha - \beta)$
$= (\cos \alpha \cos \beta - \sin \alpha \sin \beta) \cdot (\cos \alpha \cos \beta + \sin \alpha \sin \beta)$
$= \cos^2 \alpha \cos^2 \beta - \sin^2 \alpha \sin^2 \beta$
$= \cos^2 \alpha \cos^2 \beta - \sin^2 \alpha \sin^2 \beta + (\cos^2 \alpha \sin^2 \beta - \cos^2 \alpha \sin^2 \beta)$
$= \cos^2 \alpha (\cos^2 \beta + \sin^2 \beta) - \sin^2 \beta (\sin^2 \alpha + \cos^2 \alpha)$
$= \cos^2 \alpha - \sin^2 \beta$

EXAMPLE 24

446. Prove the identity

$$\sin \theta = 4 \sin \theta \cos^2 \theta - \sin 3\theta.$$

446. $4 \sin \theta \cos^2 \theta - \sin 3\theta$
$= 4 \sin \theta \cos^2 \theta - \sin 2\theta \cos \theta - \cos 2\theta \sin \theta \quad \text{by (11)}$
$= \sin \theta (4 \cos^2 \theta - \cos 2\theta) - \sin 2\theta \cos \theta$
$= \sin \theta (4 \cos^2 \theta - 2 \cos^2 \theta + 1) - \sin 2\theta \cos \theta \quad \text{by (19)}$
$= \sin \theta \cos 2\theta + 2 \sin \theta - \sin 2\theta \cos \theta \quad \text{by (19)}$
$= \sin \theta \cos 2\theta - \sin 2\theta \cos \theta + 2 \sin \theta$
$= \sin (-\theta) + 2 \sin \theta$
$= -\sin \theta + 2 \sin \theta$
$= \sin \theta$

If you cannot answer the following questions correctly, review the appropriate frames.

1. Use the addition identity for $\sin(\alpha + \beta)$ to derive the identity for $\sin 2\theta$.

2. Complete the following identities.

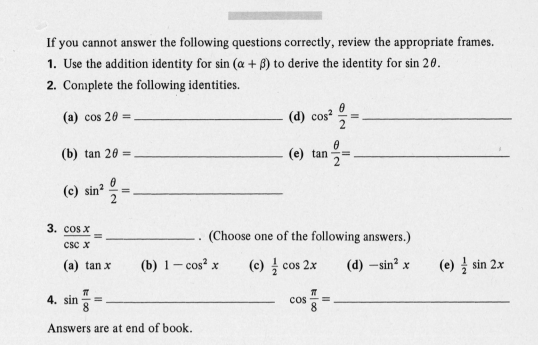

    (a) $\cos 2\theta =$ _____   **(d)** $\cos^2 \dfrac{\theta}{2} =$ _____

    (b) $\tan 2\theta =$ _____   **(e)** $\tan \dfrac{\theta}{2} =$ _____

    (c) $\sin^2 \dfrac{\theta}{2} =$ _____

3. $\dfrac{\cos x}{\csc x} =$ _____ . (Choose one of the following answers.)

    (a) $\tan x$ **(b)** $1 - \cos^2 x$ **(c)** $\tfrac{1}{2} \cos 2x$ **(d)** $-\sin^2 x$ **(e)** $\tfrac{1}{2} \sin 2x$

4. $\sin \dfrac{\pi}{8} =$ _____ $\cos \dfrac{\pi}{8} =$ _____

Answers are at end of book.

12 Inverse Trigonometric Functions

ARCSINE

Upon completing this section you should be able to

   I. Give the domain and range of the restricted sine function Sin x.

   II. Define and give the domain and range of Arcsin x.

   III. Calculate the values of Arcsin $\frac{1}{2}$, Arcsin $\left(-\frac{\sqrt{3}}{2}\right)$, etc.

   IV. Prove that Arcsin $(-x) = -$Arcsin x for all x.

   V. Give the value for sin (Arcsin x) and Arcsin (Sin x) for any x.

---

447. In the chapter on inverse functions in Volume II, we proved that a function f has an inverse f^{-1} if and only if f is one-to-one. Recall that a function $f : D \rightarrow B$ is one-to-one if and only if

_____

_____ .

---

447. each element y in the range is associated with one and only one element in the domain.

If you had difficulty, see frames 224 to 241 in Volume II on functions.

448. Furthermore we saw from its graph that a function is one-to-one if a _____ line through any point in the range meets the graph _____ .

---

448. horizontal; once and only once.

If you had difficulty, see frames 224 to 226 in Volume II on functions.

449. For functions like $f(x) = x^3 - 3x^2 + 1$, which were not one-to-one, we used the same rule but a smaller domain to get a new function that was one-to-one.

Choose a domain for which

$f_1(x) = x^3 - 3x^2 + 1$ if _____ x _____ is one-to-one.

---

449. There are three likely choices: $x \leqslant 0$, $0 \leqslant x \leqslant 2$, and $2 \leqslant x$. However, we could choose any subset of any one of these three.

If you had difficulty, see frame 241 of Volume II on functions.

---

450. We had the following definition for the inverse f^{-1} of the function.

DEFINITION: If the inverse f^{-1} of a function exists, it is a function whose domain will be the _____ of f, and whose range will be the _____ , and $f^{-1}(y) = x$ where $f(x) = y$ for all $y \in D_{f^{-1}} = \mathcal{R}_f$.

---

450. range; domain of f.

If you had difficulty, see frames 242 to 247 of Volume II on functions.

---

451. If f^{-1} exists it is also a one-to-one function and we can graph it. In graphing a function, we choose the _____ axis to
(horizontal, vertical)
represent the domain and the letter ___ to represent elements of the domain.

---

451. horizontal; x

452. If we graph a function f and its inverse f^{-1} on the same coordinate axes, with the domain of each on the x-axis, then the graph of f^{-1} is the reflection of the graph of f in

_____.

---

452. the 45° line, $y = x$.

If you had difficulty, see frames 252 to 271 of Volume II on functions.

---

453. Since the trigonometric functions are periodic, they clearly

_____ one-to-one. For example, $\sin 0 = \sin 2\pi = \sin 4\pi$
(are, are not)

and $\cos \pi = \cos 3\pi = \cos 5\pi$, etc.

---

453. are not

---

454. However, if we use the same rule for the definition but a much smaller domain, we can define a new function that is one-to-one and hence has an inverse.

In the graph of $y = \sin x$, choose an interval on which $\sin x$ is one-to-one.

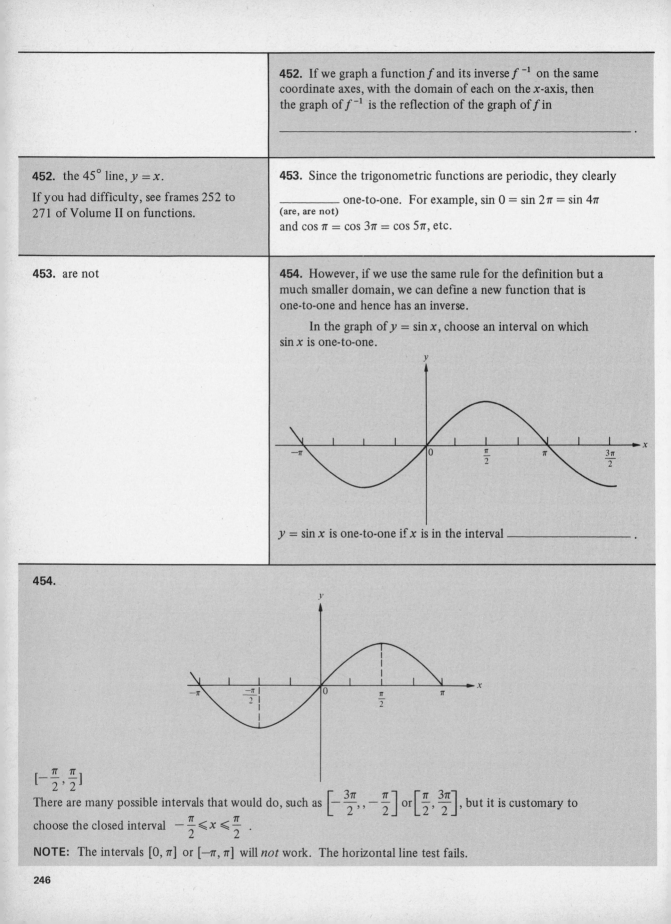

$y = \sin x$ is one-to-one if x is in the interval _____.

454.

$[-\frac{\pi}{2}, \frac{\pi}{2}]$

There are many possible intervals that would do, such as $\left[-\frac{3\pi}{2}, -\frac{\pi}{2}\right]$ or $\left[\frac{\pi}{2}, \frac{3\pi}{2}\right]$, but it is customary to choose the closed interval $-\frac{\pi}{2} \leqslant x \leqslant \frac{\pi}{2}$.

NOTE: The intervals $[0, \pi]$ or $[-\pi, \pi]$ will *not* work. The horizontal line test fails.

455. In order to distinguish it from $\sin x$ whose domain is the set of all real numbers, we shall denote our new function by $\mathrm{Sin}\, x$ with a capital S.

$$\mathrm{Sin}\, x = \sin x \quad \text{if} \quad -\frac{\pi}{2} \leqslant x \leqslant \frac{\pi}{2}.$$

That is, $\mathrm{Sin}\, x$ is the function $\sin x$ restricted to the interval

_____ .

---

455. $-\dfrac{\pi}{2} \leqslant x \leqslant \dfrac{\pi}{2}$

456. The range of $\sin x$ is $\{y \in R \mid -1 \leqslant y \leqslant 1\}$ and the range of

$\mathrm{Sin}\, x$ is $\{y \in R \mid$ _____ $\}$.

---

456. $-1 \leqslant y \leqslant 1$

457. Thus, the range of $\mathrm{Sin}\, x$ is the same as for $\sin x$. And every element y in the range of $\sin x$ is associated with one and only one

element in the _____ .

---

457. domain of $\mathrm{Sin}\, x$

458. Since $\mathrm{Sin}\, x$ is one-to-one, it has an inverse called the **Arcsine** or **inverse sine** function. It is denoted by $\mathrm{Arcsin}\, x$ or $\mathrm{Sin}^{-1} x$. The

domain of Sin^{-1} is _____ and the range

is _____ .

---

458. $\{x \in R \mid -1 \leqslant x \leqslant 1\}$;

$\left\{ y \in R \mid -\dfrac{\pi}{2} \leqslant y \leqslant \dfrac{\pi}{2} \right\}$

459. And we have the following definition:

DEFINITION: The **Arcsine** or **inverse sine** function is the function whose domain is $\{x \in R \mid -1 \leqslant x \leqslant 1\}$, and

$\mathrm{Arcsin}\, x = y$ where $x = \sin y$ and $-\dfrac{\pi}{2} \leqslant y \leqslant \dfrac{\pi}{2}$.

We have represented elements in the domain of Arcsine by the

letter ___ , and elements in the range by ___ .

---

459. $x; y$

460. The solid line on the coordinate axes represents the entire graph of $y = \text{Sin } x$. On the same axes, graph $y = \text{Arcsin } x$.

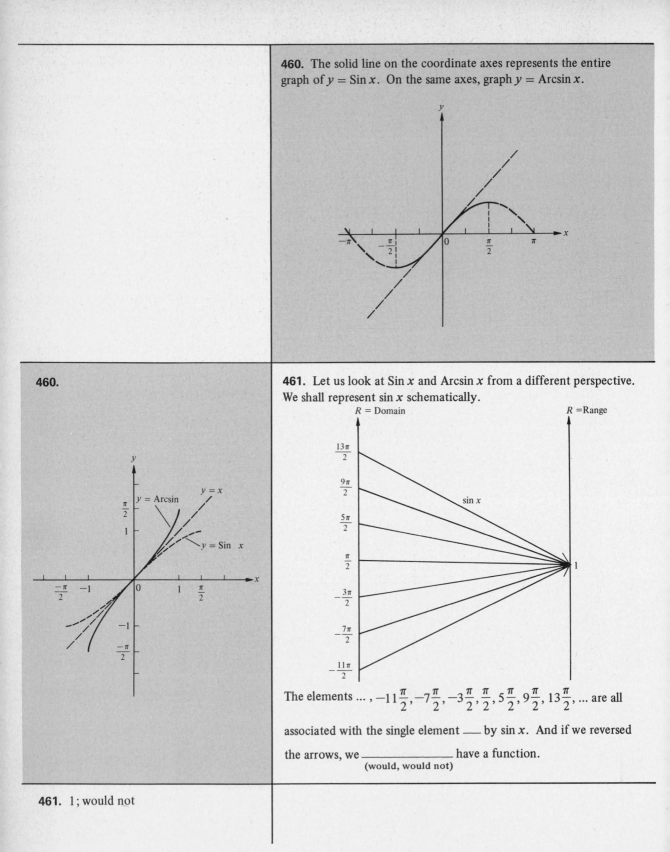

460.

461. Let us look at Sin x and Arcsin x from a different perspective. We shall represent sin x schematically.

The elements $\ldots, -11\frac{\pi}{2}, -7\frac{\pi}{2}, -3\frac{\pi}{2}, \frac{\pi}{2}, 5\frac{\pi}{2}, 9\frac{\pi}{2}, 13\frac{\pi}{2}, \ldots$ are all associated with the single element ____ by sin x. And if we reversed the arrows, we _____ have a function.
(would, would not)

461. 1; would not

248

462. However, in arbitrarily restricting the domain of $\sin x$, we chose one and only one value in the domain that is associated with 1, namely $\frac{\pi}{2}$. We call $\frac{\pi}{2}$ the **principal value** of 1. Thus, Arcsin 1 is defined as the principal value of 1. That is, Arcsin $1 = \frac{\pi}{2}$.

What is the principal value of 0? ___

That is, Arcsin $0 =$ ___ .

---

462. 0;
0

(since the domain of Sin, and hence the range of Arcsin, was taken to be $[-\frac{\pi}{2}, \frac{\pi}{2}]$)

463. $-\frac{\pi}{2}$ is the _____ of -1.

That is, Arcsin $(-1) =$ _____ .

---

463. principal value;
$-\frac{\pi}{2}$

464. For each real number y in the range $\{y \in R \mid -1 \leqslant y \leqslant 1\}$ of $\sin x$ there is a principal value in the interval _____ associated with it.

---

464. $-\frac{\pi}{2} \leqslant x \leqslant \frac{\pi}{2}$

465. And the range of the Arcsine function is the set of all these

_____ .

---

465. principal values

466. Our original trigonometric functions had as their domains sets of angles and as their ranges sets of real numbers. In calculating the values of the inverse trigonometric functions, it is often convenient to think of the inverse functions as taking on angle values. That is, we shall sometimes think of the inverse trigonometric functions as having sets of _____ for their domains and sets of _____ for their ranges.

---

466. real numbers; angles

467. By definition Arcsin $x = y$ if and only if Sin ___ = ___ .

Thus, $y = \text{Arcsin } x$ is read "y is that number whose sine is x" or

"y is that angle _____ ."

---

467. y; x;
whose sine is x

468. The domain of Sin x was restricted to be the interval

_____ and the range of

$\text{Sin } x = \{y \in R \mid$ _____ $\}$.

---

468. $-\dfrac{\pi}{2} \leqslant x \leqslant \dfrac{\pi}{2}$;

$-1 \leqslant y \leqslant 1$

469. Thus, the domain of the inverse sine, or Arcsin x, is

_____ and the range of Arcsin x is

_____ .

---

469. $\{x \in R \mid -1 \leqslant x \leqslant 1\}$;

the interval $-\dfrac{\pi}{2} \leqslant y \leqslant \dfrac{\pi}{2}$

EXAMPLE 1

470. $\text{Arcsin } \dfrac{1}{2} =$ ___ $\text{Arcsin } \dfrac{1}{\sqrt{2}} =$ ___

---

470. $\dfrac{\pi}{6}$, $\dfrac{\pi}{4}$

If you had difficulty, go on to the next
frame. If not, skip to frame 475.

471. By definition

$\text{Arcsin } \dfrac{1}{2} = y$ if and only if Sin ___ = ___ .

---

471. y; $\dfrac{1}{2}$

472. That is, we want that angle y whose Sine is $\dfrac{1}{2}$. And we see

from the diagram in this frame that $y =$ ___ .

That is $\text{Arcsin } \dfrac{1}{2} =$ ___ .

---

472. $\dfrac{\pi}{6}$; $\dfrac{\pi}{6}$

473. Similarly, $\text{Arcsin } \dfrac{1}{\sqrt{2}} = y$ if and only if _____ .

---

473. $\text{Sin } y = \dfrac{1}{\sqrt{2}}$

474. We want the angle y **(a)** _____ .

Thus, $y =$ **(b)** ____ and $\text{Arcsin } \dfrac{1}{\sqrt{2}} =$ **(c)** ____ .

---

474.   **(a)** whose sine is $\dfrac{1}{\sqrt{2}}$,

(b) $\dfrac{\pi}{4}$,

(c) $\dfrac{\pi}{4}$

EXAMPLE 2
475.

$\text{Arcsin } \left(-\dfrac{1}{2}\right) =$ **(a)** ____ $\text{Arcsin } \dfrac{\sqrt{2}}{2} =$ **(b)** ____

$\text{Arcsin } \left(-\dfrac{\sqrt{3}}{2}\right) =$ **(c)** ____

---

475. **(a)** $-\dfrac{\pi}{6}$, **(b)** $\dfrac{\pi}{3}$, **(c)** $-\dfrac{\pi}{3}$.

If you had difficulty, go on to the next frame. If not, skip to frame 480.

476. We want the principal values for $-\dfrac{1}{2}, \dfrac{\sqrt{3}}{2}$, and $-\dfrac{\sqrt{3}}{2}$. Thus,

the answers must all be in the interval _____ .

---

476. $-\dfrac{\pi}{2} \leqslant y \leqslant \dfrac{\pi}{2}$

477. Thus, if we think in terms of angles, y must be in

quadrant ____ or quadrant ____ , since $\dfrac{\pi}{2} \leqslant y \leqslant \dfrac{\pi}{2}$.

---

477. I; IV

478. Since $-\dfrac{1}{2}$ is negative, the angle $y = \text{Arcsin } \left(-\dfrac{1}{2}\right)$ will lie in

quadrant ____ . That is, y will be _____ .

                                              (positive, negative)

---

478. IV;
negative

479. Hence $\text{Arcsin } \left(-\dfrac{1}{2}\right) =$ **(a)** ____ .

Similarly, $\text{Arcsin } \left(-\dfrac{\sqrt{3}}{2}\right) =$ **(b)** ____ ,

since $\text{Arcsin } \left(+\dfrac{\sqrt{3}}{2}\right) =$ **(c)** ____ .

---

479. **(a)** $-\dfrac{\pi}{6}$,

(b) $-\dfrac{\pi}{3}$, **(c)** $\dfrac{\pi}{3}$.

If you still had difficulty, see frames 470 to 474.

480. We see from frames 470 to 479 that

Arcsin $\frac{1}{2}$ = (a) _____ and Arcsin $\left(-\frac{1}{2}\right)$ = (b) _____ ;

Arcsin $\frac{\sqrt{3}}{2}$ = (c) _____ and Arcsin $\left(-\frac{\sqrt{3}}{2}\right)$ = (d) _____ .

And, in general, if

Arcsin $x = y$, then Arcsin $(-x)$ = (e) _____ .

---

480. (a) $\frac{\pi}{6}$, (b) $-\frac{\pi}{6}$,

(c) $\frac{\pi}{3}$, (d) $-\frac{\pi}{3}$, (e) $-y$

481. Prove the identity

Arcsin $(-x) = -$Arcsin x.

---

481. If you had difficulty, go on to the next frame. If not, skip to frame 486.

482. Starting with the left-hand side we know that by definition

(1) Arcsin $(-x) = y$ if and only if _____ .

---

482. Sin $y = -x$

483. That is, (2) $-$Sin $y = x$. But we know that

(3) $-$Sin $y = $ Sin (_____).
Hence we have

$\qquad x = -$Sin $y = $ _____ .

---

483. $-y$;
Sin $(-y)$

484. And again by definition

(4) $x = $ Sin $(-y)$ if and only if _____ .

---

484. Arcsin $x = -y$

---

485. Putting these steps together we have

(1) Arcsin $(-x) = y$ if and only if _____ ,

(2) _____ if and only if $-\text{Sin } y = x$,

(3) $-\text{Sin } y = x$ if and only if _____ ,
and, by definition,

(4) _____ if and only if _____ .
Thus,

(5) Arcsin $(-x) = y$ if and only if _____ .
That is,

(6) Arcsin $(-x) = $ _____ ,
and our identity is proved.

---

485. (1) $\text{Sin } y = -x$,
    (2) $\text{Sin } y = -x$,
    (3) $\text{Sin } (-y) = x$,
    (4) $\text{Sin } (-y) = x$, $\text{Arcsin } x = -y$,
    (5) $\text{Arcsin } x = -y$,
    (6) $-\text{Arcsin } x$

486. $\text{Arcsin}\left(-\dfrac{1}{\sqrt{2}}\right) = $ _____

---

486. $-\dfrac{\pi}{4} = -\text{Arcsin}\dfrac{1}{\sqrt{2}}$.

If you had difficulty, see frames 470
to 481.

487. In the chapter on inverse functions, we proved that if
$f : D_f \to R_f$ is a one-to-one function then $f^{-1} : R_f \to D_f$ is a function,
and the composite

$\quad f \circ f^{-1} : \text{(a)} \underline{\quad} \to \underline{\quad}$

is defined by $f \circ f^{-1}(x) = \text{(b)} \underline{\quad}$ for $x \in \text{(c)} \underline{\quad}$.

---

487. (a) R_f; R_f,
(b) x, **(c)** R_f .

If you had difficulty, see frames 286
to 291 in Volume II on functions.

488. Thus, if we start with any real number x, $-1 \leqslant x \leqslant 1$, and
first apply Arcsine to x, and then apply sine to the result, we

get ____ . That is, $\sin(\text{Arcsin } x) = $ ____ for all $x \in [-1, 1]$.

---

488. x;
x

489. Thus, $\sin (\text{Arcsin } \frac{1}{8}) = $ **(a)** _____ ,

$\sin (\text{Arcsin } \frac{1}{\sqrt{2}} = $ **(b)** _____ ,

$\sin (\text{Arcsin } (-\frac{1}{5})) = $ **(c)** _____ ,

$\sin (\text{Arcsin } .7031) = $ **(d)** _____ .

---

489. **(a)** $\frac{1}{8}$, **(b)** $\frac{1}{\sqrt{2}}$,

(c) $-\frac{1}{5}$, **(d)** .7031

If you had difficulty, see frames 487 and 488.

490. Similarly, we can form Arcsin (Sin x).

Arcsin (Sin x) = _____ for all x, _____ x _____ .

---

490. x;

$-\frac{\pi}{2} \leqslant \quad \leqslant \frac{\pi}{2}$

491. Thus, $\text{Arcsin } (\text{Sin } \frac{\pi}{2}) = $ **(a)** _____ ,

$\text{Arcsin } (\text{Sin } \frac{\pi}{12}) = $ **(b)** _____ ,

$\text{Arcsin } (\text{Sin } (-\frac{\pi}{9})) = $ **(c)** _____ .

---

491. **(a)** $\frac{\pi}{2}$,

(b) $\frac{\pi}{12}$,

(c) $-\frac{\pi}{9}$

492. The domain of sin x is _____ and the range of sin x is _____ .

---

492. all real numbers (or all angles); $\{y \in R \mid -1 \leqslant y \leqslant 1\}$

493. But the domain of Sin x is _____ and the range of Sin x is _____ .

---

493. the interval

$-\frac{\pi}{2} \leqslant x \leqslant \frac{\pi}{2}$ of real numbers (or angles); $\{y \in R \mid -1 \leqslant y \leqslant 1\}$

494. Thus, the domain of Arcsin x is _____ , and the range of Arcsin x is _____ .

---

494. $\{x \in R \mid -1 \leqslant x \leqslant 1\}$;

the interval $-\frac{\pi}{2} \leqslant y \leqslant \frac{\pi}{2}$ of real numbers (or angles)

495. The domain of sin (Arcsin x) is **(a)** _____

and the range of sin (Arcsin x) is **(b)** _____

and sin (Arcsin x) = **(c)** ___ for all $x \in$ **(d)** _____ .

495. **(a)** $\{x \in R \mid -1 \leqslant x \leqslant 1\}$,
(b) $\{x \in R \mid -1 \leqslant x \leqslant 1\}$,
(c) x, **(d)** $-1 \leqslant x \leqslant 1$

496. Finally, the domain of Arcsin (Sin x) is

(a) _____ and the range of Arcsin (Sin x) is

(b) _____ and Arcsin (Sin x) = **(c)** ___ , for all

$x \in$ **(d)** _____ .

496. **(a)** the interval $-\dfrac{\pi}{2} \leqslant x \leqslant \dfrac{\pi}{2}$,

(b) the interval $-\dfrac{\pi}{2} \leqslant x \leqslant \dfrac{\pi}{2}$,

(c) x, **(d)** $-\dfrac{\pi}{2} \leqslant x \leqslant \dfrac{\pi}{2}$

QUIZ

If you cannot answer the following questions correctly, review the appropriate frames.

1. Give the domain and range of the restricted sine function Sin x and the function Arcsin x.

Function	Domain	Range
Sin x		
Arcsin x		

2. By definition Arcsin $x = y$ if and only if (iff) _____ .

3. Prove that Arcsin $(-x) = -$Arcsin x.

4. For any x in the domain of Arcsin x, sin (Arcsin x) = _____ .

5. Arcsin $\left(-\dfrac{\sqrt{3}}{2}\right) = $ _____ .

Answers are at end of book.

ARCCOSINE

Upon completing this section, you should be able to

I. Give the domain and range of the restricted cosine function $\cos x$.

II. Define and give the domain and range of $\text{Arccos } x$.

III. Prove that $\text{Arccos}\,(-x) = \pi - \text{Arccos } x$.

IV. Calculate the values for

(A) $\text{Arccos } 1$, $\text{Arccos}\left(-\dfrac{\sqrt{3}}{2}\right)$, etc.

(B) $\sin\left(\text{Arccos } \dfrac{1}{\sqrt{2}}\right)$, $\cos\left(\text{Arcsin}\left(-\dfrac{\sqrt{2}}{2}\right)\right)$, etc.

(C) $\cos\,(\text{Arccos } x)$, $\text{Arccos}\,(\cos x$, $\sin\,(\text{Arccos } x)$, and $\cos\,(\text{Arcsin } x)$.

(D) $\sin\left(\text{Arccos } \dfrac{3x}{5}\right)$ and $\cos\left(\text{Arcsin}\left(-\dfrac{x}{2}\right)\right)$, etc.

497. As we did with the sine of x, we can restrict the domains of the other trigonometric functions and form $\text{Cos } x$, $\text{Tan } x$, $\text{Csc } x$, $\text{Sec } x$, and $\text{Cot } x$, where the restricted functions are all denoted by an initial capital letter.

Look at the graph of $y = \cos x$ and choose an interval on which $\cos x$ is one-to-one and the range of $\cos x$ is still $\{y \in R \mid -1 \leqslant y \leqslant 1\}$.

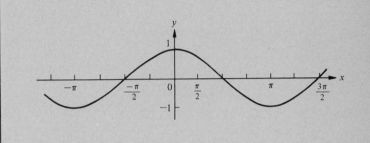

$y = \cos x$ is one-to-one if x is in the interval _____ .

497.

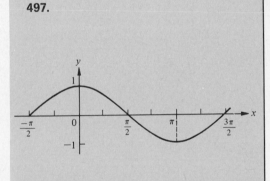

$0 \leqslant x \leqslant \pi$.

NOTE: Again, many possible intervals would do, such as $[-2\pi, -\pi]$, $[-\pi, 0]$, $[\pi, 2\pi]$. But it is customary to choose the closed interval $0 \leqslant x \leqslant \pi$.

Notice that $-\dfrac{\pi}{2} \leqslant x \leqslant \dfrac{\pi}{2}$ will not do since the horizontal line test fails on that interval.

---

498. We shall denote our restricted function by $\text{Cos } x$, with a capital C, to distinguish it from $\cos x$ whose domain is the set of all real numbers. By definition,

$\text{Cos } x = $ _____ if _____ .

---

498. $\cos x$; $0 \leqslant x \leqslant \pi$

499. Since $\text{Cos}\,x$ is one-to-one, it has an inverse called the **Arcsine** or **inverse cosine** function. We denote it by

$\text{Arccos}\,x$ or _____ .

DEFINITION: The **Arccosine** or **inverse cosine** function is the function whose domain is

$\{x \in R \mid$ _____ $\}$
and $\text{Arccos}\,x = y$ where $x = \text{Cos}\,y$.

---

499. $\text{Cos}^{-1}\,x$;
$-1 \leqslant x \leqslant 1$

---

500. Thus, the domain of $\text{Cos}^{-1}\,x$ is _____

and the range is _____ .

---

500. $\{x \in R \mid -1 \leqslant x \leqslant 1\}$;
$\{y \in R \mid 0 \leqslant y \leqslant \pi\}$ (since
$x = \text{Cos}\,y$ is defined only for
$0 \leqslant y \leqslant \pi$)

---

501. The solid line on the coordinate axes represents the entire graph of $y = \text{Cos}\,x$. Graph $y = \text{Arccos}\,x$ on the same axes.

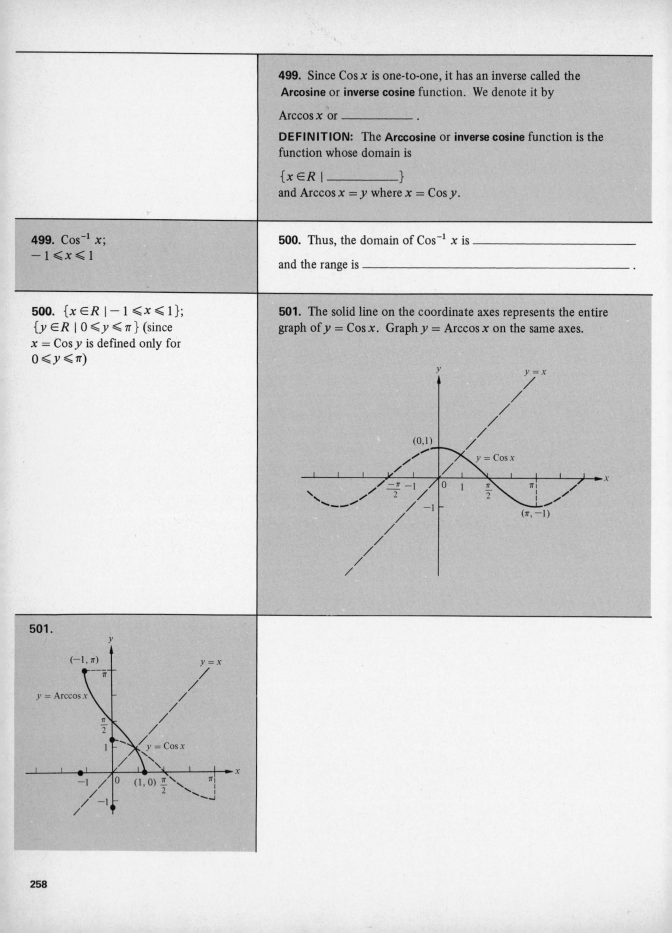

501.

258

502. As in the case of $\sin x$, each real number y in the range, $\{y \in R \mid -1 \leqslant y \leqslant 1\}$, of $\cos x$ has a principal value associated with it. This time the principal values lie in the interval

_____ x _____ .

---

502. $0 \leqslant; \leqslant \pi$

503. By definition Arccos $x = y$ if and only if _____ ,

and we read $y =$ Arccos x as "_____

_____ ."

---

503. Cos $y = x$;
y is that number or angle whose cosine is x

EXAMPLE 3

504.

Arccos $1 =$ **(a)** ____ Arccos $0 =$ **(b)** ____

Arccos $\dfrac{1}{\sqrt{2}} =$ **(c)** ____

---

504. **(a)** 0, **(b)** $\dfrac{\pi}{2}$, **(c)** $\dfrac{\pi}{4}$.

If you had difficulty, go on to the next frame. If not, skip to frame 507.

505. By definition Arccos $1 = y$ if and only if _____ .

---

505. Cos $y = 1$

506. That is, we want an angle y, in the interval $[0, \pi]$, whose cosine is 1. Thus, $y =$ **(a)** ____ . And Arccos $1 =$ **(b)** ____ .
Arccos 0 and Arccos $\dfrac{1}{\sqrt{2}}$ are similar. Arccos $0 =$ **(c)** ____ and

Arccos $\dfrac{1}{\sqrt{2}} =$ **(d)** ____ .

---

506. **(a)** 0,
(b) 0,
(c) $\dfrac{\pi}{2}$,
(d) $\dfrac{\pi}{4}$

EXAMPLE 4

507.

$\text{Arccos } \frac{1}{2} = \textbf{(a)} \underline{\hspace{1cm}} \quad \text{Arccos}\left(-\frac{1}{2}\right) = \textbf{(b)} \underline{\hspace{1cm}}$

$\text{Arccos}\,(-1) = \textbf{(c)} \underline{\hspace{1cm}} \quad \text{Arccos}\left(-\frac{1}{\sqrt{2}}\right) = \textbf{(d)} \underline{\hspace{1cm}}.$

NOTE: In general $\text{Arccos}\,(-x) \neq -\text{Arccos}\,x$. We shall soon see what $\text{Arccos}\,(-x)$ does equal.

---

507. **(a)** $\frac{\pi}{3}$, **(b)** $\frac{2\pi}{3}$, **(c)** π, **(d)** $\frac{3\pi}{4}$.

If you had difficulty, go on to the next frame. If not, skip to frame 513.

508. Arccos x associates with any x in $-1 \leqslant x \leqslant 1$ its principal value. Therefore, Arccos $x = y$ must lie in the interval

$\underline{\hspace{1cm}}\ y\ \underline{\hspace{1cm}}.$

---

508. $0 \leqslant;\ \leqslant \pi$

509. Thus, if we think in terms of angles, y must lie in

quadrant $\underline{\hspace{1cm}}$ or quadrant $\underline{\hspace{1cm}}$.

---

509. I; II

510. If x is negative, the angle $y = \text{Arccos}\,x$ will lie in quadrant $\underline{\hspace{0.5cm}}$,

y will be $\underline{\hspace{2cm}}$.
$\phantom{y \text{ will be }}$ (positive, negative)

---

510. II; positive
NOTE: y will always be positive since $y = \text{Arccos}\,x$ must always be in the range $0 \leqslant y \leqslant \pi$.

511. Thus if we think in terms of angles, to find $\text{Arccos}\left(-\frac{1}{2}\right)$, we want that angle in quadrant $\underline{\hspace{1cm}}$ whose cosine is $\underline{\hspace{1cm}}$.

---

511. II; $-\frac{1}{2}$

512. But $\text{Cos}\,\textbf{(a)} \underline{\hspace{1cm}} = -\frac{1}{2}$, and thus $\text{Arccos}\left(-\frac{1}{2}\right) = \textbf{(b)} \underline{\hspace{1cm}}.$

Similarly, $\text{Arccos}\,(-1) = \textbf{(c)} \underline{\hspace{1cm}}$ and $\text{Arccos}\left(-\frac{1}{\sqrt{2}}\right) = \textbf{(b)} \underline{\hspace{1cm}}$,

---

512. **(a)** $\frac{2\pi}{3}$, **(b)** $\frac{2\pi}{3}$, **(c)** π, **(d)** $\frac{3\pi}{4}$

513. We see from frames 504 to 512 that

$\text{Arccos } 1 = 0$ and $\text{Arccos}\,(-1) = \textbf{(a)} \underline{\hspace{1cm}}$,

$\text{Arccos }\frac{1}{\sqrt{2}} = \frac{\pi}{4}$ and $\text{Arccos}\left(-\frac{1}{\sqrt{2}}\right) = \textbf{(d)} \underline{\hspace{1cm}}$

$\text{Arccos }\frac{1}{2} = \frac{\pi}{3}$ and $\text{Arccos}\left(-\frac{1}{2}\right) = \textbf{(c)} \underline{\hspace{1cm}}$, and, in general, if

$\text{Arccos }x = y$, then $\text{Arccos}\,(-x) = \textbf{(d)} \underline{\hspace{1cm}}.$

---

513. **(a)** π, **(b)** $\frac{3\pi}{4}$, **(c)** $\frac{2\pi}{3}$, **(d)** $\pi - y$

514. Prove the identity

$\text{Arccos}(-x) = \pi - \text{Arccos}\, x.$

---

514. If you had difficulty, go on to the next frame. If not, skip to frame 519.

515. Starting with the left-hand side of the identity, we know that by definition

(1) $\text{Arccos}(-x) = y$ if and only if _____ .

---

515. $\text{Cos}\, y = -x$

516. That is,

(2) $-\text{Cos}\, y = x.$

But one of the reduction formulas shows that

(3) $-\text{Cos}\, y = \text{Cos}\, (\underline{\quad\quad}).$

---

516. $\pi - y$

517. Hence, we have $x = \text{Cos}\,(\pi - y).$

And again by definition,

[4] $x = \text{Cos}\,(\pi - y)$ if and only if _____ .

---

517. $\text{Arccos}\, x = \pi - y$

518. Putting these steps together we have by definition

(1) Arccos $(-x) = y$ if and only if _____ .

(2) _____ if and only if $-\text{Cos } y = x$.

(3) $-\text{Cos } y = x$ if and only if _____ ,
and again by definition

(4) _____ if and only if _____ .
Thus,

(5) Arccos $(-x) = y$ if and only if _____ .
That is,

(6) Arccos $(-x) = y$ if and only if _____ $= y$,
and

(7) Arccos $(-x) =$ _____ ,
which proves our identity.

---

518. (1) $\text{Cos } y = -x$,
(2) $\text{Cos } y = -x$,
(3) $\text{Cos } (\pi - y) = x$,
(4) $\text{Cos } (\pi - y) = x$; Arccos $x = \pi - y$,
(5) Arccos $x = \pi - y$,
(6) $\pi - \text{Arccos } x$,
(7) $\pi - \text{Arccos } x$

519. Arccos $(-\dfrac{\sqrt{3}}{2}) =$ _____

---

519. $\dfrac{5\pi}{6} = \pi - \dfrac{\pi}{6} = \pi - \text{Arccos } \dfrac{\sqrt{3}}{2}$

520. If we start with any real number x, $-1 \leqslant x \leqslant 1$, and first apply Arccosine to x, and then apply cosine to the result, we get **(a)** _____ . That is, cos (Arccos x) = **(b)** _____ for all x, **(c)** _____ x _____ .

---

520. (a) x,
(b) x,
(c) $-1 \leqslant; \leqslant 1$

521. Thus, cos (Arccos $\dfrac{1}{7}$) = **(a)** _____ ,

cos (Arccos $\dfrac{\sqrt{3}}{2}$) = **(b)** _____ ,

cos (Arcos $(-\dfrac{1}{3})$) = **(c)** _____ , and

cos (Arcos $(-.3201)$) = **(d)** _____ .

521.
(a) $\dfrac{1}{7}$, (b) $\dfrac{\sqrt{3}}{2}$, (c) $-\dfrac{1}{3}$,

(d) $-.3201$

522. Similarly, we can form Arccos (Cos x).

Arccos (Cos x) = ____ for all x, ____ x ____ .

522. x; $0 \leqslant ; \leqslant \pi$

523. Thus, Arccos$\left(\text{Cos } \dfrac{\pi}{9}\right)$ = **(a)** ____ ,

Arccos$\left(\text{Cos } \dfrac{\pi}{3}\right)$ = **(b)** ____ , and

Arccos$\left(\text{Cos } \dfrac{11\pi}{12}\right)$ = **(c)** ____ .

523. **(a)** $\dfrac{\pi}{9}$,

(b) $\dfrac{\pi}{3}$,

(c) $\dfrac{11\pi}{12}$

524. In discussing Arcsine and Arccosine, we have sometimes taken both the domain and the range to be subsets of real numbers, since there are many problems, especially in calculus, where an answer in angles would be meaningless. For example, the area of the shaded region is given by Area = Arcsin t.

However, as we have seen, it is sometimes convenient to consider the ranges of the inverse trigonometric functions as sets of angles. Under this assumption the domain of both Arcsine and Arccosine

is **(a)** _____ , and the range of Arcsine is the set of

angles y such that **(b)** _____ , while the range of

Arccosine is **(c)** _____ .

524. **(a)** $\{x \in R \mid -1 \leqslant x \leqslant 1\}$,

(b) $-\dfrac{\pi}{2} \leqslant y \leqslant \dfrac{\pi}{2}$,

(c) the set of angles y such that $0 \leqslant y \leqslant \pi$

525. Earlier, we considered $f \circ f^{-1}$ where $f(x) = \text{Sin } x$ and $f^{-1}(x) = \text{Arcsin } x$. If $f = \sin x$ and $g^{-1} = \text{Arccos } x$, we can still form the composite function $f \circ g^{-1}$. That is, $f \circ g^{-1}$ defined by

$$(f \circ g^{-1})(x) = f(g^{-1}(x)) = \sin(\text{Arccos } x)$$

has as its domain _____
and its range is at least contained in

_____ .

---

525. $\{x \in R \mid -1 \leqslant x \leqslant 1\}$;
$\{x \in R \mid -1 \leqslant x \leqslant 1\}$

EXAMPLE 5

526. $\sin\left(\text{Arccos } \frac{1}{2}\right) =$ _____

---

526. $\dfrac{\sqrt{3}}{2}$.

If you had difficulty, go on to the next frame. If not, skip to frame 529.

527. $\text{Arccos } \frac{1}{2} =$ _____ since by definition

$\text{Arccos } \frac{1}{2} = y$ if and only if _____ .

---

527. $\dfrac{\pi}{3} (= 60°)$;

$\text{Cos } y = \dfrac{1}{2}$

528. Thus, $\sin\left(\text{Arccos } \frac{1}{2}\right) = \sin \dfrac{\pi}{3} =$ _____ .

---

528. $\dfrac{\sqrt{3}}{2}$

529. Let us now look at a geometric interpretation of the relation between the inverse trigonometric functions and angles.

Consider again the value of $\sin\left(\text{Arccos }\frac{1}{2}\right)$. By definition $\text{Arccos }\frac{1}{2} = y$ if and only if $\text{Cos }y = \frac{1}{2}$. Thus, if we label the central angle y, we can label one of the sides of the triangle 1 and the hypotenuse is 2. Label the sides of length 1 and 2.

529.

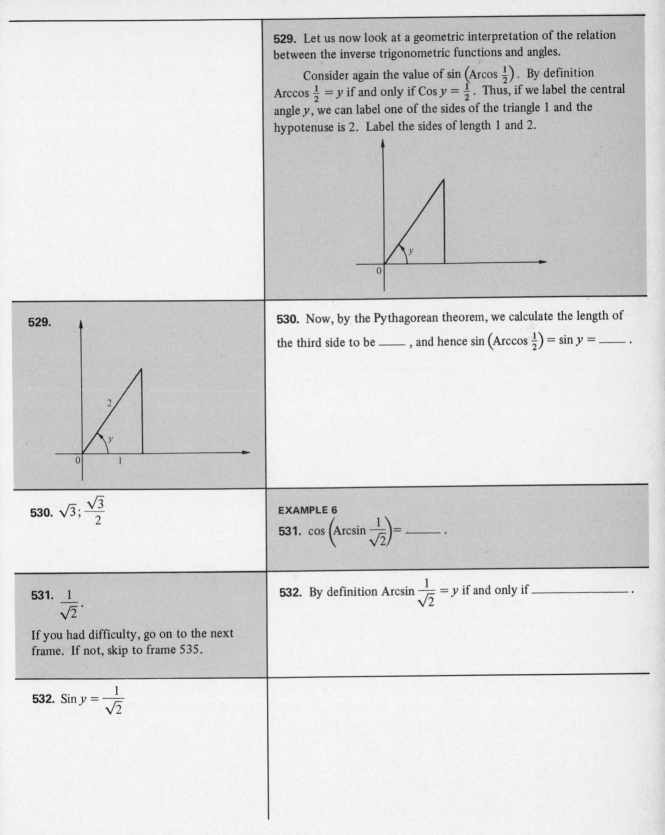

530. Now, by the Pythagorean theorem, we calculate the length of the third side to be _____ , and hence $\sin\left(\text{Arccos }\frac{1}{2}\right) = \sin y = $ _____ .

530. $\sqrt{3}$; $\dfrac{\sqrt{3}}{2}$

EXAMPLE 6

531. $\cos\left(\text{Arcsin }\dfrac{1}{\sqrt{2}}\right) = $ _____ .

531. $\dfrac{1}{\sqrt{2}}$.

If you had difficulty, go on to the next frame. If not, skip to frame 535.

532. By definition $\text{Arcsin }\dfrac{1}{\sqrt{2}} = y$ if and only if _____ .

532. $\text{Sin }y = \dfrac{1}{\sqrt{2}}$

533. Draw a triangle, label the central angle y, and label the three sides with the appropriate values.

533.

Diagram is derived from $\sin y = \dfrac{1}{\sqrt{2}}$ and the Pythagorean theorem.

534. Hence $\cos\left(\text{Arcsin }\dfrac{1}{\sqrt{2}}\right) = \cos y = \underline{\hspace{2cm}}$.

534. $\dfrac{1}{\sqrt{2}}$

EXAMPLE 7

535. $\sin\left(\text{Arccos}\left(-\dfrac{\sqrt{3}}{2}\right)\right) = \underline{\hspace{2cm}}$.

535. $\frac{1}{2}$.

If you had difficulty, go on to the next frame. If not, skip to frame 539.

536. By definition, $\text{Arccos}\left(-\dfrac{\sqrt{3}}{2}\right) = y$ if and only if $\underline{\hspace{2cm}}$.

536. $\cos y = -\dfrac{\sqrt{3}}{2}$

266

537. Draw a triangle and label the appropriate angle and the three sides.

537.

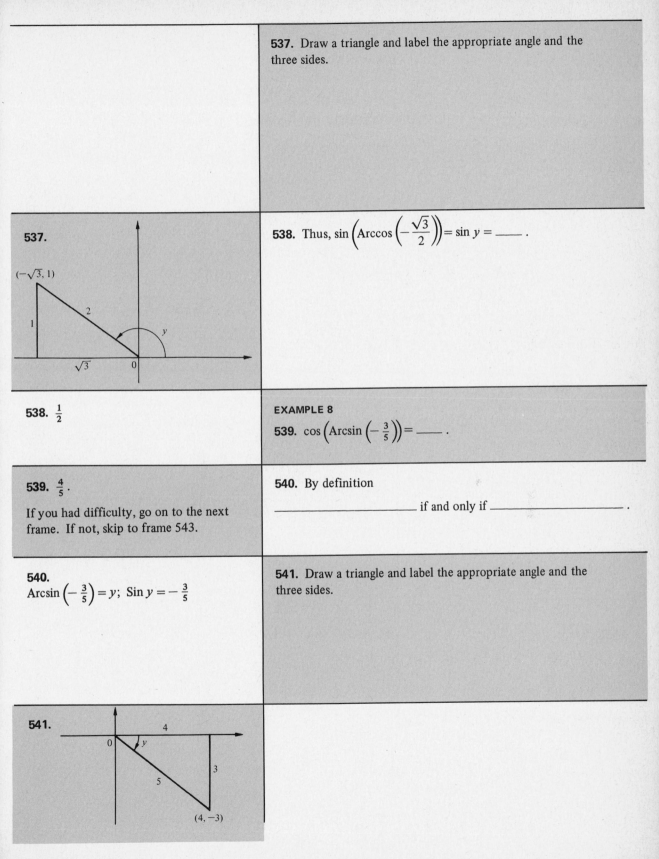

538. Thus, $\sin\left(\text{Arccos}\left(-\dfrac{\sqrt{3}}{2}\right)\right) = \sin y = $ _____ .

---

538. $\dfrac{1}{2}$

EXAMPLE 8

539. $\cos\left(\text{Arcsin}\left(-\dfrac{3}{5}\right)\right) = $ _____ .

---

539. $\dfrac{4}{5}$.

If you had difficulty, go on to the next frame. If not, skip to frame 543.

540. By definition

_____ if and only if _____ .

540.
$\text{Arcsin}\left(-\dfrac{3}{5}\right) = y$; $\text{Sin } y = -\dfrac{3}{5}$

541. Draw a triangle and label the appropriate angle and the three sides.

541.

267

542. Thus, $\cos\left(\text{Arcsin}\left(-\frac{3}{5}\right)\right) =$ _____ .

---

542. $\cos y = \frac{4}{5}$

EXAMPLE 9

543. If $0 \leqslant x \leqslant 1$, then $\sin(\text{Arccos } x) =$ _____ .

---

543. $\sqrt{1-x^2}$.

If you had difficulty, go on to the next frame. If not, skip to frame 547.

544. By definition

Arccos $x = y$ if and only if _____ .

---

544. Cos $y = x$

545. Draw a triangle and label the appropriate angle and the three sides.

545.

546. Thus, $\sin(\text{Arccos } x) = \sin y =$ _____

if $0 \leqslant x \leqslant 1$.

---

546. $\dfrac{\sqrt{1-x^2}}{1} = \sqrt{1-x^2}$

547. If $-1 \leqslant x \leqslant 0$, then $\sin(\text{Arccos } x) =$ _____ .

---

547. $\sqrt{1-x^2}$.

If you had difficulty, see frames 543 to 546. This time, draw the triangle in quadrant II.

EXAMPLE 10

548. If $0 \leqslant x \leqslant 1$, then $\cos(\text{Arcsin } x) =$ _____ .

---

548. $\sqrt{1-x^2}$.

If you had difficulty, go on to the next frame. If not, skip to frame 552.

549. By definition Arcsin $x = y$ if and only if _____ .

---

549. Sin $y = x$

550. Draw a triangle and label the appropriate angle and the three sides.

550.

551. Thus, $\cos(\text{Arcsin } x) = \cos y =$ _____ .

---

551. $\sqrt{1-x^2}$

552. Finally, if $-1 \leqslant x \leqslant 0$, then $\cos(\text{Arcsin } x) =$ _____ .

In which quadrant should you draw your triangle this time? ____

---

552. $\sqrt{1-x^2}$; IV.

If you had difficulty, see frames 548 to 551.

553. Thus, for all values of x in the domain of Arcsine and Arccosine,

$\sin(\text{Arccos } x) = \cos(\text{Arcsin } x) =$ _____ .

---

553. $\sqrt{1-x^2}$

EXAMPLE 11

554. $\cos\left(\text{Arcsin } \dfrac{3x}{5}\right) =$ _____

---

554. $\dfrac{\sqrt{25-9x^2}}{5}$.

If you had difficulty, go on to the next frame. If not, skip to frame 558.

555. By definition Arcsin $\dfrac{3x}{5} = y$ if and only if _____ .

---

555. Sin $y = \dfrac{3x}{5}$

556. Draw a triangle and label the appropriate angle y and the appropriate side $3x$. Then fill in the values for the two other sides.

556.

NOTE: We could have drawn our triangle in quadrant IV, representative of the case where $x < 0$. The result would be the same.

557. Thus, $\cos\left(\text{Arcsin } \dfrac{3x}{5}\right) = \cos y = $ _____ .

557. $\dfrac{\sqrt{25 - 9x^2}}{5}$

558. $\dfrac{\sqrt{4 - 3x^2}}{2}$.

If you had difficulty, see frames 554 to 557.

EXERCISE 1

558.

$\sin\left(\text{Arcos}\left(-\dfrac{\sqrt{3x}}{2}\right)\right) = $ _____

If you cannot answer the following questions correctly, review the appropriate frames.

1. Give the domain and range of the restricted cosine function Cos x and the function Arccos x.

Function	Domain	Range
Cos x		
Arccos x		

2. By definition Arccos $x = y$ iff _____ .

3. Prove that Arccos $(-x) = \pi -$ Arccos x.

4. Calculate the following

   (a) $\text{Arccos}\left(-\dfrac{1}{\sqrt{2}}\right)$

   (b) $\text{Arccos}(\cos x)$

   (c) $\text{Cos}(\text{Arcsin } x)$

   (d) $\sin\left(\text{Arcos}\left(-\dfrac{x}{2}\right)\right)$

Answers are at end of book.

ARCTANGENT

Upon completing this section, you should be able to

I. Give the domain and range of the restricted tangent function Tan x.

II. Define and give the domain and range of Arctan x.

III. Prove that Arctan$(-x) = -$Arctan x.

IV. Calculate values for Arctan 1, Arctan$\sqrt{3}$, etc. and tan (Arctan x) and Arctan (Tan x).

V. State whether the following are defined and, if so, calculate them.

(A) $\tan\left(\text{Arcsin } \frac{\sqrt{3}}{2}\right)$ $\cos\left(\text{Arctan}\left(-\frac{4}{3}\right)\right)$, etc.

(B) tan (Arccos x), sec (Arctan x), etc.

(C) $\cos\left(\text{Arctan } \frac{9x}{2}\right)$, $\cot\left(\text{Arcsin}\left(-\frac{\sqrt{7x}}{4}\right)\right)$, etc.

559. Now we turn to the definition of Arctangent. On the graph of $y = \tan x$, choose an interval for which $\tan x$ is one-to-one and the range of $\tan x$ is still the set of all real numbers.

$y = \tan x$ is one-to-one if x is in the interval

_____ x _____ .

---

559. $-\dfrac{\pi}{2} <; < \dfrac{\pi}{2}$.

NOTE: $\tan x$ is not defined at the end points $-\dfrac{\pi}{2}$ and $\dfrac{\pi}{2}$. Once more, there are many possible intervals, such as $-\dfrac{3\pi}{2} < x < -\dfrac{\pi}{2}$ and $\dfrac{\pi}{2} < x < \dfrac{3\pi}{2}$.
But it is customary to choose the open interval $-\dfrac{\pi}{2} < x < \dfrac{\pi}{2}$.

560. And we shall denote the restricted tangent function by $\operatorname{Tan} x$ to distinguish it from $\tan x$, which is not one-to-one.

$\operatorname{Tan} x =$ _____ if _____ x _____ .

---

560. $\tan x$;
$-\dfrac{\pi}{2} <; < \dfrac{\pi}{2}$

561. Since $\operatorname{Tan} x$ is one-to-one, it has an inverse called the **Arctangent** or **inverse tangent** function. We denote it by

Arctan x or _____ .

DEFINITION: The **Arctangent** or **inverse tangent** function is a function whose domain is _____ ,
and Arctan $x = y$ where $x = \operatorname{Tan} y$.

---

561. $\operatorname{Tan}^{-1} x$;
R, the set of all real numbers

562. Thus, the domain of $\text{Tan}^{-1} x$ is R, and the range is

_____ .

---

562. $\left\{ y \in R \mid -\dfrac{\pi}{2} < y < \dfrac{\pi}{2} \right\}$

$\left(\text{since } x = \text{Tan } y \text{ is defined only for} \right.$

$\left. -\dfrac{\pi}{2} < y < \dfrac{\pi}{2} \right)$

---

563. The dotted lines represent the graph of $\tan x$. Graph $\text{Tan } x$ with a solid line.

Then graph $y = \text{Arctan } x$ on the same axes.

563.

---

564. Each real number y in the range to $\tan x$ has a principal value

in the interval _____ associated with it.

---

564. $-\dfrac{\pi}{2} < x < \dfrac{\pi}{2}$

EXAMPLE 12
565. Arctan $0 =$ (a) _____ Arctan $\dfrac{1}{\sqrt{3}} =$ (b) _____

Arctan $\sqrt{3} =$ (c) _____ Arctan $1 =$ (d) _____

---

565. (a) 0, (b) $\dfrac{\pi}{6}$, (c) $\dfrac{\pi}{3}$, (d) $\dfrac{\pi}{4}$.

If you had difficulty, go on to the next frame. If not, skip to frame 569.

566. By definition Arctan $\dfrac{1}{\sqrt{3}} = y$ if and only if _____ .

---

566. Tan $y = \dfrac{1}{\sqrt{3}}$

567. That is, we want an angle y, in the interval _____ , whose tan is $\dfrac{1}{\sqrt{3}}$.

---

567. $-\dfrac{\pi}{2} < y < \dfrac{\pi}{2}$

568. Thus $y =$ (a) _____ . That is, Arctan $\dfrac{1}{\sqrt{3}} =$ (b) _____ .

Similarly, Arctan $0 =$ (c) _____ , Arctan $\sqrt{3} =$ (d) _____ , and

Arctan $1 =$ (e) _____ .

---

568. (a) $\dfrac{\pi}{6}$, (b) $\dfrac{\pi}{6}$, (c) 0,

(d) $\dfrac{\pi}{3}$, (e) $\dfrac{\pi}{4}$

EXAMPLE 13
569.

Arctan $\left(-\dfrac{1}{\sqrt{3}}\right) =$ (a) _____

Arctan $\left(-\sqrt{3}\right) =$ (b) _____

Arctan $(-1) =$ (c) _____

---

569. (a) $-\dfrac{\pi}{6}$, (b) $-\dfrac{\pi}{3}$, (c) $-\dfrac{\pi}{4}$.

If you had difficulty, go on to the next frame. If not, skip to frame 575.

570. Arctan x associates with any $x \in R$ its principal value. Therefore Arctan $x = y$ must lie in the interval

_____ y _____ .

---

570. $-\dfrac{\pi}{2} <;\ < \dfrac{\pi}{2}$

571. Thus, if we think in terms of angles, Arctan $x = y$ must lie in quadrant _____ or quadrant _____ .

---

571. I; IV

572. If x is negative, the angle $y = \text{Arctan } x$ will be in quadrant ___ , and y will be _____ .
(positive, negative)

---

572. IV; negative

573. Thus, to find $\text{Arctan}\left(-\dfrac{1}{\sqrt{3}}\right)$, we want the angle in quadrant ___ whose tan is ___ .

---

573. IV; $-\dfrac{1}{\sqrt{3}}$

$(\sqrt{3}, -1)$

574. And (a) $\tan$ (___) $= -\dfrac{1}{\sqrt{3}}$. Thus,

$\text{Arctan}\left(-\dfrac{1}{\sqrt{3}}\right) =$ (b) ___ . Similarly, $\text{Arctan}\left(-\sqrt{3}\right) =$ (c) ___

and $\text{Arctan}\left(-1\right) =$ (d) ___ .

---

574. (a) $-\dfrac{\pi}{6}$, (b) $-\dfrac{\pi}{6}$.

NOTE: $\tan\dfrac{5\pi}{6}$ is also equal to $-\dfrac{1}{\sqrt{3}}$, but $\dfrac{5\pi}{6}$ is *not* the principal value since it does not lie in the interval $-\dfrac{\pi}{2} < y < \dfrac{\pi}{2}$.

(c) $-\dfrac{\pi}{3}$, (d) $-\dfrac{\pi}{4}$

575. We see from frames 565 to 574 that
$\text{Arctan}\left(\dfrac{1}{\sqrt{3}}\right) =$ (a) ___ and $\text{Arctan}\left(-\dfrac{1}{\sqrt{3}}\right) =$ (b) ___ ,
$\text{Arctan}\ \sqrt{3} =$ (c) ___ and $\text{Arctan}\left(-\sqrt{3}\right) =$ (d) ___ ,
$\text{Arctan}\ 1 =$ (e) ___ and $\text{Arctan}\left(-1\right) =$ (f) ___ .
And, in general, if
$\text{Arctan } x = y$ then $\text{Arctan}\left(-x\right) =$ (g) ___ .

---

575. (a) $\dfrac{\pi}{6}$, (b) $-\dfrac{\pi}{6}$,

(c) $\dfrac{\pi}{3}$, (d) $-\dfrac{\pi}{3}$, (e) $\dfrac{\pi}{4}$,

(f) $-\dfrac{\pi}{4}$, (g) $-y$

EXERCISE 2
576. Prove the identity $\text{Arctan}\left(-x\right) = -\text{Arctan } x$.

---

576. If you had difficulty, see frames 481 to 485. The proof is the same.

577. Just as we did for Arcsin and Arccosine, we can form the composite function tan (Arctan x).

tan (Arctan x) = ___ for all x, _____

---

577. x ;
$x \in R$ (or $-\infty < x < \infty$)

578. Thus tan (Arctan 17) = **(a)** _____ ,

tan (Arctan $\sqrt{3}$) = **(b)** _____ ,

tan $\left(\text{Arctan}\left(-\dfrac{1}{\sqrt{3}}\right)\right)$ = **(c)** _____ ,

and

tan (Arctan (-142)) = **(d)** _____ .

---

578. **(a)** 17, **(b)** $\sqrt{3}$,
(c) $-\dfrac{1}{\sqrt{3}}$, **(d)** -142

579. Similarly, we can form Arctan (Tan x).

Arctan (Tan x) = ___ for all x, _____

---

579. x ;
$-\dfrac{\pi}{2} < x < \dfrac{\pi}{2}$

580. If we think of the trigonometric functions as functions from angles to real numbers, then tan (Arctan x is a function from

(a) _____ to **(b)** _____ , and
(angles, real numbers)

Arctan (Tan x) is a function from **(c)** _____ to

(d) _____ .

---

580. **(a)** real numbers,
(b) real numbers,
(c) angles,
(d) angles

EXAMPLE 14

581. We can now combine Arctan x with sin x and cos x, and tan x with Arcsin x and Arccos x. Use a triangle to evaluate sin (Arctan 1).

sin (Arctan 1) = _____

---

581. $\dfrac{1}{\sqrt{2}}$.

If you had difficulty, go on to the next frame. If not, skip to frame 585.

582. By definition

Arctan $1 = y$ if and only if _____ .

---

582. Tan $y = 1$

583. Draw a triangle, label the central angle y, and label the three sides with the appropriate values.

583.

If you had difficulty, see frames 529 to 534.

584. Sin (Arctan 1) $= \sin y =$ _____

---

584. $\dfrac{1}{\sqrt{2}}$

EXAMPLE 15

585. Evaluate tan $\text{Arccos}\left(-\dfrac{3}{5}\right)$. ____

---

585. $-\dfrac{4}{3}$.

If you had difficulty, go on to the next frame. If not, skip to frame 589.

586. By definition

Arccos $\left(-\dfrac{3}{5}\right) = y$ if and only if _____ .

---

586. Cos $y = -\dfrac{3}{5}$

587. Draw a triangle and label the appropriate angle and the three sides.

587.

588. Thus

$$\tan \left(\text{Arccos}\left(-\tfrac{3}{5}\right)\right) = \tan y = \underline{\hspace{1cm}}$$

588. $-\dfrac{4}{3}$

589. We have defined three functions Sine, Cosine, and Tangent by restricting the domains of sine, cosine, and tangent, respectively. Give the domain and range of Sine, Cosine, and Tanget.

Function	Domain	Range
Sin x		
Cos x		
Tan x		

589.

Sin x	$-\dfrac{\pi}{2} \leqslant x \leqslant \dfrac{\pi}{2}$	$-1 \leqslant y \leqslant 1$
Cos x	$0 \leqslant x \leqslant \pi$	$-1 \leqslant y \leqslant 1$
Tan x	$-\dfrac{\pi}{2} < x < \dfrac{\pi}{2}$	R, the set of all real numbers

590. Sine, Cosine, and Tangent are all one-to-one and hence have inverses. Give the domains and ranges of Arcsine, Arcosine, and Arctangent.

Function	Domain	Range
Arcsin x		
Arccos x		
Arctan x		

590.

Arcsin x	$-1 \leqslant x \leqslant 1$	$-\dfrac{\pi}{2} \leqslant y \leqslant \dfrac{\pi}{2}$
Arccos x	$-1 \leqslant x \leqslant 1$	$0 \leqslant y \leqslant \pi$
Arctan x	R	$-\dfrac{\pi}{2} < y < \dfrac{\pi}{2}$

591. In forming composite functions such as sin (Arccos x) and tan (Arcsin x), with the inverse function taken first, we have always used sin x, cos x, and tan x with small letters, to insure that the range (with the possible exception of the end points) of the inverse function is contained in the domain of the trigonometric function. If we use the restricted trigonometric functions instead, the composite function might not be defined for all values in the domain of the inverse function.

For example, consider Sin $\left(\text{Arcos}\left(-\frac{1}{2}\right)\right)$.

Arccos$\left(-\frac{1}{2}\right) =$ _____ and the domain of

Sin y is _____

591. $\dfrac{2\pi}{3}$;

$-\dfrac{\pi}{2} \leqslant y \leqslant \dfrac{\pi}{2}$

592. Thus Sin $\left(\text{Arccos}\left(-\frac{1}{2}\right)\right) =$ Sin $\dfrac{2\pi}{3}$ is not defined. However, sin $\left(\text{Arccos}\left(-\frac{1}{2}\right)\right)$ is defined and is equal to _____ , since the domain domain of sin y is _____ .

592. $\dfrac{\sqrt{3}}{2}$;

R, the set of all real numbers

593. Is Cos (Arctan (-1)) defined? _____

Why? _____

_____

593. no;

Arctan $\left(-1\right) = -\dfrac{\pi}{4}$ and the domain of

Cos y is $0 \leqslant y \leqslant \pi$.

594. However, cos (Arctan (-1)) = _____ .

594. $\dfrac{1}{\sqrt{2}}$.

If you had difficulty, see frames 539 to 542.

595. We may also run into difficulty in trying to form composite functions such as Arccos (Tan x) and Arctan (Sin x), with the inverse function taken second.

For example, consider Arccos $\left(\text{Tan } \dfrac{\pi}{3}\right)$.

Tan $\dfrac{\pi}{3}$ = ____ and the domain of Arccos y is _____.

---

595. $\sqrt{3}$;
$-1 \leqslant y \leqslant 1$

596. Thus, Arccos $\left(\text{Tan } \dfrac{\pi}{3}\right)$ is not defined. Since the domain of Arccos y is $-1 \leqslant y \leqslant 1$, Arccos (Tan x) will be defined if and only if x is such that Tan x is in the interval _____.

---

596. $-1 \leqslant$ Tan $x \leqslant 1$

597. And Tan x is in the interval $-1 \leqslant$ Tan $x \leqslant 1$ if and only if x is in the interval _____.

---

597. $-\dfrac{\pi}{4} \leqslant x \leqslant \dfrac{\pi}{4}$

598. Thus Arccos (Tan x) is defined if and only if x is in the interval _____.

---

598. $-\dfrac{\pi}{4} \leqslant x \leqslant \dfrac{\pi}{4}$

EXAMPLE 16

599. Give the following values or say they are undefined.

Arcsin (Cos π) = (a) _____   Arccos $\left(\text{Tan } \dfrac{2\pi}{7}\right)$ = (b) _____

Arctan $\left(\text{Sin } \dfrac{\pi}{2}\right)$ = (c) _____

---

599. (a) $-\dfrac{\pi}{2}$,

(b) undefined, since $\dfrac{2\pi}{7} \notin [-\dfrac{\pi}{4}, \dfrac{\pi}{4}])$,

(c) $\dfrac{\pi}{4}$.

If you had difficulty, go on to the next frame. If not, skip to frame 603.

600. To find Arcsin (Cos π) we first find Cos π.

Cos π = ____

---

600. -1

601. And, by definition,

Arcsin $(-1) = y$ if and only if _____.

---

601. Sin $y = -1$

---

602. Thus, $y = $ _____ , and Arcsin (Cos π) = _____ .

602. $-\dfrac{\pi}{2}$; $-\dfrac{\pi}{2}$

603. Similarly, Sin $\dfrac{\pi}{2} = $ _____ , and Arctan $\left(\text{Sin } \dfrac{\pi}{2}\right) = $ _____ .

603. 1; $\dfrac{\pi}{4}$

604. Just as we have formed Sine, Cosine, and Tangent, we can define Cosecant, Secant, and Cotangent (with initial capital letters) by restricting the domains of cosecant, secant, and cotangent. However, there is no agreement on the best choice of domains. One fairly common choice is to restrict Csc x to have the same domain as Sin x. That is, the domain of Csc x would be

_____ x _____ .

604. $-\dfrac{\pi}{2} \leqslant$; $\leqslant \dfrac{\pi}{2}$

605. The domain of Sec x is chosen to be the same as the domain of Cos x. Thus, the domain of Sec x would be _____ .

605. $0 \leqslant x \leqslant \pi$

606. And, as shown by the graph of cot x, a good choice for the domain of Cot x is the interval $0 \leqslant x \leqslant \pi$.

The domains of Sin x and Csc x are the same, and the domains of Cos x and Sec x are the same, but with this choice for Cot x, Cot x and Tan x do not have the same domain, since the domain of Tan x is _____ .

606. $-\dfrac{\pi}{2} < x < \dfrac{\pi}{2}$

EXAMPLE 17

607. Arcsine, Arccosine, and Arctangent occur most frequently, and if necessary may be substituted for an expression involving the other three inverse functions. Therefore, we shall not study the other inverse functions further. However, if you meet one of them, be sure you know what its range is.

We now return to some final practice in evaluating composite functions.

sec $\left(\text{Arctan } \left(-\tfrac{3}{4}\right)\right) = $ _____ .

607. $\dfrac{5}{4}$

If you had difficulty, go on to the next frame. If not, skip to frame 611.

608. By definition, Arctan $\left(-\frac{3}{4}\right) = y$ if and only if _____ .

608. Tan $y = -\frac{3}{4}$

609. Draw a triangle and label the appropriate angle and the three sides.

609.

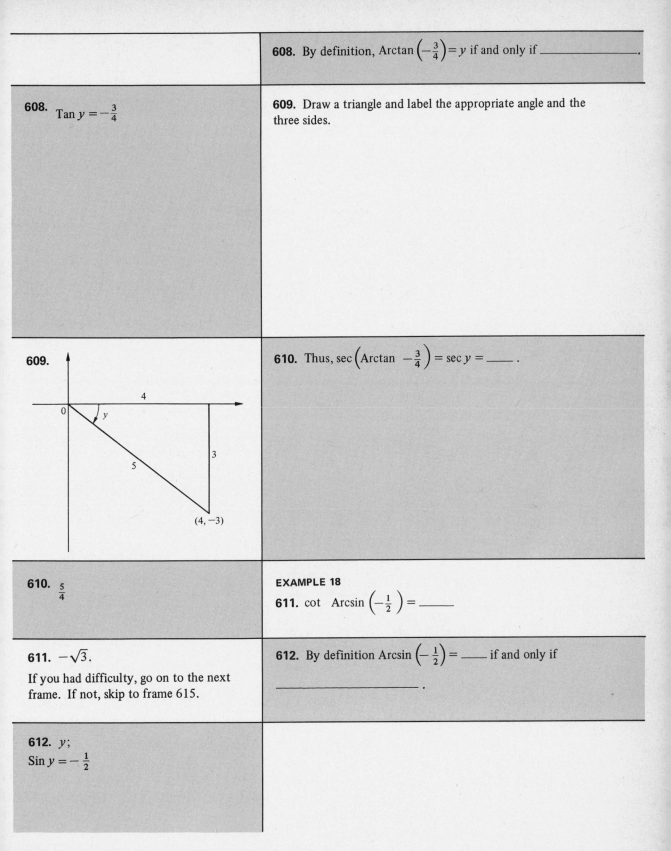

610. Thus, sec $\left(\text{Arctan} \; -\frac{3}{4}\right) = \sec y =$ _____ .

610. $\frac{5}{4}$

EXAMPLE 18

611. cot Arcsin $\left(-\frac{1}{2}\right) =$ _____

611. $-\sqrt{3}$.

If you had difficulty, go on to the next frame. If not, skip to frame 615.

612. By definition Arcsin $\left(-\frac{1}{2}\right) =$ _____ if and only if

_____ .

612. y;

Sin $y = -\frac{1}{2}$

613. Draw a triangle and label the appropriate angle and the three sides.

613.

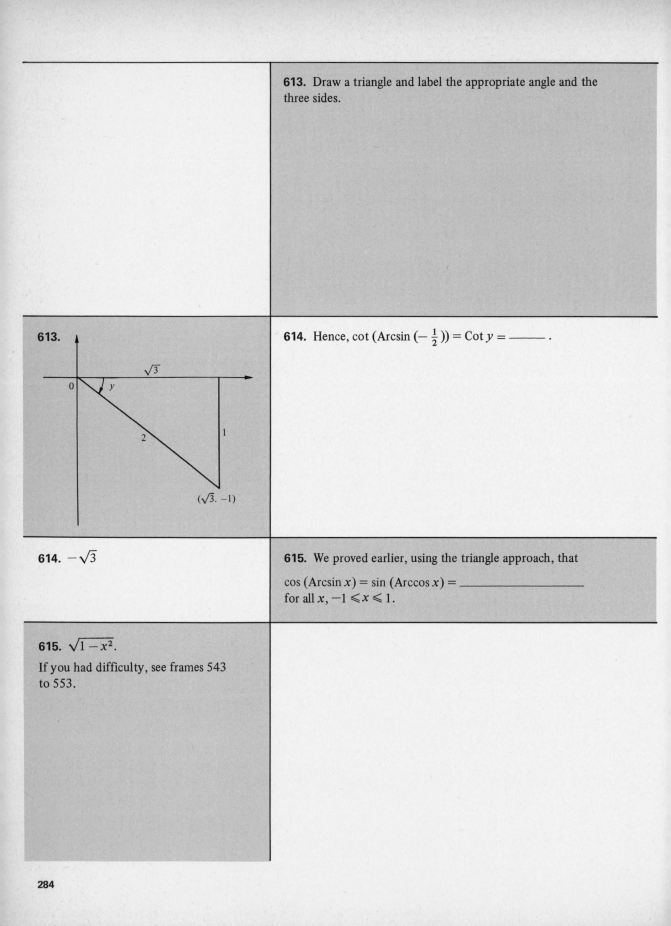

614. Hence, cot $\left(\text{Arcsin}\left(-\frac{1}{2}\right)\right) = \text{Cot } y = $ _____ .

614. $-\sqrt{3}$

615. We proved earlier, using the triangle approach, that

$\cos (\text{Arcsin } x) = \sin (\text{Arccos } x) = $ _____
for all x, $-1 \leqslant x \leqslant 1$.

615. $\sqrt{1 - x^2}$.

If you had difficulty, see frames 543 to 553.

EXAMPLE 19

616. Now draw a triangle and calculate $\tan(\text{Arccos}\,x)$.

$\tan(\text{Arccos}\,x) = \underline{\hspace{3cm}}$

---

616. $\dfrac{\sqrt{1-x^2}}{x}$.

If you had difficulty, go on to the next frame. If not, skip to frame 619.

617. By definition $\text{Arccos}\,x = y$ if and only if $\text{Cos}\,y = x$. Draw a triangle and label the appropriate angle and the three sides.

617.

NOTE: We chose x negative. However, the result is the same if y is in the first quadrant.

618. Thus, tan (Arccos x) = tan y = _____ .

---

618. $\dfrac{\sqrt{1-x^2}}{x}$

EXAMPLE 20
619. sec (Arctan x) = _____

---

619. $\sqrt{x^2+1}$.

If you had difficulty, go on to the next frame. If not, skip to frame 622.

620. By definition Arctan $x = y$ if and only if Tan $y = x$. Draw and label a triangle.

620.

NOTE: We chose x negative. However, the result is the same if y is in the first quadrant.

621. Hence sec (Arctan x) = sec y = _____ .

---

621. $\sqrt{x^2+1}$

EXAMPLE 21
622. $\cos\left(\text{Arctan } \dfrac{9x}{2}\right) =$ _____

---

622. $\dfrac{2}{\sqrt{4+81x^2}}$.

If you had difficulty, go on to the next frame. If not, skip to frame 625.

623. By definition Arctan $\dfrac{9x}{2} = y$ if and only if Tan $y = \dfrac{9x}{2}$. Draw and label a triangle. Label one side $9x$.

623.

624. Thus, $\cos\left(\text{Arctan } \dfrac{9x}{2}\right) = \text{Cos } y = $ _____ .

---

624. $\dfrac{2}{\sqrt{4 + 81x^2}}$

PROBLEM 1

625. $\tan(\text{Arcsin } x) = $ _____

---

625. $\dfrac{x}{\sqrt{1 - x^2}}$.

If you had difficulty, see frames 616 to 618.

PROBLEM 2

626. $\cot(\text{Arcsin } x) = $ _____

---

626. $\dfrac{\sqrt{1 - x^2}}{x}$.

If you had difficulty, see frames 619 to 621.

PROBLEM 3

627. $\sin\left(\text{Arctan } \dfrac{3x}{7}\right) = $ _____

---

627. $\dfrac{3x}{\sqrt{49 + 9x^2}}$.

If you had difficulty, see frames 622 to 624.

If you cannot answer the following questions correctly, review the appropriate fram⟨

1. Give the domain and range of the following functions.

Sin x

Cos x

Tan x

Arcsin x

Arccos x

Arctan x

2. Prove that Arctan $(-x) = -$Arctan x.

3. Calculate the following

  (a) Arctan $\left(-\sqrt{3}\right)$ **(c)** tan (Arcsin x)

  (b) sin (Arctan 1)   **(d)** sec $\left(\text{Arctan } \dfrac{\sqrt{5}}{2}\right)$

Answers are at end of book.

13 Trigonometric Equations

As we mentioned in the chapter on identities, a trigonometric equation is an equation in which one or more of the expressions contains a trigonometric function. In this chapter we shall consider those equations in which every expression is made up of trigonometric functions.

Any trigonometric equation separates the real numbers into three categories (or three categories of angles, if we are thinking in terms of angles).

1. The equation is undefined for some values of x,

2. the equation is a true statement for some values of x, and

3. the equation is defined but not true for some values of x.

An *identity* was defined to be an equation that is true for *all* values for which both sides are defined. A *conditional equation* is an equation that is not true for at least one value at which both sides of the equation are defined.

It is the conditional equations or "equations" that we wish to investigate in this chapter.

Before we can solve a trigonometric equation, we must know its range of possible solutions. Are the solutions to be real numbers or angles? And once we have decided this, are we to consider all real numbers, or all angles, or some restricted set of real numbers or angles such as $0 \leqslant x \leqslant 2\pi$ or $-\dfrac{\pi}{2} \leqslant x \leqslant \dfrac{\pi}{2}$?

We shall consider only real number solutions, since angle solutions are the same. And we shall indicate for each problem any restriction on the range of possible solutions.

Upon completing this chapter, you should be able to solve trigonometric equations that can be solved

I. immediately;

II. by factoring;

III. by applying a double-angle formula;

IV. by applying the square identities, $\sin^2 x + \cos^2 x = 1$, $\tan^2 x + 1 = \sec^2 x$, and $1 + \cot^2 x = \csc^2 x$.

V. by dividing by a trigonometric function;

VI. by using the identities for $\sin s + \sin t$, etc.;

VII. by dividing by $\sqrt{a^2 + b^2}$ where the equation is of the form $a \sin x + b \cos x + c = 0$.

---

628. Since an identity is true for all defined values and an equation is true only for some (possibly no) defined values, we had to prove identities, but we must solve equations.

To solve an equation, we find all real numbers that make it true or satisfy it. Such a value is called a **solution** of the equation, and the set of all solutions is called the **solution set** of the equation.

Find the solution set of the equation $\sin x = 1$.

$\{x \in R \mid x = \underline{\hspace{4cm}} \}$

628.

$\dfrac{\pi}{2} \pm 2n\pi, n = 0, 1, 2, ...$

629. $\{x \in R \mid x = \pm 2n\pi, n = 0, 1, 2, ...\}$ is the $\underline{\hspace{2cm}}$ of the equation $\cos x = 1$.

---

629. solution set

630. If the product of two factors is zero, as in

$(\sin x - 1)(\cos x - 1) = 0$,

then either $\underline{\hspace{2cm}} = 0$ or $\underline{\hspace{2cm}} = 0$ or both.

---

630. $\sin x - 1; \cos x - 1$

631. Therefore, since $\frac{\pi}{2}$ is a solution of $(\sin x - 1) = 0$, it is also a

solution of _____ .

---

631. $(\sin x - 1)(\cos x - 1) = 0$

632. Similarly, since π is a solution of $(\cos x - 1) = 0$, it is also a

solution of _____ .

---

632. $(\sin x - 1)(\cos x - 1) = 0$

633. In fact the solution set of $(\sin x - 1)(\cos x - 1) = 0$ is the

_____ of the two solution sets of the two factors:
(union, intersection)
$\sin x - 1 = 0$ and $\cos x - 1 = 0$.

---

633. union, (since
$(\sin x - 1)(\cos x - 1) = 0$ if and only if
$\sin x - 1 = 0$ **or** $\cos x - 1 = 0$)

634. Thus the solution set of
$$(\sin x - 1)(\cos x - 1) = 0$$
is $\{x \in R \mid$ _____ $\}$.

634.
$x = \frac{\pi}{2} \pm 2n\pi$ or $x = \pi \pm 2n\pi, n = 0, 1, 2, \ldots$
or
$\{x \in R \mid x = \frac{\pi}{2} \pm 2n\pi, n = 0, 1, 2, \ldots\} \cup$
$\{x \in R \mid x = 2n\pi, x = 0, 1, 2, \ldots\}$
If you had difficulty, see Volume II on Sets.

635. As in the case of identities, there is no set procedure for solving trigonometric equations. The only tools are elementary algebra and substitution using the basic identities.

However, we have illustrated one useful suggestion:
(1) If an equation can be factored or written as a product of trigonometric expressions which is equal to zero, then each factor can be set equal to zero and solved, and the solution set of the equation is the union of the

_____ .

---

635. solution sets of the factors

636. Suggestion (1) can be written symbolically as follows:

If $a \cdot b = 0$, then $a = 0$ or _____ (or both).
And
[Solution set of $a \cdot b = 0$] =
[Solution set of $a = 0$] _____ [Solution set of $b = 0$] .

---

636. $b = 0; \cup$

637. (2) A second possible approach is to express the equation in terms of only one function and only one variable by means of the basic identities. Then the equation can be solved by purely algebraic methods.

For example, if we have the equation

$$\sin x - \cos^2 x + 1 = 0,$$

we can replace $1 - \cos^2 x$ by _____ , and obtain

_____ .

---

637. $\sin^2 x$;
$\sin x + \sin^2 x = 0$

---

638. The equation is now in the form $y^2 + y = 0$. Thus we can factor

$\sin^2 x + \sin x = 0$ into _____
and solve it as we did the previous example.

---

638. $\sin x \,(\sin x + 1) = 0$

---

639. $\sin x \,(\sin x + 1) = 0$ if and only if

_____ .

---

639. $\sin x = 0$ or $\sin x + 1 = 0$

---

640. The solution set of $\sin x = 0$ is

$\{x \in R \mid$ _____ $\}$
and the solution set of $\sin x + 1 = 0$ is

_____ .

---

640. $x = \pm 2n\pi, n = 0, 1, 2, ...\}$;
$\{x \in R \mid x = \dfrac{3\pi}{2} \pm 2n\pi, n = 0, 1, 2, ...\}$

---

641. Thus the solution set of

$\sin x - \cos^2 x + 1 = \sin x \,(\sin x + 1) = 0$

is $\{x \in R \mid$ _____ .

641.
$x = \pm 2n\pi, n = 0, 1, 2, ...\} \cup$
$\{x \in R \mid x = \dfrac{3\pi}{2} \pm 2n\pi, n = 0, 1, 2, ...\}$
or
$\{x \in R \mid x = \pm 2n\pi \ \text{or} \ x = \dfrac{3\pi}{2} \pm 2n\pi,$
$n = 0, 1, 2, ...\}$

EXAMPLE 1

642. The only way to become proficient at solving equations is to know the basic identities and to practice. We illustrate several different types below.

　　In the following equations find only those solutions x that fall in the range $0 \leqslant x < 2\pi$.

Immediately solvable

Solve the equation $\cos^2 x = \frac{3}{4}$ for $0 \leqslant x < 2\pi$.

$x = $ _____

---

642. $\dfrac{\pi}{6}, \dfrac{5\pi}{6}, \dfrac{7\pi}{6}, \dfrac{11\pi}{6}$.

If you had difficulty, go on to the next frame. If not, skip to frame 649.

643. Taking the square root of both sides, we get

_____ .

---

643. $\cos x = \pm \dfrac{\sqrt{3}}{2}$

644. That is, $\cos^2 x = \frac{3}{4}$ if and only if

$\cos x = +\dfrac{\sqrt{3}}{2}$ or $\cos x = $ _____ .

---

644. $-\dfrac{\sqrt{3}}{2}$

645. Thus the solutions of both $\cos x = +\dfrac{\sqrt{3}}{2}$ and $\cos x = -\dfrac{\sqrt{3}}{2}$

are solutions of _____ .

---

645. $\cos^2 x = \dfrac{3}{4}$

646.
$\cos x = +\dfrac{\sqrt{3}}{2}$ has _____ solutions,
　　　　　　　　　　(how many?)

and $\cos x = -\dfrac{\sqrt{3}}{2}$ has _____ solutions.

---

646. 2; 2

647. The solutions of $\cos x = +\dfrac{\sqrt{3}}{2}$ are **(a)** _____ and **(b)** _____ .

And the solutions of $\cos x = -\dfrac{\sqrt{3}}{2}$ are **(c)** _____ and **(d)** _____ ,

as can be seen from the figure.

647. **(a)** $\dfrac{\pi}{6}$, **(b)** $\dfrac{11\pi}{6}$,

(c) $\dfrac{5\pi}{6}$, **(d)** $\dfrac{7\pi}{6}$

648. Thus the solution set of the equation

$\cos^2 x = \dfrac{3}{4}$ is _____ .

648. $\left\{ \dfrac{\pi}{6}, \dfrac{5\pi}{6}, \dfrac{7\pi}{6}, \dfrac{11\pi}{6} \right\}$

EXAMPLE 2

649. Solve the equation $2 \sin^2 x = 1$ for $0 \leqslant x < 2\pi$.

The solution set is _____ .

649. $\left\{ \dfrac{\pi}{4}, \dfrac{3\pi}{4}, \dfrac{5\pi}{4}, \dfrac{7\pi}{4} \right\}$.

$2 \sin^2 x = 1$ if and only if $\sin^2 x = \frac{1}{2}$.

Thus $2 \sin^2 x = 1$ if and only if $\sin x = \pm \dfrac{1}{\sqrt{2}}$

and the solutions of both $\sin x = +\dfrac{1}{\sqrt{2}}$

and $\sin x = -\dfrac{1}{\sqrt{2}}$ are solutions of

$2 \sin^2 x = 1$.

$\sin x = +\dfrac{1}{\sqrt{2}}$ has two solutions, $\dfrac{\pi}{4}$

and $\dfrac{3\pi}{4}$, and $\sin x = -\dfrac{1}{\sqrt{2}}$ has two

solutions $\dfrac{5\pi}{4}$ and $\dfrac{7\pi}{4}$.

Thus the solution set of
$\sin^2 x = \frac{1}{2}$ is

$\left\{ \dfrac{\pi}{4}, \dfrac{3\pi}{4}, \dfrac{5\pi}{4}, \dfrac{7\pi}{4} \right\}$.

EQUATIONS THAT CAN BE FACTORED

EXAMPLE 3

650. Solve the equation $\cos^2 x - \cos x - 2 = 0$ for $0 \leqslant x < 2\pi$.

The solution set is _____ .

---

650. $\{\pi\}$.

If you had difficulty, go on to the next frame. If not, skip to frame 656. If at any time you can complete the solutions, do so and skip to frame 656.

651. Since $\cos^2 x - \cos x - 2 = 0$ is expressed in terms of cosine and x only, it is of the form $y^2 - y - 2 = 0$ and we can factor it.

$\cos^2 x - \cos x - 2 = $ _____ $= 0$.

---

651. $(\cos x + 1)(\cos x - 2)$

652. Thus $\cos^2 x - \cos x - 2 = 0$ if and only if

_____ or _____ .

---

652. $\cos x + 1 = 0$;
$\cos x - 2 = 0$

653. Thus the solution set of $\cos^2 x - \cos x - 2 = 0$ is the

_____

_____ .

---

653. union of the solution sets of $\cos x + 1 = 0$ and $\cos x - 2 = 0$

654. The solution set of $\cos x + 1 = 0$ for $0 \leqslant x < 2\pi$ is _____ .

And the solution set of $\cos x - 2 = 0$ is _____ .

---

654. $\{\pi\}$; empty. That is, $\cos x \neq 2$ for any x, since $\cos x \leqslant 1$ for all x.

655. Thus the solution set of the equation

$\cos^2 x - \cos x - 2 = 0$ is _____ .

---

655. $\{\pi\}$

EXAMPLE 4

656. Solve the equation $2 \sin^2 x - \sin x - 1 = 0$ for $0 \leqslant x < 2\pi$.

The solution set is _____ .

656. $\left\{\dfrac{\pi}{2}, \dfrac{7\pi}{6}, \dfrac{11\pi}{6}\right\}$.

Since $2 \sin^2 x - \sin x - 1 = 0$ is
expressed in terms of sine and x only,
it is of the form $2y^2 - y - 1 = 0$
and can be factored. We get

$2 \sin^2 x - \sin x - 1 = (2 \sin x + 1)(\sin x - 1) = 0.$

Thus $2 \sin^2 x - \sin x - 1 = 0$ if and only if
$2 \sin x + 1 = 0$ or $\sin x - 1 = 0$.
And the solution set of
$2 \sin^2 x - \sin x - 1 = 0$ is the union of the
solution sets of
$2 \sin x + 1 = 0$ and $\sin x - 1 = 0$.

$2 \sin x + 1 = 0$ if and only if $\sin x = -\dfrac{1}{2}$

and this occurs at $x = \dfrac{7\pi}{6}$ and $\dfrac{11\pi}{6}$.

And $\sin x - 1 = 0$ at $x = \dfrac{\pi}{2}$.

Thus the solution set of
$2 \sin^2 x - \sin x - 1 = 0$ is
$\left\{\dfrac{\pi}{2}, \dfrac{7\pi}{6}, \dfrac{11\pi}{6}\right\}$.

APPLY DOUBLE-ANGLE FORMULA, THEN FACTOR

EXAMPLE 5

657. Solve $\sin 2x + \cos x = 0$ for $0 \leqslant x < 2\pi$.

The solution set is _____ .

---

657. $\left\{ \dfrac{\pi}{2}, \dfrac{7\pi}{6}, \dfrac{3\pi}{2}, \dfrac{11\pi}{6} \right\}$.

If you had difficulty, go on to the next frame. If not, skip to frame 665. If at any time you can complete the solution, do so and skip to frame 665.

658. We use the identity $\sin 2x = $ _____

to replace $\sin 2x$ by _____ .

---

658. $2 \sin x \cos x$;
$2 \sin x \cos x$

659. We get

$\sin 2x + \cos x = $ _____ $= 0$.

---

659. $2 \sin x \cos x + \cos x$

660. Now we can factor $2 \sin x \cos x + \cos x = 0$ and get

$2 \sin x \cos x + \cos x = $ _____ $= 0$.

---

660. $\cos x\,(2 \sin x + 1)$

661. Thus $\sin 2x + \cos x = 0$ if and only if

_____ or _____ .

---

661. $\cos x = 0$;
$2 \sin x + 1 = 0$

662. And the solution set of $\sin 2x + \cos x = 0$ is the

_____ of _____
(union, intersection)

_____ .

---

662. union; the solution sets of $\cos x = 0$ and $2 \sin x + 1 = 0$

663. The solution set of $\cos x = 0$ for $0 \leqslant x < 2\pi$ *is* _____ .

And the solution set of $2 \sin x + 1$ is _____ .

---

663. $\left\{ \dfrac{\pi}{2}, \dfrac{3\pi}{2} \right\}$;

$\left\{ \dfrac{7\pi}{6}, \dfrac{11\pi}{6} \right\}$

664. Thus the solution set of the equation $\sin 2x + \cos x = 0$ for $0 \leqslant x < 2\pi$ is

_____ .

664. $\left\{ \dfrac{\pi}{2}, \dfrac{3\pi}{2}, \dfrac{7\pi}{6}, \dfrac{11\pi}{6} \right\}$

EXAMPLE 6

665. Solve the equation $\sin 2x - \sin x = 0$

for $0 \leqslant x < 2\pi$.

The solution set is _____ .

665. $\left\{ 0, \dfrac{\pi}{3}, \pi, \dfrac{5\pi}{3} \right\}$

We use the identity
$\sin 2x = 2 \sin x \cos x$ and
replace $\sin 2x$, getting
$\sin 2x - \sin x = 2 \sin x \cos x - \sin x = 0$.

Now we can factor $2 \sin x \cos x - \sin x = 0$
and get
$2 \sin x \cos x - \sin x = \sin x (2 \cos x - 1) = 0$.
Thus $\sin 2x - \sin x = 0$ if and only if
$\sin x = 0$ or $2 \cos x - 1 = 0$.
And the solution set of
$\sin 2x - \sin x = 0$ is the union of the
solution sets of $\sin x = 0$ and
$2 \cos x - 1 = 0$.

The solution set of $\sin x = 0$ is $\{0, \pi\}$ and the
solution set of $2 \cos x - 1 = 0$ is
$\left\{ \dfrac{\pi}{3}, \dfrac{5\pi}{3} \right\}$.
Hence the solution set of
$\sin 2x - \sin x = 0$ is $\left\{ 0, \dfrac{\pi}{3}, \pi, \dfrac{5\pi}{3} \right\}$.

EXAMPLE 7

666. Solve $\sin x - \cos^2 x - 1 = 0$ for $0 \leqslant x < 2\pi$.

The solution set is _____ .

---

666. $\left\{ \dfrac{\pi}{2} \right\}$.

If you had difficulty, go on to the next frame. If not, skip to frame 673. If at any time you can complete the solution, do so and skip to frame 673.

667. We use the identity $\sin^2 x + \cos^2 x = 1$ to replace $\cos^2 x$ by _____ .

---

667. $1 - \sin^2 x$

668. We get

$\sin x - \cos^2 x - 1 =$ _____ $= 0$.

---

668. $\sin x + \sin^2 x - 1 - 1$,
that is, $\sin^2 x + \sin x - 2 = 0$

669. We factor $\sin^2 x + \sin x - 2 = 0$ and get

$\sin^2 x + \sin x - 2 =$ _____ $= 0$.

---

669. $(\sin x + 2)(\sin x - 1)$

670. Thus $\sin x - \cos^2 x - 1 = 0$ if and only if

_____ .

And the solution set of $\sin x - \cos^2 x - 1 = 0$ is the

_____

_____ .

---

670. $\sin x + 2 = 0$ or $\sin x - 1 = 0$; union of the solution sets of $\sin x + 2 = 0$ and $\sin x - 1 = 0$

671. The solution set of $\sin x + 2 = 0$ is _____

and the solution set of $\sin x - 1 = 0$ is _____ .

---

671. empty, $\sin x \neq -2$ any x; $\left\{ \dfrac{\pi}{2} \right\}$

---

672. Thus the solution set of the equation $\sin x - \cos^2 x - 1 = 0$ for $0 \leqslant x < 2\pi$ is _____ .

672. $\left\{ \dfrac{\pi}{2} \right\}$

EXAMPLE 8
673. Solve the equation $\cos^2 x - \sin^2 x + 1 = 0$ for $0 \leqslant x < 2\pi$.

The solution set is _____ .

673. $\left\{ \dfrac{\pi}{2}, \dfrac{3\pi}{2} \right\}$.

We use the identity
$\sin^2 x + \cos^2 x = 1$ to replace
$1 - \sin^2 x$ by $\cos^2 x$. We get
$\cos^2 x - \sin^2 x + 1 = \cos^2 x + \cos^2 x = 0.$
That is,
$\quad 2 \cos^2 x = 0 \quad \text{or} \quad \cos^2 x = 0.$
and, finally, $\cos x = 0$.

Thus $\cos^2 x - \sin^2 x + 1 = 0$
if and only if $\cos x = 0$.
And the solution set of $\cos x = 0$ and
hence $\cos^2 x - \sin^2 x + 1 = 0$ is
$\left\{ \dfrac{\pi}{2}, \dfrac{3\pi}{2} \right\}$.

EXAMPLE 9

674. Solve $\sin x = \cos x$ for $0 \leqslant x < 2\pi$.

The solution set is _____ .

---

674. $\left\{ \dfrac{\pi}{4}, \dfrac{5\pi}{4} \right\}$.

If you had difficulty, go on to the next frame. If not, skip to frame 679. If at any time you can complete the solution, do so and skip to frame 679.

675. $\sin x$ and $\cos x$ do not equal 0 at the same value of x. Therefore $\cos x = 0$ will not be a solution, and we can divide both sides of $\sin x = \cos x$ and get

_____ .

---

675. $\dfrac{\sin x}{\cos x} = 1$.

That is, $\tan x = 1$.

676. Thus $\sin x = \cos x$ if and only if _____ .

---

676. $\tan x = 1$

677. And the solution set for $\sin x = \cos x$ is the same as the solution set for _____ .

---

677. $\tan x = 1$

678. The solution set for $\tan x = 1$ and hence for $\sin x = \cos x$ is _____ .

---

678. $\left\{ \dfrac{\pi}{4}, \dfrac{5\pi}{4} \right\}$

EXAMPLE 10

679. Solve the equation $2 \sin x = \tan x$ for $0 \leqslant x < 2\pi$.

The solution set is _____ .

679. $\left\{ 0, \dfrac{\pi}{3}, \dfrac{5\pi}{3} \right\}$.

We first write
$$\tan x = \frac{\sin x}{\cos x}$$
and obtain
$$2 \sin x = \frac{\sin x}{\cos x}.$$

Since $\sin x = 0$ is clearly a solution, we can either divide by $\sin x$ and add $x = 0$ to our solution set, or we can avoid this by writing
$$2 \sin x = \frac{\sin x}{\cos x} \quad \text{as} \quad 2 \sin x - \frac{\sin x}{\cos x} = 0.$$

We can now factor out $\sin x$ and get
$$2 \sin x - \frac{\sin x}{\cos x} = \sin x \left(2 - \frac{1}{\cos x} \right).$$

Thus $2 \sin x = \tan x$ if and only if
$$\sin x = 0 \text{ or } 2 - \left(\frac{1}{\cos x} \right) = 0$$

The solution set of $\sin x = 0$ is $\{0\}$ and the solution set of $2 - \left(\dfrac{1}{\cos x} \right) = 0$

is $\left\{ \dfrac{\pi}{3}, \dfrac{5\pi}{3} \right\}$ since $2 - \left(\dfrac{1}{\cos x} \right) = 0$ if and only if $\cos x = \dfrac{1}{2}$. Thus the solution set of $2 \sin x = \tan x$ is

$\left\{ 0, \ \pi, \dfrac{5\pi}{3} \right\}$.

EXAMPLE 11

680. Solve $\cos 2x - \cos 3x = 0$ for $0 \leqslant x < 2\pi$.

The solution set is _____ .

---

680. $\left\{ 0, \dfrac{2\pi}{5}, \dfrac{4\pi}{5}, \dfrac{6\pi}{5}, \dfrac{8\pi}{5} \right\}$.

If you had difficulty, go on to the next frame. If not, skip to frame 687. If at any time you can complete the solution, do so and skip to frame 687.

681. We let $2x = s$, $3x = t$, and apply the identity

$$\cos s - \cos t = -2 \sin \left(\frac{s+t}{2} \right) \sin \left(\frac{s-t}{2} \right)$$

and get

$\cos 2x - \cos 3x =$ _____ $= 0$.

681.

$$-2 \sin \left(\frac{2x + 3x}{2} \right) \sin \left(\frac{2x - 3x}{2} \right) = 0.$$

That is,

$$-2 \sin \left(\frac{5x}{2} \right) \sin \left(\frac{-x}{2} \right) = 0$$

or

$$2 \sin \left(\frac{5x}{2} \right) \sin \left(\frac{x}{2} \right) = 0$$

since $\sin (-t) = -\sin t$.

682. Thus $\cos 2x - \cos 3x = 0$ if and only if

_____ ,

and the solution set of $\cos 2x - \cos 3x = 0$ is the

_____

_____ .

682.

$\sin \left(\dfrac{5x}{2} \right) = 0$ or $\sin \left(\dfrac{x}{2} \right) = 0$;

union of the solution sets of

$\sin \left(\dfrac{5x}{2} \right) = 0$ and $\sin \left(\dfrac{x}{2} \right) = 0$

683. The solution set of $\sin \left(\dfrac{5x}{2} \right) = 0$ is

_____ and the

solution set if $\left(\dfrac{x}{2} \right) = 0$ is _____ .

---

683. $\left\{ 0, \dfrac{2\pi}{5}, \dfrac{4\pi}{5}, \dfrac{6\pi}{5}, \dfrac{8\pi}{5} \right\}$; $\{ 0 \}$.

If you had difficulty, go on to the next frame. If not, skip to frame 687.

684. $\sin\left(\dfrac{5x}{2}\right) = 0$ if and only if $\dfrac{5x}{2} = 0, \pi, 2\pi, 3\pi, 4\pi$.

Thus $\sin\left(\dfrac{5x}{2}\right) = 0$ for $x = $ _____ .

684. $0, \dfrac{2\pi}{5}, \dfrac{4\pi}{5}, \dfrac{6\pi}{5}, \dfrac{8\pi}{5}$.

NOTE: We want only those solutions $0 \leqslant x < 2\pi$, and $\dfrac{5x}{2} = 6\pi$ gives $x = \dfrac{12\pi}{5}$, which is not in $0 \leqslant x < 2\pi$.

685. Similarly $\sin\left(\dfrac{x}{2}\right) = 0$ if and only if $\dfrac{x}{2} = $ ____ . Thus $\sin\left(\dfrac{x}{2}\right) = 0$ for $x = $ ____ .

685. $0, 0$

686. Thus the solution set of the equation

$\cos 2x - \cos 3x = 0$ for $0 \leqslant x < 2\pi$ is _____ .

686. $\left\{ 0, \dfrac{2\pi}{5}, \dfrac{4\pi}{5}, \dfrac{6\pi}{5}, \dfrac{8\pi}{5} \right\}$

EXAMPLE 12

687. Solve $\sin 5x + \sin x = 0$ for $0 \leqslant x < 2\pi$.

The solution set is _____ .

687. $\left\{0, \dfrac{\pi}{4}, \dfrac{\pi}{3}, \dfrac{2\pi}{3}, \dfrac{3\pi}{4}, \pi, \right.$
$\left. \dfrac{5\pi}{4}, \dfrac{4\pi}{3}, \dfrac{5\pi}{3}, \dfrac{7\pi}{4} \right\}.$

Let $s = 5x$ and $t = x$ and apply the identity
$$\sin s + \sin t = 2 \sin \left(\frac{s+t}{2}\right) \cos \left(\frac{s-t}{2}\right)$$
and get
$$\sin 5x + \sin x = 2 \sin \left(\frac{5x+x}{2}\right) \cos \left(\frac{5x-x}{2}\right)$$
$$= 2 \sin (3x) \cos (2x) = 0.$$

Thus $\sin 5x + \sin x = 0$ if and only if $\sin (3x) = 0$ or $\cos (2x) = 0$.

The solution set of $\sin (3x) = 0$ is
$$\left\{0, \frac{\pi}{3}, \frac{2\pi}{3}, \pi, \frac{4\pi}{3}, \frac{5\pi}{3} \right\},$$
since $\sin 3x = 0$ if and only if
$3x = 0, \pi, 2\pi, 3\pi, 4\pi,$ or 5π.
And the solution set of $\cos (2x) = 0$ is
$$\left\{\frac{\pi}{4}, \frac{3\pi}{4}, \frac{5\pi}{4}, \frac{7\pi}{4} \right\},$$
since $\cos 2x = 0$ if and only if
$$2x = \frac{\pi}{2}, \frac{3\pi}{2}, \frac{5\pi}{2}, \frac{7\pi}{2},$$
and the solution set of $\sin 5x + \sin x = 0$ is

$$\left\{0, \frac{\pi}{4}, \frac{\pi}{3}, \frac{2\pi}{3}, \frac{3\pi}{4}, \pi, \frac{5\pi}{4}, \frac{4\pi}{3}, \frac{5\pi}{3}, \frac{7\pi}{4} \right\}.$$

EQUATIONS OF THE FORM $a \sin x + b \cos x = c$. DIVIDE BOTH SIDES BY $\sqrt{a^2 + b^2}$.

EXAMPLE 13

688. To solve $\sqrt{7} \sin x + 3 \cos x = 2$ for $0 \leqslant x < 2\pi$, we divide both sides of $\sqrt{7} \sin x + 3 \cos x = 2$ by $\sqrt{(\sqrt{7})^2 + (3)^2}$ and obtain equation (A).

(A) _____ = _____ .

---

688. $\dfrac{\sqrt{7}}{4} \sin x + \dfrac{3}{4} \cos x = \dfrac{1}{2}$

689. Now $\left(\dfrac{\sqrt{7}}{4}\right)^2 + \left(\dfrac{3}{4}\right)^2 = 1$. Thus there is an α, $0 \leqslant \alpha \leqslant \dfrac{\pi}{2}$ such that $\sin \alpha = \dfrac{\sqrt{7}}{4}$, $\cos \alpha = \dfrac{3}{4}$, and $\sin^2 \alpha + \cos^2 \alpha =$ _____ .

---

689. 1

690. If we replace $\dfrac{\sqrt{7}}{4}$ by $\sin \alpha$ and $\dfrac{3}{4}$ by $\cos \alpha$ in equation (A) above, we get _____ $= \dfrac{1}{2}$.

---

690. $\sin \alpha \sin x + \cos \alpha \cos x$

691. If we apply the identity

$$\cos (x - \alpha) = \sin \alpha \sin x + \cos \alpha \cos x$$

we get _____ $= \dfrac{1}{2}$.

---

691. $\cos(x - \alpha)$

692. Thus we know that $\sin \alpha = \dfrac{\sqrt{7}}{4}$, $\cos \alpha = \dfrac{3}{4}$, and $\cos (x - \alpha) = \dfrac{1}{2}$. Therefore from the table of values $\alpha = 41°24'$ and $x - \alpha =$ _____ or _____ .

---

692. $60°$; $300°$

693. Thus **(a)** $x =$ _____ or **(b)** $x =$ _____ and the solution set of $\sqrt{7} \sin x + 3 \cos x = 2$, $0 \leqslant x < 2\pi$ is

(c) _____ .

---

693. **(a)** $101° 24'$,
(b) $341° 24'$,
(c) $\{101° 24', 341° 24'\}$

EXAMPLE 14

694. Solve $\sin x + \sqrt{3}\cos x = \sqrt{2}$.

—————————————————————— .

694. $\left\{\dfrac{5\pi}{12}, \dfrac{23\pi}{12}\right\}$.

Dividing both sides by $\sqrt{(\sqrt{3})^2 + 1^2} = 2$, we get

$$\frac{1}{2}\sin x + \frac{\sqrt{3}}{2}\cos x = \frac{\sqrt{2}}{2} = \frac{1}{\sqrt{2}}.$$

Therefore there exists an α such that

$\sin \alpha = \frac{1}{2}$ and $\cos \alpha = \dfrac{\sqrt{3}}{2}$ and

$$\sin^2 \alpha + \cos^2 \alpha = \left(\tfrac{1}{2}\right)^2 + \left(\frac{\sqrt{3}}{2}\right)^2 = 1.$$

Therefore if we replace $\frac{1}{2}$ by $\sin \alpha$

and $\dfrac{\sqrt{3}}{2}$ by $\cos \alpha$, we get

$$\sin \alpha \sin x + \cos \alpha \cos x = \frac{1}{\sqrt{2}}.$$

And after applying the identity for

$\cos(x - \alpha)$ we get $\cos(x - \alpha) = \dfrac{1}{\sqrt{2}}$.

Thus $x - \alpha = \dfrac{\pi}{4}$ or $\dfrac{7\pi}{4}$ and

$\alpha = \dfrac{\pi}{6}$ (since $\sin \alpha = \frac{1}{2}$).

Thus $x = \dfrac{\pi}{4} + \dfrac{\pi}{6}$ or $x = \dfrac{7\pi}{4} + \dfrac{\pi}{6}$.

That is, $x = \dfrac{5\pi}{12}$ or $x = \dfrac{23\pi}{12}$.

Thus the solution set of

$\sin x + \sqrt{3}\cos x = \sqrt{2}$ for $0 \leqslant x < 2\pi$ is

$\left\{\dfrac{5\pi}{12}, \dfrac{23\pi}{12}\right\}$.

EXERCISE 1

695. Solve the equation $\tan^2 x - 3 = 0$ for $0 \leqslant x < 2\pi$.

The solution set is _____ .

---

695. $\left\{ \dfrac{\pi}{3}, \dfrac{2\pi}{3}, \dfrac{4\pi}{3}, \dfrac{5\pi}{3} \right\}$.

If you had difficulty, see frames 642 to 649. The approach is the same.

EXERCISE 2

696. Solve $3 \cos x - 2 \sin^2 x = 0$ for $0 \leqslant x < 2\pi$.

The solution set is _____ .

---

696. $\left\{ \dfrac{\pi}{3}, \dfrac{5\pi}{3} \right\}$.

If you had difficulty, see frames 666 to 673. The approach is the same.

EXERCISE 3

697. Solve $\cos 2x - \sin x = 0$ for $0 \leqslant x < 2\pi$.

The solution set is _____ .

---

697. $\left\{ \dfrac{\pi}{6}, \dfrac{5\pi}{6}, \dfrac{3\pi}{2} \right\}$.

If you had difficulty, see frames 657 to 665. Use $\cos 2x = 1 - 2 \sin^2 x$ and then factor.

698. Solve $\sin 3x + \sin 4x = 0$ for $0 \leqslant x < 2\pi$.

The solution set is _____ .

698.

$$\left\{0, \frac{2\pi}{7}, \frac{4\pi}{7}, \frac{6\pi}{7}, \pi, \frac{8\pi}{7}, \frac{10\pi}{7}, \frac{12\pi}{7}\right\}.$$

If you had difficulty, see frames 680 to 687. Let $s = 3x$ and $t = 4x$.

699. Solve $\cos x = \cot x$ for $0 \leqslant x < 2\pi$.

The solution set is _____ .

---

699. $\left\{\frac{\pi}{2}, \frac{3\pi}{2}\right\}.$

If you had difficulty, see frames 674 to 679.

700. Solve $\sin 4x - \sin 2x = 0$ for $0 \leqslant x < 2\pi$.

The solution set is _____ .

700.

$$\left\{0, \frac{\pi}{6}, \frac{\pi}{2}, \frac{5\pi}{6}, \pi, \frac{7\pi}{6}, \frac{3\pi}{2}, \frac{11\pi}{6}\right\}$$

701. Solve $3 \tan^3 x - \tan x = 0$ for $0 \leqslant x < 2\pi$.

The solution set is _____ .

---

701. $\left\{0, \dfrac{\pi}{6}, \dfrac{5\pi}{6}, \pi, \dfrac{7\pi}{6}, \dfrac{11\pi}{6}\right\}$.

If you had difficulty, see frames 650 to 656.

702. Solve $\sqrt{3} \sin x - \cos x = 1$ for $0 \leqslant x < 2\pi$.

The solution set is _____ .

---

702. $\left\{\pi, \dfrac{\pi}{3}\right\}$.

If you had difficulty, see frames 688 to 694.

703. Solve $\sin^2 x - \cos^2 x = 0$ for $0 \leqslant x < 2\pi$.

The solution set is _____ .

---

703. $\left\{\dfrac{\pi}{4}, \dfrac{3\pi}{4}, \dfrac{5\pi}{4}, \dfrac{7\pi}{4}\right\}$.

If you had difficulty, see frames 666 to 673.

EXERCISE 10

704. Solve $\tan x = \sec x$ for $0 \leqslant x < 2\pi$.

The solution set is _____.

704. $\left\{\dfrac{\pi}{2}\right\}$.

If you had difficulty, see frames 674 to 679.

EXERCISE 11

705. Solve $\sec^2 x + \sec x - 2 = 0$ for $0 \leqslant x < 2\pi$.

The solution set is _____.

705. $\left\{0, \dfrac{2\pi}{3}, \dfrac{4\pi}{3}\right\}$.

If you had difficulty, see frames 650 to 656.

QUIZ

If you cannot answer the following questions correctly, review the appropriate frames.

1. Solve the equation $4\cos^2 x = 1$.

2. Solve the equation $\sin^2 x - \sin x - 2 = 0$.

3. Solve the equation $\sin 2x - \sqrt{3}\cos x = 0$.

4. Solve the equation $\sec^2 x + 2\tan x = 0$.

5. Solve the equation $\cot x = \csc x$.

6. Solve the equation $\sin 2x + \sin 4x = 0$.

7. Solve the equation $\sqrt{3}\sin x + \cos x = \sqrt{2}$.

Answers are at end of book.

Complex Numbers

PART

III

The earliest numbers used by man were the counting or *natural numbers*, 1, 2, 3, ... These numbers were inadequate for describing parts of objects, so the fractions or *rational numbers* were added to them. Each rational was expressed as a ratio p/q, $q \neq 0$, where p and q were natural numbers. Even the rationals were inadequate for indicating direction or solving subtraction problems, and so the negative numbers and zero were added to the natural numbers to form the *integers* ... , $-3, -2, -1, 0, 1, 2, 3, ...$.

While the rational numbers were adequate for all practical measurements, the early Greeks proved that there are numbers that are not rational. They used the Pythagorean theorem to show that the length of the hypotenuse of the right triangle with unit sides (shown below) is $\sqrt{2}$ and proved that the $\sqrt{2}$ is not a rational number.

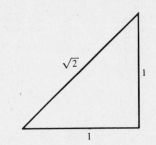

Since $\sqrt{2}$ is a non-rational number, a new kind of number, the *irrational number*, was introduced.

The rational and irrational numbers together form the *real numbers*. Any measurement problem or linear equation can be solved with real numbers.

However, not all quadratic equations have real solutions, and it is necessary to introduce one last type of number, the *complex number*.

14   Complex Numbers

Upon completing this chapter, you should be able to

   I. Express complex numbers

      (A) in rectangular form,

      (B) as ordered pairs of real numbers,

      (C) in trigonometric form.

   II. Change a complex number from rectangular to trigonometric form and vice versa.

  III. Given a complex number in any of the above forms, find

      (A) the modulus or absolute value, and

      (B) the argument.

  VI. Graph complex numbers.

   V. Add, subtract, multiply, and divide complex numbers in
rectangular form.

  VI. Multiply and divide complex numbers in trigonometric
form.

 VII. Use DeMoivre's theorem to find the powers z^n of a complex
number z.

VIII. Find the n nth roots of a complex number.

  IX. Graph the n nth roots of a complex number.

1. The equation $x^2 + 1 = 0$ has no real solutions, since

$$x^2 = -1;$$

that is, the equation can not be solved because $x = \pm\sqrt{-1}$ has no real solutions. Therefore we need a new number, which we shall denote by i and call an *imaginary* number.

$$i = \sqrt{-1}.$$

Thus, if

$$x^2 = -1,$$

there are two imaginary solutions $x =$ _____ and $x =$ _____ .

---

1. $i; -i$

2. If $x^2 + 4 = 0$, then $x^2 = -4$, and

$$x = \pm\sqrt{-4} = \pm\sqrt{4}\cdot\sqrt{-1} = \textbf{(a)} \pm \underline{\hspace{1cm}} *$$

Again we have two non-real solutions: **(b)** _____ and **(c)** _____ .
We shall call any number of the form bi, where b is a nonzero real number, *imaginary* or *pure imaginary*.

---

2. (a) $2i$
  (b) $2i$
  (c) $-2i$

3. Finally, consider the equation

$$x^2 - 2x + 2 = 0.$$

Completing the square we get

$$(x - 1)^2 + 1 = 0$$

or

$$(x - 1)^2 = -1.$$

That is,

$$(x - 1) = \pm\underline{\hspace{1.5cm}} = \pm\underline{\hspace{1.5cm}}$$

or

$$x = \underline{\hspace{2cm}}$$

---

3. $\sqrt{-1}$ $i; 1 \pm i$

---

*We shall justify these steps later.

4. $1 + i$ and $1 - i$ are non-real solutions. We shall call them *complex numbers*. In fact, we shall call any number of the form $a + bi$, where a and b are real, a complex number.

Label each of the following complex numbers either real, pure imaginary, or complex.

(a) $-3i$ _____

(b) $\sqrt{2}$ _____

(c) $-\frac{1}{2} + 7i$ _____

(d) $1 - \sqrt{2}i$ _____

(e) π _____

---

4. (a) pure imaginary **(d)** complex
(b) real **(e)** real
(c) complex

5. A complex number is of the form $a + bi$ where a and b are

_____ numbers.
(what kind?)

---

5. real

6. 7 is the **(a)** _____ part of $7 - 3i$ and -3 is the
(real, imaginary)

(b) _____ part of $7 - 3i$. So the real part of
(real, imaginary)

$4 + 5i$ is **(c)** ___ and the imaginary part of $4 + 5i$ is **(d)** ___ .

---

6. (a) real
(b) imaginary
(c) 4
(d) 5

7. In general, if a and b are real numbers, $a + bi$ is called a

(a) _____ number whose **(b)** _____ part is **(c)** ___

and whose **(d)** _____ part is **(e)** ___ .

---

7. (a) complex **(d)** imaginary
(b) real **(e)** b (not bi)
(c) a

8. Two complex numbers are equal (or the same) if and only if their real parts are equal and their imaginary parts are equal. That is,

$a + bi = c + di$

if and only if ___ = ___ and ___ = ___ .

---

8. $a; c; b; d$

EXAMPLE 1

9. Which of the following complex numbers are equal?

(a) $2-3i$ (b) $\frac{4}{2}+3i$ (c) $\frac{4}{2}-\frac{6}{2}i$ (d) $-2-3i$

(e) $-\frac{6}{3}+\frac{6}{2}i$

---

9. (a) and (c) (since $2-3i=\frac{4}{2}-\frac{6}{2}i$)

10. If $x+yi=4-3i$,

then $x=$ _____ and $y=$ _____ .

---

10. $4; -3$

11. We can define addition of two complex numbers in the natural way by adding the two real parts to form the real part of the sum and adding the two imaginary parts to form the imaginary part of the sum. That is,

$$(a+ib)+(c+id)=(a+c)+(b+d)i$$

Add the following complex numbers.

(a) $(8+2i)+(5+3i)$ = _____

(b) $(6+3i)+(5-2i)$ = _____

(c) $(-4-7i)+(-\sqrt{2}+i)=$ _____

---

11. (a) $13+5i$
(b) $11+i$
(c) $(-4-\sqrt{2})-6i$

12. We can add two complex numbers by treating them as binomials and then collecting the real and the imaginary parts together. Thus

$$(7+3i)+(5-2i)=7+3i+5-2i$$
$$=7+5+3i-2i$$
$$=12+i$$

Add the following complex numbers.

(a) $(9-4i)+(-6+3i)$ = _____

(b) $(\frac{1}{2}+i)+(2-\frac{3}{4}i)$ = _____

(c) $(\pi-6i)+(3+\sqrt{2}i)=$ _____

---

12. (a) $3-i$
(b) $2\frac{1}{2}+\frac{1}{4}i$
(c) $(\pi+3)+(\sqrt{2}-6)i$

13. In general $(e+fi)+(m+ni)=$ _____ .

---

13. $(e+m)+(f+n)i$

14. To subtract one complex number from another, we subtract the real part of the second from the real part of the first and subtract the imaginary part of the second from the imaginary part of the first. Thus

$$(a + bi) - (c + di) = \underline{\hspace{4cm}}$$

---

14. $(a - c) + (b - d)i$

15. Complete the following subtractions.

(a) $(6 + 7i) - (3 + 5i) = \underline{\hspace{2.5cm}}$

(b) $(5 + 2i) - (4 + 8i) = \underline{\hspace{2.5cm}}$

(c) $(3 + 4i) - (5 - 5i) = \underline{\hspace{2.5cm}}$

(d) $(-9 + 2i) - (-6 - i) = \underline{\hspace{2.5cm}}$

---

15. (a) $3 + 2i$
(b) $1 - 6i$
(c) $-2 + 9i$
(d) $-3 + 3i$

EXAMPLE 2

16. Find the complex number $x + yi$ such that

$$(x + yi) + (3 - \tfrac{1}{2}i) = 2 + \tfrac{1}{2}i.$$

$x + yi = \underline{\hspace{3cm}}$

---

16. $-1 + i$

17. We can define multiplication by treating each complex number as a binomial. Thus

$$(a + bi) \cdot (c + di)$$

is defined to be

$$ac - bd + (bc + ad)i$$

since $(a + bi) \cdot (c + di) = ac + bci + adi + bd(i^2)$

$= \underline{\hspace{3cm}}$ since $i^2 = \underline{\hspace{1cm}}$.

---

17. $ac - bd + (bc + ad)i; -1$

18. Multiply the complex numbers:

$(3 + 4i) \cdot (5 + 2i) = \underline{\hspace{5cm}}$.

---

18. $(15 - 8) + (20 + 6)i = 7 + 26i$

19. Multiply

$(-7 + 6i) \cdot (1 + 4i) = \underline{\hspace{5cm}}$.

19.
$(-7 - 24) + (6 - 28)i = -31 - 22i$

	20. Multiply $(5 - 3i) \cdot (8 + 2i) = $ _____ .
20. $(40 + 6) + (-24 + 10)i = 46 - 14i$	**21.** Multiply $(-6 + 4i) \cdot (3 - 5i) = $ _____ .
21. $(-18 + 20) + (12 + 30)i = 2 + 42i$	**22.** In general, $(a + bi) \cdot (c + di) = $ _____ .

22. $(ac - bd) + (bc + ad)i.$
If you had difficulty, see frame 17.
	23. Before we define division of complex numbers we need to introduce the **complex conjugate** of a complex number.
	  Suppose we have a complex number $a + bi$, by what number must we multiply it in order to obtain a real number?
	  If we multiply by $c + di$, then
	
	$(a + bi)(c + di) = $ _____ .
	
	And for this to be a real number _____ must equal 0.

23. $(ac - bd) + (bc + ad)i$; $bc + ad$	**24.** If we put $c = a$, then $bc + ad = 0$ if $d = $ ____ . That is, we get a real number if we multiply $(a + bi)$ by _____ .
24. $-b; a - bi$	**25.** $(a + bi) \cdot (a - bi) = $ _____ $(a - bi) \cdot (a + bi) = $ _____
25. $a^2 + b^2; a^2 + b^2.$ $((bi)(-bi) = -b^2 i^2$, since $i^2 = -1.)$	**26.** $a - bi$ is called the **complex conjugate** of $a + bi$. What is the complex conjugate of $8 + 5i$? _____
26. $8 - 5i$	**27.** The complex conjugate of $5 - 6i$ is _____ .
27. $5 + 6i$	**28.** And $(5 - 6i) \cdot (5 + 6i) = $ _____ .
28. $25 + 36 = 61$	

	29. The complex conjugate of $-4 + i$ is _____ . And $-4 + i$ multiplied by its conjugate is _____ .
29. $-4 - i$; $16 + 1 = 17$	**30.** And, in general, the complex conjugate of $c + di$ is _____ . And the complex conjugate of $m - ni$ is _____ .
30. $c - di$; $m + ni$	**31.** We shall denote the complex conjugate of the complex number z by $\bar{z}$. Thus if $z = 4 - 3i$, then $\bar{z} =$ _____ .
31. $4 + 3i$	**32.** If $z = 2 + 5i$, we would represent its complex conjugate by $2 - 5i =$ _____ .
32. $\bar{z} = \overline{2 + 5i}$	**33.** In general, if $u = a + bi$, the $n\bar{u} =$ _____ .
33. $a - bi$	**34.** If $u = a + bi$ and $v = c + di$ are two complex numbers, then $u + v =$ _____ .
34. $(a + c) + (b + c)i$	**35.** And the conjugate of $u + v$ is $\overline{u + v} =$ _____ .
35. $(a + c) - (b + c)i$	**36.** On the other hand, $\bar{u} =$ _____ , and $\bar{v} =$ _____ .
36. $a - bi$; $c - di$	**37.** Thus $\bar{u} + \bar{v} =$ _____ .
37. $(a + c) - (b + d)i$	**38.** Hence we have shown that (i) $\overline{u + v} = (a + b) - (b + d)\ i =$ _____ .
38. $\bar{u} + \bar{v}$	**39.** That is, the conjugate of the sum of two complex numbers is the same as the sum of the two _____ .
39. conjugates	

40.
$(a + bi)(c + di)$
$= (ac - bd) + (bc + ad)i$

40. Similarly, if $u = a + bi$, and $v = c + di$, then

$u \cdot v =$ _____ .

41. $(ac - bd) - (bc + ad)i$

41. And $\overline{u \cdot v} =$ _____ .

42. (a) $a - bi$
(b) $c - di$
(c) $(a - bi)(c - di)$
   $= (ac - bd) - (bc + ad)i$

42. On the other hand **(a)** $\overline{u} =$ _____ , **(b)** $\overline{v} =$ _____

and **(c)** $\overline{u} \cdot \overline{v} =$ _____ .

43. $\overline{u} \cdot \overline{v}$, (since $\overline{u \cdot v} = (ac - bd) -$
$(bc + ad)i = \overline{u} \cdot \overline{v}$)

43. Thus we have shown that

(ii) $\overline{u \cdot v} =$ _____ .

44. the product of the conjugates of those numbers

44. That is, the conjugate of the product of two complex numbers

is the same as _____

_____ .

45. $\overline{u} + \overline{v}$; $\overline{u \cdot v} = \overline{u} \cdot \overline{v}$

45. We have proved the following theorem.

THEOREM 1. If $u = a + bi$ and $v = c + di$ are two complex numbers, then

(i) $\overline{u + v} =$ _____

(ii) _____

SUMMARY

Theorem 1

If $u = a + bi$ and $v = c + di$ are two complex numbers, then

(i) $\overline{u + v} = \overline{u} + \overline{v}$

(ii) $\overline{u \cdot v} = \overline{u} \cdot \overline{v}$

Proof: (i) By the definition of addition

$$u + v = (a + c) + (b + d)i$$

and the conjugate of $u + v$ is

$$\overline{u + v} = (a + c) - (b + d)i$$

On the other hand, $\overline{u} = a - bi$, $\overline{v} = c - di$, and

$$\overline{u} + \overline{v} = (a + b) - (b + d)i.$$

Hence $\overline{u + v} = \overline{u} + \overline{v}$.

(ii) Similarly,

$$u \cdot v = (a + bi)(c + di) = (ac - bd) + (bc + ad)i$$

and

$$\overline{u \cdot v} = (ac - bd) - (bc + ad)i.$$

On the other hand, $\overline{u} = a - bi$, $\overline{v} = c - di$, and

$$\overline{u} \cdot \overline{v} = (a - bi)(c - di) = (ac - bd) - (bc + ad)i.$$

Hence $\overline{u \cdot v} = \overline{u} \cdot \overline{v}$. And our proof is complete.

46. As in the case of multiplication, we shall define division by treating each complex number as an ordinary binomial.

Given $\dfrac{a + bi}{c + di}$, we multiply numerator and denominator by the complex conjugate of the denominator $c - di$ to get

$$\frac{a + bi}{c + di} \cdot \frac{c - di}{c - di} = \frac{(ac + bd) + (bc - ad)i}{c^2 + d^2}$$

Thus, we define division by

$$\frac{a + bi}{c + di} = \frac{ac + bd}{c^2 + d^2} + \frac{(bc - ad)i}{c^2 + d^2}$$

$$\frac{3 + 5i}{1 + 2i} = \underline{\hspace{5cm}}$$

46.

$$\frac{3 + 5i}{1 + 2i} \cdot \frac{1 - 2i}{1 - 2i} = \frac{(3 + 10) + (5 - 6)i}{1 + 4}$$

$$= \tfrac{13}{5} - \tfrac{1}{5} i$$

47. Divide the following.

$$\frac{8 - 3i}{2 + 3i} = \underline{\hspace{5cm}}$$

47.

$$\frac{8 - 3i}{2 + 3i} \cdot \frac{2 - 3i}{2 - 3i} = \frac{(16 - 9) + (-6 - 24)i}{4 + 9}$$

$$= \tfrac{7}{13} - \tfrac{30}{13} i$$

48. Divide the following.

$$\frac{7 + 4i}{5 - 2i} = \underline{\hspace{5cm}}$$

48.

$$\frac{7 + 4i}{5 - 2i} \cdot \frac{5 + 2i}{5 + 2i} = \frac{(35 - 8) + (20 + 14)i}{25 + 4}$$

$$= \tfrac{27}{29} + \tfrac{34}{29} i$$

49. Divide the following.

$$\frac{-6 + 7i}{3 - 4i} = \underline{\hspace{5cm}}$$

49.

$$\frac{-6 + 7i}{3 - 4i} \cdot \frac{3 + 4i}{3 + 4i} = \frac{(-18 - 28) + (21 - 24)i}{9 + 16}$$

$$= \tfrac{-46}{25} - \tfrac{3}{25} i$$

	50. And, in general,
	$$\dfrac{a + bi}{c + di} = \underline{\hspace{6cm}}.$$

50.	**51.** Recall that $a + bi = c + di$ if and only if
$\dfrac{ac + bd}{c^2 + d^2} + \dfrac{(bc - ad)i}{c^2 + d^2}$.	$\underline{\hspace{6cm}}.$
If you had difficulty, see frame 46.	

51. $a = c$ and $b = d$	**52.** In particular $a + bi$ does not equal $b + ai$ unless $\underline{\hspace{2.5cm}}.$

52. $a = b$	**53.** Thus, the complex number $a + bi$ is uniquely determined by the two real numbers a and b. And we can set up a one-to-one correspondence between the complex numbers and the set of all ordered pairs of real numbers defined by $$a + bi \longleftrightarrow (a, b).$$ In fact, one way to define complex numbers is to define them as ordered pairs of real numbers. What complex number corresponds to the ordered pair $(3, -5)$? $\underline{\hspace{4cm}}$

53. $3 - 5i$	**54.** And the ordered pair that corresponds to the complex number $-\pi + 3i$ is $\underline{\hspace{2.5cm}}.$

54. $(-\pi, 3)$	**55.** We can write the real number 7 as $7 + 0i$. Hence, we can associate the ordered pair $(\underline{\hspace{0.5cm}}, \underline{\hspace{0.5cm}})$ with the real number 7.

55. $7, 0$	**56.** We can associate the ordered pair $\underline{\hspace{2cm}}$ with the real number $\sqrt{2}$.

56. $(\sqrt{2}, 0)$	

57. And, in general, we can associate the ordered pair _____ with the real number a. And there is a one-to-one correspondence between the set of real numbers R and the set of ordered pairs $(a, \underline{\quad})$ where a is a real number.

---

57. $(a, 0)$; 0

58. Thus we can think of the set of real numbers as a subsystem of the set of complex numbers. Similarly, we can write the pure imaginary number i as $0 + i$. Hence we can associate the ordered pair $(\underline{\quad}, \underline{\quad})$ with i.

---

58. 0, 1

59. Because of the correspondence between the complex numbers and the set of all ordered pairs of real numbers, there is an obvious correspondence between the complex numbers and the points in the Euclidean or geometric plane.

The complex number $3 + 5i$ corresponds to the point with coordinates $(\underline{\quad}, \underline{\quad})$.

---

59. 3, 5

EXAMPLE 3

60. Plot the following complex numbers on the Cartesian axes.

$$-2 + 2i, \qquad 3 + i, \qquad -1 - 3i \qquad 4 - 2i$$

60.

61. Thus the abscissa (or x-coordinate) a represents the _____ part of the complex number $a + bi$ and the ordinate (or y-coordinate) b represents the _____ .

---

61. real; imaginary part

62. Thus any complex number $z = a + bi$ can be represented in the plane by the point with coordinates (___ , ___). And we can call this geometrical representation of the set of all complex numbers the **complex plane.**

---

62. a, b

63. Real numbers are represented along the ___-axis and pure imaginary numbers on the _____ .

---

63. x; y-axis

64. Let $z = a + bi$ be a complex number represented in the complex plane. Then label the distance from z to the origin, r.

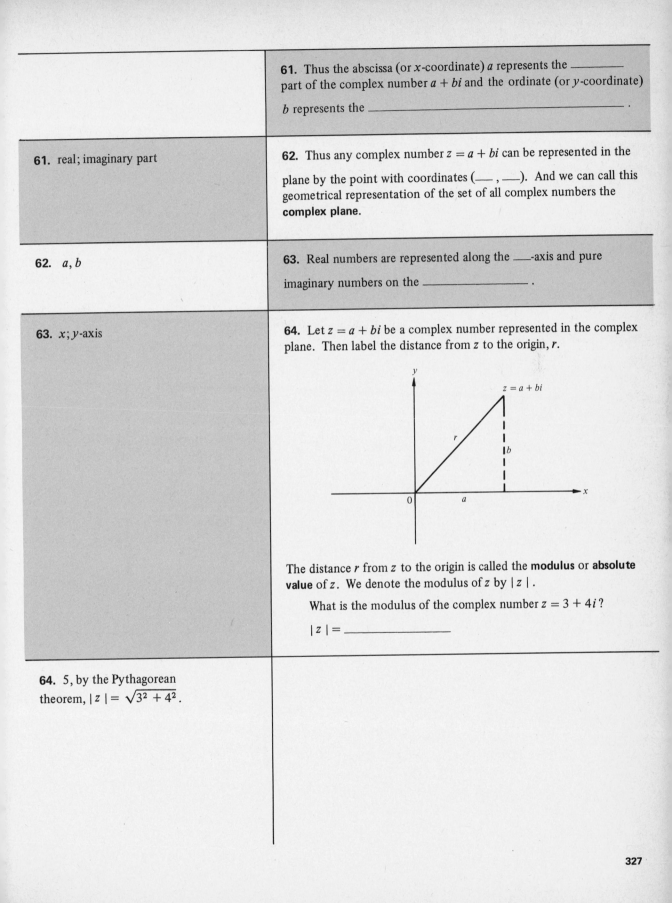

The distance r from z to the origin is called the **modulus** or **absolute value** of z. We denote the modulus of z by $|z|$.

What is the modulus of the complex number $z = 3 + 4i$?

$|z| =$ _____

---

64. 5, by the Pythagorean theorem, $|z| = \sqrt{3^2 + 4^2}$.

EXAMPLE 4

65. Plot $z = 2 - 5i$ on the axes, and find the modulus $|z|$.

$|z| = $ _____

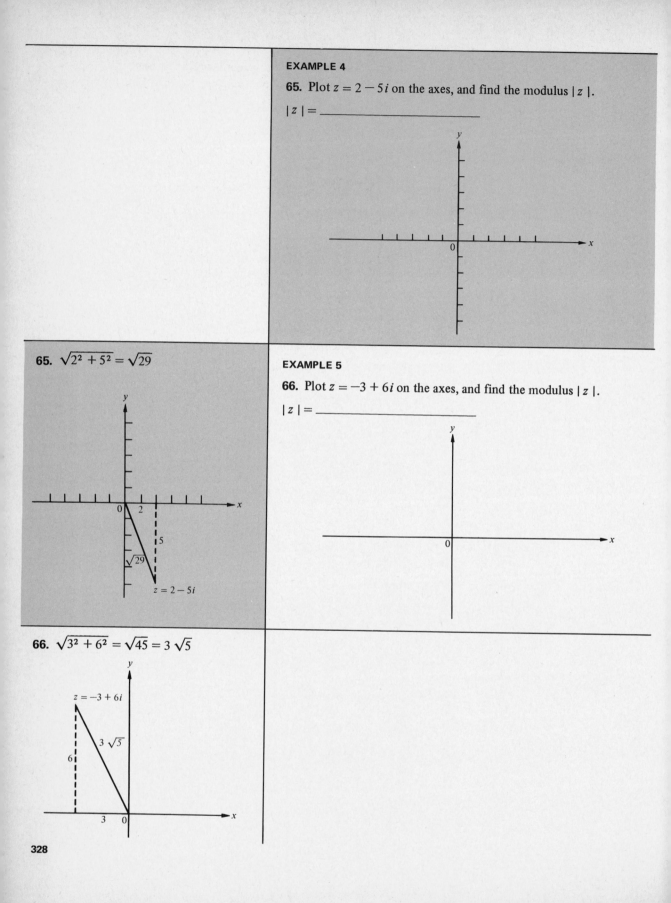

65. $\sqrt{2^2 + 5^2} = \sqrt{29}$

EXAMPLE 5

66. Plot $z = -3 + 6i$ on the axes, and find the modulus $|z|$.

$|z| = $ _____

66. $\sqrt{3^2 + 6^2} = \sqrt{45} = 3\sqrt{5}$

EXAMPLE 6

67. Find the modulus of $z = -4 - 2i$.

$|z| =$ _____

---

67. $\sqrt{4^2 + 2^2} = \sqrt{20} = 2\sqrt{5}$

68. In general if $z = a + bi$, the modulus $|z|$ is given by

_____ .

---

68. $\sqrt{a^2 + b^2}$

EXAMPLE 7

69. Now plot the number 2 on the axes, and find the modulus $|2|$.

$|2| =$ _____

---

69. 2

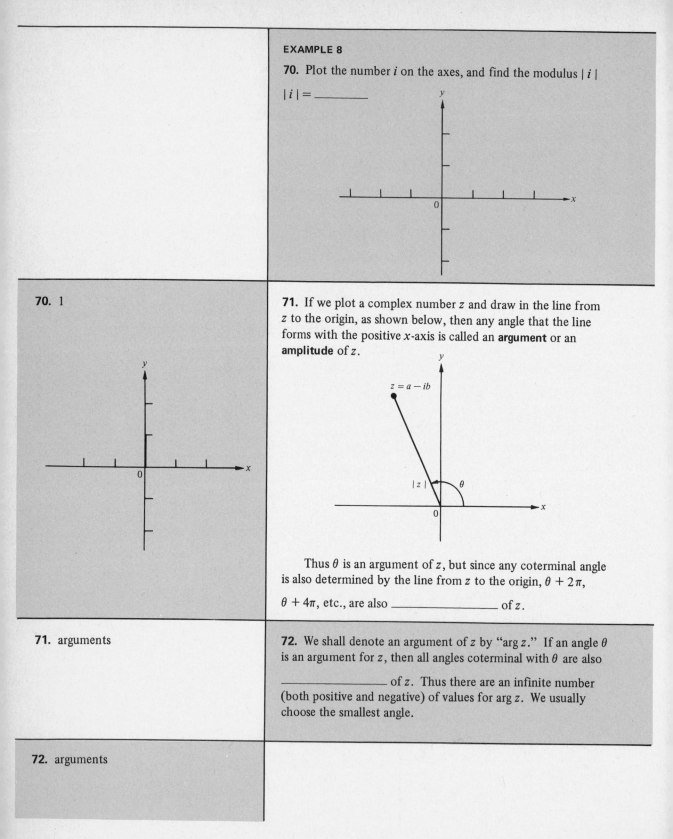

EXAMPLE 8

70. Plot the number i on the axes, and find the modulus $|i|$

$|i| = $ _____

70. 1

71. If we plot a complex number z and draw in the line from z to the origin, as shown below, then any angle that the line forms with the positive x-axis is called an **argument** or an **amplitude** of z.

$z = a - ib$

$|z|$ θ

Thus θ is an argument of z, but since any coterminal angle is also determined by the line from z to the origin, $\theta + 2\pi$, $\theta + 4\pi$, etc., are also _____ of z.

71. arguments

72. We shall denote an argument of z by "arg z." If an angle θ is an argument for z, then all angles coterminal with θ are also

_____ of z. Thus there are an infinite number (both positive and negative) of values for arg z. We usually choose the smallest angle.

72. arguments

EXAMPLE 9

73. From the diagram in frame 71 we see that if θ is an argument, then $\tan \theta = $ _____ .

Plot the number $z = 1 + i$ on the axes, and find the smallest positive argument for z.

$\arg z = $ _____

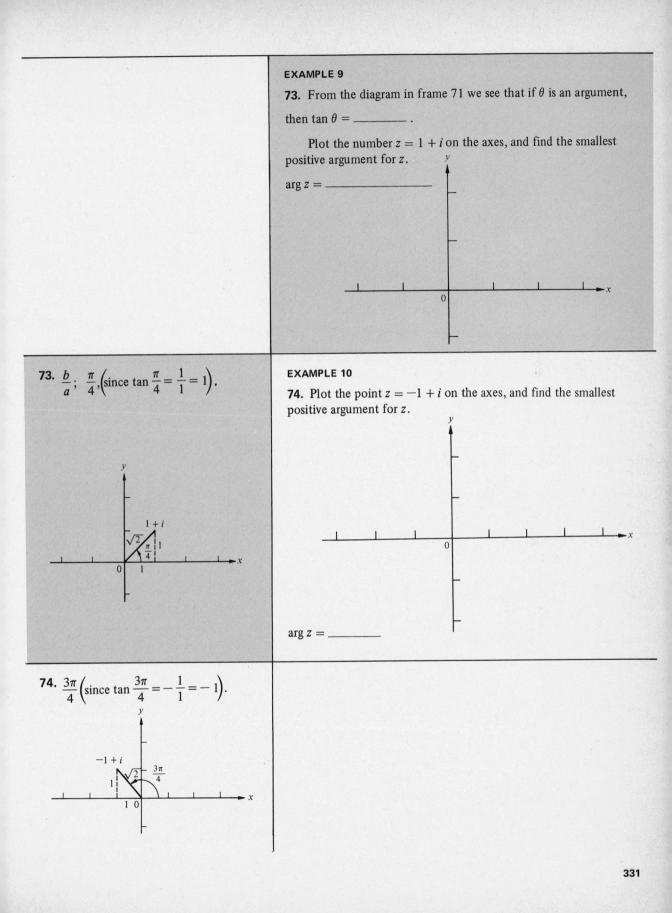

73. $\dfrac{b}{a}$; $\dfrac{\pi}{4}$, $\left(\text{since } \tan \dfrac{\pi}{4} = \dfrac{1}{1} = 1\right)$.

EXAMPLE 10

74. Plot the point $z = -1 + i$ on the axes, and find the smallest positive argument for z.

$\arg z = $ _____

74. $\dfrac{3\pi}{4}$ $\left(\text{since } \tan \dfrac{3\pi}{4} = -\dfrac{1}{1} = -1\right)$.

EXAMPLE 11

75. Plot the point $z = \sqrt{3} + i$ on the axes, and find the smallest positive argument for z.

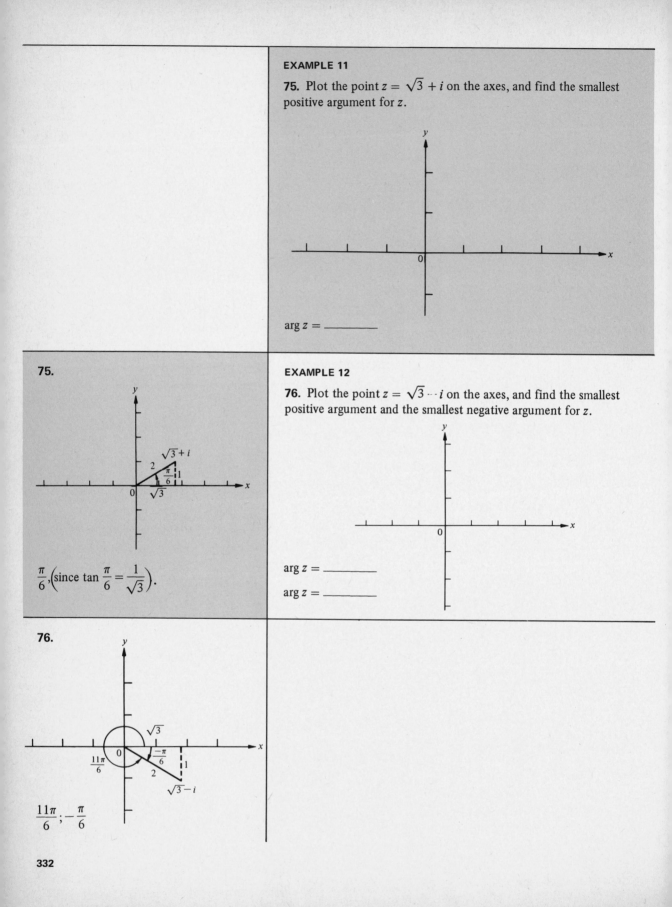

arg $z = $ _____

75.

$\dfrac{\pi}{6}, \left(\text{since } \tan \dfrac{\pi}{6} = \dfrac{1}{\sqrt{3}}\right).$

EXAMPLE 12

76. Plot the point $z = \sqrt{3} - i$ on the axes, and find the smallest positive argument and the smallest negative argument for z.

arg $z = $ _____

arg $z = $ _____

76.

$\dfrac{11\pi}{6}; -\dfrac{\pi}{6}$

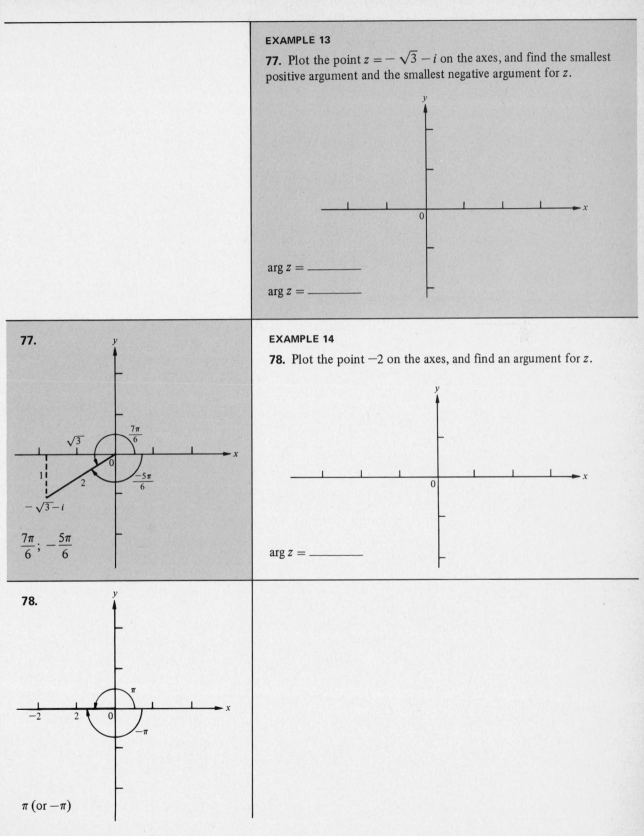

EXAMPLE 13

77. Plot the point $z = -\sqrt{3} - i$ on the axes, and find the smallest positive argument and the smallest negative argument for z.

arg $z =$ _____

arg $z =$ _____

77.

$\dfrac{7\pi}{6}, \; -\dfrac{5\pi}{6}$

EXAMPLE 14

78. Plot the point -2 on the axes, and find an argument for z.

arg $z =$ _____

78.

$\pi \; (\text{or} \; -\pi)$

EXAMPLE 15

79. Plot the point $3i$ on the axes, and find an argument for z.

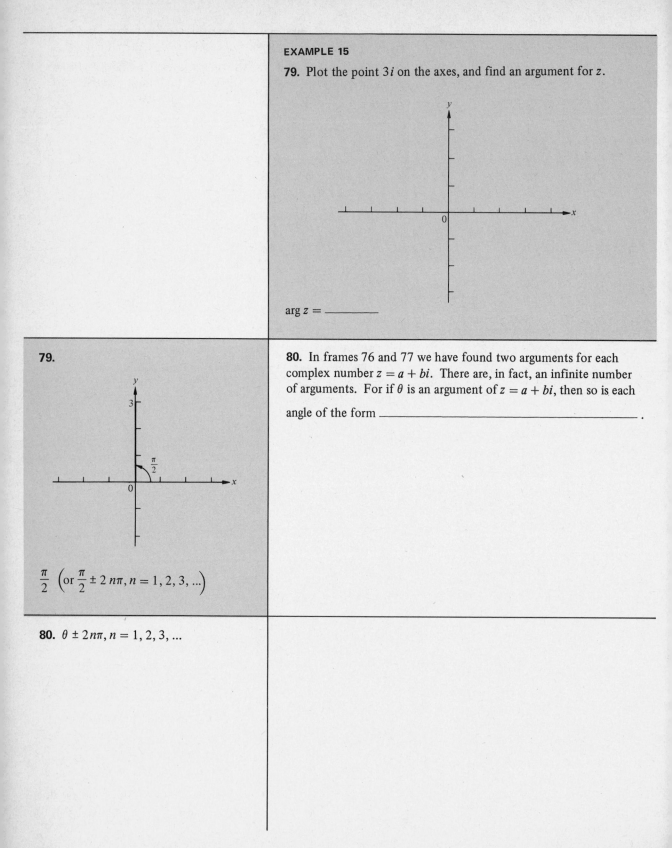

arg $z =$ _____

79.

$\dfrac{\pi}{2} \left(\text{or } \dfrac{\pi}{2} \pm 2\,n\pi, n = 1, 2, 3, ... \right)$

80. In frames 76 and 77 we have found two arguments for each complex number $z = a + bi$. There are, in fact, an infinite number of arguments. For if θ is an argument of $z = a + bi$, then so is each angle of the form _____ .

80. $\theta \pm 2n\pi, n = 1, 2, 3, ...$

81. However, the trigonometric value of an angle is completely determined by the terminal side of that angle. Thus, for each complex number $z = a + bi$ with modulus r and argument θ, as shown, there are associated the two unique values,

$a = r \cos \theta$ and $b = $ _____ .

81. $r \sin \theta$

82. Thus we can express any complex number $z = a + bi$ as

$z = a + bi = r \cos \theta + $ _____ .

82. $(r \sin \theta)i$

83. It is customary to factor out the r and to write the i before the sin θ. Thus we get $z = a + bi = $ _____ .
This is called the **trigonometric form**.

83. $r(\cos \theta + i \sin \theta)$

84. Since $\cos \theta = \cos(\theta \pm 2n\pi)$, $n = 1, 2, 3, \dots$, and

$\sin \theta = \sin($_____$)$, _____ , we get the same trigonometric form no matter which argument we choose. That is,

$r\left[\cos\left(\theta \pm 2n\pi\right) + \sin\left(\theta \pm 2n\pi\right)\right] = $ _____
for all $n = 1, 2, 3, \dots$. Thus we shall usually choose the smallest argument.

84. $(\theta \pm 2n\pi), n = 1, 2, 3, \dots$;
$r(\cos \theta + i \sin \theta)$

85. Express the complex number $z = 1 + 1$ in trigonometric form.

$z = $ _____

85. $\sqrt{2}\left(\cos \dfrac{\pi}{4} + i \sin \dfrac{\pi}{4}\right).$

If you had difficulty, see frames 73 to 81 and 84.

86. Express the complex number $z = -1 + i$ in trigonometric form.

$z = $ _____

86. $\sqrt{2}\left(\cos\dfrac{3\pi}{4} + i\sin\dfrac{3\pi}{4}\right)$.

If you had difficulty, see frames 74 and 81 to 84.

87. Express the complex number $z = \sqrt{3} + i$ in trigonometric form.

$z = $ _____

87. $2\left(\cos\dfrac{\pi}{6} + i\sin\dfrac{\pi}{6}\right)$.

If you had difficulty, see frames 75 and 81 to 84.

88. Express the complex number $z = \sqrt{3} - i$ in trigonometric form.

$z = $ _____

88. $2\left(\cos-\dfrac{\pi}{6} + i\sin-\dfrac{\pi}{6}\right)$

$\left(\text{or } 2\left(\cos\dfrac{11\pi}{6} + i\sin\dfrac{11\pi}{6}\right)\right)$.

If you had difficulty, see frames 76 and 81 to 84.

89. Express the complex number $z = -2$ in trigonometric form.

$z = $ _____

89. $2(\cos\pi + i\sin\pi)$.

If you had difficulty, see frames 78 and 81 to 84.

90. Express the complex number $z = 3i$ in trigonometric form.

$z = $ _____

90. $3\left(\cos\dfrac{\pi}{2} + i\sin\dfrac{\pi}{2}\right)$.

If you had difficulty, see frames 79 and 81 to 84.

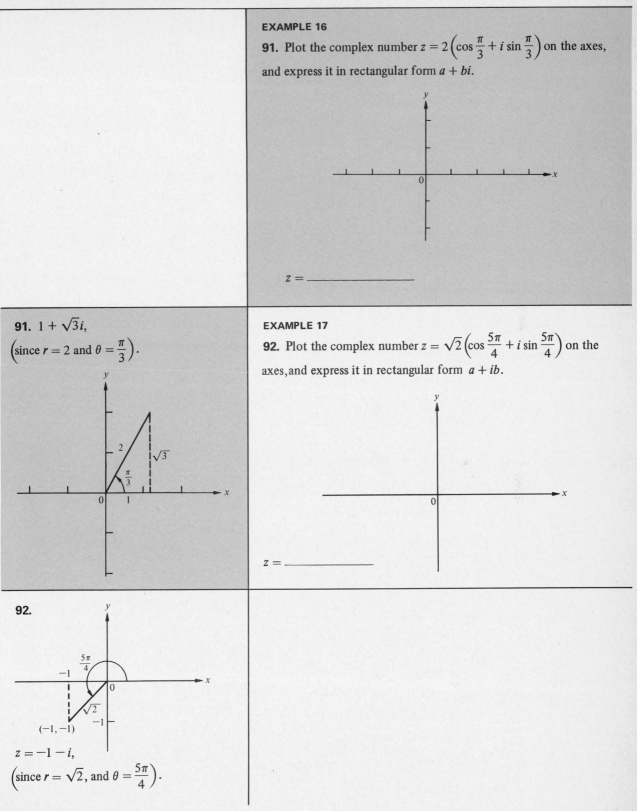

EXAMPLE 16

91. Plot the complex number $z = 2\left(\cos\dfrac{\pi}{3} + i\sin\dfrac{\pi}{3}\right)$ on the axes, and express it in rectangular form $a + bi$.

$z = $ _____

91. $1 + \sqrt{3}\,i,$

$\left(\text{since } r = 2 \text{ and } \theta = \dfrac{\pi}{3}\right).$

EXAMPLE 17

92. Plot the complex number $z = \sqrt{2}\left(\cos\dfrac{5\pi}{4} + i\sin\dfrac{5\pi}{4}\right)$ on the axes, and express it in rectangular form $a + ib$.

$z = $ _____

92.

$z = -1 - i,$

$\left(\text{since } r = \sqrt{2}, \text{ and } \theta = \dfrac{5\pi}{4}\right).$

EXAMPLE 18

93. Express the complex number $z = 2\left(\cos\left(-\dfrac{\pi}{6}\right) + i \sin\left(-\dfrac{\pi}{6}\right)\right)$ in rectangular form $a + ib$.

$z = $ _____

---

93. $\sqrt{3} - i$,

$\left(\text{since } r = 2 \text{ and } \theta = -\dfrac{\pi}{6}\right)$.

94. If a complex number z is written in trigonometric form $z = r(\cos\theta + i\sin\theta)$, then the modulus,

$|z| = $ _____

and an argument, $\arg z = $ _____ .

---

94. r; θ

EXAMPLE 19

95. Express the number $z = 2 + 2i$ in trigonometric form.

$z = $ _____

---

95. $\sqrt{8}\left(\cos\dfrac{\pi}{4} + i\sin\dfrac{\pi}{4}\right)$.

If you had difficulty, go on to the next frame. If not, skip to frame 98.

96. Plot the number $z = 2 + 2i$ on the axes below.

Since r is the modulus, we find r by $r = |z| = $

_____ .

96.

$\sqrt{a^2 + b^2} = \sqrt{(2)^2 + (2)^2} = \sqrt{8}$

338

97. Since $a = b$, the argument $\theta =$ _____ ,

since $\tan \theta =$ _____ .
and z is in quadrant I.

---

97. $\dfrac{\pi}{4}$; $\dfrac{b}{a} = \dfrac{2}{2} = 1$

EXAMPLE 20

98. Express the complex number $z = 3 - 3\sqrt{3}\,i$ in trigonometric form.

$z =$ _____

---

98. $6\left(\cos\dfrac{5\pi}{3} + i\,\sin\dfrac{5\pi}{3}\right).$

If you had difficulty, go on to the next frame. If not, skip to frame 101.

99. Plot the number $z = 3 - 3\sqrt{3}\,i$ on the axes.

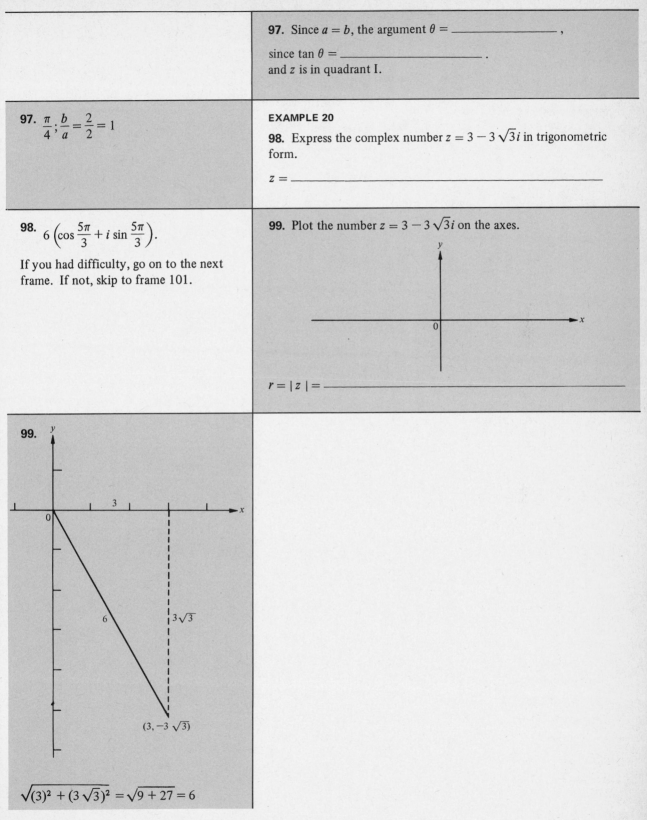

$r = |z| =$ _____

99.

$(3, -3\sqrt{3})$

$\sqrt{(3)^2 + (3\sqrt{3})^2} = \sqrt{9 + 27} = 6$

100. And **(a)** the argument $\theta =$ _____ .

since **(b)** $\tan \theta =$ _____

and **(c)** z is in quadrant _____

---

100. **(a)** $\dfrac{5\pi}{3}$ or $-\dfrac{\pi}{3}$

(b) $\dfrac{-3\sqrt{3}}{3} = -\dfrac{\sqrt{3}}{1}$

(c) IV

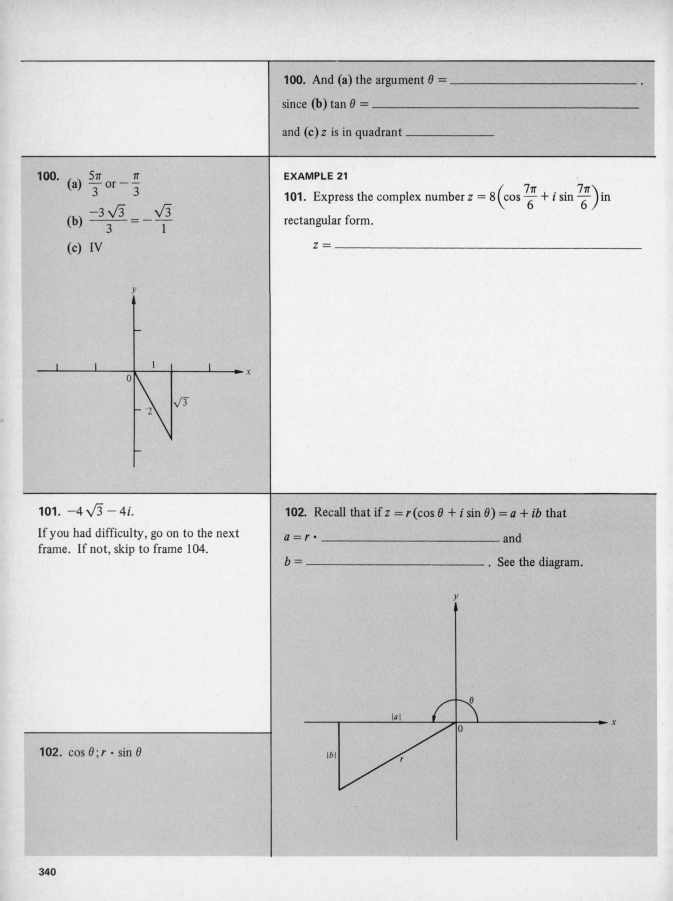

EXAMPLE 21
101. Express the complex number $z = 8\left(\cos \dfrac{7\pi}{6} + i \sin \dfrac{7\pi}{6}\right)$ in rectangular form.

$z =$ _____

---

101. $-4\sqrt{3} - 4i$.

If you had difficulty, go on to the next frame. If not, skip to frame 104.

102. Recall that if $z = r(\cos \theta + i \sin \theta) = a + ib$ that

$a = r \cdot$ _____ and

$b =$ _____ . See the diagram.

---

102. $\cos \theta$; $r \cdot \sin \theta$

103. Thus if $z = 8(\cos \dfrac{7\pi}{6} + i \sin \dfrac{7\pi}{6})$

(a) $a = 8 \cdot$ _____ = _____ and **(b)** $b =$ _____ .

That is, $z =$ **(c)** _____ .

103.

(a) $\cos \dfrac{7\pi}{6} = -4\sqrt{3}$

(b) $8 \cdot \sin \dfrac{7\pi}{6} = -4$

(c) $-4\sqrt{3} - 4i$

$(-4\sqrt{3}, -4)$

---

104. Earlier we defined addition, subtraction, multiplication, and division of complex numbers in rectangular form. There are certain advantages to using the trigonometric form for multiplication and division. We look now at multiplication in trigonometric form.

Let $z_1 = r_1(\cos \theta_1 + i \sin \theta_1)$ and $z_2 = r_2(\cos \theta_2 + i \sin \theta_2)$ be two complex numbers. Then

$z_1 \cdot z_2 = r_1(\cos \theta_1 + i \sin \theta_1) \cdot r_2(\cos \theta_2 + i \sin \theta_2)$

$= r_1 r_2 [\cos \theta_1 \cos \theta_2 + i \sin \theta_1 \cos \theta_2 + i \cos \theta_1 \sin \theta_2 + i^2 \sin \theta_1 \sin \theta_2]$

$= r_1 r_2 [\cos \theta_1 \cos \theta_2 + i (\sin \theta_1 \cos \theta_2 + \cos \theta_1 \sin \theta_2) - \sin \theta_1 \sin \theta_2]$

$= r_1 r_2 [(\cos \theta_1 \cos \theta_2 - \sin \theta_1 \sin \theta_2) + i (\sin \theta_1 \cos \theta_2 + \cos \theta_1 \sin \theta_2)]$

But we have two identities that give us

(a) $\cos (\theta_1 + \theta_2) =$ _____

and

(b) $\sin (\theta_1 + \theta_2) =$ _____

Thus **(c)** $z_1 \cdot z_2 =$ _____ .

104.

(a) $\cos \theta_1 \cos \theta_2 - \sin \theta_1 \sin \theta_2$

(b) $\sin \theta_1 \cos \theta_2 + \cos \theta_1 \sin \theta_2$

(c) $r_1 \cdot r_2 [\cos (\theta_1 + \theta_2) + i \sin (\theta_1 + \theta_2)]$

---

105. Thus if $z_1 = r_1(\cos \theta_1 + i \sin \theta_1)$ and $z_2 = r_2(\cos \theta_2 + i \sin \theta_2)$, then the modulus of the product,

$|z_1 \cdot z_2| =$ _____ and an argument of the product,

$\arg z_1 \cdot z_2 =$ _____ .

---

105. $r_1 r_2 \, ; \theta_1 + \theta_2$

---

106. If $z_1 = 5\left(\cos \dfrac{\pi}{3} + i \sin \dfrac{\pi}{3}\right)$ and $z_2 = 7(\cos \pi + i \sin \pi)$,

then $z_1 \cdot z_2 =$ _____ .

---

106. $35\left(\cos \dfrac{4\pi}{3} + i \sin \dfrac{4\pi}{3}\right).$

If you had difficulty, see frames 104 and 105.

107. If $z_1 = 3\left(\cos\dfrac{13\pi}{12} + i\sin\dfrac{13\pi}{12}\right)$ and

and $z_2 = 4\left(\cos\dfrac{3\pi}{4} + i\sin\dfrac{3\pi}{4}\right)$,

then $z_1 \cdot z_2 = $ _____ .

---

107. $12\left(\cos\dfrac{11\pi}{6} + i\sin\dfrac{11\pi}{6}\right)$.

If you had difficulty, see frames 104 and 105.

EXAMPLE 22

108. Express $z_1 = -3$ and $z_2 = 2 + 2\sqrt{3}\, i$ in trigonometric form and find $z_1 \cdot z_2$.

(a) $z_1 = $ _____

(b) $z_2 = $ _____

(c) $z_1 \cdot z_1 = $ _____

108.
(a) $3\left(\cos\pi + i\sin\pi\right)$

(b) $4\left(\cos\dfrac{\pi}{3} + i\sin\dfrac{\pi}{3}\right)$

(c) $12\left(\cos\dfrac{4\pi}{3} + i\sin\dfrac{4\pi}{3}\right)$

109. We now want to turn our attention to division in trigonometric form. First we must find the complex conjugate of a number in trigonometric form.

If $z = a + bi$, then the complex conjugate $\bar{z}$ in rectangular form is

$\bar{z} = $ _____ .

---

109. $a - bi$

110. Give the complex conjugate $\bar{z}$ of $z = 1 + i$.

$\bar{z} = $ _____

---

110. $1 - i$

111. To change to trigonometric form

(a) $a = $ _____ , and **(b)** $b = $ _____ .
Thus in trigonometric form

(c) $z = a + ib = $ _____ and

(d) $z = a - ib = $ _____ .

---

111. (a) $r\cos\theta$
 (b) $r\sin\theta$
 (c) $r\left(\cos\theta + i\sin\theta\right)$
 (d) $r\left(\cos\theta - i\sin\theta\right)$

112. Now express $z = 1 + i$ and $\overline{z} = 1 - i$ in trigonometric form.

$z =$ _____

$\overline{z} =$ _____

112. $\sqrt{2}\left(\cos\dfrac{\pi}{4} + i\sin\dfrac{\pi}{4}\right)$;

$\sqrt{2}\left(\cos\dfrac{\pi}{4} - i\sin\dfrac{\pi}{4}\right)$

113. If $z = -\sqrt{3} + i$, then **(a)** $z =$ _____ and in trigonometric form

(b) $z =$ _____

and **(c)** $z =$ _____ .

113. **(a)** $-\sqrt{3} - i$

(b) $2\left(\cos\dfrac{5\pi}{6} + i\sin\dfrac{5\pi}{6}\right)$

(c) $2\left(\cos\dfrac{5\pi}{6} - i\sin\dfrac{5\pi}{6}\right)$

114. If $z = -1 - \sqrt{3}\,i$, then **(a)** $z =$ _____ and in trigonometric form

(b) $z =$ _____

and **(c)** $z =$ _____ .

114. **(a)** $-1 + \sqrt{3}\,i$

(b) $2\left(\cos\left(-\dfrac{2\pi}{3}\right) + i\sin\left(-\dfrac{2\pi}{3}\right)\right)$

(c) $2\left(\cos\left(-\dfrac{2\pi}{3}\right) - i\sin\left(-\dfrac{2\pi}{3}\right)\right)$

115. Finally, if $z = \sqrt{3} - i$, then **(a)** $z =$ _____ and in trigonometric form

    (b) $z =$ _____

    and **(c)** $z =$ _____ .

---

115. (a) $\sqrt{3} + i$

    (b) $2\left(\cos\left(-\dfrac{\pi}{6}\right) + i\sin\left(-\dfrac{\pi}{6}\right)\right)$

    (c) $2\left(\cos\left(-\dfrac{\pi}{6}\right) - i\sin\left(-\dfrac{\pi}{6}\right)\right)$

116. And, in general, if $z = r(\cos\theta + i\sin\theta)$, then

$\bar{z} =$ _____ .

---

116. $r(\cos\theta - i\sin\theta)$

117. If $z = 9\left(\cos\dfrac{9\pi}{13} + i\sin\dfrac{9\pi}{13}\right)$, the the complex conjugate

$\bar{z} =$ _____ .

---

117. $9\left(\cos\dfrac{9\pi}{13} - i\sin\dfrac{9\pi}{13}\right)$

118. If $z_1 = r_1(\cos\theta_1 + i\sin\theta_1)$ and $z_2 = r_2(\cos\theta_2 + i\sin\theta_2)$, we divide by multiplying the numerator and denominator of

$$\frac{z_1}{z_2} = \frac{r_1(\cos\theta_1 + i\sin\theta_1)}{r_2(\cos\theta_2 + i\sin\theta_2)}$$

by the complex conjugate

$\bar{z}_2 =$ _____ .

---

118. $r_2(\cos\theta_2 - i\sin\theta_2)$

119. We get

$$\frac{z_1}{z_2} = \frac{r_1(\cos\theta_1 + i\sin\theta_1)}{r_2(\cos\theta_2 + i\sin\theta_2)} \cdot \frac{(\cos\theta_2 - i\sin\theta_2)}{(\cos\theta_2 - i\sin\theta_2)} \left(\text{since } \frac{r_2}{r_2} = 1\right)$$

$$= \frac{r_1(\cos\theta_1\,\cos\theta_2 + i\sin\theta_1\,\cos\theta_2 - i\cos\theta_1\,\sin\theta_2 - i^2\,\sin\theta_1\,\sin\theta_2)}{r_2(\cos^2\theta_2 - i^2\,\sin^2\theta_2)}$$

$$= \frac{r_1[\cos\theta_1\,\cos\theta_2 + i(\sin\theta_1\,\cos\theta_2 - \cos\theta_1\,\sin\theta_2) + \sin\theta_1\,\sin\theta_2]}{r_2[\cos^2\theta_2 + \sin^2\theta_2]}$$

$$= \frac{r_1}{r_2}\left[\frac{\cos\theta_1\,\cos\theta_2 + \sin\theta_1\,\sin\theta_2 + i(\sin\theta_1\,\cos\theta_2 - \cos\theta_1\,\sin\theta_2)}{\cos^2\theta_2 + \sin^2\theta_2}\right]$$

But we have the three identities

(1) $\cos\theta_1\,\cos\theta_2 + \sin\theta_1\,\sin\theta_2 =$ _____ ,

(2) $\sin\theta_1\,\cos\theta_2 - \cos\theta_1\,\sin\theta_2 =$ _____ ,

and

(3) $\cos^2\theta_2 + \sin^2\theta_2 =$ _____ .

Thus

(4) $\dfrac{z_1}{z_2} =$ _____ .

119.

(1) $\cos(\theta_1 - \theta_2)$

(2) $\sin(\theta_1 - \theta_2)$

(3) 1

(4) $\dfrac{r_1}{r_2}(\cos(\theta_1 - \theta_2) + i\sin(\theta_1 - \theta_2))$

120. This if $z_1 = r_1(\cos\theta_1 + i\sin\theta_1)$ and $z_2 = r_2(\cos\theta_2 + i\sin\theta_2)$, then the modulus of the quotient,

$$\left|\frac{z_1}{z_2}\right| = \text{_____} \text{ and an argument of the quotient,}$$

$$\arg\frac{z_1}{z_2} = \text{_____} .$$

120. $\dfrac{r_1}{r_2}; \theta_1 - \theta_2$

121. If $z_1 = 10\left(\cos\dfrac{3\pi}{2} + i\sin\dfrac{3\pi}{2}\right)$ and

$z_2 = 5\left(\cos\dfrac{\pi}{4} + i\sin\dfrac{\pi}{4}\right)$, then

$\dfrac{z_1}{z_2} = \underline{\hspace{6cm}}$.

---

121. $2\left(\cos\dfrac{5\pi}{4} + i\sin\dfrac{5\pi}{4}\right).$

If you had difficulty, see frames 119 and 120.

122. If $z_1 = 3\left(\cos\dfrac{\pi}{2} + i\sin\dfrac{\pi}{4}\right)$ and

$z_2 = 6\left(\cos\dfrac{3\pi}{4} + i\sin\dfrac{3\pi}{4}\right)$, then

$\dfrac{z_1}{z_2} = \underline{\hspace{6cm}}$.

---

122. $\dfrac{1}{2}\left(\cos\left(-\dfrac{\pi}{4}\right) + i\sin\left(-\dfrac{\pi}{4}\right)\right)$

If you had difficulty, see frames 119 and 120.

123. Express the complex numbers $i, -1, z_1 = 1 + i$, and $z_2 = \sqrt{3} + i$ in trigonometric form.

(a) $i = \underline{\hspace{5cm}}$

(b) $-1 = \underline{\hspace{5cm}}$

(c) $z_1 = 1 + i = \underline{\hspace{4cm}}$

(d) $z_2 = \sqrt{3} + i = \underline{\hspace{4cm}}$

---

123. (a) $i = \left(\cos\dfrac{\pi}{2} + i\sin\dfrac{\pi}{2}\right)$

(b) $-1 = \left(\cos\pi + i\sin\pi\right)$

(c) $z_1 = \sqrt{2}\left(\cos\dfrac{\pi}{4} + i\sin\dfrac{\pi}{4}\right)$

(d) $z_2 = 2\left(\cos\dfrac{\pi}{6} + i\sin\dfrac{\pi}{6}\right)$

124. Now use the trigonometric form to find iz_1, iz_2, and plot z_1, z_2, iz_1, and iz_2 on the axes below.

$i \cdot z_1 =$ _____

$i \cdot z_2 =$ _____

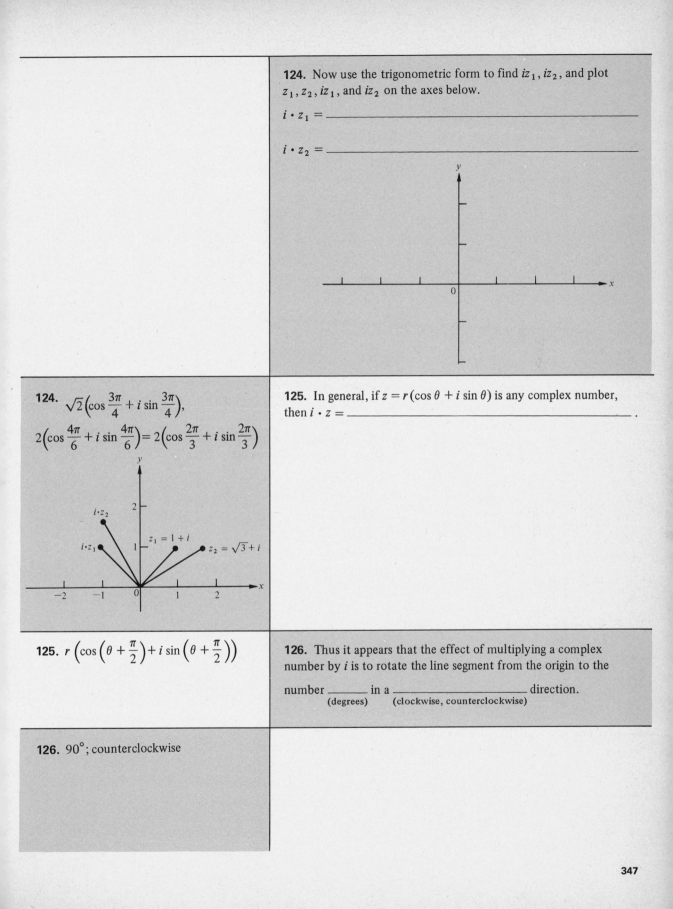

124. $\sqrt{2}\left(\cos\dfrac{3\pi}{4} + i\sin\dfrac{3\pi}{4}\right),$

$2\left(\cos\dfrac{4\pi}{6} + i\sin\dfrac{4\pi}{6}\right) = 2\left(\cos\dfrac{2\pi}{3} + i\sin\dfrac{2\pi}{3}\right)$

125. In general, if $z = r(\cos\theta + i\sin\theta)$ is any complex number, then $i \cdot z =$ _____ .

125. $r\left(\cos\left(\theta + \dfrac{\pi}{2}\right) + i\sin\left(\theta + \dfrac{\pi}{2}\right)\right)$

126. Thus it appears that the effect of multiplying a complex number by i is to rotate the line segment from the origin to the number _____ in a _____ direction.
  (degrees)   (clockwise, counterclockwise)

126. $90°$; counterclockwise

EXAMPLE 23

127. Now we find $\dfrac{z_1}{i}$ and $\dfrac{z_2}{i}$ where $z_1 = 1 + i$ and

$z_2 = \sqrt{3} + i$, as before. Plot $z_1, z_2, \dfrac{z_1}{i}$, and $\dfrac{z_2}{i}$ on the axes below.

$\dfrac{z_1}{i} =$ _____

$\dfrac{z_2}{i} =$ _____

---

127. $\sqrt{2}\left(\cos\left(-\dfrac{\pi}{2}\right) = i\sin\left(-\dfrac{\pi}{4}\right)\right);$

$2\left(\cos\left(-\dfrac{2\pi}{6}\right) + i\sin\left(-\dfrac{2\pi}{6}\right)\right)$

128. In general, if $z = r(\cos\theta + i\sin\theta)$ is any complex number,

then $\dfrac{z}{i} =$ _____ .

---

128. $r\left(\cos\left(\theta - \dfrac{\pi}{2}\right)\right) + i\sin\left(\theta - \dfrac{\pi}{2}\right)\right)$

129. Thus the effect of dividing a complex number by i is to rotate the line segment from the origin to the number _____ degrees in a _____ direction.

---

129. $90°$; clockwise

EXERCISE 1

130. If $z_1 = 5 \left(\cos \dfrac{7\pi}{6} + i \sin \dfrac{7\pi}{6} \right)$

and

$$z_2 = 2 \left(\cos \dfrac{2\pi}{3} + i \sin \dfrac{2\pi}{3} \right),$$

then $\dfrac{z_1}{z_2} = $ _____ .

---

130. $\dfrac{5}{2} \left(\cos \dfrac{\pi}{2} + i \sin \dfrac{\pi}{2} \right)$

EXERCISE 2

131. If $z_1 = 3 \left(\cos \dfrac{3\pi}{4} + i \sin \dfrac{3\pi}{4} \right)$

and $z_2 = 7 \left(\cos \left(-\dfrac{\pi}{4} \right) + i \sin \left(-\dfrac{\pi}{4} \right) \right),$

then $\dfrac{z_1}{z_2} = $ _____ .

---

131. $\dfrac{3}{7} \left(\cos \pi + i \sin \pi \right)$

132. And, in general, if
$$z_1 = r_1 (\cos \theta_1 + i \sin \theta_1)$$
and $z_2 = r_2 (\cos \theta_2 + i \sin \theta_2),$

then $\dfrac{z_1}{z_2} = $ _____ .

---

132. $\dfrac{r_1}{r_2} (\cos (\theta_1 - \theta_2) + i \sin (\theta_1 - \theta_2)).$

If you had difficulty, see frame 119.

133. $r^2(\cos(\theta + \theta) + i\sin(\theta + \theta))$
$= r^2(\cos 2\theta + i\sin 2\theta)$

134. $r^3(\cos 3\theta + i\sin 3\theta)$, since
$z \cdot z^2 = r(\cos\theta + i\sin\theta) \cdot r^2(\cos 2\theta + i\sin 2\theta) = r^3(\cos(\theta + 2\theta) + i\sin(\theta + 2\theta))$

135. $r^4(\cos 4\theta + i\sin 4\theta)$;
$r^5(\cos 5\theta + i\sin 5\theta)$

136. $r^n(\cos n\theta + i\sin n\theta)$

137. (a) $9\left(\cos\dfrac{2\pi}{3} + i\sin\dfrac{2\pi}{3}\right)$
(b) $27(\cos\pi + i\sin\pi)$
(c) $729(\cos 2\pi + i\sin 2\pi)$

If you had difficulty, see frames 133 to 136.

---

133. Now let us consider powers of complex numbers. If $z = r(\cos\theta + i\sin\theta)$, then

$z^2 = z \cdot z = $ _____ .

134. $z^3 = z \cdot z^2 = $ _____

135. $z^4 = z \cdot z^3 = $ _____

$z^5 = $ _____

136. And in general, it is true that if $z = r(\cos\theta + i\sin\theta)$, then

$z^n = $ _____ .

This result is known as DeMoivre's theorem. We shall not prove it here.

EXAMPLE 24

137. If $z = 3\left(\cos\dfrac{\pi}{3} + i\sin\dfrac{\pi}{3}\right)$, find z^2, z^3, and z^6.

(a) $z^2 = $ _____

(b) $z^3 = $ _____

(c) $z^6 = $ _____

EXAMPLE 25

138. If $z = \sqrt{2}\left(\cos\dfrac{\pi}{12} + i\sin\dfrac{\pi}{12}\right)$, find z^3 and z^8.

$z^3 = $ _____

$z^8 = $ _____

138.

$2\sqrt{2}\left(\cos\dfrac{\pi}{4} + i\sin\dfrac{\pi}{4}\right);$

$16\left(\cos\dfrac{2\pi}{3} + i\sin\dfrac{2\pi}{3}\right).$

If you had difficulty, see frames 133 to 136.

ROOTS OF COMPLEX NUMBERS

139. We began this chapter by showing that the equation $x^2 + 1 = 0$ had no real solutions. We have seen that $x^2 + 1 = 0$ has two complex solutions, namely _____ and _____ .

---

139. $i; i$

140. In fact we know by the Fundamental Theorem of Algebra that any polynomial of the form

$$a_0 x^n + a_1 x^{n-1} + \ldots + a_{n-1}x + a_n = 0$$

where the a's are real or complex numbers, has a complex number solution. In particular the polynomial equation

$$x^n - a = 0$$

has a complex number solution. In fact we shall show that $x^n - a = 0$ has exactly n distinct complex number solutions.

The two solutions of $x^2 = 1$ are _____ and _____ , where the real numbers are considered a subsystem of the complex numbers.

---

140. $1; -1$

141. The two solutions of $x^2 = 2$ are _____ and _____ .

---

141. $\sqrt{2}; -\sqrt{2}$

142. $-\sqrt{2}$

142. $\sqrt{2}$ is the positive square root of 2 and _____ is the negative square root of 2.

143. The two square roots of -1 are _____ and _____ .

143. i; $-i$.
If you had difficulty, see frame 139.

144. That is, $(i)^2 =$ _____ and $(-i)^2 =$ _____ .

144. -1; -1

145. In general if we are given a complex number a, then a square root of a is a complex number z such that _____ $= a$.

145. z^2

146. We shall use the trigonometric form and DeMoivre's theorem to find the square roots of a complex number. First recall the following fact. Since θ and $\theta + 2k\pi$, $k = ..., -2, -1, 0, 1, 2, ...$, are coterminal,

$$a = r(\cos(\theta + 2k\pi) + i\sin(\theta + 2k\pi)) = \underline{\hspace{3cm}}$$
for any integer k.

146. $r(\cos\theta + i\sin\theta)$

147. Let $a = 4\left(\cos\dfrac{\pi}{4} + i\sin\dfrac{\pi}{4}\right)$, if z is a square root of a, then

$$\underline{\hspace{4cm}} .$$

147. $z^2 = a$

148. If $z = r(\cos\theta + i\sin\theta)$, then $z^2 = a$ becomes in trigonometric form

$$\underline{\hspace{3cm}} = 4\left(\cos\dfrac{\pi}{4} + i\sin\dfrac{\pi}{4}\right)$$
$$= 4\left(\cos\dfrac{\pi}{4} + 2k\pi\right) + i\sin\left(\dfrac{\pi}{4} + 2k\pi\right)\right), k = \pm 1, \pm 2, ...$$

148. $r^2(\cos 2\theta + i\sin 2\theta)$

149. If $r^2(\cos 2\theta + i\sin 2\theta)$ and
$4\left(\cos\left(\dfrac{\pi}{4} + 2k\pi\right) + i\sin\left(\dfrac{\pi}{4} + 2k\pi\right)\right)$
represent the same complex number, then
$r^2 =$ _____ and $2\theta =$ _____ for some k, $k = ..., -2, -1, 0, 1, 2, ...$

149. $4; \dfrac{\pi}{4} + 2k\pi$

150.
$2; \dfrac{\pi}{8} + k\pi$

151. That is, if z is a square root of

$$4 \left(\cos \frac{\pi}{4} + i \sin \frac{\pi}{4} \right.$$

$$= 4 \left(\cos \left(\frac{\pi}{4} + 2k\pi \right) + i \sin \left(\frac{\pi}{4} + 2\,k\pi \right. \right.$$

then $z =$ _____
for some k; $k = ..., -2, -1, 0, 1, 2, ... $.

151.
$2 \left(\cos \left(\frac{\pi}{8} + k\pi \right) + i \sin \left(\frac{\pi}{8} + k\pi \right) \right)$

152. If $k = 0$, then one square root is

$z_1 =$ _____ .

152.
$2 \left(\cos \dfrac{\pi}{8} + i \sin \dfrac{\pi}{8} \right)$

153. And if $k = 1$, the second square root is

$z_2 =$ _____ .

153.
$2 \left(\cos \dfrac{9\pi}{8} + i \sin \dfrac{9\pi}{8} \right)$

154. We can check that z_1 and z_2 are in fact square roots of
$a = 4 \left(\cos \dfrac{\pi}{4} + i \sin \dfrac{\pi}{4} \right)$ since

$(z_1)^2 =$ _____
and
$(z_2)^2 =$ _____ .

154.
$$4 \left(\cos \left(2 \cdot \frac{\pi}{8} \right) + i \sin \left(2 \cdot \frac{\pi}{8} \right) \right)$$

$$= 4 \left(\cos \frac{\pi}{4} + i \sin \frac{\pi}{4} \right);$$

$$4 \left(\cos \left(2 \cdot \frac{9\pi}{8} \right) + i \sin \left(2 \cdot \frac{9\pi}{8} \right) \right)$$

$$= 4 \left(\cos \frac{18\pi}{8} + i \sin \frac{18\pi}{8} \right),$$

which is the same complex number as
shown above.

155. And z_1 and z_2 are the only square roots, for if $k = 2$, then

$z_3 =$ _____ ,

which is the same complex number as z_1.

---

155. $2 \left(\cos \left(\frac{\pi}{8} + 2\pi \right) + i \sin \left(\frac{\pi}{8} + 2\pi \right) \right)$

156. And all other values of k give either z_1 or z_2. Thus the complex number $a = 4\left(\cos\dfrac{\pi}{4} + i \sin\dfrac{\pi}{4}\right)$ has exactly two distinct square roots.

$z_1 =$ _____

$z_2 =$ _____

---

156. $2\left(\cos\dfrac{\pi}{8} + i \sin\dfrac{\pi}{8}\right);$

$2\left(\cos\dfrac{9\pi}{8} + i \sin\dfrac{9\pi}{8}\right)$

EXAMPLE 26

157. Find the square roots of the complex number

$a = 5\left(\cos\dfrac{2\pi}{3} + i \sin\dfrac{2\pi}{3}\right).$

$z_1 =$ _____

$z_2 =$ _____

---

157. $\sqrt{5}\left(\cos\dfrac{\pi}{3} + i \sin\dfrac{\pi}{3}\right);$

$\sqrt{5}\left(\cos\dfrac{4\pi}{3} + i \sin\dfrac{4\pi}{3}\right).$

If you had difficulty, go on to the next frame. If not, skip to frame 164.

---

158. We must find a complex number $z = r\,(\cos\theta + i \sin\theta)$ such that

_____ $= a,$

or in trigonometric form

_____ $= 5\left(\cos\dfrac{2\pi}{3} + i \sin\dfrac{2\pi}{3}\right)$

$= 5\left(\cos\left(\dfrac{2\pi}{3} + 2k\pi\right) + i \sin\left(\dfrac{2\pi}{3} + 2k\pi\right)\right), k = ..., -2, -1, 0, 1, 2, ...$

---

158. z^2; $r^2\,(\cos 2\theta + i \sin 2\theta)$

---

159. Thus $r^2 =$ ____ and $2\theta =$ _____.

---

159. 5;

$\dfrac{2\pi}{3} + 2k\pi, k = ..., -2, -1, 0, 1, 2, ...$

---

160. Therefore $r =$ ____

and $\theta =$ _____.

---

160. $\sqrt{5}; \dfrac{\pi}{3} + k\pi, k = 0, \pm 1, \pm 2, ...$

161. Thus the two square roots are of the form

$$z = \underline{\hspace{7cm}}$$

for some k, $k = 0, \pm 1, \pm 2, \ldots$.

161.
$$\sqrt{5}\left(\cos\left(\frac{\pi}{3} + k\pi\right) + i\sin\left(\frac{\pi}{3} + k\pi\right)\right)$$

162. If $k = 0$, $z_1 = \underline{\hspace{4cm}}$

and

if $k = 1$, $z_2 = \underline{\hspace{4cm}}$.

---

162. $\sqrt{5}\left(\cos\frac{\pi}{3} + i\sin\frac{\pi}{3}\right)$;

$\sqrt{5}\left(\cos\frac{4\pi}{3} + i\sin\frac{4\pi}{3}\right)$

163. Thus the two square roots of

$$5\left(\cos\frac{2\pi}{3} + i\sin\frac{2\pi}{3}\right) \text{ are}$$

$z_1 = \underline{\hspace{6cm}}$ and

$z_2 = \underline{\hspace{6cm}}$.

---

163. $\sqrt{5}\left(\cos\frac{\pi}{3} + i\sin\frac{\pi}{3}\right)$;

$\sqrt{5}\left(\cos\frac{4\pi}{3} + i\sin\frac{4\pi}{3}\right)$

EXAMPLE 27

164. Find the square roots of the complex number i.

$z_1 = \underline{\hspace{3cm}}$ $z_2 = \underline{\hspace{3cm}}$

---

164. $\left(\cos\frac{\pi}{4} + i\sin\frac{\pi}{4}\right)$;

$\left(\cos\frac{5\pi}{4} + i\sin\frac{5\pi}{4}\right)$.

If you had difficulty, go on to the next frame. If not, skip to frame 172.

165. First write i in trigonometric form.

$i = \underline{\hspace{6cm}}$

---

165. $1\left(\cos\frac{\pi}{2} + i\sin\frac{\pi}{2}\right)$

166. Now find the square roots of $i = 1\left(\cos \dfrac{\pi}{2} + i \sin \dfrac{\pi}{2}\right)$.

$z_1 = \underline{\hspace{4cm}}$ $z_2 = \underline{\hspace{4cm}}$

---

166. $\left(\cos \dfrac{\pi}{4} + i \sin \dfrac{\pi}{4}\right)$;

$\left(\cos \dfrac{5\pi}{4} + i \sin \dfrac{5\pi}{4}\right)$.

If you still had difficulty, go on to the next frame. If not, skip to frame 172.

167. We must find $z = r\left(\cos \theta + i \sin \theta\right)$ such that

$\underline{\hspace{4cm}} = 1\left(\cos \dfrac{\pi}{2} + i \sin \dfrac{\pi}{2}\right)$

$= \underline{\hspace{4cm}}$, $k = 0, \pm 1, \pm 2, \dots$.

---

167. $r^2\left(\cos 2\theta + i \sin 2\theta\right)$;

$1\left(\cos\left(\dfrac{\pi}{2} + 2k\pi\right) + i \sin\left(\dfrac{\pi}{2} + 2k\pi\right)\right)$

168. Thus $r^2 = \underline{\hspace{1cm}}$ and

$2\theta = \underline{\hspace{5cm}}$.

---

168. 1; $\dfrac{\pi}{2} + 2k\pi$, $k = 0, \pm 1, \pm 2, \dots$

169. Therefore $r = \underline{\hspace{1cm}}$ and

$\theta = \underline{\hspace{5cm}}$.

---

169. 1; $\dfrac{\pi}{4} + k\pi$, $k = 0, \pm 1, \pm 2, \dots$

170. Thus the two square roots of

$i = 1\left(\cos \dfrac{\pi}{2} + i \sin \dfrac{\pi}{2}\right)$ are of the form

$z = \underline{\hspace{5cm}}$

for some k, $k = 0, \pm 1, \pm 2, \dots$.

170.
$1\left(\cos\left(\dfrac{\pi}{4} + k\pi\right) + i \sin\left(\dfrac{\pi}{4} + k\pi\right)\right)$

171. That is, the two square roots of

$$i = 1 \left(\cos \frac{\pi}{2} + i \sin \frac{\pi}{2} \right) \text{ are}$$

$z_1 = $ _____ if $k = 0$

and

$z_2 = $ _____ if $k = 1$.

---

171. $\cos \dfrac{\pi}{4} + i \sin \dfrac{\pi}{4}$;

$\cos \dfrac{5\pi}{4} + i \sin \dfrac{5\pi}{4}$

EXAMPLE 28

172. Express $z_1 = \cos \dfrac{\pi}{4} + i \sin \dfrac{\pi}{4}$ and $z_2 = \cos \dfrac{5\pi}{4} + i \sin \dfrac{5\pi}{4}$ in rectangular form and plot them on the axes.

$z_1 = $ _____ $z_2 = $ _____

172. $\dfrac{1}{\sqrt{2}} + \dfrac{1}{\sqrt{2}} i$; $-\dfrac{1}{\sqrt{2}} - \dfrac{1}{\sqrt{2}} i$

173. In a similar way we can find the three cube roots of a complex number a. If z is a cube root of a, then _____ $= a$.

---

173. z^3

174. If $a = 8 \left(\cos \dfrac{3\pi}{2} + i \sin \dfrac{3\pi}{2} \right)$ and z is a cube root of a
$z = r(\cos \theta + i \sin \theta)$, then

$$\underline{\hspace{4cm}} = 8\left(\cos \dfrac{3\pi}{2} + i \sin \dfrac{3\pi}{2} \right)$$

$$= 8\left(\cos\left(\dfrac{3\pi}{2} + 2k\pi \right) + i \sin\left(\dfrac{3\pi}{2} + 2k\pi \right) \right), k = 0, \pm 1, \pm 2, \dots.$$

---

174. $z^3 = r^3(\cos 3\theta + i \sin 3\theta)$

175. Thus $r^3 =$ _____ , and

$3\theta =$ _____ .

---

175. $8; \dfrac{3\pi}{2} + 2k\pi, k = 0, \pm 1, \pm 2, \dots$

176. And $r =$ _____ , and

$\theta =$ _____ .

---

176. $2; \dfrac{\pi}{2} + \dfrac{2k\pi}{3}, k = 0, \pm 1, \pm 2, \dots.$

NOTE: Because we want cube roots, we had 3θ and we must divide $\dfrac{3\pi}{2} + 2k\pi$ by 3 to get θ.

177. Hence the cube root

$z =$ _____
for some k, $k = 0, \pm 1, \pm 2, \dots.$

177.
$2\left(\cos\left(\dfrac{\pi}{2} + \dfrac{2k\pi}{3} \right) + i \sin\left(\dfrac{\pi}{2} + \dfrac{2k\pi}{3} \right) \right)$

178.
If $k = 0$, $z_1 =$ _____ .

---

178. $2\left(\cos \dfrac{\pi}{2} + i \sin \dfrac{\pi}{2} \right)$

179.
If $k = 1$, $z_2 =$ _____ .

---

179. $2\left(\cos \dfrac{7\pi}{6} + i \sin \dfrac{7\pi}{6} \right)$

180.
And if $k = 2$, $z_3 =$ _____ .

---

180. $2\left(\cos \dfrac{11\pi}{6} + i \sin \dfrac{11\pi}{6} \right)$

181. three

182. Plot $a = 8\left(\cos\dfrac{3\pi}{2} + i\sin\dfrac{3\pi}{2}\right)$ and its three cube roots on the axes and express them in rectangular form.

(a) $a \;=$ _____

(b) $z_1 \;=$ _____

(c) $z_2 \;=$ _____

(d) $z_3 \;=$ _____

182. (a) $-8i$
   (b) $2i$
   (c) $-\sqrt{3} - i$
   (d) $\sqrt{3} - i$

If you had difficulty, see frames 172 and 173.

183. In general if $a = r(\cos\theta + i\sin\theta)$, then $z = s(\cos\alpha + i\sin\alpha)$ is a square root of a if _____ $= a$.

---

183. z^2

184. Or in trigonometric form

_____ $= r(\cos\theta + i\sin\theta)$.

---

184. $s^2(\cos 2\alpha + i\sin 2\alpha)$

185. Hence $s^2 = $ ____ and $2\alpha = $ _____ ,
$k = 0, \pm1, \pm2, \dots$.

---

185. r ; $\theta + 2k\pi$,

186. And $s = $ _____ and

$\alpha = $ _____ .

---

186. $\sqrt{r}$;
$\dfrac{\theta + 2k\pi}{2} = \dfrac{\theta}{2} + k\pi, k = 0, \pm1, \pm2, \dots$

187. Therefore the two square roots of $a = r(\cos\theta + i\sin\theta)$ are of

the form $z = $ _____
where $k = 0$ or 1.

187.
$\sqrt{r}\left(\cos\left(\dfrac{\theta}{2} + k\pi\right) + i\sin\left(\dfrac{\theta}{2} + k\pi\right)\right)$
or
$\sqrt{r}\left(\cos\left(\dfrac{\theta + 2k\pi}{2}\right) + i\sin\left(\dfrac{\theta + 2k\pi}{2}\right)\right)$

188. And the three cube roots of $a = r(\cos\theta + i\sin\theta)$ are of the

form $z = $ _____
where $k = 0, 1,$ and 2.

188.
$\sqrt[3]{r}\left(\cos\left(\dfrac{\theta + 2k\pi}{3}\right) + i\sin\left(\dfrac{\theta + 2k\pi}{3}\right)\right)$.

If you had difficulty, see frames 173 to 186.

189. The four fourth roots of $a = r(\cos\theta + i\sin\theta)$ are of the form

$z = $ _____ ,

where $k = $ _____ .

189.
$\sqrt[4]{r}\left(\cos\left(\dfrac{\theta + 2k\pi}{4}\right) + i\sin\left(\dfrac{\theta + 2k\pi}{4}\right)\right)$;

0, 1, 2, and 3.

If you had difficulty, go on to the next frame. If not, skip to frame 192.

190. If we want the fourth roots of $a = r(\cos\theta + i\sin\theta)$, we want $z = s(\cos\alpha + i\sin\alpha)$ such that _____ $= a$ or, in trigonometric form,

_____ $= r(\cos\theta + i\sin\theta)$

$= r\left[\cos(\theta + 2k\pi) + i\sin(\theta + 2k\pi)\right],\, k = 0, \pm 1, \pm 2, \dots.$

---

190. z^4; $s^4(\cos 4\alpha + i\sin 4\alpha)$

191. Thus **(a)** $s =$ _____ , **(b)** $\alpha =$ _____ ,
and the fourth roots of $r(\cos\theta + i\sin\theta)$ are of the form

(c) $z =$ _____

where **(d)** $k =$ _____ .

---

191. (a) $\sqrt[4]{r}$

(b) $\dfrac{\theta + 2k\pi}{4}$, $k = 0, \pm 1, \pm 2, \dots$

(c) $\sqrt[4]{r}\left(\cos\left(\dfrac{\theta + 2k\pi}{4}\right) + i\sin\left(\dfrac{\theta + 2k\pi}{4}\right)\right)$

(d) $0, 1, 2,$ and 3

192. And, finally, if for any natural number n, we want the nth roots of $a = r(\cos\theta + i\sin\theta)$, we want $z = s(\cos\alpha + i\sin\alpha)$ such

that _____ $= a$ or in trigonometric form

_____ $= r(\cos\theta + i\sin\theta).$

---

192. z^n; $s^n(\cos n\alpha + i\sin n\alpha)$

193. Thus $s =$ _____ , and $\alpha =$ _____ .

---

193. $\sqrt[n]{r}$; $\dfrac{\theta + 2k\pi}{n}$, $k = 0, \pm 1, \pm 2, \dots$

194. And the n distinct roots of $r(\cos\theta + i\sin\theta)$ are of the form

_____

where $k =$ _____ .

194.

$\sqrt[n]{r}\left(\cos\left(\dfrac{\theta + 2k\pi}{n}\right) + i\sin\left(\dfrac{\theta + 2k\pi}{n}\right)\right)$;

$0, 1, 2, \dots, n - 1$

EXAMPLE 29

195. Find the four fourth roots of $16\left(\cos\dfrac{4\pi}{3} + i\sin\dfrac{4\pi}{3}\right).$

(a) $z_1 = $ _____

(b) $z_2 = $ _____

(c) $z_3 = $ _____

(d) $z_4 = $ _____

---

195. (a) $2\left(\cos\dfrac{\pi}{3} + i\sin\dfrac{\pi}{3}\right)$

(b) $2\left(\cos\dfrac{5\pi}{6} + i\sin\dfrac{5\pi}{6}\right)$

(c) $2\left(\cos\dfrac{4\pi}{3} + i\sin\dfrac{4\pi}{3}\right)$

(d) $2\left(\cos\dfrac{11\pi}{6} + i\sin\dfrac{11\pi}{6}\right)$

If you had difficulty, go on to the next frame. If not, skip to frame 198.

196. By frame 194, the fourth roots of

$16\left(\cos\dfrac{4\pi}{3} + i\sin\dfrac{4\pi}{3}\right)$ will be of the form

_____

where $k = 0, 1, 2,$ and $3.$

196.

$$\sqrt[4]{16}\left(\cos\left(\frac{\frac{4\pi}{3} + 2k\pi}{4}\right) + i\sin\left(\frac{\frac{4\pi}{3} + 2k\pi}{4}\right)\right)$$

$$= \sqrt[4]{16}\left(\cos\left(\frac{\pi}{3} + \frac{k\pi}{2}\right) + i\sin\left(\frac{\pi}{3} + \frac{k\pi}{2}\right)\right)$$

197. (a) $2\left(\cos\dfrac{\pi}{3} + i\sin\dfrac{\pi}{3}\right)$

(b) $2\left(\cos\dfrac{5\pi}{6} + i\sin\dfrac{5\pi}{6}\right)$

(c) $2\left(\cos\dfrac{4\pi}{3} + i\sin\dfrac{4\pi}{3}\right)$

(d) $2\left(\cos\dfrac{11\pi}{6} + i\sin\dfrac{11\pi}{6}\right)$

EXAMPLE 30

198. Plot z_1, z_2, z_3, and z_4 on the axes and express them in rectangular form.

(a) $z_1 =$ _____

(b) $z_2 =$ _____

(c) $z_3 =$ _____

(d) $z_4 =$ _____

198. (a) $1 + \sqrt{3}i$

(b) $-\sqrt{3} + i$

(c) $-1 - \sqrt{3}i$

(d) $\sqrt{3} - i$

199. Look back at frames 172, 182, and 198. What geometric pattern can you see for the roots of a complex number?

If z_1 and z_2 are the square roots of $a = r(\cos\theta + i\sin\theta)$,

then z_1 and z_2 are equally spaced around the circle of radius _____ whose center is at the origin.

---

199. $\sqrt{r}$

200. If z_1, z_2, and z_3 are the cube roots of $a = r(\cos\theta + i\sin\theta)$,

then z_1, z_2, and z_3 lie on the circle of radius _____ , and the

difference in the arguments of any two of them is _____ degrees.

---

200. $\sqrt[3]{r}$; 120

201. If z_1, z_2, z_3, and z_4 are the fourth roots of $a = r(\cos\theta + i\sin\theta)$, then z_1, z_2, z_3, and z_4 lie on the circle of

radius _____ , and the difference in the arguments of any two

adjacent roots is _____ degrees.

---

201. $\sqrt[4]{r}$; 90

202. This pattern holds true for all n, so that the nth roots of $a = r(\cos\theta + i\sin\theta)$ are equally spaced around the circle of radius

_____ . That is, the difference in the arguments of any two adjacent

roots is _____ degrees.

---

202. $\sqrt[n]{r}$; $\dfrac{360}{n}$

364

EXAMPLE 31

203. Find the five fifth roots of 1.

(a) $z_1 = $ _____

(b) $z_2 = $ _____

(c) $z_3 = $ _____

(d) $z_4 = $ _____

(e) $z_5 = $ _____

---

203. (a) $\cos 0 + i \sin 0$

(b) $\cos \dfrac{2\pi}{5} + i \sin \dfrac{2\pi}{5}$

(c) $\cos \dfrac{4\pi}{5} + i \sin \dfrac{4\pi}{5}$

(d) $\cos \dfrac{6\pi}{5} + i \sin \dfrac{6\pi}{5}$

(e) $\cos \dfrac{8\pi}{5} + i \sin \dfrac{8\pi}{5}$

If you had difficulty, go on to the next frame. If not, skip to frame 207.

204. First express 1 in trigonometric form.

$1 = $ _____

---

204. $1 (\cos 0 + i \sin 0)$

205. Now find the five fifth roots of 1. They will be of the form

_____

where $k = 0, 1, 2, 3,$ and 4.

205.

$$\sqrt[5]{1} \left(\cos \frac{2k\pi}{5} + i \sin \frac{2k\pi}{5} \right)$$

206. Thus **(a)** if $k = 0, z_1 = $ _____ ,

(b) if $k = 1, z_2 = $ _____ ,

(c) if $k = 2, z_3 = $ _____ ,

(d) if $k = 3, z_4 = $ _____ ,

and **(e)** if $k = 4, z_5 = $ _____ .

---

206. (a) $\cos 0 + i \sin 0,$

    (b) $\cos \dfrac{2\pi}{5} + i \sin \dfrac{2\pi}{5}$

    (c) $\cos \dfrac{4\pi}{5} + i \sin \dfrac{4\pi}{5}$

    (d) $\cos \dfrac{6\pi}{5} + i \sin \dfrac{6\pi}{5}$

    (e) $\cos \dfrac{8\pi}{5} + i \sin \dfrac{8\pi}{5}$

207. Plot the five fifth roots of 1 on the axes. Plot z_1, and then plot the remainder geometrically.

207.

If you had difficulty, see frames 199 to 202.

EXAMPLE 32

208. Find the five fifth roots of i.

(a) $z_1 =$ _____

(b) $z_2 =$ _____

(c) $z_3 =$ _____

(d) $z_4 =$ _____

(e) $z_5 =$ _____

208.

(a) $\cos \dfrac{\pi}{10} + i \sin \dfrac{\pi}{10}$

(b) $\cos \dfrac{\pi}{2} + i \sin \dfrac{\pi}{2}$

(c) $\cos \dfrac{9\pi}{10} + i \sin \dfrac{9\pi}{10}$

(d) $\cos \dfrac{13\pi}{10} + i \sin \dfrac{13\pi}{10}$

(e) $\cos \dfrac{17\pi}{10} + i \sin \dfrac{17\pi}{10}$

If you had difficulty, go on to the next frame. If not, skip to frame 212.

209.

In trigonometric form $i =$ _____ .

---

209. $1 \left(\cos \dfrac{\pi}{2} + i \sin \dfrac{\pi}{2} \right)$

210. And the five fifth roots of i will be of the form

_____

where $k =$ _____ .

210.

$$\cos \left(\dfrac{\dfrac{\pi}{2} + 2k\pi}{5} \right) + i \sin \left(\dfrac{\dfrac{\pi}{2} + 2k\pi}{5} \right) ;$$

0, 1, 2, 3, and 4

211. Thus the five fifth roots of i will be

(a) $z_1 = $_____ ,

(b) $z_2 = $_____ ,

(c) $z_3 = $_____ ,

(d) $z_4 = $_____ ,

(e) $z_5 = $_____ .

211.

(a) $\cos \dfrac{\pi}{10} + i \sin \dfrac{\pi}{10}$,

(b) $\cos \dfrac{\pi}{2} + i \sin \dfrac{\pi}{2}$,

(c) $\cos \dfrac{9\pi}{10} + i \sin \dfrac{9\pi}{10}$,

(d) $\cos \dfrac{13\pi}{10} + i \sin \dfrac{13\pi}{10}$

(e) $\cos \dfrac{17\pi}{10} + i \sin \dfrac{17\pi}{10}$

212. Plot the five fifth roots of i on the axes. Plot z_2, and then plot the remainder geometrically.

212.

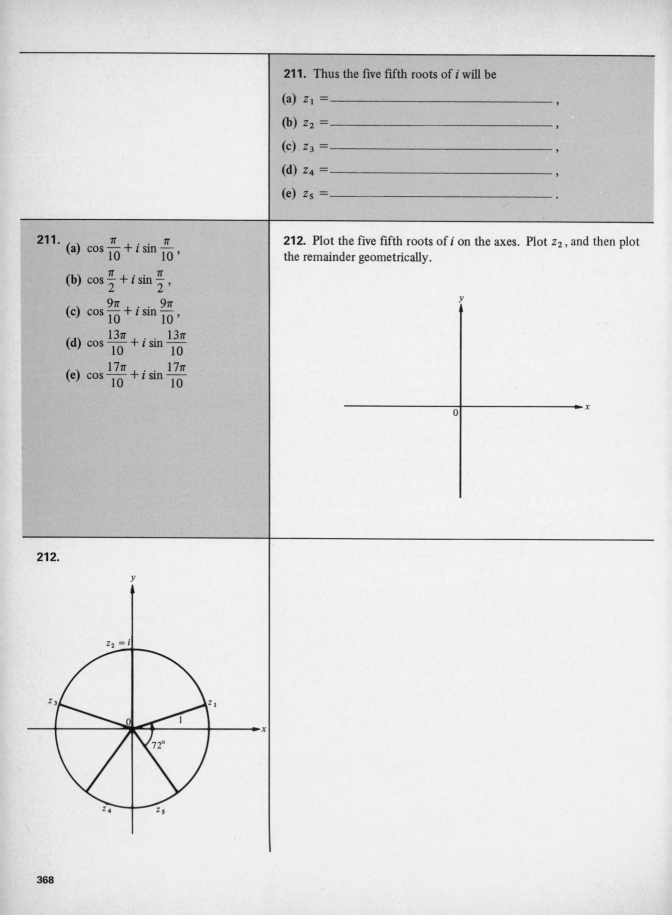

EXAMPLE 33

213. Find the nine ninth roots of

$a = \cos\dfrac{3\pi}{4} + i \sin\dfrac{3\pi}{4}$. They are of the form

$z_{k+1} = $ _____

where $k = 0, 1, 2, ..., 8$.

213.
$$\cos\left(\dfrac{\dfrac{3\pi}{4} + 2k\pi}{9}\right) + i \sin\left(\dfrac{\dfrac{3\pi}{4} + 2k\pi}{9}\right)$$
$$= \cos\left(\dfrac{\pi}{12} + \dfrac{2k\pi}{9}\right) + i \sin\left(\dfrac{\pi}{12} + \dfrac{2k\pi}{9}\right)$$

214.

If $k = 0$, $z_1 = $ _____

214.
$$\cos\dfrac{\pi}{12} + i \sin\dfrac{\pi}{12}$$

215. And since $\dfrac{\pi}{12}$ radian is ____ degrees, we can plot z_1 as shown below.

Plot the remainder of the ninth roots of $a = \cos\dfrac{3\pi}{4} + i \sin\dfrac{3\pi}{4}$ geometrically on the axes. The argument of each root will differ from the argument of the preceding root by ____ degrees.

---

215. 15; 40

EXAMPLE 34

216. Find the six sixth roots of -1.

(a) $z_1 =$ _____ ,

(b) $z_2 =$ _____ ,

(c) $z_3 =$ _____ ,

(d) $z_4 =$ _____ ,

(e) $z_5 =$ _____ ,

(f) $z_6 =$ _____ .

---

216. (a) $\cos \dfrac{\pi}{6} + i \sin \dfrac{\pi}{6}$

(b) $\cos \dfrac{\pi}{2} + i \sin \dfrac{\pi}{2}$

(c) $\cos \dfrac{5\pi}{6} + i \sin \dfrac{5\pi}{6}$

(d) $\cos \dfrac{7\pi}{6} + i \sin \dfrac{7\pi}{6}$

(e) $\cos \dfrac{3\pi}{2} + i \sin \dfrac{3\pi}{2}$

(f) $\cos \dfrac{11\pi}{6} + i \sin \dfrac{11\pi}{6}$

If you had difficulty, see frames 194 and 208 to 211.

217. Find the n nth roots of 1. They are of the form

$z_{k+1} =$ _____ ,

where $k =$ _____ .

---

217. $\cos \dfrac{2k\pi}{n} + i \sin \dfrac{2k\pi}{n}$;

$0, 1, 2, ..., n-1$.

If you had difficulty, see frames 194 and 203 to 207.

218. These n complex numbers are called the "nth roots of unity." If $k = 1$,

$z_2 =$ _____ and

$z_2^2 =$ _____ .

---

218. $\cos \dfrac{2\pi}{n} + i \sin \dfrac{2\pi}{n}$;

$\cos \dfrac{4\pi}{n} + i \sin \dfrac{4\pi}{n} = z_3$

219.

$z_2^3 =$ _____ $=$ _____ .

---

219. $\cos \dfrac{6\pi}{n} + i \sin \dfrac{6\pi}{n} = z_4$

220. (a) $z_2^4 =$ _____ , **(b)** $z_2^5 =$ _____ and finally

(c) $z_2^n =$ _____ $=$ **(d)** _____ .

---

220. (a) z_7
  (b) z_6
  (c) $\cos \dfrac{2n\pi}{n} + i \sin \dfrac{2n\pi}{n}$
  (d) 1

221. The seventeen 17th roots of units are of the form

$z_{k+1} =$ _____ ,

where $k =$ _____ .

---

221. $\cos \dfrac{2k\pi}{17} + i \sin \dfrac{2k\pi}{17}$;

$0, 1, ..., 16$

222. If $z_2 = \cos \dfrac{2\pi}{17} + i \sin \dfrac{2\pi}{17}$, then

$z_2^{17} =$ _____ .

---

222. $\cos \dfrac{2\pi 17}{17} + i \sin \dfrac{2\pi 17}{17}$

$= \cos 2\pi + i \sin 2\pi = 1 + (i \cdot 0) = 1$

QUIZ

1. Label each of the following numbers either real, pure imaginary, or complex.

  (a) $\frac{1}{2} i$ **(b)** $\sqrt{5} - 3i$

  (c) e **(d)** $-2 + 2i$

  (e) $-i$

2. If $x + yi = \sqrt{5} - 3i$, then $x =$ _____ and $y =$ _____ .

3. Given $z_1 = 7 - 3i$ and $z_2 = -4 + 5i$, find

  (a) $z_1 + z_2$ **(b)** $z_1 - z_2$

  (c) $z_1 \cdot z_2$ **(d)** $\dfrac{z_1}{z_2}$

4. Given $z = 1 + \sqrt{3}\, i$,

  (a) express z in trigonometric form ;

  (b) find the absolute value $|\, z\, |$;

  (c) find the argument $\arg z$;

  (d) graph z on the axes on the right.

5. Given $z = 4\left(\cos\dfrac{\pi}{6} + i \sin\dfrac{\pi}{6}\right),$

   (a) express z in rectangular form;

   (b) find the absolute value $|z|$;

   (c) find the argument $\arg z$;

   (d) graph z on the axes on the right.

6. Given $z_1 = 3\left(\cos\dfrac{\pi}{5} + i \sin\dfrac{\pi}{5}\right)$ and $z_2 = 5\left(\cos\dfrac{\pi}{3} + i \sin\dfrac{\pi}{3}\right)$, then

   (a) $z_1 \cdot z_2 = $ _____ ;

   (b) $z_1/z_2 = $ _____ .

7. If $z = 2\left(\cos\dfrac{\pi}{8} + i \sin\dfrac{\pi}{8}\right)$, then

   (a) $z^3 = $ _____ ;

   (b) $z^7 = $ _____ .

8. If $a = 243\left(\cos\dfrac{5\pi}{6} + i \sin\dfrac{5\pi}{6}\right)$, find the five fifth roots of a and graph them.

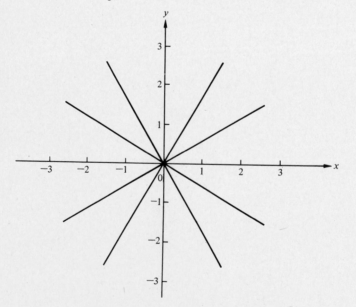

ANSWERS

Page 16

1. (a) terminal side, (b) vertex, (c) initial side, (e) negative, (f) III
   (d)

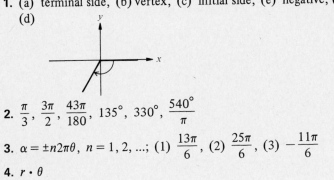

2. $\dfrac{\pi}{3}$, $\dfrac{3\pi}{2}$, $\dfrac{43\pi}{180}$, $135°$, $330°$, $\dfrac{540°}{\pi}$

3. $\alpha = \pm n2\pi\theta$, $n = 1, 2, ...$; (1) $\dfrac{13\pi}{6}$, (2) $\dfrac{25\pi}{6}$, (3) $-\dfrac{11\pi}{6}$

4. $r \cdot \theta$

Page 33

PROBLEMS

1. $\sin\theta = \dfrac{\sqrt{3}}{2}$, $\tan\theta = -\sqrt{3}$, $\csc\theta = \dfrac{2}{\sqrt{3}}$, $\sec\theta = -2$, $\cot\theta = -\dfrac{1}{\sqrt{3}}$

2. $\sin\theta = -\dfrac{4}{\sqrt{17}}$, $\cos\theta = -\dfrac{1}{\sqrt{17}}$, $\csc\theta = -\dfrac{\sqrt{17}}{4}$, $\sec\theta = -\sqrt{17}$, $\cot\theta = \dfrac{1}{4}$

3. $\cos\theta = \dfrac{\sqrt{3}}{2}$, $\tan\theta = -\dfrac{1}{\sqrt{3}}$, $\csc\theta = -2$, $\sec\theta = \dfrac{2}{\sqrt{3}}$, $\cot\theta = -\sqrt{3}$

4. $\sin\theta = \dfrac{2}{\sqrt{13}}$, $\cos\theta = \dfrac{3}{\sqrt{13}}$, $\tan\theta = \dfrac{2}{3}$, $\csc\theta = \dfrac{\sqrt{13}}{2}$, $\sec\theta = \dfrac{\sqrt{13}}{3}$

QUIZ

1. $\sin\theta = \dfrac{y}{r}$, $\cos\theta = \dfrac{x}{r}$, $\tan\theta = \dfrac{y}{x}$, $\csc\theta = \dfrac{r}{y}$, $\sec\theta = \dfrac{r}{x}$, $\cot\theta = \dfrac{x}{y}$

2. $\cos\theta$, $\tan\theta$, $\sin\theta$, $\tan\theta$

3.

4. III, $-\frac{4}{5}$

5.

θ	$30° = \frac{\pi}{6}$	$45° = \frac{\pi}{4}$	$60° = \frac{\pi}{3}$
$\sin \theta$	$\frac{1}{2}$	$\frac{1}{\sqrt{2}}$	$\frac{\sqrt{3}}{2}$
$\cos \theta$	$\frac{\sqrt{3}}{2}$	$\frac{1}{\sqrt{2}}$	$\frac{1}{2}$
$\tan \theta$	$\frac{1}{\sqrt{3}}$	1	$\sqrt{3}$
$\csc \theta$	2	$\sqrt{2}$	$\frac{2}{\sqrt{3}}$
$\sec \theta$	$\frac{2}{\sqrt{3}}$	$\sqrt{2}$	2
$\cot \theta$	$\sqrt{3}$	1	$\frac{1}{\sqrt{3}}$

Page 55

PROBLEMS

1. decreases, $0, -1$; increases, unbounded negative values, -1
2. decreases, $0, -1$; increases, 0, unbounded positive values
3. decreases, -1, unbounded negative values; decreases, 0, unbounded negative values

QUIZ

1. (a) 0, (b) $\frac{\pi}{2}$, (c) π, (d) $\frac{3\pi}{2}$

2.

θ	$0° = 0$ radian	$90° = \frac{\pi}{2}$ radian	$180° = \pi$ radian	$270° = \frac{3\pi}{2}$ radian
$\sin \theta$	0	1	0	-1
$\cos \theta$	1	0	-1	0
$\tan \theta$	0	undefined	0	undefined
$\csc \theta$	undefined	1	undefined	-1
$\sec \theta$	1	undefined	-1	undefined
$\cot \theta$	undefined	0	undefined	0

3. (a) decreases, $0, -1$; (b) increases, $-1, 0$

(c) increases, 0, unbounded positive $(+\infty)$; (d) increases, unbounded negative $(-\infty), -1$

(e) decreases, -1, unbounded negative $(-\infty)$; (f) decreases, unbounded positive $(+\infty), 0$

4.

Function	Domain	Range
$\sin \theta$	set of all angles	$\{y \in R \mid -1 \leqslant y \leqslant 1\}$
$\cos \theta$	set of all angles	$\{y \in R \mid -1 \leqslant y \leqslant 1\}$
$\tan \theta$	all angles except $\left\{\frac{\pi}{2} \pm n\pi\right\}$	R, set of all real numbers
$\csc \theta$	all angles except $\{\pm n\pi\}$	$\{y \in R \mid y \leqslant -1 \text{ or } y \geqslant 1\}$
$\sec \theta$	all angles except $\left\{\frac{\pi}{2} \pm n\pi\right\}$	$\{y \in R \mid y \leqslant -1 \text{ or } y \geqslant 1\}$
$\cot \theta$	all angles except $\{\pm n\pi\}$	R, set of all real numbers

Page 85

PROBLEMS

1. $\dfrac{1}{2}, -\dfrac{\sqrt{3}}{2}, -\dfrac{1}{\sqrt{3}}$ **2.** $-\dfrac{1}{\sqrt{2}}, -\dfrac{1}{\sqrt{2}}, 1$

3. $-\dfrac{1}{\sqrt{2}}, -\dfrac{1}{\sqrt{2}}, 1$ **4.** $-\dfrac{\sqrt{3}}{2}, \dfrac{1}{2}, -\sqrt{3}$

QUIZ

1. $-\sin \theta, \ \sin \theta, \ -\sin \theta$ **2.** $\cos \theta, \cos \theta$
$-\cos \theta, -\cos \theta, \ \cos \theta$ $\qquad \quad$ $\sin \theta, -\sin \theta$
$\tan \theta, -\tan \theta, \ -\tan \theta$ $\qquad \quad$ $\cot \theta, \ -\cot \theta$

3. $+\dfrac{1}{2}, -\dfrac{\sqrt{3}}{2}, -\dfrac{1}{\sqrt{3}}$

Page 94

2.

Function	Domain	Range
$\sin t$	R, set of all real numbers	$\{y \in R \mid -1 \leqslant y \leqslant 1\}$
$\tan t$	$\{t \in R \text{ except } \frac{\pi}{2} \pm n\pi\}$	R, all reals
$\sec t$	$\{t \in R \text{ except } \frac{\pi}{2} \pm n\pi\}$	$\{y \in R \mid y \leqslant -1 \text{ or } y \geqslant 1\}$

PROBLEMS

1. $\dfrac{2\pi}{3}$ **2.** $\dfrac{\pi}{2}$ **3.** $\dfrac{\pi}{2}$ **4.** 2π

5. 2π **6.** $\dfrac{\pi}{2}$ **7.** π **8.** $\dfrac{\pi}{2}$

9. $\leqslant \dfrac{\pi}{2}$ **10.** $\leqslant \dfrac{\pi}{2}$ **11.** $\leqslant \dfrac{2\pi}{3}$ **12.** $\leqslant 2\pi$

QUIZ

1. there exists a real number $p > 0$ such that $f(x + p) = f(x)$ for all x in the domain of f.

2. period $= 2$ **3.** period $= \dfrac{\pi}{2}$ **4.** period $= 2\pi$ **5.** period $= 2\pi$

6. (a) $\dfrac{p}{a}$, (b) p, (c) p, (d) $\leqslant p$, (e) $\leqslant p$, (f) $\leqslant p$

Page 138

1.

Function	Period
sin x	2π
cos x	2π
tan x	π

Function	Period
cot x	π
csc x	2π
sec x	2π

2. and 3.   **4. and 5.**

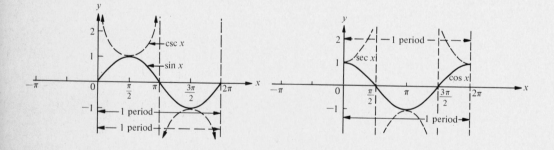

6.

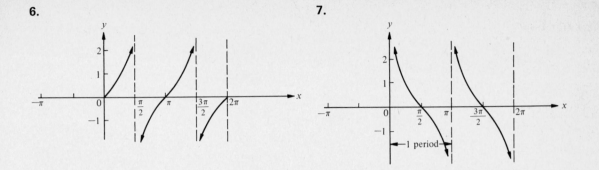

7.

Page 176

PROBLEMS

1. Amplitude $= 3$, period $= \dfrac{2\pi}{3}$, phase shift $= 0$

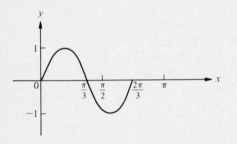

2. Amplitude $= 1$, period $= \dfrac{\pi}{2}$, phase shift $= 0$

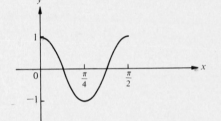

3. Amplitude $= 1$, period $= 2\pi$, phase shift $= -\dfrac{\pi}{3}$

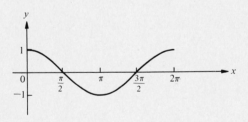

4. Amplitude $= 2$, period $= 2\pi$, phase shift $= 0$

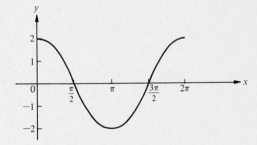

5. Amplitude = 3, period = 2π,

phase shift = $+\dfrac{\pi}{2}$

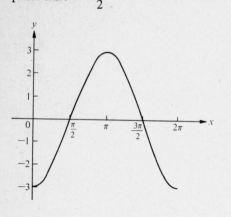

6. Amplitude = 1, period = 4π,

phase shift = $-\pi$

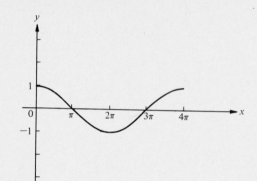

7. Amplitude = 1, period = π,

phase shift = $-\dfrac{\pi}{2}$

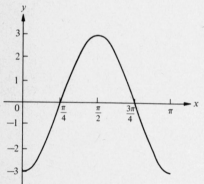

8. Amplitude = ∞, period = 4π,

phase shift = $+\dfrac{\pi}{2}$

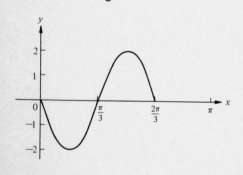

9. Amplitude = 2, period = $\dfrac{2\pi}{3}$,

phase shift = $-\dfrac{\pi}{2}$

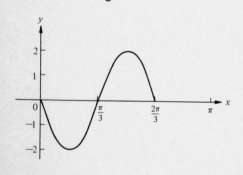

10. Amplitude = 3, period = 2π,

phase shift = $+\dfrac{\pi}{2}$

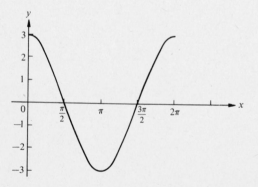

QUIZ

1. period $= \dfrac{2\pi}{3}$

2. phase shift $= -\dfrac{\pi}{4}$

3. phase shift $= +\dfrac{\pi}{4}$, period $= \dfrac{\pi}{2}$

4. amplitude $= 3$

5. amplitude $= 3$, period $= \dfrac{\pi}{2}$,

   phase shift $= +\dfrac{\pi}{4}$

6.

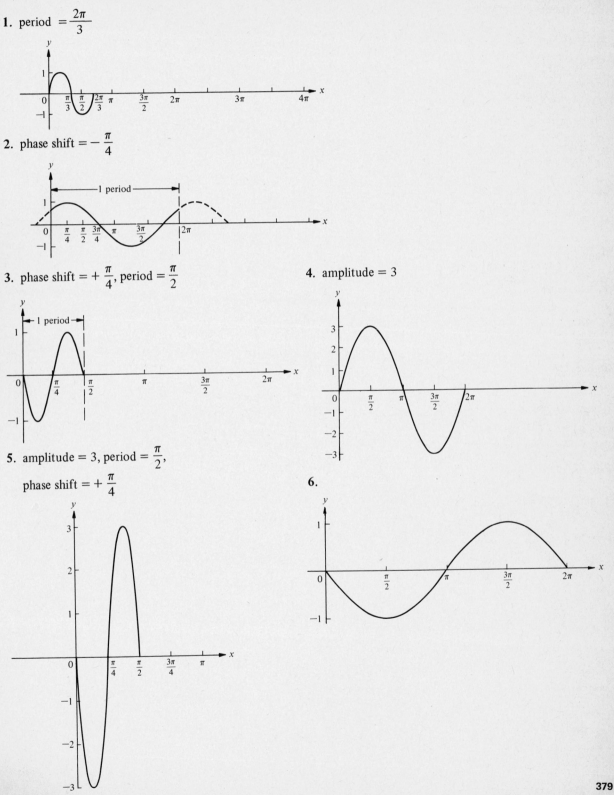

Page 194

1. See frames 275 to 284.

2.
$$\csc x = \frac{1}{\sin x} \qquad \sec x = \frac{1}{\cos x}$$

$$\cot x = \frac{1}{\tan x} \qquad \tan x = \frac{\sin x}{\cos x}$$

$$\cot x = \frac{\cos x}{\sin x} \qquad \sin^2 x + \cos^2 x = 1$$

$$1 + \tan^2 x = \sec^2 x \qquad \cot^2 x + 1 = \csc^2 x$$

3.
$$\frac{\sin^2 x}{1 - \cos x} = \frac{1 - \cos^2 x}{1 - \cos x}$$

$$= \frac{(1 - \cos x)(1 + \cos x)}{1 - \cos x}$$

$$= 1 + \cos x$$

Page 222

1. See frames 310 to 318 and the summary.
2. $\cos \alpha \cos \beta - \sin \alpha \sin \beta$,
   $\cos \alpha \cos \beta + \sin \alpha \sin \beta$,
   $$\frac{\tan \alpha - \tan \beta}{1 + \tan \alpha \tan \beta}$$
3. See frames 329, 330, and the summary.
4. See frame 380.
5. $\sin \dfrac{\pi}{12} = \dfrac{\sqrt{3} - 1}{2\sqrt{2}}$, $\cos \dfrac{\pi}{12} = \dfrac{\sqrt{3} + 1}{2\sqrt{2}}$

Page 243

1. $\sin(\alpha + \beta) = \sin \alpha \cos \beta + \cos \alpha \sin \beta$
   $\sin 2\theta = \sin(\theta + \theta) = \sin \theta \cos \theta + \cos \theta \sin \theta$
   $$= 2 \sin \theta \cos \theta$$

2. (a) $\cos^2 \theta - \sin^2 \theta$ or $1 - 2 \sin^2 \theta$ or $2 \cos^2 \theta - 1$; (b) $\dfrac{2 \tan \theta}{1 - \tan 2\theta}$;

   (c) $\dfrac{1 - \cos \theta}{2}$; (d) $\dfrac{1 + \cos \theta}{2}$

   (e) $\sqrt{\dfrac{1 - \cos \theta}{1 + \cos \theta}}$ or $\dfrac{\sin \theta}{1 + \cos \theta}$ or $\dfrac{1 - \cos \theta}{\sin \theta}$ 3. $\dfrac{1}{2} \sin 2x$

4. $\sqrt{\dfrac{\sqrt{2} - 1}{2\sqrt{2}}}$, $\sqrt{\dfrac{\sqrt{2} + 1}{2\sqrt{2}}}$

Page 255

1.

Function	Domain	Range
Sin x	$-\dfrac{\pi}{2} \leqslant x \leqslant \dfrac{\pi}{2}$	$-1 \leqslant y \leqslant 1$
Arcsin x	$-1 \leqslant x \leqslant 1$	$-\dfrac{\pi}{2} \leqslant y \leqslant \dfrac{\pi}{2}$

2. Sin $y = x$

3. (1) Arcsin $(-x) = y$ iff   Sin $y = -x$
   (2)   Sin $y = -x$ iff $-$Sin $y = x$
   (3) $-$Sin $y = x$ iff   Sin $(-y) = x$
   (4)   Sin $(-y) = x$ iff   Arcsin $x = -y$
   Thus, Arcsin $(-x) = y$ iff   Arcsin $x = -y$
   and Arcsin $(-x) = -$Arcsin x

4. x **5.** $-60°$ or $-\dfrac{\pi}{3}$

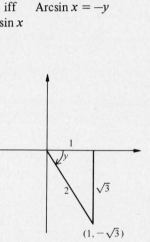

Page 271

1.

Function	Domain	Range
Cos x	$0 \leqslant x \leqslant \pi$	$-1 \leqslant y \leqslant 1$
Arccos x	$-1 \leqslant x \leqslant 1$	$0 \leqslant y \leqslant \pi$

2. Cos $y = x$

3. (1) Arccos $(-x) = y$ iff   Cos $y = -x$
   (2)   Cos $y = -x$ iff $-$Cos $y = x$
   (3) $-$Cos $y = x$ iff   Cos $(\pi - y) = x$
   (4)   Cos $(\pi - y) = x$ iff   Arccos $x = \pi - y$
   Thus, Arccos $(-x) = \pi - $Arccos x

4. (a) $\dfrac{3\pi}{4}$, (b) x, (c) $\sqrt{1 - x^2}$, (d) $\dfrac{\sqrt{4 - x^2}}{2}$

1.

Function	Domain	Range
Sin x	$-\dfrac{\pi}{2} \leqslant x \leqslant \dfrac{\pi}{2}$	$-1 \leqslant y \leqslant 1$
Cos x	$0 \leqslant x \leqslant \pi$	$-1 \leqslant y \leqslant 1$
Tan x	$-\dfrac{\pi}{2} < x < \dfrac{\pi}{2}$	R
Arcsin x	$-1 \leqslant x \leqslant 1$	$-\dfrac{\pi}{2} \leqslant y \leqslant \dfrac{\pi}{2}$
Arccos x	$-1 \leqslant x \leqslant 1$	$0 \leqslant y \leqslant \pi$
Arctan x	R	$-\dfrac{\pi}{2} < y < \dfrac{\pi}{2}$

2. (1) $\quad$ Arctan $(-x) = y \qquad$ iff $\qquad$ Tan $y = -x$
(2) $\qquad$ Tan $y = -x \qquad$ iff $\qquad$ $-$Tan $y = x$
(3) $\qquad$ $-$Tan $y = x \qquad$ iff $\qquad$ Tan $(-y) = x$
(4) $\qquad$ Tan $(-y) = x \qquad$ iff $\qquad$ Arctan $x = -y$
Thus, Arctan $(-x) = y \qquad$ iff $\qquad$ Arctan $x = -y$
$\quad$ and Arctan $(-x) = -$Arctan x

3. (a) $-\dfrac{\pi}{3}$, (b) $\dfrac{1}{\sqrt{2}}$, (c) $\dfrac{x}{\sqrt{1-x^2}}$, (d) $\dfrac{3}{2}$

Page 312

1. $\left\{ \dfrac{\pi}{3}, \dfrac{5\pi}{3} \right\}$ $\quad$ **2.** $\left\{ \dfrac{3\pi}{2} \right\}$ $\quad$ **3.** $\left\{ \dfrac{\pi}{3}, \dfrac{\pi}{2}, \dfrac{2\pi}{3}, \dfrac{3\pi}{2} \right\}$ $\quad$ **4.** $\left\{ \dfrac{3\pi}{4}, \dfrac{7\pi}{4} \right\}$ $\quad$ **5.** $\{0\}$

6. $\left\{ 0, \dfrac{\pi}{3}, \dfrac{\pi}{2}, \dfrac{2\pi}{3}, \pi, \dfrac{4\pi}{3}, \dfrac{3\pi}{2}, \dfrac{5\pi}{3} \right\}$ $\quad$ **7.** $\left\{ \dfrac{\pi}{12}, \dfrac{7\pi}{12} \right\}$

Page 371

1. (a) pure imaginary; (b) complex; (c) real; (d) complex; (e) pure imaginary
2. $x = \sqrt{5}$, $y = -3$ $\quad$ **3.** (a) $3 + 2i$, (b) $11 - 8i$, (c) $-13 + 47i$,

$\quad$ (d) $-\dfrac{43}{41} - \dfrac{23}{41}i$

4. (a) $2(\cos \dfrac{\pi}{3} + i \sin \dfrac{\pi}{3})$, (b) 2, (c) $\dfrac{\pi}{3}$, (d) see figure $\quad$ **5.** (a) $2\sqrt{3} + 2i$,

$\quad$ (b) 4, (c) $\dfrac{\pi}{6}$, (d) see figure

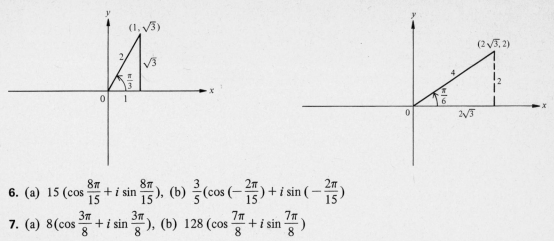

6. (a) $15 \left(\cos \dfrac{8\pi}{15} + i \sin \dfrac{8\pi}{15} \right)$, (b) $\dfrac{3}{5} \left(\cos \left(-\dfrac{2\pi}{15} \right) + i \sin \left(-\dfrac{2\pi}{15} \right) \right)$

7. (a) $8 \left(\cos \dfrac{3\pi}{8} + i \sin \dfrac{3\pi}{8} \right)$, (b) $128 \left(\cos \dfrac{7\pi}{8} + i \sin \dfrac{7\pi}{8} \right)$

8. (a) $3 \left(\cos \dfrac{\pi}{6} + i \sin \dfrac{\pi}{6} \right)$, (b) $3 \left(\cos \dfrac{17\pi}{30} + i \sin \dfrac{17\pi}{30} \right)$, (c) $3 \left(\cos \dfrac{29\pi}{30} + i \sin \dfrac{29\pi}{30} \right)$,

(d) $3 \left(\cos \dfrac{41\pi}{30} + i \sin \dfrac{41\pi}{30} \right)$, (e) $3 \left(\cos \dfrac{53\pi}{30} + i \sin \dfrac{53\pi}{30} \right)$

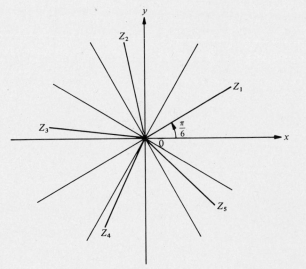

TABLE I   SINES AND COSINES

SINES

Deg.	.0°	.1°	.2°	.3°	.4°	.5°	.6°	.7°	.8°	.9°		
0°	0.000	002	003	005	007	009	010	012	014	016	0.017	89°
1°	0.017	019	021	023	024	026	028	030	031	033	0.035	88°
2°	0.035	037	038	040	042	044	045	047	049	051	0.052	87°
3°	0.052	054	056	058	059	061	063	065	066	068	0.070	86°
4°	0.070	071	073	075	077	078	080	082	084	085	0.087	85°
5°	0.087	089	091	092	094	096	098	099	101	103	0.105	84°
6°	0.105	106	108	110	111	113	115	117	118	120	0.122	83°
7°	0.122	124	125	127	129	131	132	134	136	137	0.139	82°
8°	0.139	141	143	144	146	148	150	151	153	155	0.156	81°
9°	0.156	158	160	162	163	165	167	168	170	172	0.174	80°
10°	0.174	175	177	179	181	182	184	186	187	189	0.191	79°
11°	0.191	193	194	196	198	199	201	203	204	206	0.208	78°
12°	0.208	210	211	213	215	216	218	220	222	223	0.225	77°
13°	0.225	227	228	230	232	233	235	237	239	240	0.242	76°
14°	0.242	244	245	247	249	250	252	254	255	257	0.259	75°
15°	0.259	261	262	264	266	267	269	271	272	274	0.276	74°
16°	0.276	277	279	281	282	284	286	287	289	291	0.292	73°
17°	0.292	294	296	297	299	301	302	304	306	307	0.309	72°
18°	0.309	311	312	314	316	317	319	321	322	324	0.326	71°
19°	0.326	327	329	331	332	334	335	337	339	340	0.342	70°
20°	0.342	344	345	347	349	350	352	353	355	357	0.358	69°
21°	0.358	360	362	363	365	367	368	370	371	373	0.375	68°
22°	0.375	376	378	379	381	383	384	386	388	389	0.391	67°
23°	0.391	392	394	396	397	399	400	402	404	405	0.407	66°
24°	0.407	408	410	412	413	415	416	418	419	421	0.423	65°
25°	0.423	424	426	427	429	431	432	434	435	437	0.438	64°
26°	0.438	440	442	443	445	446	448	449	451	452	0.454	63°
27°	0.454	456	457	459	460	462	463	465	466	468	0.469	62°
28°	0.469	471	473	474	476	477	479	480	482	483	0.485	61°
29°	0.485	486	488	489	491	492	494	495	497	498	0.500	60°
30°	0.500	502	503	505	506	508	509	511	512	514	0.515	59°
31°	0.515	517	518	520	521	522	524	525	527	528	0.530	58°
32°	0.530	531	533	534	536	537	539	540	542	543	0.545	57°
33°	0.545	546	548	549	550	552	553	555	556	558	0.559	56°
34°	0.559	561	562	564	565	566	568	569	571	572	0.574	55°
35°	0.574	575	576	578	579	581	582	584	585	586	0.588	54°
36°	0.588	589	591	592	593	595	596	598	599	600	0.602	53°
37°	0.602	603	605	606	607	609	610	612	613	614	0.616	52°
38°	0.616	617	618	620	621	623	624	625	627	628	0.629	51°
39°	0.629	631	632	633	635	636	637	639	640	641	0.643	50°
40°	0.643	644	645	647	648	649	651	652	653	655	0.656	49°
41°	0.656	657	659	660	661	663	664	665	667	668	0.669	48°
42°	0.669	670	672	673	674	676	677	678	679	681	0.682	47°
43°	0.682	683	685	686	687	688	690	691	692	693	0.695	46°
44°	0.695	696	697	698	700	701	702	703	705	706	0.707	45°
	.9°	.8°	.7°	.6°	.5°	.4°	.3°	.2°	.1°	.0°	Deg.	

Deg.	.0°	.1°	.2°	.3°	.4°	.5°	.6°	.7°	.8°	.9°		
45°	0.707	708	710	711	712	713	714	716	717	718	0.719	44°
46°	0.719	721	722	723	724	725	727	728	729	730	0.731	43°
47°	0.731	733	734	735	736	737	738	740	741	742	0.743	42°
48°	0.743	744	745	747	748	749	750	751	752	754	0.755	41°
49°	0.755	756	757	758	759	760	762	763	764	765	0.766	40°
50°	0.766	767	768	769	771	772	773	774	775	776	0.777	39°
51°	0.777	778	779	780	782	783	784	785	786	787	0.788	38°
52°	0.788	789	790	791	792	793	794	795	797	798	0.799	37°
53°	0.799	800	801	802	803	804	805	806	807	808	0.809	36°
54°	0.809	810	811	812	813	814	815	816	817	818	0.819	35°
55°	0.819	820	821	822	823	824	825	826	827	828	0.829	34°
56°	0.829	830	831	832	833	834	835	836	837	838	0.839	33°
57°	0.839	840	841	842	842	843	844	845	846	847	0.848	32°
58°	0.848	849	850	851	852	853	854	854	855	856	0.857	31°
59°	0.857	858	859	860	861	862	863	863	864	865	0.866	30°
60°	0.866	867	868	869	869	870	871	872	873	874	0.875	29°
61°	0.875	875	876	876	877	878	879	880	881	882	0.883	28°
62°	0.883	884	885	885	886	887	888	889	889	890	0.891	27°
63°	0.891	892	893	893	894	895	896	896	897	898	0.899	26°
64°	0.899	900	900	901	902	903	903	904	905	906	0.906	25°
65°	0.906	907	908	909	909	910	911	911	912	913	0.914	24°
66°	0.914	914	915	916	916	917	918	918	919	920	0.921	23°
67°	0.921	921	922	923	923	924	925	925	926	927	0.927	22°
68°	0.927	928	928	929	930	930	931	932	932	933	0.934	21°
69°	0.934	934	935	935	936	937	937	938	938	939	0.940	20°
70°	0.940	940	941	941	942	943	943	944	944	945	0.946	19°
71°	0.946	946	947	947	948	948	949	949	950	951	0.951	18°
72°	0.951	952	952	953	953	954	954	955	955	956	0.956	17°
73°	0.956	957	957	958	958	959	959	960	960	961	0.961	16°
74°	0.961	962	962	963	963	964	964	965	965	965	0.966	15°
75°	0.966	966	967	967	968	968	969	969	969	970	0.970	14°
76°	0.970	971	971	972	972	972	973	973	974	974	0.974	13°
77°	0.974	975	975	976	976	976	977	977	977	978	0.978	12°
78°	0.978	979	979	979	980	980	980	981	981	981	0.982	11°
79°	0.982	982	982	983	983	983	984	984	984	985	0.985	10°
80°	0.985	985	985	986	986	986	987	987	987	987	0.988	9°
81°	0.988	988	988	988	989	989	989	990	990	990	0.990	8°
82°	0.990	991	991	991	991	991	992	992	992	992	0.993	7°
83°	0.993	993	993	993	993	994	994	994	994	994	0.995	6°
84°	0.995	995	995	995	995	995	996	996	996	996	0.996	5°
85°	0.996	996	996	997	997	997	997	997	997	997	0.998	4°
86°	0.998	998	998	998	998	998	998	998	998	999	0.999	3°
87°	0.999	999	999	999	999	999	999	999	999	999	0.999	2°
88°	0.999	999	000	000	000	000	000	000	000	000	1.000	1°
89°	1.000	000	000	000	000	000	000	000	000	000	1.000	0°
	.9°	.8°	.7°	.6°	.5°	.4°	.3°	.2°	.1°	.0°	Deg.	

TABLE II TANGENTS AND COTANGENTS

TANGENTS

Deg.	0°	.1°	.2°	.3°	.4°	.5°	.6°	.7°	.8°	.9°		
0°	0.000	002	003	005	007	009	010	012	014	016	0.017	89°
1°	0.017	019	021	023	024	026	028	030	031	033	0.035	88°
2°	0.035	037	038	040	042	044	045	047	049	051	0.052	87°
3°	0.052	054	056	058	059	061	063	065	066	068	0.070	86°
4°	0.070	072	073	075	077	079	080	082	084	086	0.087	85°
5°	0.087	089	091	093	095	096	098	100	102	103	0.105	84°
6°	0.105	107	109	110	112	114	116	117	119	121	0.123	83°
7°	0.123	125	126	128	130	132	133	135	137	139	0.141	82°
8°	0.141	142	144	146	148	149	151	153	155	157	0.158	81°
9°	0.158	160	162	164	166	167	169	171	173	175	0.176	80°
10°	0.176	178	180	182	184	185	187	189	191	193	0.194	79°
11°	0.194	196	198	200	202	203	205	207	209	211	0.213	78°
12°	0.213	214	216	218	220	222	224	225	227	229	0.231	77°
13°	0.231	233	235	236	238	240	242	244	246	247	0.249	76°
14°	0.249	251	253	255	257	259	260	262	264	266	0.268	75°
15°	0.268	270	272	274	275	277	279	281	283	285	0.287	74°
16°	0.287	289	291	292	294	296	298	300	302	304	0.306	73°
17°	0.306	308	310	311	313	315	317	319	321	323	0.325	72°
18°	0.325	327	329	331	333	335	337	338	340	342	0.344	71°
19°	0.344	346	348	350	352	354	356	358	360	362	0.364	70°
20°	0.364	366	368	370	372	374	376	378	380	382	0.384	69°
21°	0.384	386	388	390	392	394	396	398	400	402	0.404	68°
22°	0.404	406	408	410	412	414	416	418	420	422	0.424	67°
23°	0.424	427	429	431	433	435	437	439	441	443	0.445	66°
24°	0.445	447	449	452	454	456	458	460	462	464	0.466	65°
25°	0.466	468	471	473	475	477	479	481	483	486	0.488	64°
26°	0.488	490	492	494	496	499	501	503	505	507	0.510	63°
27°	0.510	512	514	516	518	521	523	525	527	529	0.532	62°
28°	0.532	534	536	538	541	543	545	547	550	552	0.554	61°
29°	0.554	557	559	561	563	566	568	570	573	575	0.577	60°
30°	0.577	580	582	584	587	589	591	594	596	598	0.601	59°
31°	0.601	603	606	608	610	613	615	618	620	622	0.625	58°
32°	0.625	627	630	632	635	637	640	642	644	647	0.649	57°
33°	0.649	652	654	657	659	662	664	667	669	672	0.675	56°
34°	0.675	677	680	682	685	687	690	692	695	698	0.700	55°
35°	0.700	703	705	708	711	713	716	719	721	724	0.727	54°
36°	0.727	729	732	735	737	740	743	745	748	751	0.754	53°
37°	0.754	756	759	762	765	767	770	773	776	778	0.781	52°
38°	0.781	784	787	790	793	795	798	801	804	807	0.810	51°
39°	0.810	813	816	818	821	824	827	830	833	836	0.839	50°
40°	0.839	842	845	848	851	854	857	860	863	866	0.869	49°
41°	0.869	872	875	879	882	885	888	891	894	897	0.900	48°
42°	0.900	904	908	910	913	916	920	923	926	929	0.933	47°
43°	0.933	936	939	942	946	949	952	956	959	962	0.966	46°
44°	0.966	969	972	976	979	983	986	990	993	997	1.000	45°
	.9°	.8°	.7°	.6°	.5°	.4°	.3°	.2°	.1°	.0°		Deg.

TANGENTS

Deg.	0°	.1°	.2°	.3°	.4°	.5°	.6°	.7°	.8°	.9°		Deg.
45°	1.000	004	007	011	014	018	021	025	028	032	1.036	44°
46°	1.036	039	043	046	050	054	058	061	065	069	1.072	43°
47°	1.072	076	080	084	088	091	095	099	103	107	1.111	42°
48°	1.111	115	118	122	126	130	134	138	142	146	1.150	41°
49°	1.150	154	159	163	168	171	175	179	183	188	1.192	40°
50°	1.192	196	200	205	209	213	217	222	226	231	1.235	39°
51°	1.235	239	244	248	253	257	262	266	271	275	1.280	38°
52°	1.280	285	289	294	299	303	308	313	318	322	1.327	37°
53°	1.327	332	337	342	347	351	356	361	366	371	1.376	36°
54°	1.376	381	387	392	399	402	407	412	418	423	1.428	35°
55°	1.428	434	439	444	450	455	461	466	472	477	1.483	34°
56°	1.483	488	494	499	505	511	517	522	528	534	1.540	33°
57°	1.540	546	552	558	564	570	576	582	588	594	1.600	32°
58°	1.600	607	613	619	626	632	638	645	651	658	1.664	31°
59°	1.664	671	676	684	691	698	705	711	718	725	1.732	30°
60°	1.732	739	746	753	760	768	775	782	789	797	1.804	29°
61°	1.804	812	819	827	834	842	850	857	865	873	1.881	28°
62°	1.881	889	897	905	913	921	929	938	946	954	1.963	27°
63°	1.963	971	980	988	997	*006	*015	*023	*032	*041	2.050	26°
64°	2.050	059	069	078	087	097	106	116	125	135	2.145	25°
65°	2.145	154	164	174	184	194	205	215	225	236	2.246	24°
66°	2.246	257	267	278	289	300	311	322	333	345	2.356	23°
67°	2.356	367	379	391	402	414	426	438	450	463	2.475	22°
68°	2.475	488	500	513	526	539	552	565	578	592	2.605	21°
69°	2.605	619	633	646	661	675	689	703	718	733	2.748	20°
70°	2.748	763	778	793	808	824	840	856	872	888	2.904	19°
71°	2.904	921	938	954	971	989	*006	*024	*042	*056	3.078	18°
72°	3.078	096	115	133	152	172	191	211	231	251	3.271	17°
73°	3.271	291	312	333	354	376	398	420	442	465	3.487	16°
74°	3.487	511	534	558	582	606	631	655	681	706	3.732	15°
75°	3.732	758	785	812	839	867	895	923	952	981	4.011	14°
76°	4.011	041	071	102	134	165	198	230	264	297	4.332	13°
77°	4.332	366	402	437	474	511	548	586	625	665	4.705	12°
78°	4.705	745	787	829	872	915	959	*005	*050	*097	5.145	11°
79°	5.145	193	242	292	344	396	449	503	558	614	5.671	10°
80°	5.671	730	789	850	912	976	*041	*107	*174	*243	6.314	9°
81°	6.314	386	460	535	612	691	772	855	940	*026	7.115	8°
82°	7.115	207	300	396	495	596	700	806	916	*029	8.144	7°
83°	8.144	264	386	513	643	777	915	*058	*205	*357	9.514	6°
84°	9.514	9.677	9.845	10.02	10.20	10.39	10.58	10.78	10.99	11.21	11.43	5°
85°	11.43	11.66	11.91	12.16	12.43	12.71	13.00	13.30	13.62	13.95	14.30	4°
86°	14.30	14.67	15.06	15.46	15.90	16.35	16.83	17.34	17.89	18.46	19.08	3°
87°	19.08	19.74	20.45	21.21	22.02	22.90	23.86	24.90	26.03	27.27	28.64	2°
88°	28.64	30.15	31.82	33.69	35.80	38.19	40.92	44.07	47.74	52.08	57.29	1°
89°	57.29	63.66	71.62	81.85	95.49	114.6	143.2	191.0	286.5	573.0	∞	0°
90°	∞											
		.9°	.8°	.7°	.6°	.5°	.4°	.3°	.2°	.1°	.0°	Deg.

TABLE III SECANTS AND COSECANTS

SECANTS

Deg.	.0°	.1°	.2°	.3°	.4°	.5°	.6°	.7°	.8°	.9°		
											1.000	90°
0°	1.000	000	000	000	000	000	000	000	000	000	1.000	89°
1°	1.000	000	000	000	000	000	000	000	000	001	1.001	88°
2°	1.001	001	001	001	001	001	001	001	001	001	1.001	87°
3°	1.001	001	002	002	002	002	002	002	002	002	1.002	86°
4°	1.002	003	003	003	003	003	003	003	004	004	1.004	85°
5°	1.004	004	004	004	004	005	005	005	005	005	1.006	84°
6°	1.006	006	006	006	006	006	007	007	007	007	1.008	83°
7°	1.008	008	008	008	008	009	009	009	009	010	1.010	82°
8°	1.010	010	010	011	011	011	011	012	012	012	1.012	81°
9°	1.012	013	013	013	014	014	014	015	015	015	1.015	80°
10°	1.015	016	016	016	017	017	017	018	018	018	1.019	79°
11°	1.019	019	019	020	020	020	021	021	022	022	1.022	78°
12°	1.022	023	023	023	024	024	025	025	025	026	1.026	77°
13°	1.026	027	027	028	028	028	029	029	030	030	1.031	76°
14°	1.031	031	032	032	032	033	033	034	034	035	1.035	75°
15°	1.035	036	036	037	037	038	038	039	039	040	1.040	74°
16°	1.040	041	041	042	042	043	043	044	045	045	1.046	73°
17°	1.046	046	047	047	048	049	049	050	050	051	1.051	72°
18°	1.051	052	053	053	054	054	055	056	056	057	1.058	71°
19°	1.058	058	059	060	060	061	062	062	063	064	1.064	70°
20°	1.064	065	066	066	067	068	068	069	070	070	1.071	69°
21°	1.071	072	073	073	074	075	076	076	077	078	1.079	68°
22°	1.079	079	080	081	082	082	083	084	085	086	1.086	67°
23°	1.086	087	088	089	090	090	091	092	093	094	1.095	66°
24°	1.095	095	096	097	098	099	100	101	102	102	1.103	65°
25°	1.103	104	105	106	107	108	109	110	111	112	1.113	64°
26°	1.113	114	115	115	116	117	118	119	120	121	1.122	63°
27°	1.122	123	124	125	126	127	128	129	130	132	1.133	62°
28°	1.133	134	135	136	137	138	139	140	141	142	1.143	61°
29°	1.143	144	146	147	148	149	150	151	152	154	1.155	60°
30°	1.155	156	157	158	159	161	162	163	164	165	1.167	59°
31°	1.167	168	169	170	172	173	174	175	177	178	1.179	58°
32°	1.179	180	182	183	184	186	187	188	190	191	1.192	57°
33°	1.192	193	195	196	198	199	201	202	203	205	1.206	56°
34°	1.206	208	209	211	212	213	215	216	218	219	1.221	55°
35°	1.221	222	224	225	227	228	230	231	233	235	1.236	54°
36°	1.236	238	239	241	242	244	246	247	249	250	1.252	53°
37°	1.252	254	255	257	259	260	262	264	266	267	1.269	52°
38°	1.269	271	272	274	276	278	280	281	283	285	1.287	51°
39°	1.287	289	290	292	294	296	298	300	302	304	1.305	50°
40°	1.305	307	309	311	313	315	317	319	321	323	1.325	49°
41°	1.325	327	329	331	333	335	337	339	341	344	1.346	48°
42°	1.346	348	350	352	354	356	359	361	363	365	1.367	47°
43°	1.367	370	372	374	376	379	381	383	386	388	1.390	46°
44°	1.390	393	395	397	400	402	404	407	409	412	1.414	45°
	.9°	.8°	.7°	.6°	.5°	.4°	.3°	.2°	.1°	.0°		Deg.

SECANTS

Deg.	.0°	.1°	.2°	.3°	.4°	.5°	.6°	.7°	.8°	.9°		
45°	1.414	417	419	422	424	427	429	432	434	437	1.440	44°
46°	1.440	442	445	447	450	453	455	458	461	464	1.466	43°
47°	1.466	469	472	475	477	480	483	486	489	492	1.494	42°
48°	1.494	497	500	503	506	509	512	515	518	521	1.524	41°
49°	1.524	527	530	534	537	540	543	546	549	552	1.556	40°
50°	1.556	559	562	566	569	572	575	579	582	586	1.589	39°
51°	1.589	592	596	599	603	606	610	613	617	621	1.624	38°
52°	1.624	628	632	635	639	643	646	650	654	658	1.662	37°
53°	1.662	666	669	673	677	681	685	689	693	697	1.701	36°
54°	1.701	705	710	714	718	722	726	731	735	739	1.743	35°
55°	1.743	748	752	757	761	766	770	775	779	784	1.788	34°
56°	1.788	793	798	802	807	812	817	821	826	831	1.836	33°
57°	1.836	841	846	851	856	861	866	871	877	882	1.887	32°
58°	1.887	892	898	903	908	914	919	925	930	936	1.942	31°
59°	1.942	947	953	959	964	970	976	982	988	994	2.000	30°
60°	2.000	006	012	018	025	031	037	043	050	056	2.063	29°
61°	2.063	069	076	082	089	096	103	109	116	123	2.130	28°
62°	2.130	137	144	151	158	166	173	180	188	195	2.203	27°
63°	2.203	210	218	226	233	241	249	257	265	273	2.281	26°
64°	2.281	289	298	306	314	323	331	340	349	357	2.366	25°
65°	2.366	375	384	393	402	411	421	430	439	449	2.459	24°
66°	2.459	468	478	488	498	508	518	528	538	549	2.559	23°
67°	2.559	570	581	591	602	613	624	635	647	658	2.669	22°
68°	2.669	681	693	705	716	729	741	753	765	778	2.790	21°
69°	2.790	803	816	829	842	855	869	882	896	910	2.924	20°
70°	2.924	938	952	967	981	996	*011	*026	*041	*056	3.072	19°
71°	3.072	087	103	119	135	152	168	185	202	219	3.236	18°
72°	3.236	254	271	289	307	326	344	363	382	401	3.420	17°
73°	3.420	440	460	480	500	521	542	563	584	606	3.628	16°
74°	3.628	650	673	695	719	742	766	790	814	839	3.864	15°
75°	3.864	889	915	941	967	994	*021	*049	*077	*105	4.134	14°
76°	4.134	163	192	222	253	284	315	347	379	412	4.445	13°
77°	4.445	479	514	549	584	620	657	694	732	771	4.810	12°
78°	4.810	850	891	931	973	*016	*059	*103	*148	*194	5.241	11°
79°	5.241	288	337	386	436	487	540	593	647	702	5.759	10°
80°	5.759	816	875	935	996	*059	*123	*188	*255	*323	6.392	9°
81°	6.392	464	537	611	687	765	845	927	*011	*097	7.185	8°
82°	7.185	276	368	463	561	661	764	870	979	*091	8.206	7°
83°	8.206	324	446	571	700	834	971	*113	*259	*411	9.567	6°
84°	9.567	728	895	10.07	10.25	10.43	10.63	10.83	11.03	11.25	11.47	5°
85°	11.47	11.71	11.95	12.20	12.47	12.75	13.03	13.34	13.65	13.99	14.34	4°
86°	14.34	14.70	15.09	15.50	15.93	16.38	16.86	17.37	17.91	18.49	19.11	3°
87°	19.11	19.77	20.47	21.23	22.04	22.93	23.88	24.92	26.05	27.29	28.65	2°
88°	28.65	30.16	31.84	33.71	35.81	38.20	40.93	44.08	47.75	52.09	57.30	1°
89°	57.30	63.66	71.62	81.85	95.49	114.6	143.2	191.0	286.5	573.0	∞	0°
90°	∞											
	.9°	.8°	.7°	.6°	.5°	.4°	.3°	.2°	.1°	.0°	Deg.	

Index